DATE DUE

**Three (3) week loans are subject
to recall after one week**

PARADISE
MISLAID

Books by E. J. Applewhite

Cosmic Fishing: An Account of Writing Synergetics
with Buckminster Fuller

*Washington Itself: An Informal Guide to the Capital
of the United States*

*Paradise Mislaid: Birth, death & the human
predicament of being biological*

and as Fuller's collaborator

Synergetics
Synergetics 2
*Synergetics Dictionary: The Mind
of Buckminster Fuller* (four volumes)

PARADISE MISLAID

Birth, death
& the human
predicament of
being biological

———————❧———————

E. J. Applewhite

ST. MARTIN'S PRESS NEW YORK

PARADISE MISLAID. Copyright © 1991 by E. J. Applewhite. All rights reserved. Printed in the United States of America. No part of this book may be used or reproduced in any manner whatsoever without written permission except in the case of brief quotations embodied in critical articles or reviews. For information, address St. Martin's Press, 175 Fifth Avenue, New York, N.Y. 10010.

Design by Diane Stevenson, SNAP·HAUS GRAPHICS

Library of Congress Cataloging-in-Publication

Applewhite, E. J.
   Paradise mislaid : life, death, and the biological predicament of
being human / E.J. Applewhite.
       p. cm.
   "A Thomas Dunne book."
   ISBN 0-312-05944-2
   1. Birth (Philosophy) 2. Life. 3. Death. 4. Man. 5. Science.
6. Life (Biology) 7. Knowledge, Theory of. 8. Artificial
intelligence. I. Title.
   BD443.A66   1991
   128—dc20   90-27309
                                                               CIP

Pages 459–460 constitute an extension of this copyright page.

First Edition: June 1991

10 9 8 7 6 5 4 3 2 1

To the memory of my parents

MABEL AGNES METZLER APPLEWHITE

b. *Paradise, Pennsylvania   24 January 1879*
d. *New York City   15 December 1974*

EDGAR JARRATT APPLEWHITE

b. *Southampton Co., Virginia   1 January 1873*
d. *Newport News, Virginia   1 August 1941*

PROEM

Darwin supplied the keystone of the arch connecting our understanding of the destiny of the atom with that of the destiny of man.

—*Theodosius Dobzhansky,*
MANKIND EVOLVING, 1962

What could be more consoling than the thought that we are not alone in our love affair with destiny? Atoms have destiny too.

CONTENTS

Contents

A note to the reader

My children—two sons and two daughters, now married and with families of their own—have not asked me whether I expect to go to heaven, but I have written this book for them anyway. It is about how I have come to feel about the definition of life (hard to define) and the meaning of death (very little meaning).

In my later years, after I had lost the solace of religion, I found I was nevertheless still obstinately concerned with salvation. This seemed hardly fair: If I had abandoned the church from disdain for the supernatural, shouldn't I also relinquish any claim to deliverance? In forsaking the mystical realm of Christian doctrine for the physical world of nature as described by science, I still wonder whether there might be some prospect of a kind of secular salvation, a survival of individual consciousness after death—ordained by biological evidence rather than religion.

The result is that, though I am not a biologist or a philosopher, I have come up with a book raising biological and philosophical questions about the limitations of natural life and the prospects of artificial life. For this I plead the curiosity of the layman and the license of the essayist.

These chapters plunder without shame the books and papers of biologists. For some of the many quotations I may have approached the limits of fair use. Whether their language is paraphrased or in quotation marks, I have in every case attempted to credit my sources. I hope they will be charitable enough to regard my pillaging as not stealing but borrowing.

I spent five years of my life in the U.S. Navy, and 25 years in the CIA. I joined the latter (as I wrote in my book

Cosmic Fishing) because I couldn't bear for anyone to have any secrets I didn't know about. After leaving the government at the age of 50, I spent a decade working with Buckminster Fuller in the writing of *Synergetics*, his system of philosophical geometry. In this book I have drawn a number of personal allusions with an indulgence approaching the autobiographical. In the case of Fuller, I realize that not everyone shares the taste I acquired many years ago for his maverick genius; as my mentor, his spirit dwells in these pages, and I quote from him copiously in anticipation of his rightful place in the world of letters.

E.J.A.

1517 30th Street NW
Washington, D.C. 20007
November 1990

I

DESCRIBING LIFE

———————— ❧ ————————

*T*HIS IS A BOOK ABOUT THE SIMPLE FACT
that we are all biological creatures. Like other animals we have sensations and emotions; unlike other animals we have myths and beliefs and—worse—questions. Men of science can tell us much about our physical and chemical nature, perhaps something about the way we behave, but really nothing about our spiritual and intellectual nature. In fact, biologists can tell us more about our physiology as human beings than they can about the general phenomenon of the appearance of life in the universe.

We have no idea about how life originated or where it may have come from. There are theories, but such theories command far less scientific attention than the dubious—and controversial—attempts to map the human genome or trap the ultimate particle in the supercollider.

This first section of the book is speculative rather than systematic. It explores problems of defining life in general. Then it surveys various descriptions of life, none of which are exhaustive or sufficient. This is followed by a brief review of life as the chemical interaction of molecules; the views of life formulated by the particle physicist Erwin Schrödinger; a series of pronouncements on the impulse to replicate; and a final medley of some metaphoric approaches to the essence of living.

This section introduces the theme that it seems easier to define life in common, everyday terms—in the vernacular—than in the disciplined language of law and biology.

I
No agreed definitions

WHERE IS THE PHYSICAL THRESHOLD?

In the fall of 1985 I went around the corner from my house in northwest Washington, D.C., to the Washington Hebrew Congregation to hear an address by a newly arrived astronomer from Harvard who had just been installed as president of the American University, located a little further up Massachusetts Avenue. The university had no suitable assembly hall and the synagogue—the largest in the city—had for years generously made its facilities available to AU. The astronomer-president was Dr. Richard Berendzen, and his address was a review of cosmology. In the course of his grand description of the latest picture of the cosmos—illustrated with large dark slides of wonderful pink and white galaxies glowing from deep space—he said, arrestingly, that "stars had to die in order for life to occur." Stars had to die to form atoms and the elements of earthly matter. Matter had to exist to make organisms. And then he asserted dogmatically that "DNA is alive and amino acids are not."

This arresting statement galvanized my longtime preoccupation with the nature of the threshold between the living and the nonliving. Here was the first time I had heard a pronouncement from a qualified man of science on my growing obsession with the question: Where does life begin?

There I had it: Amino acids are not alive, but DNA, with the capacity to code for the sequences of amino acids that make up proteins, is indeed living. Is this the threshold of my absorption, the threshold between the living and the not-living, between the animate and the inanimate?

Well, what Berendzen said might or might not be logically defensible. But I found it not altogether persuasive to conclude that a large molecule of one shape is alive while an equally large one of another shape is not. Live molecules exist only in particular contexts. And here we get into the relationship of gene and organism, and from that point on there is no stopping place, no end to it. From atom to molecule to cell to organism—somewhere the biological mechanisms of life arise from out of the whole ensemble. And somehow the animals that people are come into the picture.

Hence this book. The only animals I like are people. How did we find ourselves among the beasts?

THERE ARE NO AGREED DEFINITIONS OF LIFE

The question *What is life?* is a naïve one. When Pontius Pilate asked *What is truth?* he took on the armor of irony as a defense against mockery. But when we ask what is life, where is the defense against derision? We ask it knowing that a simple expository answer is unlikely. But we do not ask it rhetorically (as Pilate surely did), because our curiosity about life is artless. The curiosity is anchored in disdain for the myths and folklore of our ancestors, it is goaded by a faith transferred from the dogma of religion to the integrity of science in a secular age. The question stretches the limits of our investigatory capacities, hovering at the margins between gravity and bathos. It is, in short, naïve.

If we start out in ignorance and turn to science for an answer, we will learn many wonderful things about life, but we will probably end up at a point very close to the innocence from which we started. There are two reasons for this. First is the elusive nature of life itself. In our present state of knowledge life is profoundly—*into the abyss*—unfathomable. And second, there is the very possible incapacity of science to deal with what might be a nonscientific question.

It is not a problem of language. We probably have the words to describe life if we only had a conceptual scheme that all could agree on.

The dawning recognition that an exact definition of life is as yet, and perhaps always may be, beyond the grasp of science has not deterred me from a stubborn search for what scientists, particularly biologists, have to say in the matter. In a way, this search has resulted in an unexpected survey of how much biologists have to tell us about life without having bothered to define it, or at least mustering much rigor in its description.

Dictionaries start out with the sorry practice of defining life in only negative terms. They say it is "opposed to death" (*Oxford English Dictionary*) or "the quality that distinguishes a being from a dead body or purely chemical matter" (*Webster 3*). But living matter is no less chemical than dead. In fact, it is more so; it is highly chemical. Next to fireworks what *could* be more chemical?

Note the abstraction of the word *being.—a being*. It is a noun, and not even a gerund; and there are few words in English harder to pronounce (or harder for lip readers to fathom.) *Being* is a concept that craves a philosophical context: the dictionary provides none. (Philosophically, the theory of *being*, ontology, is the primary element in metaphysics, the doctrine of the categories, the first of categories.)

Have we no verbs to rise to the occasion? There is a growing literature on the self-organization of matter, and life as a self-organizing phenomenon. But *self-organize* as a verb is, so far, exotic, unfamiliar and not part of our daily experience. The self-organization of matter is still one of the youngest and most immature of scientific disciplines. As a verb it has yet to become a common idiom of our language, and as a concept it is yet to enter our culture.

Science dictionaries are no better than general ones. Few of them even have an entry for *life*, and when they do, they say that it is just the quality that distinguishes living matter from nonliving matter. Did the word *quality* ever have to bear such freight? The unresolved distinction is the reason you looked the word up in the first place.

Among the biological disciplines look for no generally agreed definitions of life. Textbooks supply no comprehensive description of living matter, including every case and excluding the rest.

The conclusion is inescapable. Defining life is not the proper business of science. Scientists make no pretence of having established the full range of criteria for life. The description of life is an incidental by-product—but not an obligation—of biology. Philosophy beckons where empiricism falters.

In the pages that follow there are many descriptions of the processes of life from varying points of investigation. Some are arbitrary, some contradictory; but most are rich in insights, illuminating the resistance of life to generalizability as well as the ambiguity of our attitudes toward it. No grand synthesis emerges from a survey of the annals of biology. It remains ironic that life is more difficult to define than death.

The 20th century began with the conceptual prodigies of relativity and quantum mechanics putting physics in the driver's seat. But as the century closes, biology overtakes physics as the preeminent science. Yet, unlike every other scientific discipline, biology enjoys no consensus among its practitioners of its proper field of concern. The scope of concern may be so broad that ambivalence is inherent. Between the theoretical macropicture of the evolutionary biologist and the reductionist micropicture of the molecular biologist there is no easy accommodation. This absence of any familiar middle ground exacerbates the remoteness of biology from our everyday experience.

When it comes to describing where life begins and where it ends, there is not much to be gained by appealing

7

to members of other concerned professions. Lawyers, doctors, and ministers flourish in that hiatus between birth and death. With regard to human beings, their professional involvement in the act of birth and the fact of death ranges from the intimate to the ceremonial. But they have no common view of what life *is* at those thresholds.

In matters such as contraception, abortion, and euthanasia, the lawyers and doctors and scientists—the courts and hospitals and expert witnesses—have no common agreement even within their respective disciplines. This is an area in which in our Western culture we are temperamentally disposed to look to science for empirical answers upon which the axioms of other disciplines may be built. But to little avail. Definitions of life at the itchy threshold end up by default at the doorstep of the layman. What are the professions for if they cannot *profess* on the very questions of most concern in our daily lives? I find this predicament a bleak one. Search not biology for solace.

Neither scientists nor any other academics were any help to the U.S. Supreme Court when it had to make its first major ruling on the legality of abortions. The justices were so intimidated by the obscurity of life that they rejected any attempt to define it.

> **We need not resolve the difficult question of when life begins. When those trained in the respective disciplines of medicine, philosophy and theology are unable to arrive at any consensus, the judiciary at this point in the development of man's knowledge is not in a position to speculate. [From the majority opinion in the U.S. Supreme Court ruling in *Roe* v. *Wade*, 410 US 113, 1973]**

We have had to wait for a practicing physician and science writer, Dr. Lewis Thomas, to articulate our sense of dismay.

> **One thing that is wrong with us and eats away at us [is that] we do not know enough about ourselves. We are ignorant about how we work, about where we fit in, and most of all**

about the enormous imponderable system of life in which we are embedded as working parts. We do not really understand nature, at all.... Just think, two centuries ago we could explain everything about everything, out of pure reason, and now most of that elaborate and harmonious structure has come apart before our eyes. We are *dumb.*

There is a great array of biological specialties and disciplines, and many of them are described at the end of this book. But a survey of the disciplines only compounds the problem as each biological specialty tends to describe the life process it studies in terms of a particular apparatus or technique of investigation.

In the 1960s the physicist James E. Lovelock was engaged in a NASA project to determine whether there is life on Mars. He started out by reasoning that any life on Mars must be much the same as life on Earth, but he was frustrated that he could find nowhere in the scientific literature a comprehensive definition of life as a physical process. He was driven to an analogy of technical people trying to describe a TV set in terms only of their individual specialties:

Data galore had been accumulated on every conceivable aspect of living species ... but in the whole vast encyclopedia of facts the crux of the matter, life itself, was almost totally ignored. At best, the literature read like a collection of expert reports, as if a group of scientists from another world had taken a television receiver home with them and had reported on it. The chemist said it was made of wood, glass, and metal. The physicist said it radiated heat and light. The engineer said the supporting wheels were too small and in the wrong place for it to run smoothly on a flat surface. But nobody said what it was....

Our recognition of living things, both animal and vegetable, is instant and automatic, and our fellow creatures in the animal world would appear to have the same facility.... Anything living may be edible, lethal, friendly, aggressive, or a potential mate, all questions of prime significance for

**our welfare and continued existence. However, our auto-
matic recognition system appears to have paralyzed our capacity for conscious thought about a definition of life.**

The recognition of forms of life by other forms of life is
instinctive, evolving no doubt as a powerful but unconscious survival factor. In our generation it has become artificial, or at least civilized. Most of us see fish only through
the glass walls of fish bowls and aquariums, and bears only
in zoos. (Yet, thanks to our subconscious animal memories,
residents of Manhattan are said to dream of snakes as often
as natives of Africa.)

Mature human beings, whatever their social or cultural
position, are often preoccupied with matters of life and
death. And the preoccupation seems to be inherent and
persistent in the routine dailiness of life of all adult members of the species—at least until the point at which they
become practicing biologists. None of the catalog of specialists who devote their careers to experiment and measurement at the threshold of biological discovery seem at
all preoccupied with the problem of defining life as the
layman understands it, although it is the life process alone
that makes their field of study so absorbing. Biologists are
of course concerned with the broader contexts and implication of their specialized research in the laboratory. Workers in AIDS and cancer research do care—probably even
more than the rest of us—whether a cure can be found for
the scourges they explore. But concern for the very threshold, the point at which matter organizes itself into life or
disorganizes itself into the death of the host and not just of
the cell—that does not seem to preoccupy the microbiologist or oncologist at all.

An Australian bushman seeing a creature in his path
knows intuitively how to distinguish a living, threatening
creature from a harmless, inert dead body; and he makes
the distinction so essential for his survival in a fraction of
a second, and with no recourse to molecular biology or
computers. The common man—voters and laymen—seems

to have less trouble resorting to his inherited instincts in recognizing the living from the dead than do his scientific and judicial mentors.

NET DEFINITIONS

Most science dictionaries have no entry for the definition of life. This suggests not indifference or oversight, but simple recognition that the word is not an absolute term of science. Science dictionaries having an entry for life usually concede that no acceptable definition has been found that covers all aspects of living matter and excludes all nonliving matter. "Life" is a fuzzy idea, and it is hard to find any single criterion that is not equally applicable to some form of inanimate matter. The definition remains fuzzy because the full range of vital phenomena are consequent upon an as yet not remotely exhausted body of data.

Here, in chronological order, are some of the more serious attempts by highly qualified authorities at a net definition. The broad range of approaches attests to the intractability of their target.

- *Herbert Spencer* gives us what is perhaps the most famous effort to define life in a single phrase: "The continuous adjustment of internal relations to external relations." (*Principles of Biology*, 1864.)
- *Friedrich Engels*. "Life is the mode of existence of proteins, and this mode of existence essentially consists in the constant self-renewal of the chemical constituents of these substances." (*Anti-Duhring*, 1892.) That may sound a little better in the original German.
- *J. Shaxel*, a German biologist: "Living processes and living materials as such simply do not exist save as parts of single whole organisms." (*Grundzuge der Theorienbildung in der Biologie*, 1922.)
- *J. D. Bernal*. "Life is a partial, continuous, progressive, multiform and conditionally interactive self-realization

of the potentialities of atomic electron states." (*The Origin of Life*, 1967.)

- *Paul Weiss* (Rockefeller University). "A living system that does not behave is dead; life is process, not substance." (*The Living System*, 1969.)
- *Marcel Florkin* presents us with "the cellular polyphasic system of integrated macromolecules, commonly known as life." (*A History of Biochemistry*, 1972.)
- *R. Buckminster Fuller* asserts that "life is the eternal present in the temporal." (*Synergetics*, 1975.)
- *Ernest Borek* says we live because of the processes of enzymes. "Life may be defined as a system of integrated, cooperating enzyme reactions." (*The Atoms Within Us*, 1980.)
- *Harold Morowitz*. "We have recently come to view life as a property of very special molecular arrangements called cells." (1984.)
- *Eric Chaisson*. "Living systems stay alive by steadily maintaining themselves far from equilibrium. . . . in fact, unachieved equilibrium can be taken as an essential premise, even an operational definition, of all life." (*The Life Era*, 1987.)
- *Renato Dulbecco*. "Life is the expression of coded instructions contained in a chemical present in all living organisms: DNA." (*The Design of Life*, 1987.)
- *Gerard Piel*. "We have come to recognize life as a geological, cosmic force engaged in the great physical and chemical cycles of our small world's atmosphere, hydrosphere, and lithosphere." (*Address to American Institute of Biological Sciences*, 12 November 1987.)
- *Christopher Langton*. "Life is a property of *form*, not *matter*, a result of the organization of matter rather than something that inheres in the matter itself." (*Artificial Life: SFI Studies in the Sciences of Complexity*, 1989.)

The question of whether life is a property of the organism or whether the organism is a manifestation of life remains unanswered. We do not know whether the "unit of selection" is the individual, the family, the population, or the species. . . . But life is certainly more than an *engagement.* Where is the self that does the self-organizing? Economical as these one-liners are, they provide us in the ensemble a flash of insight into the elusive character of the processes of being alive. Though they come to us from a wide range of different intellectual directions, they appear to accommodate each other remarkably well and without any jarring contradictions. Still, the chasm between physical and metaphysical remains unbridged.

SOME MINIMUM ATTRIBUTES OF LIVING ORGANISMS

If people cannot define life, they at least try to describe it by listing what they see as its inescapable characteristics. This search for life's minimum attributes has as wide an array of approaches as the net definitions just examined. Here is a listing of numbers of minimum characteristics or obligatory properties characterizing living organisms as discerned by a variety of biologists and other scientists.

Three minimum properties. Lawrence J. Henderson, in *The Fitness of the Environment,* 1913, wrote ". . . the natural characteristics of the environment promote and favor complexity, regulation, and metabolism, the three fundamental characteristics of life." L. J. Henderson was both a biochemist and a sociologist. His work cited has the interesting subtitle: *An inquiry into the biological significance of the properties of matter.*

John Maynard Smith, in *The Problems of Biology,* 1986, stated that "Entities with the properties of multiplication, variation, and heredity are alive, and entities lacking one or more of those properties are not."

Jacques Monod, in *Chance and Necessity,* 1971, says that "Life is a system that has three properties: *autonomous morphogenesis,* which means that the system can operate as a self-contained system; *teleonomy*, which means that the system is endowed with a purpose; and *reproductive invariance*, the capacity to reproduce highly ordered structure." Note that purposiveness is specifically defended by Monod as a necessary condition.

Five minimum characteristics. As discussed by Richard Lewontin: "Living organisms are characterized by five properties: they reproduce, they evolve, they recognize themselves, they develop, and they feel." (*The Science of Metamorphoses*, 1989.) Lewontin includes self-recognition, for which there is no general mechanism but which is most commonly manifest in the physiology of higher animals as the formation of antibodies.

Seven physiological functions:
eating,
metabolizing
excreting
breathing
moving
growing
response to external stimuli
—*Britannica 3*

Ten important features of living things:
complexity
organization
uniqueness
emergence
holism
unpredictability—"cows, plants and geraniums are in no
sense inevitable products of evolution"
openness
interconnectedness—"life is fully meaningful only in the
context of the entire biosphere"
disequilibrium
evolution
—Paul Davies, *The Cosmic Blueprint*, 1989

The formulas differ as much in their style as in the intellectual landscape of their authors. But is it not like the story of the blind men describing an elephant?

A BLURRING OF THE DISTINCTIONS

Why are biologists so insouciant about the problem of defining life? Perhaps partly because the imperatives for definition appear to be psychological and philosophical—indeed metaphysical—not scientific. Some of us with a longing for identity or at least an itch for tidiness are haunted by this deficiency at the core of biological studies. It would comfort the laymen to see the question of what life *is* resolved by biologists themselves rather than by theologians and philosophers who do not shirk the issue, but cannot bring to bear the kind of firsthand factual authority we expect from men of science. Without resorting to the authority of scripture and without going into the coterie language of semantics, is there not—should not there be—some agreed definition of life that satisfies our commonsense experience without doing violence to the facts of science?

Many of the most prominent and articulate authorities have assumed postures ranging from indifference to hostility or even scorn. Professor Gal-Or of the Technion-Israel Institute in Haifa dismisses any attempt at such discrimination: "... the distinction between living and nonliving, which was widely discussed at the turn of the century, has lost much of its relevance in the light of accumulative evidence against it—in particular—of the now established characteristics of genes and viruses which may be characterized as "living" or "nonliving" *without* loss of scientific relevance!"* (*Cosmology, Physics, and Philosophy,* 1983.)

* *In remarkably similar language the 15th edition of the* Encyclopedia Britannica *of 1978, vol. 12, p 873, says, "The distinction between living and nonliving, which was widely discussed at the turn of the century, has lost much of its interest for current biology." We must be on to something.*

For the Nobel laureate Sir Peter Medawar the peace of mind afforded by definition can be "too dearly bought." "What is the meaning of the word *life*," he asks. "There is no true meaning," he answers: "There is a *usage* that serves the purposes of the working biologists well enough."

When the French biologist André Lwoff was invited to deliver the Thompson lectures at MIT in 1959, he acknowledged at the outset that "Life is difficult to define, and the easiest solution is to decide, as so many people have done, that its definition is impossible. In his book *The Nature of Life*, Szent-Gyorgi writes: 'Life as such does not exist; nobody has ever seen it. . . . The noun "life" has no sense, there being no such thing.' "

Back in 1937 one of the leading biologists of his day, the Oxford biochemist N. W. Pirie, issued a somber injunction in the learned journal *Perspectives in Biochemistry*, vol. 11, persuading his colleagues to abandon all attempts "to define life" once and for all. The bald title of his article was "The meaninglessness of the terms 'life' and 'living.' " However meaningless those terms may be, he at least managed to combine them into an interesting phrase. In 1953, Pirie asserted that "life" and "living" are words the the scientist has borrowed from the layman. "Life," he says, "is not a thing or a philosophical entity: it is an attitude of mind toward what is being observed." Then he goes on to concede (using a term of which he would deny his colleagues the use) that "No other place and time seem more suitable for the appearance of life than here and now."

When noted scientists like Pirie and Medawar and Szent-Gyorgi say that the word "life" makes no sense, they betray the scientist's penchant for the mathematical description of physical quantities. They display a profound distrust for the notion that mere words can have a true and fixed inner meaning. For Sir Peter Medawar, *life* is simply one of the common terms in science which have been "pirated from the vernacular"—one that science apparently has had to borrow, to its discomfiture, from everyday speech, rather regrettably from the vulgar tongue.

I am haunted by an unwelcome premonition: Could it be at this point in the development of man's knowledge that science has so restricted its domain that our common concern for the distinction between life and nonlife is reduced to a vernacular concept? Does all this herald the advent—and possible supersession—of what we know as natural life by artificial life?

IRRELEVANCE OF ATTEMPTS TO DEFINE LIFE

The terms 'life' and 'living' are examples of ordinary English words the meaning of which—so the biologist finds —become more and more indefinite as biological knowledge accumulates.
> —W. H. Thorpe
> Biology and the Nature of Man, *1962*

Plain men know what they mean when they say a system is alive; scientists do not.
> —André Lwoff
> Biological Order, *1968*

More than anything else it is distaste—rather than neglect or indifference—that prompts many leading biologists to fail to come to grips with the task of defining the life process. Distaste to the point of antagonism. They regard efforts at definition as simplistic and making no contribution to the advancement of research. Energy thus expended might be not just wasted but counterproductive.

We have it on the authority of Ernst Mayr that attempts to define life are futile because "there is no special substance, object or force that can be identified with life." Mayr is the Alexander Agassiz Professor of Zoology at Harvard. He is the author of the monumental *The Growth of Biological Thought* (1982), and he is widely regarded as a leading commentator of his generation on biology. Mayr maintains that "the explanatory equipment of the physical sciences is insufficient to explain complex living systems." Were anyone but he to say this, I would think it a position that verges on nihilism. The literature of biology convinces us that living organisms exhibit processes and possess attributes—such as complexity, macromolecular structure, and genetic program—that differentiate them from inanimate objects. The difference is certainly in degree, and one would presume also in kind. And yet ambiguities persist, hovering at the brink of reductionism, and they are sufficient to cause giants like Mayr to scorn attempts to fudge them.

Perhaps it is unfair to single out *life* as elusive of definition. Without getting further into semantics, *matter* and *energy* are likewise not so easy to define as abstract concepts. Matter and energy can exist without life, but life cannot manifest itself in the world of physical experience without both. Scientists are invariably uneasy with dependence on abstract nouns, even those so closely related to the physical world of nature. Abstract nouns express concepts that are susceptible to scientific measurement only with great difficulty and under controlled circumstances.

As adherents of a descriptive science, biologists can and do deny that there is such a thing as life per se; the only objects of observation and description are living organisms. Professor H. Sandon says:

> **Talk about the "forms of life" suggests comparison with the forms of matter or of energy, limited in number and evolving into one another in fixed predictable ways. Life does not evolve, but complex populations of living organisms do, and their evolution results from their mutual interactions with equally complex environments. The results are almost infinitely varied and unpredictable.**

Organic manifestations are too complex and conceptual tools are apparently too weak for biology to be a predictive science. (Astronomers can tell us the exact moment of the next solar eclipse, but biologists haven't a clue about the next species.) Biology can increasingly describe a number of processes of living organisms—with no apparent upper limit in sight. Living processes yield to the microscope and the taxonomist; they yield to observation and description; but life itself remains elusive. Lancelot Hogben, the British scholar who wrote *Mathematics for the Millions*, has gone so far as to assert that "Biology is not the science of life. Science is not about the study of abstract nouns."

According to Thomas S. Hall, a professor of biology at Washington University in St. Louis, life and matter are not coordinate concepts, ". . . and matter comes closer than life to being a sophisticatedly scientific concept." Hall has written a two-volume history of *Ideas of Life and Matter: studies in the history of general physiology: 600 B.C. to 1900 A.D.* He did not embark on such an ambitious project without some foreknowledge of the murky landscape into which he was venturing:

> When I was a graduate student of biology at Yale, my professor and mentor, the late Alexander Petrunkevitch, admonished me to temper my ambitions and not to hope to "discover the difference between living and nonliving things." While accepting this advice, I was tantalized by it and made up my mind to find out, when time should allow, what major thinkers of the past had thought about this most central of biological questions. [Thomas S. Hall, *Ideas of Life and Matter* (vol. I), 1969]

He had been warned. And at the end of his sweeping survey Hall concludes that life and matter are "conceptual artifacts"—useful fictions, but troublesome ones, "with a notorious tendency to take on an illusory concreteness."

Unlike Hall, I have had no one to warn me.

SCIENTIFIC VS. VERNACULAR LANGUAGE

Scientific language eschews abstract nouns: They are vulnerable to problems of meaning, and science likes terms that are value-neutral. Science counts and measures. Its ideal language is mathematical and its preferred sentences are generalizable formulas—screening out the special case. Our common language is full of fuzz, and it has become a bane of software programmers that computers can deal only with data from which all the fuzz has been removed. Yet fuzz—unprogrammable data—remains the stuff of meaning.

Since some scientists regard attempts to define life as a vernacular impulse, we might as well explore vernacularity and some of its implications. Vernacular speech and design are cultural artifacts and inherently unsuitable for scientific precision. According to Eric Partridge's etymological dictionary *Origins*, the word *vernacular* is from the medieval Latin *vernaculus*, meaning "born in one's master's house." It was used specifically to describe the provenance of a slave born as a member of the household. Partridge qualifies the term as "o.o.o." (of obscure origin) and he suggests that it may have come down to us from the Etruscans. The term is used chiefly to describe certain types of language and architecture. In the former case it applies to idiomatic, native, or dialect speech as opposed to standard or literary usage; in the latter it is descriptive of architecture without professional architects such as the indigenous dwellings of untutored and semiprimitive societies. The architecture of the Cotswold village or the Mediterranean hillside town or the pleasant carpenter's Gothic of 19th-century America or the adobe settlements of New Mexican Indians are all vernacular, and, though esthetic values vary from generation to generation, they are generally regarded as virtuous and associated with a golden past.

As long as scientists have not defined life for us in the technical terminology of their discipline, we may perhaps be forgiven when it comes to *usage*—pirates though we be—for lapsing into language from our golden past. Likewise, in a later section (see page 83), I will assert that the threshold between the animate and the inanimate can be described in no language other than that of common everyday speech. Is this perhaps because such thresholds embody metaphysical echoes in the language of our Indo-European ancestors?

2
Describing life

—————⌁—————

We have started out by examining the limits of attempts to define life, and we found that the limits are inescapable and probably beyond the reach of science for the foreseeable future. But much comfort and compensation for such limits can be found in simple contemplation of the great variety of manifestations of living organisms and their self-organizing processes. The descriptions that follow are from a range of sources—not all of them biologists—and they are illustrative rather than exhaustive. The appeal of these descriptions is that they all delineate certain necessary conditions of life, but the enigma remains that none of them, even all taken together, are sufficient conditions.

LIFE AS ORGANIZATION OF CARBON AND WATER

That the vital functions of natural organisms are largely *chemical* is the chief reason that carbon and water are so essential to life. Vital functions may be seen as indirectly mechanical (as in muscles) or even potentially electronic (as in the semiconductors of artificial life), but plants and animals as we know them are manifests of organic chemistry, hence aqueous and carbonaceous. Carbon and water can make structures, particularly the chemical structure of protein foldings; proteins can make muscle, but they cannot make mechanical structures in the ordinary sense.

Carbon. Natural organisms entail the chemical transformation of elemental atoms and small molecules into large molecules with long stable chains of great precision and complexity. Carbon is the only element we know that can bind itself in long chains without a great expense in energy.

The carbon atom with its four bonding potentials arrayed outwardly from a common center generates the form of a pyramid with a triangular base: a tetrahedron. These bonds splay out from each other like a photographer's tripod (at the conventional *tetrahedral angle* of 109° 28' 16"), accommodating chemical bonds with as many as four other atoms. This protean arrangement is not available to any other element in our established chemical repertory. (One of the leading scientific journals of organic chemistry has the simple title of *Tetrahedron.*) Carbon maximizes—indeed (with silicon) virtually monopolizes—the unique geometry of the tetrahedron.

The carbon atom because of its small size and the four electrons in its outer shell can form four strong covalent bonds with other atoms. Equally important, it can join other carbon atoms to form chains and rings and generate large molecules with no apparent upper limit to their size. In this configuration carbon has a particular affinity for bonding with the hydrogen molecule to generate the hydrocarbons so integral to metabolic processes. The history of biochemistry suggests that only life making use of carbon can come into use spontaneously. As the 20th century closes, scientists speculate on the creation of artificial life based on silicon (see Chapter 18), but such life would be secondhand, the result of human intervention; it appears unable to evolve spontaneously.

Although carbon is widely distributed, it is not plentiful, as it makes up only about 0.2 percent of the earth's crust. At ordinary temperatures it is very unreactive; it is difficult to oxidize and it does not dissolve in any solvent. But carbon is nonpareil in its ability to form large molecules. Only silicon—a poor second—comes anywhere close. Silicon is also a four-valent element and it performs a structuring function in the mineral kingdom as carbon does for the organic world.

Carbon among all the elements is uniquely fecund in its proclivity for the formation of compounds. Organic chemists have described more than a million carbon compounds, and scores of new ones are being added every working day. More than nine-tenths of all identified and catalogued chemical compounds contain carbon. (By contrast, the repertoire of silicon-based compounds available to inorganic chemistry is less than 100,000.)

Water. It is not possible for carbon to perform these tasks without an internal environment and an external environment of water. (There is probably not enough available time and available energy for carbon to perform the task of organizing life without water.) We know of no other life than that based on carbon compounds in liquid water.

Water accounts for 70 percent of the weight of cells, and most reactions within the cell occur in an aqueous environment. If we disregard water, all but a minor fraction of the molecules of a cell are carbon compounds. Water, with its high freezing point and low boiling point, is liquid in the temperature range of most of the earth's surface.

The chemical functions and the mechanical functions of water are virtually integral and inseparable. As a recent article by two chemists puts the matter:

> **Solid as we may seem, we are all liquid beings: nearly two-thirds of the human body, by volume, consists of water— about ten gallons of it, encapsulated in trillions of cells. Water is the universal medium for all biological activity; it dissolves, dilutes, transports, and reacts with every chemical essential for life. In tears, it cleanses the eye; in saliva, the**

enzymes it contains break down food; in lymph fluid, it flushes out bacteria and foreign particles. After flowing through the stomach and reaching the intestines, water passes directly into the bloodstream; 90 percent of the fluid component of the blood, the plasma, is water. Blood, in turn, is continuously filtered through the kidneys, which secrete the aqueous solution urine; excess water is also purged from the cells and eliminated from the lungs and the skin during breathing and sweating. Water constitutes at least half the volume of each organ—from the liver to the brain; even bones, dry and unyielding as they appear, are 10 to 30 percent liquid.

Next to air—of which we are normally unconscious—water is the most immediate, familiar component of our environment, as anyone who has experienced thirst can attest. Water is the universal substrate for plant and animal organization. People who know no other chemical formula know the significance of H_2O.

Within living organisms the water is almost never fresh. Within most living cells the saltwater is 10 times as rich in potassium as in blood plasma, lymph fluids, or the open sea.

Water appears to be essential to life because it maintains the three-dimensional structure of membranes, RNA proteins, and many other important biological molecules. Proteins are useless when dry. In biochemical terms, the most important properties of water are its polarity and cohesiveness; water solvates polar molecules and weakens ionic and hydrogen bonds. The theme of chemical organization of life is further developed in the discussion of macromolecules that follows (see Chapter 3).

LIFE AS A MODULATOR OF SUNLIGHT

All organic life derives its ultimate source of energy from the sun. Only life has the capacity to convert photons of light into macromolecules of digestible energy, but there are myriad scenic routes, backwaters, and holding patterns by which solar radiation ends up in self-propagating biological organisms.

There are three key processes of life triggered by sunlight acting on simple surfaces of earthly molecules.

Photosynthesis. The most familiar effect of sunlight as studied in the textbooks is photosynthesis, by which plants and some bacteria capture sunlight for the energy needs of all forms of life. Photosynthesis is the biological process by which electromagnetic energy in the form of light is converted into chemical energy. Somehow, within the tissues of plants and microorganisms, energy is taken from sunlight to pump electrons into carbon dioxide so that it can combine with water to form carbohydrates, the ultimate power source for all life. The process evolved first in bacteria before becoming manifest in plants. Photosynthesis is the most important chemical reaction on earth. (Nitrogen fixation is probably the second.)

Vision. The second result of sunlight is vision, exploited by animals in a variety of eyes and other detectors to respond to signals that can be interpreted to control locomotion—toward food, for example, or away from danger. The perception and processing of visible light in organisms is of great antiquity. In the prodigal evolution of animals, the eye, an integral part of the brain and the window of the mind, developed independently in different species at least 40 times in at least 40 different ways. Over the eons sunlight found 40 different channels of getting through to and registering on the brain; or, conversely, the brain and nervous system discovered as many different pathways of capturing the energy and information of the impinging sunlight. The human eye is just one of the 40 ways.

In the mammalian line that led to man, sensory development witnessed a transition from an olfactory and tactile mode of life to a visual mode. The lateral position of the eyes as in horses and cows was fine for grazing; but the eyes moved to the front to provide the binocular overlap for the carnivores so they could better prey on other animals. In humans the rate of visual input is so enormous that mental processes filter out all data ruled irrelevant in order to prevent visual overload. It seems to make evolutionary sense that perception works in such a way that consciousness has no access to the raw data.

Photoperiodism. The third effect of sunlight, called photoperiodism, is the least obvious; and it applies to both plants and animals, all of which have evolved mechanisms for responding to daily cycles of light and dark and annual cycles of intensity. Photoperiodism provides the seasonal schedule for the flowering of plants, the pupation of insects, and the nesting of birds.

Biological life is universally attuned to the regularity of variations, the periodicities in the intensity of light on the time scales of day and year. They are in fact determined by the fundamental constants of nature. Months are manifests of the peculiar lunar harmonics. Not so weeks, which have their basis in physiological rhythms more profound than mere cultural artifacts, but seeming to have no relation to periodicities in the intensity of light.

The interplay of matter and energy invites a high level of generalization, and few can have risen to the occasion better than Albert Szent-Gyorgi, holder of two Nobel laureates, in his opening remarks at a symposium on "Light and Life" held at Johns Hopkins University, Baltimore, in 1961:

It is common knowledge that the ultimate source of all our energy and negative entropy is the radiation of the sun. When a photon interacts with a material particle on our globe it lifts one electron from an electron pair to a higher level. This excited state, as a rule, has but a very short lifetime and the electron drops back within 10^{-7} to 10^{-8} seconds to the ground state, giving off its excess energy in one way or another. Life has learned to catch the electron in the excited

> state, uncouple it from its partner and let it drop back to the
> ground state through its biological machinery, utilizing its
> excess energies for the processes. . . .
>   . . . while Life [sic] is continuous, radiation is intermit-
> tent and the possibilities of storing high-energy electrons are
> very limited.

The mind's picture of this has an almost sexual charge . . .
life catching the electron in the excited state.

The currency of the ATP molecule. Szent-Gyorgy goes
on to celebrate nature's discovery of a method of preserving
the electronic free energy "in a rather sophisticated form,
as part of the ATP molecule." ATP stands for adenosine
triphosphate, a complex molecule that functions in plants
at the heart of the photosynthetic process of transforming
the energy of visible light into the chemical energy of food
molecules. In animals it powers all physical activity from
growth to muscle contraction. It functions as the molecular
current of energy for virtually all biological processes, and
it does so very rapidly, without generating heat. A given
molecule of ATP survives no more than a minute after its
manufacture. It has been calculated that in a twenty-four-
hour period the human body manufactures more than its
own weight in ATP.

The primary event in photosynthesis is the light-acti-
vated transfer of an electron from one substance to another
. . . as in the pumping of protons across a membrane. "In
essence," says Lubert Stryer in describing the synthesis of
ATP, "life is powered by proton batteries that are ultimately
energized by the sun."

At the same Baltimore symposium of 1961 Bentley
Glass, a biologist at Johns Hopkins, summarized its final
report with the conclusion that the acquisition of energy
and its entrapment in suitable chemical compounds is the
primary business of life. This is most effectively accomplished by absorbing radiant energy. The radiation from the
sun with the highest energies has wavelengths too short to

be trapped by living mechanisms because their direct effect would be to destroy enzymes and mutate the genes. The invisible radiation, with wavelengths longer than light waves, consists of quanta of insufficient energy to drive the machinery of metabolism. As Bentley Glass describes it:

An enormous range in frequency and wavelength of solar radiation bathes our earth, yet most of this is of no avail to life.

In the single octave of radiation with wavelengths between 3500 A and 7000 A, comprising the near ultraviolet and visible portions of the spectrum, living organisms find it possible to subsist between disintegration and inertia. Life is thus ultimately a photochemical phenomenon.

Isn't this an echo of the grand theme of all literature: to carry out the business of life in subsistence between disintegration and inertia?

On a global scale, of the total energy from the sun fixed daily by photosynthesis, human civilization consumes about one-fifteenth of that received by the vegetation on the earth's surface. (In biology, "fix" means to convert nitrogen into biologically stable and assimilable compounds.) If we continue to increase our energy at the same rate as over the past two decades, the human species will, by 2050, be using as much energy as all land animals and plants put together.

There is always a spoiler some place, and the elegant generalization that life gets all of its energy ultimately from the sun has since been challenged. In 1977 marine biologists first discovered thriving communities of animals (not just bacteria) living 8,000 feet below the surface in total darkness. Most deep-sea animals live on organic matter falling from the surface, particulate debris settling weeks, months, years after sinking from the sunlit ocean wave tops. But there are newly discovered creatures that live near hydrothermal vents spewing mineral-rich water from which they find an exotic source of energy that is not the sun. As Boyce

Rensberger reported in *The Washington Post*, "comprising colorfully fringed worms, mussels, clams and crabs . . . they constitute a food chain that derives its energy from . . . chemicals exuded by the vents, mainly compounds of sulfur and oxygen called sulfides." The sulfides are metabolized by bacteria that live symbiotically in the gills and guts of clams and mussels. "The bacteria employ a metabolic process [that is] fundamentally different from that of conventional bacteria." The sulfides are not derived even indirectly from sunlight through photosynthetic and organic processes. Though the sulfur and oxygen in the sulfates are not solar in origin, they are remotely related to the heavens in the sense that all elements are ultimately astral.

LIFE HAS EVOLVED

Evolution may not be directly intuitive, but it is naive to conceive of life, of any living thing, except in the context of never-ending metamorphosis and development. Cells have a more ancient lineage than species, species than populations, populations than individuals. Every individual organism in the biosphere of the current, contemporary moment is only a freeze-frame, snapshot takeout of an irreversible scenario.

The essential quality of life is that it be not only complex but dynamic, and the chief dynamic element in life is evolution, the sine qua non, the unvarying condition, is that *life must have evolved.* Life evolves by remembering and building on its past achievements. Biology is not just a descriptive science; it is a historical one. Here is Gunther Stent on the matter:

> **The most profound thing that can be said about life—not just human life but *all* life—is that it is a historical process, thanks to which every individual now alive embodies the past experience of his ancestors. Furthermore, the modern theory of evolution . . . is explanatory rather than predictive.**

This feature removes the study of evolution from the realm of "hard science" and places it within the domain of general history, which explains the present in terms of the past but cannot predict the future.

Hard science likes results reproducible in the laboratory. Biology is different. The historical uniqueness of living systems—wherever they have been found on earth—means that the concrete content of biological information in any particular gene or molecule cannot be deduced from the laws of physics and chemistry without reference to the history of their evolution.

Natural selection. Only the realm of biology evolves by the operation of natural selection. Natural selection is a unique mechanism for turning rare events into common events. Speaking genetically: the slow accumulation of minor variations will in time produce unpredictable and magnificent biological results, such as orchids. Speaking culturally and sociologically, human beings employ institutions and committees for similar purposes in crude imitation of biological mutations. The source of creativity among humans remains elusive. (Artificial life—when it comes—may or may not evolve. If it does not evolve, it will be nothing like the natural life of our history on this planet. If it does evolve, it seems improbable that it will be able to do so by any mechanism approaching natural selection.)

The uniquely biological phenomena of the world are ontogenies and phylogenies. The process of ontogeny is the history of an organism from its conception to its birth and maturity and death. The process of phylogeny is the ancestral lineage of generations of organisms. We have it on the authority of a neuroanatomist that

Life is not a DNA molecule or a nerve cell or a kumquat or a wolf spider; life is not a particular thing at a given time. Life is a special set of sequences; it is the autonomous and recurrent stereotyped re-creation of certain very complex

patterns. Life is a child growing and becoming a mother and eventually a grandmother.

Truly biological entities ... have ancestors, and they beget progeny.

Evolution itself is a fact as well as a theory. That evolution works through a process of natural selection and mutation is a theory—the Darwinian theory. But that we have evolved is a fact beyond theory.

In the biological world there are many instances in which the same adaptation has evolved separately and independently. This phenomenon is known to evolutionary biologists as *convergence*. Echolocation, for example, has evolved independently in bats, birds, dolphins, and whales.

Evolution does not always proceed irreversibly in the direction of increasing complexity. Both from the fossil record and the current studies of species, evolutionary and development biologists find many examples of degeneration and decline in complexity. Despite recurring patterns of regression, however, the overall tendency of evolution is toward increasing complexity—at least in the animal kingdom; in the case of plants the pattern is more questionable. But there is no question that without evolution life would never have become so interesting. No scientist will concede that any natural processes of evolution are inevitable, much less goal-oriented. And yet we can all sense that plants and animals have organized themselves somewhat better than the blind-chance tactics of natural selection would have dictated. Has there really been enough time for all of us to have gotten where we are without the operation of some factors other than pure chance?

There is, however, much popular hostility—some of it quite vocal—to the notion of evolution. Fundamentalist Christians prefer the dogma of creationism. Once in a White House press conference President Ronald Reagan was asked if he believed in evolution, and the best response he could muster was that he felt "there must be a catch in it some-where."

It is a common hypothesis that nothing in biology makes sense except in the light of evolution. It is not only species that evolve; so do physiological organs and bio-chemical pathways. The problem that remains is that, al-though evolution is an unvarying condition of life, it is not an exclusive or definitive one; evolution is a phenomenon shared with the rest of creation. Life evolves, but so does everything else . . . the 109 elements, mountains and shore-lines, clouds, stars, and galaxies—they all evolve in time.

Once atoms have evolved, they persist in inanimate aggregates or are captured in organisms feeding on organ-isms. Inanimate evolution was slow, proceeding without benefit of natural selection. . . . Organic evolution has been much more rapid with vertebrate mammals and primates suddenly appearing as burgeoning creatures throughout all of the most recent geologic era.

LIFE AS MATTER, ENERGY, AND INFORMATION

Biomolecules are like meaningful sentences: they have in-formation content.
  —*Ilya Prigogine*, Nobel medalist in Chemistry, 1989

Why can't we cozy up to information the way we can cozy up to matter? Information is so abstract, uncongenial to our reflex for the tangible. We can never wrap ourselves up in a truckload of slick computer paper printouts the way we can wrap ourselves up in a fuzzy old hooked rug. Only the blind touch information.

We think of matter as just the most fundamental stuff of a physical universe. Since the revolution in modern phys-ics, we have learned that matter and energy are inseparable, and their theoretical treatment has come to be subsumed under a joint caption: Matter & Energy. We have more recently been told, particularly with the advances in micro-technologies, that information itself can make just as plausible a claim to being an inseparable aspect of the physical world.

Our intuition, however, lags behind scientific discovery. Most of us are more comfortable thinking of matter as the real basic stuff. We are at the point where intangible information has become tangible. It has only recently become respectable to recognize information as essential to a description of the natural world and how it operates. Perhaps this intuitive lag is because we are told that matter and energy fulminated at the moment of the Big Bang 15 billion years ago, and we sense that though information may be universally pervasive now, we have no reason to believe it was present at the creation.

Intuitively, we sense that matter and energy are as incommensurable as words and pictures. We find romance but no comfort in recognizing that matter and energy are equatable only in the language of mathematics: Einstein's equation. Journalistic accounts of the interaction of matter and energy in the experiments in supercolliders are exotic but unconvincing. We have as yet no literature in which matter and energy and information are commensurate—or, as Buckminster Fuller would say, intercommensurable or even (as he did say) omniintercommensurable.

In recent years biological descriptions have become increasingly expressed in terms of matter, energy, and information. Journals of research in molecular biology bring cumulative reports of new messenger systems and new forms of information transmission being discovered within the protein molecules of organisms and within and between their constituent cells.

The study of the structure of solid matter—crystallography—is a venerable one that achieved its first flowering around 1660. It is a crystallographer, Alan Mackay of Birkbeck College, University of London, who has given us a synoptic picture of the role of information in the description of life:

> The greatest discovery of our century has been that, parallel
> to the structure of proteins and the other substances which
> make up the biochemical pathways of all living matter, there
> is an information system made of the same atoms which
> describe the proteins in another language: that of DNA. It
> is as if an anthropologist, come from another world to study
> our material civilization, had left the Ethnographic Gallery
> of the British Museum and wandered into the Reading
> Room. . . . Nature is dialectical. . . . Informational structures
> are material, like the rest of the organism, and subject to
> the same laws of chemistry.

Mackay's statement is as dogmatic as it is exuberant; it
embraces the notion that information organizes itself *physically* at the molecular level. That is an extremely powerful
formulation. But there is an unresolved ambiguity in the
notion that information—unaided—can organize itself. The
resolution requires some kind of physical scaffold and agent
to do the organizing. The scaffold is the molecule; the agent
is somewhere in the mechanics of genes; the theater is the
cell (see Chapter 25).

Virtually all of contemporary molecular biology functions within the domain of information in the shape of the
DNA-RNA helix. A biochemical description of life sees organisms as systems containing reproducible hereditary information coded in molecules of nucleic acid. Proteins and
enzymes that make up the pathways of all living matter
contain an information system—like a word processor or a
library catalog—describing their functions and structure in
the discrete language of DNA. Here is the recognition that
information can have concrete physical *shape* conforming
directly to the laws of chemistry. Such patterns at the molecular level design and control the transformation of organs
and organisms from one phase of transition to another.

It is an oversimplification, however, to conceive of organic information as originating solely within the gene—
like a computer program on a floppy disk. Genes are inseparable from the cells that envelop them, and the infor-

mation they express is not a one-way export into a substrate or neutral cellular environment. The reality is that genes are only part of a system where information flows both ways; information is a two-way street in which gene and cell interact.

The most arresting aspect of the formula is that it prescribes organization at the *molecular* level. Atoms may be complex, but molecules are inevitably more so. What we are dealing with is the lowest possible level in nature at which information can be organized. Information thus becomes identified with physical form.

An irreducible property of any system of life as we know it is that at the cellular or creature level it must have a chemical basis for the storage of genetic information. In our human society we have learned how to store information mechanically and electronically—that is, culturally—but the kind of information required by organisms at first hand appears to be uniquely susceptible to only chemical storage.

Information exchange in natural systems is not limited to the molecular level: in developing organisms it occurs mainly through patterns at the surface of cells; ants and mammals employ chemical signals; in human societies communication is uniquely characterized by language.

Possibly the greatest biological discovery of our century is that nature is dialectical. There exists a tension and interconnectedness between matter and information in the same kind of sweeping generalization that Karl Marx resorted to when he used the language of dialectics to utter a social dogma prescribing how history and economics are interdependent.

LIFE AS PATTERN AND PROGRAM

Conventionally speaking, the occurrence of regular patterns in nature—except for crystals—is associated with organic life. The concurrent manifestation of an intrinsic program is also associated with life. These are rather elementary descriptions. The electromagnetic spectrum, the solar system, the biospheric model of the Gaia hypothesis (see page 283), the plate tectonics of geology all postulate cosmic and terrestrial patterns and processes that transcend the limits of biology as familiarly appreciated.

An appreciation of pattern in nature may be found in a work of fiction by a grandson of the eminent Victorian Thomas Henry Huxley, Aldous Huxley, in *Time Must Have a Stop*, 1944:

> **The difference between a piece of stone and an atom is that an atom is highly organized, whereas the stone is not. The atom is a pattern, and the molecule is a pattern, and the crystal is a pattern; but the stone, although it is made up of these patterns, is just a mere confusion. It's only when life appears when you begin to get organization on a larger scale. Life takes the atoms and molecules and crystals; but, instead of making a mess of them like the stone, it combines them into new and more elaborate patterns of its own.**

Huxley does not explore the way geological properties and forces of gravity tend to leave traces of pattern in almost any piece of stone or rock. But such forces are comparatively inert. Huxley is addressing the randomness of rock. There are not nearly as many words in the language for organization as there are for its opposite. Huxley's word is *confusion*. A stone can be very complex, but complexity without organization is of little interest. Living systems are constituted of relatively few of the common chemical elements, yet what makes living matter unique is the way its limited number of elementary constituents are put together in time and space: the way they are organized.

There appears, however, to be an inherent tension between the inertness of matter and the dynamics of organisms. Modern textbooks of biology recognize an organizing program as the essence of life.

Textbooks have been neglected as a literary genre; they are not often thought of as charming. A recent college-level work by Salvador E. Luria, Stephen Jay Gould, and Sam Singer (*A View of Life*, 1981) is nothing less than that. In presenting the phenomenon that Aldous Huxley treated as metaphor, they describe their area of concern as the programming of organisms. They postulate that there are only two classes of organisms on our planet. One class is inert and inorganic, obeying the physical forces in a purely mechanical way; the second consists of what we call *organisms*, which includes plants, animals, and bacteria in a rich and practically infinite variety. The peculiarity of all organisms is that they reproduce; they have heredity; they incorporate a set of instructions specifying the property of their descendants.

> **The possession of an intrinsic program [is] the central property of organisms. This program, lodged in the DNA sequence of chromosomes, is a set of instructions that directs the building of form, regulates function, and produces evolution through historical change.**
>
> **Life is directed by a program, and this program may, with some reason, be called the secret of life.**

Not many textbooks talk about secrets—even reasonable secrets—but this one does. Perhaps talk of secrets is more seductive of students than mathematical formulas.

LIFE ASSEMBLES ITSELF

The most satisfactory approach to a description of the mechanics of life that I have come across was written not by a scientist but by Boyce Rensberger, a science writer:

> **The concept of self-assembly . . . is crucial to understanding how life works. Under the right conditions, atoms or small molecules automatically link—like water molecules assembling themselves into snowflakes—to form predictable combinations. Life's chemistry generally involves larger, more**

complex molecules but these too assemble themselves into predictable structures. The discovery of self-assembly explains many events in cells that once seemed utterly mysterious.

It is the collective interactions of ... chemicals that constitute the phenomenon called life.

Life itself, at least as biologists usually understand it, is the collective interaction of molecules assembling themselves into larger structures and hundreds of enzymes mediating a vast network of chemical processes. The arena for most of these events is the individual cell.

In order for molecules to assemble themselves in the cellular theater they must draw upon sources of energy from elsewhere in their environment. Living organisms maintain themselves in a fantastically improbable state. They are able to accomplish this because they operate as open systems rather than closed ones.* The primal molecules survive from the Cenozoic through the Holocene era as exquisite examples of their capacity to diminish their own improbability.

Living organisms ... preserve their order in spite of continuous irreversible processes and even proceed, in embryonic development and evolution toward ever higher differentiations. ... In open systems with intake of matter rich in high energy, maintenance of a high degree of order and even advancement toward higher order is thermodynamically permitted. (Ludwig von Bertalanffy, *General Systems Theory*, 1968)

(The theme of self-organization is further discussed in Chapter 17.)

---

* A closed system in equilibrium does not need energy for its preservation; nor can energy be obtained from it. Living organisms are open systems, in von Bertalanffy's theory, and as such they can maintain themselves in a state of high statistical improbability, of order and organization (von Bertalanffy, 1968).

LIFE REGULATES ITSELF

Self-regulation is a prolonged rearguard action by the individual against counterattacks at the population and species levels. Self-regulation is a struggle against probability, against the sink of entropy. There is throughout the physical world a prevailing tendency for things to arrange themselves in the least complicated, most probable way. It is a universal characteristic of natural life to resist this tendency. (It is only an occasional—when built-in—characteristic of machines to resist the tendency.)

The mechanism of self-regulation is called homeostasis. It is a phenomenon that operates at every biological level from cell to organism to ecosystem. It maintains the integrity of any particular living system under the thermodynamic stresses of changing environmental conditions.

When I was a junior in college I encountered my first homeostatic device. I joined the Naval Reserve and sailed off as a midshipman in the USS *Arkansas* on a training cruise to Guantanamo Bay, Cuba. I was fascinated to learn how every gun turret of the battleship had its servomechanism, an automatic device—rugged but highly sensitive—to keep turret and gun barrel trained on target despite the roll, yaw, and pitch of the vessel. It performed this by the action of tapered rods in hydraulic fluid valving a perforated filter, providing error-sensing feedback like an automatic pilot well before the days of electronics. The point is that homeostasis (like so many attributes of life) is also available in such special cases to inanimate systems.

The word *homeostasis* was introduced to us in 1932 by Dr. Walter B. Cannon in a book called *The Wisdom of the Body*. (Cannon was the first neurologist to use X rays.) He observed that the body has its own equilibrium, an active process in which deviations from the norm induce reactions in the opposite direction. The effect is to maintain uniform conditions by continuous and delicate compensations. Blood and tissue fluids require a constant optimum temperature to function effectively independent of the body's external environment. Dr. Cannon assigned this regulatory function to the nervous system, and he called it homeostasis.

Homeostasis operates overlappingly on at least four concurrent conceptual levels:

At the *physiological* level it maintains relatively stable internal conditions in animal organisms—such as a constant degree of body heat, or water balance within the body, or the oxygen content of the blood, or even the amount of light that reaches the retina of the eye.

At the *psychological* level homeostasis maintains a relatively stable condition in the individual with respect to disparate drives and motivations. (At least most of the time.)

At the *sociological* level it manifests itself as a tendency toward relatively stable social conditions with respect to various competing factors—such as food supply or population pressures among animals or competing political or cultural factors among men.

Homeostasis also operates on an *evolutionary* level, in which species respond to the challenges of the environment.

Life is, in general, an improbable state of matter; it is really a tour de force achieved against heavy odds, by means of a slow ascent through evolution. If it is not to be snuffed out by hostile environments, life must at all times maintain, and whenever possible improve, its adaptedness to its surroundings. Changing environments present the severest challenges, since it is quite unlikely that the genetic endowments formed in response to the old environments will be, by accident, fully suited to the new ones. [Theodosius Dobzhansky, *The Biology of Ultimate Concern*, 1967]

Where homeostasis succeeds, life prevails; where it fails, death ensues. It is a primary engine of evolution.

In 1948 Norbert Wiener popularized the concept of Cybernetics with its concept of negative feedback in the control of physiological and mechanical systems—in neural networks, computers, and automatic control systems. Man has built machines that regulate themselves, like servo-mechanisms on battleships. Man might even build machines that can build machines that can regulate themselves. When men can do that they probably will, and thus open the prospect of their own obsolescence—and even eventual irrelevance.

LIFE REPAIRS ITSELF

Organic life is under constant threat of degradation from the spontaneous breakage of chemical bonds at the molecular level and from multiple assaults from sun, wind, fire, and accident and the hostility of other creatures at the level of the environment. Plants and animals exhibit remarkable powers of recovery from internal infections and from traumatic shock.

There are delicate limitations to the capacity of self-repair. Some traumas are beyond repair. Were it not so, were self-repair effective to the point of rejuvenescence, then the dread specter of immortality would be invoked.

> It seems paradoxical that the most important organ in the body—the brain—is the least able to cope with damage. In the course of evolution the central nervous system of the higher animals seems to have lost its capacity to regenerate. To compensate, the skull and spine afford protection against all but the most severe damage, but vulnerable to the accidents of our high-speed automotive society. [Eugene Mallove, *The Quickening Universe*, 1987.]

LIFE AS THE REPLICATION OF IDENTITIES

Throughout the physical universe of matter there are many patterns of similarity—even symmetry—constantly repeating themselves. But in the inanimate world they are virtually never identical, at least in the macro scale above elemental particularity. Stars and galaxies have similar patterns as do rocks. Crystals have a very limited repertoire of symmetries available for their organization, but no two examples are exactly identical. The myriads of snowflakes all conform to hexagonal symmetry, yet they are archetypically nonalike.

DNA by itself makes nothing, not even more DNA. DNA together with RNA are parts of a complex molecular ensemble, all of which must be in place and functioning for the production of proteins, the stuff of which bodies are made. Only through this process in all the natural world can bodies make direct replicas of other bodies. All of the higher organisms—animal and vegetable—can reproduce only indirectly and only through the mechanical agency of these genetic molecules. Only the organic complexity of nature manifests the capacity of endlessly recurring replication of identical macromolecules. In the world of plants and animals there are various staple protein molecules that exist in absolutely identical copies. "If this were produced by chance alone, without the aid of natural selection," wrote Francis Crick, "it would be regarded as almost infinitely improbable."

Given the level of complexity, the melody of an organic program will never get played the same way twice, however recognizable it is to an observer.

LIFE IS WARM

Temperature and radiation are easy to measure in precise numbers, but the feeling of warmth is hard to describe in words. It is felt by the entire body. The skin is the only organ directly involved in the sensation of heat, but all of the senses are involved.

In the twilight zone of waking, feelings of warmth and coolness are prior to consciousness itself. In the words of the physicist Hans von Baeyer:

> [We] might conjecture that because warmth is required by
> a fetus long before it registers any other sensory stimuli, the
> sensation of warmth is more deeply etched in the psyche
> and represents a transition between the perceptions of the
> body and those of the spirit.
>
> Unlike gravity, which we take for granted, we talk about
> warmth in minute detail. We worry when it is wrong, rejoice
> when it is right, and share our concern in endless redundancy
> with all who will listen. The ambient warmth is among the
> most reliable staples of human communication.

Life is warm but never hot. Some energy levels—certainly
above 4000°C—are radically inimical to homeostasis. A theoretical biological threshold of 4000°C is proposed because
that is about the limit for chemical processes to function;
above that point physics takes over from chemistry. The
temperature range within which life is permitted corresponds with that within which water is a liquid; the con-
gruence appears to be more of a condition than a
coincidence.

LIFE MOVES

When I was an apprentice seaman in boot camp in 1941, I
learned the U.S. Navy's first law of survival: If it moves,
salute it; if it doesn't move, paint it.

We know of no life that is utterly static and immobile.
Coral reefs are pretty stable, but they grew in the first place.
Sea anemones and giant clams don't move around; naturalists call them *sessile*, but they move their organs of ingestion and sensing. Prairie dogs standing sentinel on the
mounds of their compounds know they are safe from predators, for they will not be recognized as living creatures as
long as they remain immobile.

Capacity for motion. Plants are anchored in roots but
they grow, twist, and wither. Flowers turn in response to

stimulus from the sun, as do the leaves of trees and vines. Even the internal structures of seeds and eggs change their patterns in an enormous range of time spans. Cells change their shape and are propelled by their flagella; even those lacking motility move things around in their insides with their microtubules, their centrioles, and their spindles. Two theoretical biologists have described the process in the context of evolution: "The evolution of biological process is not the infusion of motion into a static system . . . but the modulation of chaotic motion, which is the natural state of existence for complex systems."

The problem of motion marks one of the crucial differences between the animate and the inanimate. In common opinion it is to living things only that belongs the power of movement, the capacity to initiate motion. Material things like billiard balls can only react to impulses from other objects. Living systems express motion not only in relation to their neighbors in place, but to their antecedents in time, ranging from population to bodily organs. One of the most striking features of living systems is their cyclic nature; the processes from birth to death repeat through generations, as do annual cycles in populations. In addition to the monthly and circadian rhythms, there are, on a shorter time scale, the periodicities of experimental physiology such as the repetitive discharge of neurons, the heart beat, and the slower rhythms of breathing.

Purposeful motion implies the processing of information. The most primitive bacteria or jellyfish have to have a sensory system to connect with the environment and guide their propulsion. It has even been proposed that the impulse to purposeful motility was the original cause for the development of the nervous system, and that the nervous system as centralized in the brain has ultimately impelled organisms toward culture. It may have all begun with motion and reaction to motion.

LIFE & ENVIRONMENT INTERACT

Life and the environment are inextricably and reciprocally linked. Life scouts at every margin; it tests all possible niches, it flourishes where extremity occurs. Life adapts relentlessly and ingeniously to constraints of temperature, moisture, light, and atmosphere. In the process, life keeps the environment suitable for its survival. The flora and fauna of life inform the geological record with their past variety and endow the environment with sentience.

Jonas Salk has put the matter in the historical perspective of evolution: "The organism, and the cells and molecules that compose it, cannot be thought of separately from their environments as each evolved in a series of previous environments."

Dialectical biology recognizes the complex integration of natural forces at three different magnitudes—those of gene, organism and environment. It is a school of biological thought that seeks to apply some of the methodologies of Marx and Engels to compensate for the shortcomings of Cartesian reductionism. Among its chief proponents are Richard Levins and Richard Lewontin. As the latter wrote in 1983, "What dialectical biology attempts to do is to break down the alienation of subject and object, to insist on the interpenetration of gene, organism, and environment" . . . emphasizing "the way in which organisms define and alter their environment in the process of their life activities."

To put the matter most neatly, organisms do not evolve in an environment; rather organisms and their environment coevolve. It is this phenomenon that British geneticist C. H. Waddington has termed the epigenetic landscape. Epigenetic effects are those due to environmental influences rather than built-in programming in the cell. Over the evolutionary long haul and through the feedback of natural selection, the flow of information from the environment eventually leaves its markers in the gene pool.

It is not only on genes, cells, and organisms that the environment leaves its markers. Modern industrial technology, with its threat of the supersession of nature by culture, has brought with it an environment that is predominantly built rather than given, a development that is indelibly leaving its epigenetic imprint on both the habitat and psyche of human beings (see Chapter 26).

THE INNATE COMPLEXITY OF LIFE

Complexity affords a clue to how we might reconcile, how we might come to live with, the lacunae and contradictions in this chapter's mosaic of overlapping descriptions of life.

Although the living organism is a highly ordered structure, its orderliness is not the simple periodic order of a crystal. The organism is always the product of a combination of overlapping and diverse periodicities subtly woven together into a self-sustaining pattern—a complex. The genes themselves, which guide the entire structure, are complex patterns of periodicities acting as templates for the orderly processes in, and the precise reproduction of, each cell.

Contemplating the complexity of living matter, one may wonder whether such matter is governed by the same laws of nature that govern inanimate matter; and we can ask how two such different states of matter can obey the same laws. The behavior of matter is very much a function of its state of organization. In the beginning was chaos. The physical results of chaos are infinitely sensitive to initial conditions. Some physicists view life or consciousness as a phenomenon that arises when a particular level of physical complexity is attained. In this view chaotic systems exhibit behaviors at the margin of life and death, or as John D. Barrow says, "on the verge of all the interesting questions."

Organisms not only lack the kind of periodic order found in crystals, they are nonlinear in the sense that they cannot be divided into parts without significant loss of information. Structures are complex when their initial conditions cannot be specified exactly. The complexity of organisms means that they cannot be described completely, hence they are dynamic, hence they are unpredictable.

Murray Gell-Mann, who gave us the quark, has come up with another word to describe the interaction of chaos and the impulse to order in the physical world. His new word is *plectics*—the study of simplicity and complexity, a concern for the details of the world around us: galaxies, the earth, forms of life, and the characteristics of human beings, all of which can be described as "complex adaptive systems," and all of which are "dependent on a large number of unpredictable accidents as well as on the fundamental laws of physics."

Current trends in physics, chemistry, and biology reveal increasing emphasis on attempts to model complexity and self-organization. The study of complexity offers the most serious and persuasive challenge to the reductionist view in biology.

In 1985 the Union of Biological Sciences held a symposium in Budapest on the theme of "Biology and Complexity." The preamble to its report declared (in the high-tech mandarin style of such literature) that

> **an essential feature of the complexity underlying biological organization is the ability to regulate and correlate the various activities in both space and time according to the system's past history and to the environmental conditions; to store past experience as well as to generate or exchange information; and to evolve toward new form and functions.**

There you have a manifesto in one sentence with only two semicolons; a manifesto opening a vista where physics and mathematics and the life sciences would converge in a conceptual scheme of mutual congeniality.

After conceding the elusiveness of the subject, the report goes on to present a definition of complexity. It warns that complexity should not be confused with the "complication limit" arising from the practical impossibility of describing a system where an excessively large number of degrees of freedom is involved. They assert (in the same patois) that

> the organized complexity of a system is intimately related with the possibility to display a rich space-time correlation spectrum superimposed to noise, in much the same way as, say, sound waves are superimposed to random molecular motion. The ability to extract these correlations implies that statistical laws are at work [and thus an approach based on] the tools of statistical physics and thermodynamics is appropriate.

A concluding paper of the symposium states the matter far more concretely in resorting to a formulation of Francois Jacob. Jacob expresses the idea of complexity very forcefully by stating that the genetic system is a form of memory registering the past of the species and the immune system is a form of memory registering the past of the individual, while the nervous system invents and shapes the future.

Complexity has also been viewed by the biologist Joseph G. Hoffman as a source of the tenacity of life:

> It is a great tribute to the robustness of complexity that the far-fetched occurrence of spontaneous death is far more likely in virus and yeasts, and much less likely in metazoa and mammals. Apparently, the more complex the system the better its chances of besting the hazards of statistical mechanics.

See also page 292.

3
Life as the chemical interaction of macromolecules

Atoms may have destiny, but they do not acquire much biological function on earth until they are incorporated into molecules. Biological processes require not just molecules, but macromolecules—nucleic acids, enzymes, and proteins—in order to create complex organisms. There are myriad interstellar atoms, some interstellar molecules, and a few interstellar macromolecules. Here on earth most of the macromolecules are tied up in biota or the debris of biota. This chapter takes a view of life as incorporated in complex macromolecular aggregates.

A CHEMICAL DEFINITION OF LIFE

The most useful definition of life, entirely adequate for molecular biology, is that life consists of cells composed of nucleic acids and proteins. Proteins and nucleic acids are molecules, indeed very large molecules. The atoms in those molecules are the same kind of atoms that compose nonliving things. But the structure and complication—and interaction—of life's large molecules distinguish them very sharply from the molecules of nonliving things. All of this is a necessary condition of life; the only trouble is that it is not sufficient. The same description would apply to a recently killed animal or a bunch of cut flowers: what is missing is the big *je ne sais quoi.*

What can the chemistry of macromolecules tell us about how the organism rises from the inorganic background? Physics deals with the nucleus, the internal affairs of the atom. Chemistry deals with the low energies contained in the clouds of electrons surrounding atomic nuclei.* The goal of biochemistry is to discover the patterns and regularities by which matter in its multitude of aggregations interacts with energy in its many forms to produce organic life.

The molecules of biology may be divided into two great classes: (1) those molecules that store genetic information —genes; and (2) those that preserve, support, and protect the genes—proteins. Each class is useless without the other.

In its simplest form, the DNA molecule contains about 10 billion atoms. Molecules not only have geometrical shape, they are dynamic; they are always vibrating. Although molecules are diagrammable as rigid geometrical objects, there is always a more or less implicit flexibility— many of them writhe and twist and roll and unroll. (One of the most intricate research frontiers of molecular biology is protein-*folding.*)

In biology there are two main languages, molecular and electrical. As a result, the chemical definition of life has been challenged from a very unconventional quarter. A former aerospace engineer, Dwight H. Bulkely, has come up with an "Electromagnetic Theory of Life" in which he rejects the model of life as a chemical phenomenon, replacing it with a new paradigm of life as physics. "Life is not a function of a series of chemical reactions (with mere electron transfers between donor and acceptor molecules)," says

* *The violation of this principle is what made the physicists dismiss Dr. Pons of Utah as a galling interloper when he made his abortive claim to chemical achievement of cold fusion in the spring of 1989.*

Bulkely, "but a function of flows of electrons as currents in microcircuits, with a powerful electric field ordering replications and motilities."

In physics, matter cannot exist below a certain degree of organization. The quantum principle intervenes. So it is in chemistry; below a certain degree of organization, life cannot exist. A quantum principle, if it operates in biochemistry, is still latent and unrecognized.

LIFE AS A PROPERTY OF MATTER

The nature of matter is mysterious enough, but the phenomenon of life is more so. The only thing more mysterious than matter is life. And the question of the possibility of life in the absence of matter is not very congenial to anyone. Here is Thomas S. Hall (*Ideas of Life and Matter* [vol. 1], 1969) on the subject:

> ... an enterprise as old as science itself [is] the effort to associate life with certain kinds or conditions of matter ... even where life has been viewed as an immaterial entity or agent ... it has been generally thought to require for its active expression a proper material vehicle or substrate.

What is a substrate? It is the base on which an organism lives in much the same way as the soil is the substrate of most seed plants. Within the cell a substrate may be a complex of matter, an organization of elemental atoms, or another molecule. In the biology textbooks a substrate is a nutritive medium, a source of reactive material, a substance acted upon by an enzyme. Enter the enzyme: enter life.

Chemistry. To accept a chemical definition of life, you have to accept the notion that life is a property of matter, albeit a very peculiar property of matter. And the most peculiar property of living matter is that it is made up of enormously large and complex molecules. One point that all biologists seem to agree on is that the molecule is the lowest level of integration in the biological hierarchy. The molecules of a typical inorganic substance contain only one or two atoms. The molecules of such common organic substances as carbohydrates, fats, and oils are somewhat larger, but they rarely contain more than a few dozen atoms. However, the components of living cells that seemed to be most lifelike in their properties are found to have molecules containing thousands or tens of thousands of atoms.

Of the 92 natural elements, 99 percent of living matter is made up of just four: hydrogen, oxygen, nitrogen, and carbon. George Wald claims that wherever life appears—not just on earth but anywhere in the universe—it will be made up of those four elements because of their unique properties critical to biological organization. Carbon and nitrogen are "the only elements that form real double and triple chemical bonds."

Elements are the letters of the chemical alphabet, while compounds can be compared with words. The analogy is not perfect, since molecular combinations are not linear but three-dimensional. The most important atomic elements for the composition of living structures are six of the lighter elements: carbon, hydrogen, oxygen, nitrogen, phosphorus, and sulfur. They each have single-letter symbols—making up the rubric CHONPS—and are all tangent to each other in the upper right-hand corner of the periodic table of the elements. "CHONPS . . . catchily sums up all the atomic constituents of the decisive polymers of life; the nucleic acids, most proteins, the sugars, structural substances such as collagen, cellulose and chitin, the lipids of cell membranes and even the simpler common currency of metabolism, such as the energy donor ATP and all the gears of the Krebs chemical engine producing that ubiquitous active fuel."

ENZYMES: A MOLECULE AT THE THRESHOLD

Enzymes are protein molecules that act as catalysts, causing other proteins to undergo specific chemical reactions or making them combine with other substances. They are the essential link for all biological activity. No organism is known that does not contain enzymes, and all known enzymes are special forms of protein.

Enzymes speed up chemical reactions to more than a billion times their normal rate. If it were not for their intense catalytic capacity, the chemical actions of biorganisms would proceed so slowly that life could scarcely exist. There would not have been enough time, not since the Big Bang, for Nature to have arrived. Virtually all the reactions in an organism depend upon the virtuosity of a cast of thousands of enzymes peforming within the proscenium of the cell. A single cell in the human body contains an estimated 100,000 enzyme molecules to catalyze between 1,000 and 2,000 kinds of different chemical reactions. Biochemists harbor a dream of some day coming up with a periodic table of the enzymes comparable to Mendeleyev's periodic table of the elements.

Specificity. It is the shapes of enzymes that endows them with their specific capacities. A chain of them has the discriminatory power to select just one of a large number of available reaction pathways, arriving at a unique complementarity between stimulus and response. Biochemical processes bind the substrate molecule at a far higher rate of chemical reaction than is achieved by any man-made catalysis.

In the Introduction I described Dr. Berendzen's dogmatic view that the threshold between the organic and the inorganic lies just between the amino acids and how they are organized by DNA. Other authorities say that organic life begins at the level of the enzyme. Hans Zinsser has stated the matter a little more circumspectly in *Rats, Lice and History* (1934). "It is not easy to define life. An enzyme that could expend energy and build up new energy for that which it expends, in automatically regulated cycles, would be alive—though soluble and not organized in cellular form."

The biochemist Arthur Kornberg became a Nobel medalist for his discoveries in a lifetime devoted to research on enzymes. Early in his career he pronounced the dictum that every chemical event in the cell depends on the action of an enzyme. In a personal reminiscence he has this to say about enzymes:

In my marriage to enzymes, I have found a level of complexity that suits me. I feel ill at ease grappling with the operations of a cell, let alone those of a multicellular creature. I also feel inadequate in probing the fine chemistry of small molecules. Becoming familiar with the personality of an enzyme performing in a major synthetic pathway is just right. To gain this intimacy, the enzyme must first be purified, and I have never felt unrewarded for any effort expended this way.

Cyril Ponnamperuma, director of the Laboratory of Chemical Evolution at the University of Maryland, has put the matter most poignantly: "If I can demonstrate a replicating molecule," he said, "I'll dic a happy man."

4
Erwin Schrödinger: What is life?

———————— ❧ ————————

One of the most influential books on biology of this century was written by a physicist in exile in the middle of World War II. It remains in print, and a classic, which is why I want to discuss it in some detail.

ERWIN SCHRÖDINGER: **WHAT IS LIFE?**

In my quest for definitions of life—the theme of this book—I turned first to Erwin Schrödinger's seminal essay, starkly titled *What Is Life?* Its subtitle is "The physical aspect of the living cell," and Schrödinger's objective was to account for living organisms solely in terms of the known mechanics of physics and chemistry. Published in 1944, when Schrödinger, a Viennese, was living as an anti-Nazi exile in Ireland, it was to become the most influential single book on the subject thus far.

Beautifully written in clear language, the book is a model of scientific exposition. Though now dated in many particulars, it has stood the test of time in anticipating an integrated view of physics and biology. With its engaging and lively style, it remains robustly in print. It is the first book I found devoted exclusively to its subject . . . not the origins of life, but the makeup of life, a still thorny but more tractable business.

In 1933 Schrödinger became a Nobel laureate in physics for his contribution to the theory of quantum mechanics. He developed the basic mathematical equation describing the dynamics of particles: the wave equation that bears his name. Many authorities attest that Schrödinger's wave equation has many demonstrably powerful applications as a statistical tool dealing with probabilities. It has also been described incomprehensibly as "a partial differential equation with imaginary coefficients." And a serious article celebrating the centenary of his birth in *New Scientist,* 27 August 1987, asserts that (like so much of quantum mechanics) "nobody really knows what it means." I am willing to let it go at that.

Schrödinger has had his detractors, purists deploring that a physicist should make such forays into the precincts of biology. "A physicist stands amazed at genetics," wrote one reviewer dismissively. I was gratified to learn much later that, even though it preceded the greatest biological discovery of the century—that of the genetic code—it remains a classic and has in fact been credited with attracting many physics students into the field of molecular biology, the study of those very large protein molecules that distinguish life from inanimate matter. It was Schrödinger who first hit on the idea that the chromosome is a message written in code. This was after the Second World War, when, according to their own accounts, many physicists working in the shadow of the atomic bomb felt their calling had become the science of death, and were prompted to move to biology, the science of life.

I looked up James D. Watson's book describing the birth of molecular biology, *The Double Helix,* for confirmation. In his first sentence Watson derogates his famous collaborator with the charge that "I have never seen Francis Crick in a modest mood." Thus I was surprised to find that he mustered enough generosity to pay a tribute to Schrödinger:

"A major factor in [Francis Crick's] leaving physics and developing an interest in biology had been the reading in 1946 of *What Is Life?* by the noted theoretical physicist Erwin Schrödinger. This book very elegantly propounded the belief that genes were the key components of living cells and that, to understand what life is, we must know how genes act."

The molecular biologist Gunther Stent said *What Is Life?* stirred up passions that made it the *Uncle Tom's Cabin* of the revolution in biology.

To understand life we must understand how genes act chemically; i.e., in terms of molecules. I had thought—as had many biologists up until the early half of this century—that genes were not necessarily molecules, but merely a useful way of looking at things.

Schrödinger has a flair for reducing chemical abstractions to graphic images, and his description of crystals has often been quoted. He writes:

> the most essential part of a living cell—the chromosome fiber—may suitably be called *an aperiodic crystal*. In physics we have dealt hitherto only with *periodic crystals*. . . . compared with the aperiodic crystal, they are rather plain and dull. The difference in structure is as that between an ordinary wallpaper in which the same pattern is repeated again and again . . . and a masterpiece of embroidery, say a Raphael tapestry, which shows . . . an elaborate coherent, meaningful design.

A periodic crystal can carry only a small amount of information, while an aperiodic crystal can carry an almost unlimited amount. Schrödinger went on to recognize the chromosome as an aperiodic crystal with unusual stability and information-storing capabilities, bearing a "codescript" for heredity, for transmitting information from one generation to the next.

The unfolding of events in the life cycle of an organism is controlled by a supremely well-ordered group of atoms, which represent only a very small fraction of the sum total in every cell. Schrödinger says an organism has the "astonishing gift" of concentrating a "stream of order" on itself, "drinking orderliness" from the environment—a process dependent upon the presence of aperiodic crystals—and thus escaping the decay into atomic chaos. The chromosome molecules represent the highest degree of atomic association we know of. The principle is the maintenance of order from order, anticipating the soon to be discovered role of DNA . . . a paragon of orderliness unknown anywhere else in nature except within living matter.

Schrödinger noted that living systems display two basic processes. One he calls "order from order," the other "order from disorder." The first is characterized by the genetic code. The second involves apparent contradictions between biological processes and the universal entropy decreed by the second law of thermodynamics. (The second law says, in effect, that nature can't break even because disorder is always on the increase, and entropy is irreversible. Entropy is not an easy intuitive concept; in one of Schrödinger's rare lapses into mathematics he describes it as "the logarithm of molecular disorder.")

He describes life as a nonequilibrium dissipative structure, maintaining its high degree of local organization at the *expense* of the larger budget of environmental entropy. The paradox admits the life processes as an apparent violation of the second law. Organisms, he says, feed on negative entropy, as does evolution itself in building up to higher emergent levels of organization.

Schrödinger's account provided me with the most satisfactory net statement so far about the nature of life. It is so generalized that it applies not only to natural organisms; it anticipates—or at least would admit of—the kinds of artificial life contemplated with the advent of computers. He says, "When is a piece of matter said to be alive? When it goes on "doing something, moving, exchanging material with its environment . . . for a much longer period than we would expect an inanimate piece of matter to keep going under similar circumstances.": It's a little bit like the dictionaries saying life is everything except that which is nonlife, but I have found no one who has put it more simply.

If I ever get a terminal illness, it is Schrödinger's book I will take with me to the hospice to prepare for the maximum entropy that is his definition of death.

5
Life as the impulse to replicate

————— ❧ —————

APHORISMS

Evolutionary biologists still brood over the central question of whether gene or organism is the proper target of selection. Among biological concepts this is one of the most abstract, and despite its centrality, it remains unresolved. In fact, the dilemma has entered our folk language: Which came first, the chicken or the egg?

I suppose I was in college when I first heard of Samuel Butler's sardonic formulation: "A hen is only an egg's way of making another egg." It is a mischievous notion, subversive of logic, if not of good order and discipline. The phrase has always stuck in my craw. There are two Samuel Butlers, at least two famous ones, both English writers, one 17th century, the other 19th. It is the 19th-century Samuel Butler who is responsible for the phrase in question, and it gratified me to learn that it came from the man who wrote *The Way of All Flesh*. There appears to be no limit to the man's profound skepticism of the Victorian illusion of eternal progress. An egg as the end, a chicken as the means. Indeed.

Thus, long before I ever got interested in writing about biology, I had been haunted by the logical absurdity of that morsel of doggerel. And now I might almost say that this book itself is an exercise in trying to make sense of a scrap of nonsense.

Several years ago I stumbled on Edward O. Wilson's stab at a similar exaggerated epigram: ". . . the organism is only DNA's way of making more DNA." This was the original resonance. From then on, the further accumulation of variations on the theme was a succession of happy accidental surprises in my collateral reading about biological matters. Strung together as they are here below, they have gained in dignity, and I have elevated them from doggerel to aphorisms.

A hen is only an egg's way of making another egg.
—Samuel Butler (1835–1902)
Life and Habit, 1877

. . . the organism is only DNA's way of making more DNA.
—Edward O. Wilson
Sociobiology: The New Synthesis, 1976

A physicist is an atom's way of knowing about atoms.
—George Wald, 1986

A person is only a gene's way of making another gene.
—Melvin Konner
The Tangled Web, 1985

Is an organism just a genome's way of making another genome?
—Niles Eldredge
Unfinished Synthesis, 1985

A human being might simply be a sophisticated machine which a germ cell uses to produce further immortal germ cells.
—Rodney Cotterill
The Cambridge Guide
to the Material World,
1985

The reader is just a microbe's means of making another microbe.

> —*Dorion Sagan and Lynn Margulis*
> Garden of Microbial Delights, *1988*

RNA molecules develop life as a continuation of their evolution.

> —*Murray Gell-Mann*
> *15 March 1989*

Samuel Butler exercised the freedom of the amateur in the field of philosophy, and his egg-hen-egg sequence may have arisen not just from skepticism but from a mid-Victorian preoccupation with the relationship between mechanism and life. He asserts that, while we human beings have no sense of our continuity with ourselves as infants, the inference is "irresistible, that the . . . egg remembers the course pursued by the eggs from which it sprung." "Why the fowl should be considered more alive than the egg [is a question] perhaps most answerable by considering the conceit of man, and his habit . . . of ignoring all that does not remind him of himself, hurt him, or profit him . . . perhaps, after all, the real reason is that the egg does not cackle." Perhaps also it would be fairer to say that the fowl is not more alive, but that it represents a second-order biological capacity and thus has more options. And Butler concludes in a broader generalization, anticipating some of his successors: ". . . in truth, a hen, or any other living creature, is only the primordial cell's way of going back upon itself."

That life goes back on itself is a notion that seems to persist intuitively.

Edward O. Wilson started out as a biologist with the study of social insects, mainly ants, and has capped his career as the founder of sociobiology, which proposes the coordinate evolution of genes and culture. He suggests that one of the most interesting things about individual organisms—including human beings—is their role as a "vehicle, an elaborate device to preserve and spread [genes] with the least possible biochemical perturbation. . . . Social behavior and social structure can be studied as extensions of genes that continue to exist because of their superior adaptive value."

George Wald is a Nobel laureate and an apologist for the notion that, given the natural environment of this planet, the origin of life was inevitable. His aphorism shows the anthropic fallacy (the notion that somehow natural laws are a consequence of our capacity for observing them) in its most vulnerable form.

Like Samuel Butler, Melvin Konner claims no originality for his little epigram; they do not know who said it first and treat it virtually as part of the folk heritage. In acknowledging the oversimplification involved, Konner says that the gene "has no machinery of awareness itself. It simply arranges the chemicals of life as a conduit through point mutations and changes in gene frequency contingent on the adaptive success of the gene carrier." The carrier, in the human case, is us.

Niles Eldredge is an exponent of the modern synthesis of evolutionary biology (although he might be uncomfortable with any description of his posture less than the length of his own books). In *Unfinished Synthesis*, following his aphoristic query as it appears above, he reverses the proposition, suggesting that genomes might equally be regarded as "just an organism's way of (1) staying alive (somatic genome) and (2) making more organisms (germ-line genome)." He concedes that both positions can be defended and the answer to either question is yes, but that it is logically impossible to establish the primacy of one view over the other. . . . Here we hover at the dizzy brink of logical regress in the wilderness of genetic mirrors.

Rodney Cotterill's pedestrian formulation gains a little luster from its concession that a human being is sophisticated—and from its context, the culmination of a passage in which he has just said that for most cells there is a limit of about fifty doublings, after which they degenerate and die out. There are only two mammalian cell types, he tells us, which avoid the inevitability of death: malignant cancer cells and reproductive germ cells. This is a somber rationale for the mortality of human beings and the immortality of cancer and disease. He attributes it to the suspicion that cancer and germ cells might have a "common mechanism of gene reshuffling." One can infer that those microorganisms shuffle, or even reshuffle, better than us macroorganisms.

Lynn Margulis and her son Dorion Sagan provide us with a bacteriocentric approach in which human beings are seen as late-comers and by-products in a natural world dominated by one-celled creatures. They say that we dwellers of today's world are "a mere epiphenomenon." (A phenomenon is the first item of experience or reality; an epiphenomenon is an accidental or accessory event, a secondary and perhaps unintentional aftereffect.) Margulis and Sagan are enthralled by the nonhuman splendor of the microbial world, invisible to the human eye. Vertebrates, and especially human beings, share only a small fraction of the microbe's life history on earth; and make only a tiny fraction of the organic biomass. Bacteria found the organization of many-celled animals, including vertebrates and humans, an effective strategy for coping with a world transformed by the advent of oxygen in the biosphere.

For Murray Gell-Mann the predicament of RNA is comparable to the desperation of patriotism; he explicitly compares his prescription with that of Clausewitz on war as a continuation of politics by other means.

In these bald formulations Butler's hen, Wilson's organism, Wald's physicist, Konner's person, Eldredge's organism, Cotterill's human being, Sagan and Margulis's reader, and Gell-Mann's RNA give us brash oversimplifications—irreverent, ranging from the ovocentric to the genocentric and the anthropocentric, perhaps more provoking than provocative.

Is the egg or the DNA or even the physicist an end in itself? Does replication require the egg, gene, or germ cell to go through such elaborate organic complexity to reproduce itself? Is the gene more important than the individual or the group in determining patterns of evolution? Or is the complexity of the physicist, human being, or reader an anthropocentric illusion, more apparent than real?

The premises of chicken-versus-egg substitute brute processes for considerations of design or final cause. So much for the distant goals of teleology. Coarse reductionist generalizations have a heuristic appeal; they may serve to advance inquiry or analysis. But when a partial *aperçu* is served up as a grand explanation of everything, all the subtlety of human experience is lost in the accounting.

The viewpoint is parochial rather than cosmic. The trouble with such axioms is that they tend to acquire more weight than they were perhaps intended to.

The evolutionary process is inexorable, and the biological imperatives are much faster then geological ones. It has remained for a metallurgist, Cyril Stanley Smith of MIT, to introduce the idea of nature in a hurry: "Deoxyribonucleic acid is simply a mechanism to save time in reaching higher levels of organization." To save time . . .

In the last analysis these aphorisms illustrate memorably that the gene and the organism are hostages to each other. Considered alone, both gene and organism are manifestly mortal; only in their conjunction do they offer a prospect of immortality. Evolution is inherently dual. Chicken and egg co-evolute. Coevolution inheres in the reciprocity of organism and gene.

These aphorists are suggesting by analogy that local and holistic evolutionary functions are not contradictory. They envision life processes functioning as a servomechanism, an automatic device for mutually stabilizing very large systems by means of very small systems and correcting performance by error-sensing feedback. The notions are arresting, but they seem to work at the brink of logical fallacy. Dr. Richard Restak, a Washington neurologist, describes the absurdity of regression (as of the label on the Pet Milk can holding another label of a Pet Milk can and so on)—regression without resolution.

> **When the human brain studies the human brain, a self-referential paradox is created similar to what occurs when an artist sets out to paint everything in his studio including, of course, himself in the studio in the act of painting his studio, which contains everything including himself painting the studio and so on. . . .**
>
> **The world of our inner experience partakes of the complementarity that we share with the subatomic particles that comprise us.**

The regression is infinite and the contemplation of shrinking wheels within wheels is disturbing and devoid of comfort. This catalog of aphorisms illustrates the lure of the abstract, the counterpoise of the macroworld and the microworld, as well as the inadequacy, or rather the inappropriateness, of science for dealing with questions of causation. Nor does the exercise contribute much to the definition of life in terms of everyday familiarity.

6
Metaphoric approaches
———————— ❧ ————————

METAPHORS

It may be perverse to be preoccupied with oblique approaches to the description of biological life. I have been offended by the notion of life as a disease of matter; and I have been both attracted and repelled by the idea of life—particularly individual human life—as the abstract notion of a pattern integrity. I had been filing such sophisticated —tortured, romantic, artful, even conceited—approaches under the caption of "metaphoric aspects of life." After putting these pieces down in black and white, I realized that it is not life that has metaphoric properties. Metaphors are not a property of life but of observation and communication. So it may even be the other way round: life as a property of metaphor.

Who of us nowadays could muster the courage of a New England transcendentalist like Emerson? He said, "Parts of speech are metaphors, because the whole of nature is a metaphor of the human mind."

To describe all of Western civilization as but a footnote to Plato (as people have) is a conceit, pure and simple. To describe nature as a metaphor of mind simply puts science out of business. But most metaphors are not that extravagant and many of them illuminate corners of our imagination not otherwise accessible.

Metaphors function implicitly; they can communicate only within the framework of a richly shared cultural experience. They are a phenomenon of language. The sequence seems to be metaphors come from observation and communication, which is a property of consciousness, which is a property of self, which, biologically, is a property akin to the immune system.

We are dealing here with certain approaches to the problem of defining what life is that are so deeply immersed in cultural experience that they transcend any ability of science to capture them. (For another metaphoric approach in these pages see "Life as borrowing," page 138.)

LIFE AS A DISEASE OF MATTER

Abraham Cowley, who Milton thought was the third greatest English poet (after Shakespeare and Spenser), wrote in a letter to Dr. Scarborough, "life is an incurable disease."

The common phrase evokes the kind of brash obscenity found scrawled on the stalls of public toilets on a college campus, where indeed I think I first encountered it. I found its message a haunting one, and I had thought that such a nihilistic slogan must be first of all German, and second post-war modern, rather than from the pen of a late metaphysical English poet. It had seemed reminiscent of a Berlin cabaret, perhaps a line from Bertolt Brecht. And then just recently I found that the most authentic recurrence of the theme is indeed modern, and German:

> **And life? Was it perhaps only an infection, a sickening of matter? Was that which one might call the original procreation of matter only a disease ... the first step toward evil, toward desire and death ... that pathologically luxuriant morbid growth. ... This was the Fall. ... the birth of**

> the organic out of the inorganic ... only another fatal stage
> in the progress of the corporeal toward consciousness.
> [Thomas Mann, *The Magic Mountain*, 1927]

The view of living as a disease, an inevitably fatal disease, continues to have lure for the poet. In "For Annie," Edgar Allan Poe tells us from the brink of bathos.

> *Thank Heaven! the crisis,*
> *The danger is past,*
> *And the lingering illness*
> *Is over at last—*
> *And the fever called "Living"*
> *Is conquered at last.*

George Bernard Shaw, who was not given to understatement, also saw morbidity rampant. He wrote: "Life is a disease; and the only difference between one man and another is the stage of the disease at which he lives."

Preoccupation with the notion of life as a disease of matter is not limited to the literary imagination. Two distinguished, and eccentric, astronomers, Sir Fred Hoyle and N. C. Wickramasinghe, pronounced a quite unverifiable theory of the origin of life in a work published in 1978 with the title *Diseases from Space*. It argued that life was created in cosmic clouds of interstellar dust—space being a congenial place for the assembly of biochemicals. The organic molecules from space were riddled with disease. Cancer results when genetic instructions from space "intended to promote the budding of yeast, are received accidentally by animal or plant cells." The implication is that the interstellar dust was stable and content until invaded by living processes and their concomitant afflictions.

Almost all of our knowledge of human biology comes to us from medical science: the study of disease. Cell biologists have established that not all cancer comes to us from the alteration of normal cell growth by tobacco smoke, toxic waste, or radiation. In 1976 Dr. Michael Bishop and

Dr. Harold Varmus demonstrated that certain genes found in cancer-causing viruses—oncogenes—are only slightly modified copies of normal genes found in virtually all vertebrate animals. In 1989 these two doctors were awarded the Nobel Prize for their description of proto-oncogenes, in which cancer arises not from invading viruses but from normal growth-regulating genes. As Dr. Bishop put it on receiving the award: "We have the seeds of cancer in our own genetic dowry."

The study of disease is the chief context of medicine in which healthy life arises as only a temporary triumph.

Malignancy as a catalyst. From a laboratory perspective, a standard textbook, *Cell Physiology* by Arthur C. Giese, creeps up on the disease of matter as a portal to immortality. "Possibly the only way a cell of a mammal or bird can acquire immortality—in the sense of indefinitely continued doubling [of the cycles of cell divisionings]—is for it to become malignant or cancerous." But as a practical matter, once the cancer has destroyed the host it commits suicide by exhausting its substrate—unless it is lucky enough to be popped into a petrie dish to court the immortality of the laboratory.

HeLa cells were named for the patient from whose uterine cervical cancer they were obtained and isolated in 1951. The patient was a young black woman, whose name (Helen Lane, Helen Larson or Henrietta Lacks?—the record is unclear) has been abbreviated, HeLa cells from her biopsy grew well in culture. She is no longer among us, but her cells are potentially immortal, surviving as a disease of matter. Since then, they have been continuously cultured in laboratories and are extensively used in research to test chemical and radiation therapies. Part of their utility for research is that cancer cells generally grow at an exponential rate comparable to that of microorganisms.

The Nobel medalist Linus Pauling in a paper written in 1964 with a fellow chemist, E. Zuckerkandl, evokes disease as the very trigger of evolution (which is matter in its most dynamic manifestation). "To evolve," they write, "must most often have amounted to suffering from a disease. And these diseases were of course molecular. . . . a molecular disease that turned out to be evolution."

When Bishop and Varmus were awarded the Nobel Prize in 1989, one of their colleagues, Peter Vogt, observed that retroviral oncogenes are present in all humans. "Many go way down the evolutionary ladder, and you will find quite a few even present in such lowly organisms as yeast. They are very highly conserved over long, long distances in evolution, which means that they must be very important to life."

It is haunting to reflect that the closest thing we have in nature, the nearest thing in magnitude or mechanism, to a self-replicating molecule is a virus. And that requires an organic substrate before it can produce its virulent disease.

ORIGINAL SIN

To Platonism, a human being is a fallen spirit; to Christian doctrine, a man inherits his guilt from Adam; to science, a person is a risen animal. To Richard Dawkins, humans share with other creatures the selfishness of the gene. To Dawkins, in fact, they don't share it, they are a hostage to it: in his system a gene is more important than the individual or the group in determining patterns of evolution. There is a theory (associated with Linus Pauling, among others) that evolution itself arose from a molecular disease. That's all you need for the genesis of good and evil. Only some men in some conditions can look back upon that kind of a genetic situation and construe it as a painful expulsion from Paradise.

Richard Dawkins says that the essential nature of our hereditary genetic material is selfish. But he allows that this base inheritance—the inescapable dialectic of A-C-T-G base pairs—can be overcome by a confluence of selfish genes and thinking brains; for instance, such elaborate arrangements as human society and in such totally unanticipated impulses as education are very surprising to discover from an evolutionary point of view. "Species selection has favored those species in which individual self-interest is best served by their own apparent altruism." (Richard Dawkins, *The Blind Watchmaker*, 1986, p. 268.)

A secular salvation. The process operates in the genes. The idea of a mechanical dialectic at work in a vessel of flesh and bone suggests that the original molecular disease may contain the formula for its own self-correction. Not so far from what Christians call salvation. Not so far from redemption.

Disease, the impairment of normal vital functions, began in history at the molecular level. The event has an analogy in the origin of good and evil in the Garden of Eden, but mutation and error, a disease of matter, was the engine of evolution.

LIFE AS A PATTERN INTEGRITY

While staying with Buckminster Fuller one evening in his high apartment overlooking all of Philadelphia, I asked him what the role and definition of an individual human being was in his philosophical system. Is a human being a *structure*? I asked. Of course not, he replied. Then it must be a *system*? I ventured. But he said no, not a system. What human beings are in his view of the world are *pattern integrities*. "A pattern has an integrity independent of the medium by virtue of which you have received the information that it exists. Each of the chemical elements is a pattern integrity. The pattern integrity of the human individual is evolutionary and not static." (*Synergetics*, 1975.)

Arguing from a possibly different set of premises, biologists describing complexity come uncannily close to Fuller's description of a pattern integrity. Compare specifically the extract from the report of the Union of Biological Sciences (quoted earlier in this chapter), which says that living organisms display "a rich space-time correlation spectrum superimposed to noise," in much the same way as sound waves are superimposed on random molecular motion.

One of the chief philosophical complementarities in Fuller's cosmic system is the opposition of the abstract and the energetic. The abstract is the integrity of a design (metaphysical, therefore timeless). The energetic is the manifestation of the design in the world of our senses (purely physical, and therefore temporary). Abstract vs. energetic. None of the physical elements in our bodies is older than seven years, the rate at which one's body is totally replaced. Nails grow, hair grows; skin regenerates. What alone persists is the integrity of the pattern.

Every individual is an evolutionary pattern integrity. Each individual's environment of the moment is different from that of the next moment and from that of every other individual, though two or more individuals may think that they are mutually experiencing the same environment. The individual is the product and servant of a plurality of semisimilarities of mutual tuned-in-ness. [*Synergetics*, 1975]

Among Fuller's contemporaries was his friend and colleague Cyril Stanley Smith, the widely recognized metallurgist. Smith had a flair for the perception of similarities between organic and inorganic manifestations of pattern.

The principles of pattern formation, aggregation, and transformation seem to be the same in matter and in the human brain, and if properly formulated they may provide a kind of visual metaphor that will serve to join and mutually illuminate physics on the one hand and geological, biological, and social history on the other—with art in between. [*A Search for Structure*, 1981]

THE IMPROBABILITY OF LIFE

As Dr. George E. Palade of The Rockefeller Institute put it, "Life—human life included—is the outcome of an elaborate organization based on trivial ingredients and ordinary forces. . . . life depends on an extensive organization in depth, on a superimposition of patterns which amount to infinitely more order than matter usually tolerates." Dr. Palade raises the specter of the intolerability of matter. To say that the appearance of living things is thermodynamically improbable is one thing; to imply that there are physical limits to order is another. But it is *improbable*, both in the sense of unlikely and in the sense of difficult to fathom.

The astronomer Sir James Jeans gives us a stark view of mere life as an accidental result of other cosmic or energetic processes.

It does not at present look as though Nature had designed the Universe primarily for life; the normal stars and the normal nebula have nothing to do with life except making it impossible. Life is the end of a chain of byproducts: it seems to be the accident, and torrential deluges of life-destroying radiation the essential.

Genesis could have no more profane alternative than such accounts of origins based on chance.

II

THE THRESHOLD BETWEEN THE ANIMATE & INANIMATE

---

*T*HE MARGINS BETWEEN ORGANIC AND inorganic forms of matter are elusive; for some observers the margin is more of a continuum than a threshold. In this section we discuss several hypotheses about the organization of matter in both evolutionary and physiological terms. There is a point at which a group of undifferentiated cells assemble themselves into a viable individual organism: The text in Chapter 8 deals with the distinction as it applies to the life of human beings.

Our definitions of life inevitably affect our view of its sanctity. The oblique perspectives of astrology and sex are given brief consideration.

Viruses and tardigrades are described as exemplars of living organisms with a capacity for inertia.

7
The very threshold

―――――――――――――― ⌒℘ ――――――――――――――

A BABY MAMMOTH

When a baby woolly mammoth weighing something over 100 pounds was found in a chunk of Siberian ice preserved for 40,000 years, *The Washington Post* reported that "some of the animal's molecules were still alive when the beast was found."

Nothing better illustrates the problem of defining the functions of life at the very threshold. There is no such thing as a *dead* molecule: If it is a molecule, it is neither dead nor alive. Life appears to be too complex to operate at such a low level in the hierarchy. Complex molecules like enzymes and amino acids are peculiar to life, but they are alive only as an ensemble. And there is nothing that distinguishes a simple molecule per se from its occurrence in an old leather slipper or a moth or a mammoth.

Atoms per se are not peculiar to life or to nonlife. There are a few of the basic 92 elements of which biological patterns appear as yet to have made no use. Most of the basic atoms appear in organic (at least as trace elements) as well as inorganic agglomerations.

Molecules. There are many molecules—aggregations of atoms—shared by animate and inanimate objects. And there are some molecules that are peculiar to life. This is where we get into the area of threshold. And when James D. Watson in his *Molecular Biology of the Gene* says that "the current extension of our understanding of biological phenomena to the technical level (molecular biology) will soon enable us to understand all the basic features of the living state," his hopes may be in vain. Molecular biology has made much progress in determining the mechanisms by which hereditary characteristics are transferred, which is something quite different from saying that we understand life. The word *life* "is simply not encompassed by a molecule," René Dubos (1980) reminds us, ". . . Life implies an organization, an ability to adapt to change." Life resides in the ensemble.

What had survived in that young woolly mammoth were some of the molecules that are indeed peculiar to life, and they had retained some of the genetic traces—the DNA sequences—from which the forms of life might conceivably be reconstituted. They had become dry and inert but gave every evidence of once having lived.

There were some large intact proteins, albumin and collagen, which bore the hope of providing intact strands of DNA from which fossil geneticists seek to determine the genetic structure of extinct species and their relation to existing species. But in this case, whatever DNA there may have been had been degraded in the process of leaching and aging: There appears to be a "statute of limitations" to the length of time genetic material can survive after death of its host organism. The fossil geneticists succeeded, however, in eventually solubilizing some of the mammoth's albumin molecules to prepare them for further analysis. The molecules bore evidence that they had been generated and captured by life. Even if the DNA strands had been recovered and reconstituted, they would have been only templates or patterns for the possible reconstitution of life. "Some day it may be possible to insert genes recovered from a fossil into another creature." The newspaper has speculated that such techniques might mean we could "bring back the Beatles." . . . The threshold survives, and bridging it—however tempting a reunion with the Beatles—remains elusive.

As the 20th century progresses, the distinction between the animate and the inanimate is becoming increasingly blurred—a prospect kept company by the growing perception that life itself may have arisen as a series of blunders. The army of experts in the vineyards of cybernetics and artificial intelligence and in the laboratories of biochemistry toil at the very threshold undisturbed by philosophical implications.

Yet the animate-inanimate distinction is possibly the most profound in human experience. Certainly, I find it inescapable that understanding what it means to be alive comes before anything else; only after that can you consider understanding what it is to be human.

In a 1968 book called *Biological Order*, André Lwoff describes the peculiar integrity of the living process:

> **The living organism is an integrated system of macromolecular structures and functions able to reproduce its kind. Waves and particles are the complementary aspects of the atom. Structures and functions are the complementary aspects of the organism. Separated from its context—that is, extracted from the cell—any structure, either a nucleic acid or a protein, is just an organic molecule. Such a thing as living substance or living matter does not exist. Life can only be the appanage of the organism as a whole. Only organisms are alive.**

Lwoff is a Nobel medalist and a professor at the Sorbonne and the Institut Pasteur in Paris. His summary is scrupulous. In his cosmos everything agrees with physics' understanding of matter. Nothing appears *de novo*. It is the opposite of abiogenesis (the notion that life arose spontaneously from inorganic matter). Living systems are endowed with the genetic continuity of preexisting organisms.

They are complex integrations of static structure and dynamic function. Biological structure and function have a molecular basis. The genetic basis of the structure is DNA, which generates the templates for the macromolecules that operate within the cells and govern cellular interactions. In the case of the baby woolly mammoth the molecules survived, even the woolly mammoth's body survived; but life did not survive.

Professor Lwoff in resorting to the word *appanage* has brought us very close to our elusive threshold. What is this appanage? From Latin *panis*, it originally meant "to provide with bread." In medieval legal usage it described a suitable grant by a sovereign of land, revenues, or perquisites to a younger son or daughter—a grant for the support of dependents. Figuratively this has come to mean "a customary or rightful endowment or adjunct." Here at the very threshold Lwoff brings in a word that is technical only in an obsolete legal sense; it is certainly not scientific. Searching for the razor's edge, we end up with vernacular fudge.

COMMON SENSE

Common sense is a uniquely intuitive faculty, a part of every man's natural endowment. It is not susceptible to enhancement by education. Its true nature appears to be quite beyond the grasp of experimental psychology, and its potency seems to lack any apparent correlation to individual intellectual capacity. (The familiar cartoon of the absent-minded professor suggests, in fact, an inverse ratio.) Common sense remains mysterious, intractable, untidy. Yet it exhibits a versatility and a rock-bottom capacity of discrimination-of-last-resort denied to more sophisticated and logical strategems.

From a commonsense point of view in most of our daily life, we have no trouble telling the difference between what is alive and what isn't. Common sense invokes the unreflected opinions of the ordinary person exercising his natural capacity for spontaneous intuitions without benefit of technical considerations. Common sense is a naïve capacity inaccessible to computers, disdained by textbooks, uncongenial to the tactics of the law, and indifferent to the protocols of science. It is uniquely the domain of the layman. Indeed, among professional people the precincts of common sense are invaded only by such licensed generalists as journalists and editorial writers. (Artists and poets may also resort to commonsense intuition since they are in most cultures not bound by academic restrictions.)

When the U.S. Supreme Court issues its occasional pronouncements on the constitutionality of abortion, the front porch of its courthouse in Washington is besieged by hundreds of acrimonious partisans exercising their certain conviction that life begins at conception or that a woman's right of choice is inalienable. Here is where the layman comes into his own. The viewpoints could not be more antithetical, yet adherents in either camp are devoid of doubt. They are faced with a question of social policy, where science is as irrelevant as scripture. (The courts sometimes pay attention to what science has to say—on fetal viability, for instance—and they sometimes pay no attention at all.)

Where does life begin? The crux of the matter is that the question really isn't justiciable. The question is not only susceptible to common sense, it is more than that—it is susceptible to no arena *other* than that of common sense. Science is of no avail in defining the potentiality of life; and the nature of life may be such that science will never resolve it in terms of use to the court. Not that the wisdom of the layman, in our present state of political grace, affords an easy resolution to a thorny question of social policy. Common sense is available to use and abuse—to the point of jihad—by both camps.

In attempts at the definition of life we have turned to vernacular language by default, just as, in confronting the abyss between the animate and the inanimate, we turn to common sense as a last resort.

The metaphor of life in the universe. The issue of abortion has concentrated popular attention on that brief span of human life between conception and birth. But abortion is not the only front on which technology has brought critical attention to the definition of life. Space travel and science fiction have greatly enlarged our imagination on the question of extraterrestrial life. NASA has spent millions of dollars to find out which aspects of life on earth are essential ones. Their problem is they cannot easily plan to find life in the galaxies, or plan for its transportation to other worlds, until they can generalize a better grasp of the nature of life from the incidental record of its brief history here on earth.

CRYSTAL THRESHOLD

The molecules of the fossil woolly mammoth, inert and long frozen, still bear traces of a high degree of genetic organization in the few remaining intact strands of DNA . . . a geometry so complex that it could have been accomplished only by once-living organisms. In the inanimate realm, few molecules even approach such elaborate design.

It was an aphorism of Linnaeus that "Stones grow; Plants grow and live; Animals grow and live and feel." He must have had crystals in mind, for ordinary stones do not grow—except smaller. Otherwise his progression comports with common sense.

Crystals represent the highest degree of organization of which nonliving matter is capable. Crystals are not alive, but they do grow by accretion, adding new material to what is already there, in exquisite response to an external environment. Here is a structural threshold where life is profoundly different from nonlife. Cells and organisms respond to organizing forces and patterns in their internal environment, growing dynamically from inside-out. Crystals are modified by outside forces only.

Crystals in their paracrystalline or liquid crystal form

—states of matter intermediate between the random orientation of a liquid and the almost absolute rigidity of a true crystal—approach most closely the realm of the living. In this state their internal structure and directional properties are closely related to living systems, and animate organisms appear to contain many components of a para-crystalline nature.

THE TEMPLATE HYPOTHESIS

A template is a device for the replication of any number of standard objects. Observing that molecules can indirectly organize other molecules into copies of themselves, biologists have hypothesized a template for this purpose. One of the consequences of this view of life is that, while the molecules themselves are mortal, the templates always survive: they are immortal.

There is every evidence that we now know where the very animate-inanimate threshold operates in the physical world of nature. The threshold manifests itself somewhere within cellular organisms in the arena of nucleic acid and protein enzyme interactions. Inaccessible as these areas are to common understanding, there is nevertheless no evidence that they cannot be ultimately described in terms of the ordinary laws of chemical and physical science.

During the process of reproduction in the natural world the genetic material of the organism is replicated by the mechanism of template copying, one strand of DNA acting as a template for the next. This is a peculiar property of nucleic acids, providing the molecular basis for inheritance. But so far as we know, this process occurs only within the highly organized context of the living cell. The replication of the genome and the reproduction of the organism are mutually dependent processes. As Joseph Hoffman writes,

> **the living world is essentially a vast number of templates, each one reduplicating itself with matter it takes from the**

surrounding organic world which may be either dead or living. Matter in the form of atoms in molecules moves from one pattern into another, or, we should say, goes from the influence of one template to that of another. Literally all of the organic material spread so tenuously over the earth's surface is being fought for by the templates in living things.

The cell is the only theater for the immortal template. If ever artificial life comes to compete with the life of nature, there will have to be mechanical devices at the molecular level to perform a template function in either some artificial cell or some extracellular mode.

CONTINUUM

When does life start? This is a deeply troubling question in modern society, where authorities and institutions provide only mixed signals, and where every individual in the final analysis has to decide for himself where life begins. Beginnings and endings are not characteristic of life. As human beings, we are no more at home with the intimations of our origins than we are with the forebodings of our ends.

Life is an everlasting flow, a process of reversing disorder. The physical body makes its independent appearance with birth. But when it began is meaningless: With marriage of the parents? With their sexual activity prior to conception? The continuum of life is beyond the total reach of science.

The individual self does not arise at a given moment in gestation, but rather is "the product of processes of continuing genesis, beginning *in utero*, but continuing well after birth. Self almost certainly is not actually present during the first two months of development, although it becomes increasingly imminent. In these terms the period of reasonable certainty that no semblance of self exists ends with the appearance of spontaneous and responsive behavior."

The middle ground. Harvard's eminent evolutionary biologist George Gaylord Simpson has told us not to worry about boundaries between the organic and inorganic. He tells us, albeit in a footnote to a textbook, that we should dwell on the middle ground:

> In the light of the important discoveries that began to emerge in the late 1950s ... the boundary between the living and the nonliving is becoming increasingly indefinite. Today biochemists can place purified nucleic acids and other appropriate organic materials in a test-tube system and synthesize both duplicates of these nucleic acids and specific protein molecules. Many of the essential features of life can thus be made to arise experimentally without cellular organization. The various physical and chemical properties of living organisms did not originate all at once, and some, perhaps all, of the vital reactions can be made to occur separately and outside of cells. To this extent there is a continuous spectrum from nonliving to living, with a middle ground between the two where application of either term is more or less arbitrary.

Even contemporary philosophers go along with their scientific cohorts and tell us not to worry too much about the animate-inanimate distinction. Listen to Professor Paul Churchland of the department of philosophy at the University of California, San Diego:

> Let us start with the common conception ... that evolution has two large and discontinuous gaps to bridge: the gap between nonlife and life, and the gap between unconsciousness and consciousness. Both of these distinctions, so entrenched in common sense, embody a degree of *mis*conception. In fact, neither distinction corresponds to any well-defined or unbridgeable discontinuity in nature. ... The wiser lesson is that living systems are distinguished from nonliving systems only by degrees. There is no metaphysical gap to be

bridged; only a smooth slope to be scaled, a slope measured in degrees of order and in degrees of self-regulation.

As might be expected, the secretary of the Smithsonian Institution has put the matter in an even broader context:

> It is debatable whether there are certain boundaries, or only uncertainties, around life and conscious thought. . . . A clear consensus on definitions or boundaries is also not to be found within the domain of biology, as intensifying scientific interest in primitively reproducing, energy-processing molecules and even prebiotic evolution attests.

8
Quickening

―――――――――――⌇―――――――――――

Quickening describes that stage of pregnancy when the fetus can be felt to move in the womb, the uterus. The ancients identified the phenomenon of quickening as the time when life commenced. Aristotle said about 40 days after conception and Hippocrates said 30; both speculated on a slightly longer interval for female embryos as opposed to males. Only the Stoics said that the fetus did not become animate until it breathed at birth. Later Roman law prescribed 40 days after conception as the commencement of life (for both sexes), and this was accepted by Galen.

St. Thomas Aquinas (*Summa Theologica*), having shown that life was identified by knowledge and movement, proposed that *animus* (life or soul) entered the body of the unborn infant when it turned or moved in the womb; the rule of common law in England concurred. "Life," said Blackstone, "begins in contemplation of law as soon as the infant is able to stir in the mother's womb."

It is a convention, not universally accepted, that prenatal life may be subdivided into three periods: the preembryonic, the embryonic, and the fetal. For the first two weeks the phenomenon is an ovum or conceptus or preembryo. From the third to the fifth week the human offspring is described as an embryo. Fetus describes the unborn young from the end of the seventh or eighth week to the moment of birth—the seventh or eighth week being the earliest reported capacity for response to a stimulus. (Miscarriage is a premature expulsion of a fetus from the uterus; a spontaneous event. Abortion is a termination of pregnancy without regard to the potential of the fetus for survival; an induced event.)

In America the legal significance of quickening varies from state to state. A Wisconsin state court ruling of 1923 described the dilemma of defining the onset of individual human life in terms happily congenial to both the law and to common sense.

In a strictly scientific and physiological sense there is life in an embryo from the time of conception, and in such sense there is life in the male and female elements that unite to form the embryo. But law for obvious reasons cannot in its classifications follow the latest or ultimate declarations of science. It must for purposes of practical efficiency proceed upon more everyday and popular conceptions, especially as to definitions of crime that are *malum in se*. These must be of such a nature that the ordinary normal adult knows it is morally wrong to commit them. That it should be less of an offense to destroy an embryo in a stage where human life in its common acceptance has not yet begun than to destroy a quick child is a conclusion that commends itself to most men.

In federal law under the Supreme Court's decision in *Roe* v. *Wade* (1973) no reason is required for abortion in the first two trimesters of pregnancy and a variety of reasons, such as preservation of the life or health of the mother, will suffice in the third. Quickening does not appear to be a factor.

The word *quicken* is not a scientific word; it comes from Old English and meant originally to restore or return to life. When a mother uses a needle to remove a splinter from a child's fingertip she may slip into the quick. The flight deck crews on aircraft carriers—during launches and takeoffs they are constantly dodging propellers and trip wires—used to say (in biblical language) that among their number there were only the quick and the dead. *Quicksilver* and *quicksand* dramatize the sense of elusive mobility. Here is another case where the vernacular tongue illuminates a corner of life not easily susceptible to scientific description. Shakespeare uses *quick* to mean endowed with life, pregnant. ". . . the poor wench is cast away; she's quick; the child brags in her belly already." (*Love's Labour's Lost*: V. II.)

The notion has even been translated from the human to the astronomic scale in a recent book by Eugene Mallove called *The Quickening Universe: Cosmic Evolution and Human Destiny*. In the author's metaphor the process of quickening has the double meaning of both coming to life and accelerating.

> . . . as science grows in understanding of matter, chemistry, and life itself, the more apparent it seems that "life" is the inevitable offspring of senseless matter—given the proper environment. The universe quickens and looks back on itself with a smile. . . . Quickening is also the stage of pregnancy in which the movement of the fetus can first be felt. So it seems highly appropriate to suggest that the laws of physics are literally *pregnant* with life—complexity.

There are quite enough ambiguities in the threshold between embryo and fetus, but that is hardly the end of the matter. In recent years there has been an increase of scientific and medical attention to embryo research because of its relevance to four persistent medical problems: inherited diseases, congenital handicaps, contraception, and infertility. The last of these has given rise to in vitro (test-tube) fertilization (IVF) and embryo transfer (IVFET), with the first successful conception of a child by IVFET in July 1978. These developments have brought questions of the sanctity of human life from the cloister into the laboratory, the hospital, and the courtroom.

The original purpose of in vitro fertilization was to overcome the obstructed fallopian tubes of an infertile female. Current IVF techniques result in the production of multiple follicles and multiple ova for fertilization in the test tube, with the result that only a few prospective embryos are returned to the mother's womb and an embarrassment of fertilized conceptuses remain in the glass tube on the laboratory bench. These surplus fertilized entities are the source of an exquisite moral dilemma: Should they be destroyed, donated to other infertile recipients, or be made available for scientific experimentation?

As a result of marked advances in research on human embryology, there has been a concentration of interest in the notion of the *preembryo*, the first 14 days after conception, proposed as the outer limit for research on embryos produced by in vitro fertilization. In this view an embryo does not come into being until the first two weeks after conception; the initial fertilized entity is a preembryotic conceptus. Laboratory technicians can manipulate very young conceptuses under laboratory conditions only for that first protean fortnight; after two weeks an embryo cannot survive outside the womb and no way has been found to convert a one-celled fertilized ovum into a person except by implanting it in the wall of the uterus.

About 15 days after conception fetal cells begin to arrange themselves in what is termed the "primitive streak," which marks the onset of individuality, the last point, for instance, at which identical twins can occur. In England the Warnock Committee of Inquiry into Human Fertilization and Embryology of 1986 proposed the use of the preembryo in medical research as a way to obviate the question of when a human embryo assumes human rights and entitlements.

What distinguish a functioning organism from a mass of disorganized cells are the hormonal and nervous systems that provide a network for growth and internal coordination. But in the fetus organization commences through the mechanisms of embryogenesis before the glands and nerves become manifest—and even before the future parents may be aware that they are going to have a baby. Not until at least the first 30 days does the identity of an individual begin to emerge. Hear how this process is described in the words of Jonathan Cooke, an embryologist in the United Kingdom:

> **In a majority of embryo types . . . organization is essentially complete within the first day or two after fertilization. Even in the particular version of development that begins the life of human beings, the crucial processes . . . occur early. They are complete in outline by little more than a month after human conception. Thus at a time when, for the majority of the world's population pregnancy is not suspected or thought about, the plan of the future individual's body has been designated, leaving only a precise schedule of growth and of the maturation and differentiation of the descendants of the founder cells to be played out. Along with the neural and hormonal systems, embryogenesis must rank as one of the three great integrative systems underlying the multi-cellular mode of life.**

Conception and birth are the only clear finite limits of fetal development; the first limit does not lend itself to direct observation, while the second is dramatically evident to all parties concerned. The actual threshold of viability is hypothetical. Between the limits of conception and birth there is some point (perhaps less arbitrary than the 14-day or 30-day signposts) at which the fetus becomes viable— when it can survive outside the womb. When the landmark Supreme Court decision *Roe* v. *Wade* was handed down in 1973, it provided that once a fetus is viable it could be left to the states to regulate abortion, provided that the mother's health was not at stake.

The court says that the interest of the state in the potential life of the fetus does not become compelling until the point of viability; a point that varies with advances in medical technology. In 1973 viability was pretty well recognized as about 28 weeks, providing a period of roughly seven months to decide whether to continue a pregnancy. But recent advances in medical technology have lowered the threshold considerably, to about 24 weeks, and the new medical specialty of neonatology, functioning with the facilities of a modern hospital, manages to keep alive babies weighing as little as two to three pounds, at even 22 or 23 weeks. The critical survival factor is lung function, since respiratory difficulties are the greatest risk for premature babies.

NEONATOLOGY & ABORTION

Sustaining the life of prematurely born infants with the indiscriminate application of advanced technology—say, for instance, the three-pound baby of a teenage drug-addict mother in a South Bronx hospital—is a heroic extravagance and a blatant indulgence in its cost to society. As the hard-edge, uncheerful conservation biologist Garrett Hardin tells us,

> **the smaller a preemie is, the greater is the cost of saving it. Indeed, an outside observer of the earthly scene—the proverbial Martian—would be justified in deducing that humans believe that the smaller and less mature a life is, the greater is its value. If a two-pound baby is worth a quarter of a million dollars, what is the value of a one-pound baby? A million dollars? Ten million? How about a one-ounce embryo? No doubt such a rescue will soon be technically possible.**

The later life of a surviving neonate is often a relentless susceptibility to chronic medical troubles, not to mention the distorted quality of life in a family whose resources must be dedicated to such flawed human beings. Heroic intervention with premature infants is a program clothed in nobility of motive but too often wanton in insidiousness of effect.

Recent advances in techniques for monitoring fetal development include hormonal assay of blood and urine, amniocentesis, fetoscopy, and ultrasonography. They are now generally available for screening of embryos and fetuses for possible genetic defects. Although these measures have refined our knowledge of the nature of fetal development, they have not resolved any of its ambiguities.

Biology provides no easy answer to the question of when human life begins. The absolute notion that life begins from conception results from a misleading oversimplification. For most of its long history the Catholic Church subscribed to St. Augustine's doctrine of "animation"— that the fetus is alive when it begins to stir. In 1963 Pope John XXIII appointed a commission of theologians, gynecologists, psychologists, demographers, and married couples to study the question of the use of contraceptives. The majority of the panel urged the pope to define doctrine so that mechanical and chemical methods of birth control would be morally licit. In 1968 Pope Paul VI declined the advice of the commission and delivered his encyclical *Humanae Vitae*, pronouncing for the Church for the first time that life begins with conception.*

The Catholic Church celebrated the 20th anniversary of *Humanae Vitae* on 12 November 1988 with renewed efforts to enforce the encyclical including opposition to the use of condoms even to prevent the spread of AIDS. Pope John Paul II said that any questioning of the church's ban on contraception would be tantamount to doubting "the very idea of God's holiness." Msgr. Carlo Caffarra, head of the John Paul II Institute for the Study of Marriage and the Family, underlined the extent of that dubiety by conceding in a press conference that nearly 80 percent of Catholic couples use birth control, while 70 percent of confessors condone it.

---

*Instruction on Respect for Human Life in Its Origin and on the Dignity of Procreation. *(In the title of this document the word 'dignity' takes on a baroque resonance.)*

The Catholic position accords to the instant conceptus the legal rights and individual sanctity granted to mature members of society. Colman McCarthy is one of the Church's most articulate apologists on the issue, and on the anniversary of the encyclical in his newspaper column of 27 November 1988 he took the argument to its logical extreme:

> **A growing coalition . . . is arguing that life-and-death control shouldn't belong to anyone in any issue. Not . . . mercy-killers, not judges or juries who sanction executions, not militarists who despatch the young to war . . . and not destroyers of human life when found in its weakest form, the fetal state.**
>
> **A human life created by rape or incest has the same rights to continue its growth as a human life created by a loving couple. No one chooses the conditions of his or her conception.**

The logic may be impeccable given the premises; but the premises have no sanction in science and no reinforcement in common sense. Colman McCarthy's argument brings little comfort to those of us who would otherwise defend the weak. His crazy logic makes human society—fragile as it is—a hostage to the unborn. A growing uncertainty among believers in the infallibility of Church doctrine seems to reinforce a ritual extremism on this specific issue. It has become the *Crusade de nos jours*.

For McCarthy, "violence to the fetus" is a sufficient definition of abortion to qualify it as a crime and a sin. Just one of the troubles with that dogma is that it takes no account of the violence to the mother. The uninvited fetus is perhaps a joy and perhaps a distress. In either case, the option of the mother is more important than the option of the fetus. The violence to the fetus is doctrinal; the violence to the mother is real. Abortion grants relief to mothers and families where birth control has failed. Do we want to live in a world where fetuses are more important than people

. . . more important than mothers? This might have been true of Eve, but not in a world of more than two billion mothers.

Compare this with the concept of brain death, which continuously gains wider recognition in the medical care of the terminally ill. Such a practical definition of death recognizes that the intellect and personality of the individual depend on the intact functioning of the neocortical tissue. Might there not be some comparable recognition of brain birth? . . . some recognition that no individual personality could possibly have developed prior to the organization of the nervous system and its tissues. An undue preoccupation with the *potential* for personality at one end of the spectrum or with the lingering *perpetuation* of same at the other end not only lacks the sanction of any scientific imperative but exacts an enormous toll in human suffering and societal costs.

Gestation is too complex to permit easy answers. There is something inherently absurd about according to a few dozen undifferentiated cells the dignity of an individual human being, especially during those initial 14 days when some of the cells might become a brain stem, while others could become extra-embryonic matter such as a placenta or an umbilical cord. Dignity resides not here.

It is not only the individual cells that have an uncertain (or at least so far undetermined) destination. Most conceptuses in the womb at that stage do not arouse the awareness of the mothers who are their hosts. Does it not lend some perspective to reflect that the majority of early embryos fail to implant themselves to the uterine wall and are lost to natural processes before either parent could know they were there?

This is an area where not just physiological forces are at work but also unfathomable imperatives of instinct and psychology. The rate of human reproduction derives from largely unpredicted (and perhaps unpredictable) forces: Biological demographers estimate that on a worldwide basis somewhere between 65 to 75 percent of all children born were not deliberately planned or wanted.

Some scientists feel that special-interest groups can misrepresent the preembryo concept for ideological reasons or to adduce false authority for abortion legislation. Speaking at the plenary session of the 154th national meeting of the American Association for the Advancement of Science in Boston in 1988, Dr. John Biggers of the Laboratory of Human Reproduction and Reproductive Biology, Harvard Medical School, in an address on the biological nature of life, asserted that it is arbitrary to assign special significance to the 14-day preembryo. The term preembryo "has no scientific validity, because development [like life] is a continuous process. . . . the proposal to use specific cut-off times in development as a basis for making ethical decisions is both uninformed and fraught with pitfalls."

Abortion. Therapeutic abortion is an unhappy phrase for an unhappy situation. An abortion should not be described as therapeutic when the object, the ultimate beneficiary of the therapy—the putative infant or the anguished mother or the affected family or the concerned society—is so ambiguous. Surely this is more of an exercise in prophylaxis than in therapy.

To me there is a compelling and commonsense argument in support of compassionate intervention that addresses itself directly to the fate of the child. As a medical ethicist, Millard S. Everett, wrote in 1954:

> **My personal feeling—and I don't ask anyone to agree with me—is that eventually, when public opinion is prepared for it, no child shall be admitted into the society of the living who would be certain to suffer any social handicap—for example, any physical or mental defect that would prevent marriage or that would make others tolerate his company only from a sense of mercy. . . . Life in early infancy is very close to non-existence, and admitting a child into our society**

is almost like admitting one from potential to actual existence, and viewed in this way only normal life should be accepted.

And what about if a pregnancy is perfectly normal, but unwanted? Isn't an infant who wasn't longed for more apt to grow up unloved and emotionally crippled ... a prospective burden not only to the family but to the supporting social community? Surely it can be argued that to bring such a child into the world is more morally reprehensible than abortion.

On a Sunday in April 1989 hundred of thousands of mainstream Americans—mostly family groups, particularly large numbers of mothers and daughters—marched up to the West Front of the Capitol in Washington to demonstrate support for the legality of abortions. The event was occasioned by a pending U.S. Supreme Court review of an act of the Missouri legislature that had declared by simple fiat that "life begins with conception." The main theme of the marchers was not in favor of abortion per se, but merely that the woman—not the state and not the church—should make the decision. One demonstrator carried a poster illustrating the essential neutrality of the pro-choice position. It said simply: "If you don't believe in abortions—don't have them."

Abortion is an issue that does not lend itself to compromise, and thus it invites increasing militancy in each camp. To the doctrinaire antiabortionist all sex is construed as functionally procreative; hence, not only can contraception and sterilization be conceived of as murder, but also masturbation and coitus interruptus.

On the crazier fringe of trying to apply strict logic where science and religion are at odds, two other signs in the march read "Masturbation and menstruation are murder" and "If men could get pregnant, abortion would be a sacrament." One faction's travesties of another.

On that same occasion a group of 167 scientists and physicians, including 11 Nobel laureates, submitted a friend-of-the-court brief to the court declaring simply that "There is no scientific consensus that a human life begins at conception, at a given stage of fetal development, or at birth." *Or even at birth.*

The chief rationales for therapeutic abortion are threats to the health of the mother and indications of abnormal physical development in the prospective infant. Such threats cannot often be anticipated in advance of conception, but when they are, the expedient of contraception is available. But of course the major use of birth control is for personal, family, and social reasons having nothing to do with therapeutic intentions.

"The moral property of women": RU-486. In 1986 the gynecologist Etienne Baulieu at the Hôpital de Bicetre in France invented a substance known as RU-486—affording a completely novel method of birth control. It is designed to intervene in the process of conception not prior to coitus but shortly thereafter—the long-awaited "morning after" pill. The procedure interferes with the action of progesterone and causes the uterine lining to slough off as are unfertilized eggs in the regular menstrual process. Technically it is a menses inducer, and the French Minister of Health has recognized it as "the moral property of women." The intervention can be accomplished not just the morning after coitus but up to ten days after a missed menstrual period. The increasing adoption of RU-486 by women in France is demonstrating the capacity to terminate pregnancies without significant side effects. It provides, for the first time, a morning-after option with highly sought-after physiological advantages and without the stigma and psychological stress of abortion.

To its proponents, RU-486 offers the prospect of a safe, convenient, and, above all, after-the-fact method of avoiding or frustrating pregnancy: an abortifacient. Certainly it entails much less emotional stress and would seem to be the procedure of choice in cases of rape, incest, or those occasions—ranging from the bizarre to the merely

inopportune—in which coitus occurs without any prospect
that the two people involved are prepared to provide the
family support that childbirth mandates. To its opponents,
RU-486 is considered as aggression against the unborn; to
its adherents and to its sponsors, it is described as *contra-
gestation*, the simple stimulation of a menstrual period.

At the threshold of conception new technologies continue
to intervene without elucidating the point at which a new
individual is created but without any threat to life's seam-
less continuum. The most recent biotechnological research
only reinforces the conclusion that gestation is a continuum
rather than a discrete—or quantum—process.

   To abort a viable fetus during the last months of pregnancy is manifestly repugnant, an act if not analogous to
murder at least freighted with anguish even in the most
exonerating circumstances. By contrast, a ten-day-old fetus
is nothing like a human being, not even a very primitive
one, and the notion of aborting it invokes nothing like the
same range of moral and philosophical objections.* (Abhor-
rence of aborting a fetus in the last trimester of pregnancy
is a common sensibility in contemporary Western societies.
But it was not ever thus; among Eskimos and Polynesians
infanticide of infants up to a year old was a common practice
for regulating the population; and in parts of China the
practice is condoned to the present day.)

   Some recognize an individual entitled to moral rights
at fertilization; others when the embryo implants in the
womb; some, like the Wisconsin court, suggest the time of
quickening; while still others would say individuality cannot be recognized until the fetus is capable of independent
life outside the womb, some time at the end of the second
trimester; and still others would defer recognition until par-

---

* *In the United States over half of all reported abortions are performed eight
weeks or less after the last menstrual period, and over 90 percent are performed
in the first trimester.*

turition at the commencement of the process of birth. Each of these criteria is as arbitrary as the next, and will likely remain so for the foreseeable future.

Speaking at the same session cited above, Dr. Biggers argued that to say life begins at conception is to make nonsense of scientific fact. "Life never ends, it is a continuous process. . . . Fertilization is merely one process in the cycle of life." Scripture cryptically addresses the dilemma—but fails to resolve it—in telling us that life is begotten not made. For all of us but Adam (who was created, not born) the navel serves as fleshly testament to the unbroken chain of amniotic continuity.

CONTINUUM EFFECT

Gestation, like the grander biological process of evolution itself, is an almost imperceptibly gradual business. Like every other living organism a human infant was at one ineffable moment a single cell. That first single cell develops into a conceptus—a blastocyst from which both placenta and embryo derive—which, though not yet an embryo, is a newly formed human organism biologically distinct from both its parents. How something that is not a person becomes something that is a person remains a miracle and a mystery.

This is a matter to which religion and myth bring some crazy authority where science has none: orthodox Jews, without saying what happens to baby girls, specify that a male child acquires entity—being a person unto itself—only with the act of circumcision.

As long as there is no apparent moment, organization, structure, event, or quantum jump that marks the advent of being human, as long as there is no natural threshold of individuality, the scientists, lawyers, philosophers, and theologians will find no easy accommodation of the ambiguities at the heart of gestation, a continuous process, apparently devoid of fault lines. Perhaps the process of human procreation presents the threshold between self and non-self at its most dramatic limit of unresolvability.

The claim that life begins at conception is wrong on two counts. First, life doesn't begin at all (and it possibly never has); life can only *continue*. This is the doctrine of abiogenesis: Life arises only from life. Second, there is no moment of conception; it is a physical process—and an elaborate one—that requires time, time for boy and girl to grow up, time for the gleam in the lover's eye to consummate, time for egg and sperm to fuse into a single cell (the origin of the potentiality for singleness), time for the fused cell to divide into the blastocyst, time for the blastocyst to form placenta and embryo. The process is not instantaneous, even as death is not instantaneous. The arena is a continuum in which the generations overlap.

Martin Johnson, a reader in experimental embryology at the University of Cambridge, has put it this way:

> **My emergence as a unique individual with my own identity began back in the ovaries and testes of my parents when they themselves were embryos in the grandparental womb. . . . Just as anthropologists cannot define an exact and absolute point during evolutionary time when our ancient ancestors became human, so I cannot define any single developmental transition at which I became an individual with a clear identity. The evolution of humans and the development of my own identity are both continuous processes.**

There is an effect known as *embryonic induction* that was discovered by Hans Spemann in experiments on newt embryos, for which he was awarded the Nobel Prize in 1935. He found that the ligaturing (binding and tying) of an embryo into halves at an early stage of development always resulted either in its death or in the development of a whole embryo; never in two half-embryos. The integrity of gestation resides in the entire conceptus, not in its parts.

Embryonic newt tissue always gives rise to newt organs

even when transplanted to a frog embryo. Embryonic tissue responds to induction from foreign tissue but has the potential to develop only into organs of the species from which it originated. These phenomena are known as embryonic induction.

[Hans] Spemann . . . held the view that the development of fetal life can best be understood by assuming that the maternal and fetal bodies are in some respect a single unit. That is to say, there is a reciprocity so intimate that it is more realistic and more accurate to treat the living system-of-two, rather than one-plus-one individuals. . . . the regions in which the fetal eye or ear develop, for example, are constantly being impressed by life forces as wholes. . . . The phenomenon would almost smack of the miraculous were it not a demonstration that the laws are constant, from the larger aggregate to the more particular.

The influence exerted by various regions of an embryo controls the subsequent development of cells into specific organs and tissues. If a group of undifferentiated cells is planted in the eye region of an embryo, they will turn into eye tissue; if they are planted in the ear region they became ear tissue. We are standing and walking with parts of our body which we could have use for thinking if they had been developed in another position in the embryo.

A DEMENTI ON THE SANCTITY OF LIFE

There is really no rational imperative—no moral requirement—for the human race to generate the maximum, rather than the optimum, number of human beings. On the basis of genetics and human physiology, the naturalist, Daniel B. Luten, has calculated that better than one trillion trillion people are conceivable each year, and yet only a minute fraction of them—100 million—are born. The unborn are legion; there is not space on earth to write their names.

In his posthumous message to posterity Buckminster Fuller (*Cosmography*, 1991) put the matter starkly—at the brink of atrocity—with all the ferociousness of a Francis Bacon portrait of a screaming, bleeding cardinal or a butchered, outraged beast: "Some religious bodies battle politically and morally against abortion, which inherently eliminates their most lucrative raison d'être—humans and more humans and their concomitant adversity and suffering, and their need of ministry."

A regard for the sanctity of each human individual life does not mandate a policy of forcing fecundity. Where is the grace in fulfilling all potential procreativity at any cost? (Particularly in the face of the current crisis, where the world population is growing at a net gain of 10,000 people per hour—births over deaths.)

Fuller's formulation may appear hermetic. In the context of all his writing on the subject of religion it is clear that he bears no animosity towards the Church or its ministers, merely regarding them as victims of a mistaken mythology. The business of the church is salvation—in the world to come life everlasting—the promise of hope and redemption and glory. To justify itself the Church has to value human life, even vestiges thereof, at all costs. But that rationale for the institution derives from what is for Fuller a chicanery: There is no basis for the promise of survival after we have died. How many of us are there who really believe otherwise?

Schopenhauer was equally stark in describing the dependence of religion on the fear of death: "All religious and philosophical systems are principally directed toward comforting us concerning death, and are thus primarily antidotes to the terrifying certainty of death."

Unconscious life as a waiver of sanctity. That there can be no real living without consciousness is a dogmatic view, but an attractive one. Does the sanctity of life apply to the not-yet-conscious or to the irreversibly unconscious? Is not the lack of brain development at birth as distressing as brain death in the dying? It is my view—probably a minority one in our society—that prolonging and supporting life without consciousness is a cruelty to all involved.

Incidentally, there seems to be little communication between people concerned, pro or con, with euthanasia and those concerned, pro or con, with abortion. Could the dilemmas of one illuminate the dilemmas of the other? Our courts have long been preoccupied with the doctrine of *wrongful death*; a growing literature dealing with the legal issues in human reproduction, particularly with test-tube babies and surrogate mothers, is now beginning to document the legal concept of *wrongful birth*. Human intervention, augmented by advancing technologies, at either end of the spectrum of human life invites mischief.

The circuitry of a baby's nervous system buzzes with activity long before his birth. Some aspects of mammalian sensation—taste buds, for instance—are relatively mature by the time of birth. The olfactory system seems to function before birth as the introduction of odorous substances in the amniotic fluid can stimulate suckling behavior. The fetus cannot see, but photoreceptor cells are already well enough developed to make the connections demanded by the drastic change at birth from a liquid to a gaseous environment.

There is a body of literature attesting to memories and dreams and experiences of awareness and sensation prior to birth—recaptured after the event by the conscious individual. R. D. Laing has produced the startling hypothesis that conscious life might begin with the "primal relationship" between the fetus and the placenta, and he goes on to suggest that even further back the implantation of the blastocyst within the endometrium might be the source of yet more archaic recollections. Here are speculations beyond the reach of experimental biological science. They offer little hope that greater knowledge of brain development in the fetus might provide a criterion for a point after which abortions might be considered unacceptable.

Buckminster Fuller tells us dogmatically that life is not physical, that life is "not the organism which employs it. . . . A fetus is just physical life, a bundle of reflexes like a chicken running around with its head cut off.* Consciousness and identity begin not with conception but with birth. Awareness, that's the thing! . . . that's what begins with birth."

A fetus in the womb experiences taste, touch, and sound. The upheaval of birth adds sight to the repertory. The newborn, although it has the capacity to register certain physical stimuli, is devoid of adult sensibilities and lacks any systematic contexts that might serve as a scaffold for consciousness. Not only prior to the moment of birth, but for many days thereafter, the nervous system of infants provides them with experiences better characterized as awareness than as consciousness. And as for a sense of identity, many months will pass before the infant realizes that his feet and toes are indeed his own.

A VIEW THAT LIFE BEGINS AT PARTURITION

Buckminster Fuller sees the threshold of human life at the point when the body of the infant gradually acquires independent metabolism. At birth the importing of energy not only exceeds the exporting of energy, it becomes independent—except for breastfeeding—of any maternal mechanism. There is no other basis for an independent awareness. I find the viewpoint esthetically and pragmatically attractive. At parturition the umbilicus ephemerates.

The political, religious, and judicial controversies prevailing in the late 1970s with regard to abortion and "the right to life" will ultimately be resolved by . . . popular comprehen-

* ". . . our own early life is, experientially, a complete blank. . . . Behavior during the prenatal period, and for some time after birth, thus appears to be controlled subcortically." (Munn, 1965)

sion of science's discovery . . . that the physical and chemical organism of humans consists entirely of inanimate atoms. . . . It follows that the *individual life* does not exist until the umbilical cord is cut and the child starts its own metabolic regeneration; prior to that the life in the womb is merely composed of the mother organism, as is the case with any one individual egg in her ovary. Life begins with individually self-started and sustained energy importing and dies when that independent importing ceases.

Until the epochal event of parturition there is no independent vulnerability. It has been common American practice for centuries to recognize birth as the commencement of an individual's life. Like all other societies we do not count ages from the date of conception. We do not tax or grant civic privileges to the unborn. To count pregnant women twice in our censuses would instantly increase our population by about three million.

ASTROLOGY

Astrology is an ancient and undiminished set of beliefs about the relevance of the heavens to ordinary life. Astrology, though it traffics in prediction, is not a discipline, but it is at least one of the rare vocations that offers certainty on the question of when life begins. In astrology life starts at birth, not conception.

To prepare a horoscope for an individual the astrologer has to know a lot more than what "sign" of the Zodiac governs your fate. For their horoscoping astrologers not only want to know the exact day of birth but the hour of emergence from the womb. In the astrological system there is no question but that life commences at the moment of birth. This is nine months and a country mile away from the position of the Catholic Church, in which the Vatican— like the legislature of the state of Missouri—pronounces that life begins with conception.; these theological and gubernatorial decrees express what remains a minority doctrine.

Astrology is a much older pursuit than astronomy. More people in the world earn their living as astrologers than as astronomers, and more acreage of newspaper space is devoted to horoscopes than to astrophysics.

I don't know any astrologers, so I don't know how defensive they may be about their calling. Some of them must be defensive, for they have proposed a new name for themselves with all the attributes of a discipline: *cosmobiology* no less. This is a legitimate intention to bring objectivity to an ancient practice, to seek statistical evidence of correlations between career choice or achievement and the position of the planets. No results are yet available.

THE SEX ACT

Ever since an evolutionary back alley invented sex, DNA has increased its opportunities to impose change: it has unquestionably accelerated diversity. *H. sapiens* differs from other vertebrates, indeed other mammals. in performing the sex act. No female mammals except women experience orgasm. All mammals copulate, often breeding at limited periods of fertility; no creatures except men and women have coitus. In humans the pleasure of orgasm involves the center of our experience in the nervous system and creates momentarily an altered state of consciousness; it enhances the act of sex much as taste is basic to nutrition. Among mammals man is one of the few species who adopt prolonged pair-bonding, an alliance lasting not only through the period of gestation, parturition, and lactation, but extending through the rearing of the young.

An increased participation of the husband, the prospective father, in the act of parturition is one of the most dramatic indexes of civility in mainstream 20th-century American society. The human birth process, despite all the advances in obstetrical care and intervention, remains one of the most difficult in the animal kingdom. The inescapable partnership of the husband in the birth process is now the transcendent social event of the family. In the early decades of this century it would not have been conceivable as a common domestic practice. It is an extremely recent phenomenon in American cultural evolution; and it may even come to rival the central role of the marriage ceremony of couples living together. (In weddings, the video camera recorder has already begun to supplant the Church as a ritual witness to the occasion.)

In human societies the sex act has assumed a major hedonistic significance beyond the simple function of procreation. Throughout human history sexuality has been an element of social control. All pleasure is idiosyncratic and sexual pleasure is particularly so; it is a mark of modernity that men and women become more concerned with the idiosyncratic character of sexuality than they are with its social efficiency. An evolutionary response to overpopulation may be something of a hidden factor here—as it may operate also in the incidence of homosexuality.

9
Viruses

Viruses do not seem to be going out of fashion. They are marginal organisms, pathological agents disturbing their environments whether ancient (hoof and mouth disease) or new (AIDS).

Viruses are so minuscule that they can pass through the finest porcelain filters that trap even the smallest one-celled bacteria. They are, most of them, an order of magnitude smaller than bacteria: The mass of a virus is to the mass of a human being as that of a human being is to the earth. The smallest viruses are one-thousandth the diameter of a hydrogen atom (that is, one angstrom)—smaller than the wavelengths of visible light. They are too small to be seen with ordinary light microscopes and can be studied only indirectly, as when they are dried and stained and ions are bounced off them through a scanning electron microscope. When thus enlarged several hundred thousand times and made visible as an aggregate of individual protein molecules they invariably reveal an extremely high degree of structural symmetry—complex polyhedra in the shape of sea anemones, soccer balls, helical pine cones or lunar modules.

Some viruses represent the largest crystalline chemical molecules so far described . . . inert structures with a potential for copying themselves. Viruses are primordial and unique threshold agents that find some infectious niche in virtually every living species, especially man, and some trophic (nutrient) role in virtually every ecosystem. As such they have attracted the most intense scientific scrutiny. As virulent bandits of matter they are admitted to some textbooks as microorganisms and excluded from others; they are taxonomic orphans and genetic nomads.

In 1942 the first electron micrographs were published clearly revealing the head-and-tail structure of a viral strain now known as bacteriophage T-2 (phage = eater). These eaters of bacteria were equipped with an attachment like a hypodermic syringe driving a needle through the membrane of a target bacterium, injecting sufficient DNA to make some 100 parasitic phage particles in 20 minutes.

Several decades later R. W. Horne, a researcher specializing in crystallographic aspects of biology, said that "Viewing the micrographs one has the impression of being shown how the inanimate world of atoms and molecules shades imperceptibly into the world of forms possessing some of the attributes of life. . . . Viruses are the smallest biological structures that embody all the information needed for their own reproduction."

Viruses do not grow in any conventional sense, since they do not increase in size. Their chromosome serves as a template for the direct synthesis of a new virus. (Chromosomes are threadlike structures which contain hereditary material.)

Viruses are obligate intracellular parasites, able to survive only when introduced into specific host cells (of certain bacteria, plants, or animals) in order to obtain the metabolism they need to reproduce and to cause the diseases which alone have brought them to our attention. As a result of this essential dependence, viruses are more closely related to their host cells—genetically and by chemical structure—than they are to each other. They can be as lifeless as a grain of sand, kept in stable suspense virtually forever, and yet remain virulent when brought into contact with a host cell. More than half of all human illnesses are caused by viral infections, and although viruses are important tools of biological research, no infallible antiviral drugs are yet available.

With the advent of the electron microscope viruses came to serve a role for the biologist that the hydrogen atom had long done for the physicist: bundles of energy too small to be seen but whose study would prove exceedingly fruitful in accounting for observed phenomena in the macro world. Stripped of inessential complications, the bacteriophage is an ideal experimental tool.

Viruses can have a beneficial effect on their hosts by conferring a capacity to resist offensive proteins. Viral infections are incidentally the cause of many of the beautiful and variegated colors of cultivated tulips. The virus of herpes simplex is probably older than human culture. It is undoubtedly one of the oldest domesticated organisms we know, older even than man's best friend, the dog.

The theoretical mathematician John von Neumann, a herald of cybernetics, introduced the principle that self-organizing mechanical systems require a certain minimum degree of complexity in order to reproduce themselves. This suggests an analogy with biological organisms (see discussion of artificial intelligence in Chapter 18), implying that any molecule or living organism must have a minimum size and a minimum number of constituent atoms to permit the requisite complexity for self-replication. No exact limit for the size of a free-living bit of protoplasm has yet been established, but whatever that threshold is, viruses must come very close to it.

Classifiers are relentless pigeonholers; they abhor both the miscellaneous and the sui generis. In the world of nature the taxonomist is almost always able to assign any new beast, blossom, or bug to one of the five available kingdoms of life on earth (whether single cells or complexes of cells): Monera, Protoctista, Fungi, Animalia, Plantae. Since the virus is not an abstraction of thought or a man-made artifact, why not assign it to the sixth and last of the great kingdoms, the mineral kingdom? Because it is not always inert; it can initiate chemical activity; and it enshrines nucleic acid, which is present in all living matter and has the capacity to transmit the DNA/RNA genetic code.

A virus is not a cell and it is not composed of cells. If it were, we could create a new phylum for it—but not casually; as of present writing and depending on which systematist is keeping score, there are only somewhere between 32 and 39 phyla in the animal kingdom, and in any event only two new phyla have been added since 1900. Thus the deadly elusive viruses have ended up in a limbo of their own beyond the broad reaches of the taxonomists' vast kingdoms. They are on a precarious perch between the animal and the mineral, between the potential and the inert. As Martin Gardner laments:

> **Viruses lie on a continuous spectrum of structural complexity. The spectrum fades back into the nonliving world of crystals and 'dead' organic molecules. It fades forward into simple, one-celled forms of plants and animal life. A virus is like a blue-green object which can be called either green or blue. It is a structure in the twilight zone—a living dead thing which our language is not yet rich enough to classify.**

But maybe this is a place where our language should be impoverished. Maybe we shouldn't expect language to make up our minds for us. Viruses may be even beyond the grasp of pronouns. Viruslike symbionts include viroids, virinos, mycoplasmas, plasmids, and prions. They are all homeless, wandering minstrels, shreds and patches of DNA or RNA encased in an elaborate helical or polyhedral shell of symmetrical protein. In fact they have been called bad news wrapped in a protein package. A preexisting virus is necessary to the production of a new one.

Unlike viruses, bacteria are independently alive and can be killed. How can viruses be living when 1) they do not grow, 2) they do not die, and 3) in fact, they cannot even be killed.*

---

* *In Sabin vaccine they are made inert with formaldehyde.*

10
Tardigrades

———————&———————

The deserts of Saudi Arabia cover more than a million square miles, and the southern stretches are so remote from the sea, so barren of vegetation—a desert within a desert— so enormous and so desolate that even the Bedouin call it the *Rub al Khali* or Empty Quarter. When rainfall does occur, its appearance is both local and rare: A shower may cover only a few acres, falling on sands that have felt no rain for 25 years. But even there, seeds that have remained long dormant blossom into a sudden patch of wildflowers. Wilfred Thesiger, one of the great English travelers among the desert tribes, tells us that:

> **Eskimos enduring the cold and darkness of the arctic winters can count the days till the sun appears, but here in southern Arabia the Bedu have no certainty of spring. Often there is no rain, and even if there is, it may fall at any time of the year. Generally the bitter winds turn to blazing summers over a parched and lifeless land. Bin Kabina told me now that he only remembered three springs in his life. Occasional springtimes such as these were all the Bedu ever knew of the gentleness of life.**

Harsh and extreme as all that sounds, we are still not surprised by the capacity of seeds to engender the gentleness of life. Seeds retain their potency, their vital power, through long periods of chemical inertia with no imports of energy—on basement shelves or in tombs or buried in the sands. They are just about our longest-lived biological tissues. But we are less familiar with the fact that there are forms of animal life that have a *similar capacity*, and most notable among these are the *tardigrades*.

Tardigrades are also known as water bears, which is what the naturalist Thomas Huxley called them because of their pawing locomotion on four pairs of stumpy legs, each with four bearlike claws. The largest of them are barely over one millimeter. Taxonomically they are usually considered as a class (with about 350 species) lying somewhere in evolutionary development between annelid worms and arthropods, such as insects and crustaceans. And, in the most explicit sense of the term, they are cosmopolitans; that is, they are widely distributed and common in most parts of the world and under a variety of ecological conditions. Some are marine, some live in fresh water, and some are terrestrial. Their habitations range from polar ice floes and glaciers to hot springs on the brink of steaming geysers and fumaroles.

Their name, tardigrade, comes from the Latin *tardus*, slow, and *gradus*, step, which is descriptive of the way they creep and crawl among the damp mosses and plants on which they feed—although some species are carnivorous and predatory, feeding on the juices of other animals including other species of tardigrades. The most remarkable characteristic of these survivors of Precambrian marine invertebrates is their physical tolerance for severe dessication, extreme temperatures, and intense radiation exposure. They manifest a phenomenon known as *anhydrobiosis*, life without water, or the capacity to assume a dry state of suspended animation and then be revived by water. (Anhydrobiosis is a subset of *anabiosis*, the ability to resuscitate from an apparently deathlike condition.) The tardigrades can survive almost complete dehydration and then, when they are moistened—even after decades—they survive.

When hatched, tardigrades start life about one-third the full size of an adult. Although they regularly molt (that is, shed their skin), they retain the same number of cells with which they were born; that is, they grow by the enlargement of existing cells (rather than by the usual increase in the number of cells through mitosis). Tardigrades mature and metabolize without defined respiratory or regulatory systems. Gases and food simply diffuse in their body liquids; carbon dioxide and oxygen are exchanged directly through the surface of their skin. Water usually takes up about 85 percent of a tardigrade's body weight. This compares with most land animals, including human beings, which are about three-fourths water. As the British biologist J. B. S. Haldane famously put it, "even the Pope is 70 percent water,"

Dehydration appears to be not just an idiosyncrasy but a prerequisite condition for the tardigrade imperative for survival. It is this trait that has attracted biologists to subject these creatures to environmental extremes under laboratory conditions. There is a record of specimens having been kept for eight days in a vacuum, then transferred for three days into helium gas at room temperature, and then exposed for several hours at $-270°$ C—at the brink of absolute zero—only to come to life again when returned to normal room temperature. Sixty percent of some specimens kept in liquid oxygen for 21 months managed to survive when restored to normal conditions. These creatures have also been allowed to dry at room temperature for 18 months; placed in water, they returned to life in about two hours.

When tardigrades begin to dry out they contract into a motionless form called a *tun*, a term borrowed from the wine industry whose casks they resemble. There is speculation that this procedure somehow minimizes the gross mechanical damage to tissues and organs that desiccation would otherwise involve. In the tun state the tardigrade can survive for something like a century!

One of the great disadvantages of the scanning electron microscope is that it cannot examine life *in vivo*; specimens have to be killed by freeze-drying before being submitted to the scanning apparatus. But not so with tardigrades; when they are carefully dehydrated for the scanning electron camera, they can come back to life. Almost like Japanese paper flowers. Just add water.

Of course, the scanning microscope also subjects the target to intense electron radiation. Here again the tardigrades show their extraordinary resistance. In the case of humans, 500 roentgens of X-ray exposure is considered a lethal dose. Tardigrades have survived a staggering radiation dosage of 570,000 roentgens for 24 hours.

Tardigrades may have been involved in the first scientific explorations demonstrating that the threshold between life and death is far from clear-cut. In 1702 Anton van Leeuwenhoek reported to the Royal Society in London that he had seen "animalcules" in his primitive microscope: "I found that when all the water was evaporated . . . the creature . . . then contracted itself into an oval figure [preserving] that shape unhurt." And he discovered that the state of suspended animation was reversible; when he returned the oval figures to water they began "swimming about the glass." Leeuwenhoek's report has been cited in intervening centuries to support theories of resurrection and spontaneous generation. Preoccupied as man is with his own mortality, he is irresistibly fascinated with the prospect that any organism could return to life after death—even such a putative death.

Thus the term anabiosis with its resurrectionist implication of "return to life" is somewhat misleading. In 1959 a Cambridge University biologist, David Keilin, proposed the term *cryptobiosis*—"hidden life"—as a more appropriate description of the phenomenon.

Cryptobiotic reactions appear to be triggered as a response to adverse environmental conditions—or perhaps even in psychic anticipation of reward? . . . the deliberate postponement of pleasures? In any event, it represents a way of coping with the diminution of the essential life-supporting functions afforded by water, oxygen, and heat—

at least one of which is usually absent in the cryptobiotic state, and all of which are normally viewed as essential for the biochemical and physiological integrity of living organisms.

The study of cryptobiotes has apparently not yet determined whether they experience a total cessation of metabolism or merely a deceleration of metabolic functions similar to hibernation. (In hibernation metabolism falls to about one-hundredth of the normal level; in cryptobiosis the metabolism is virtually undetectable—it is called anhydrobiosis because there is simply not enough water left to support any ordered chemistry.) Tardigrades, rotifers, and brine shrimp exemplify life not as a process but as a set of organisms retaining interlocked molecular structures with the potential to carry out metabolism in the presence of water.

We normally define death as a state of an organism in which metabolism has ceased. Perhaps further study of cryptobiosis will require us to redefine life in terms of the continuity of organized structural integrity. This terminology has been proposed to avoid the logical quandary of defining life in terms of metabolism. Then death would be defined not as the absence of metabolism but as the violation of structure.

Some organisms exhibit cryptobiosis in only the early stages of their growth, such as spores of bacteria and fungi, the seeds of the higher plants, the larvae of some insects, and the cystic eggs of a few crustaceans. Other organisms can enter the cryptobiotic state at almost any stage of their life history. It is estimated that a tardigrade has a normal life span of less than a year if it never enters the cryptobiotic state, whereas an individual that alternates the active state with the latent or hibernating-type of state might extend its life for as long as 60 years.

Though the cryptobiotic process becomes rarer as one ascends the evolutionary ladder, it is always accompanied by extension of life span and could conceivably be developed in more complex organisms. This presents a vista of the possibilities of new paradigms to bridge the gap between the organic and the inorganic—a glimpse of reciprocities between protoplasmic function and crystalline structure, between natural life and artificial or mechanical life.

Judging solely from man's own local experience on the planet Earth, intelligence as manifested in the universe appears to be a hostage to the highest form of organic life. Could the long periods of time required for space travel (in term of human life spans) be accommodated by applying cryptobiotic strategies to the extension of the life spans of *Homo sapiens*? Or, more abstractly, could such strategies modulate the continuity and transport through space of organized structural integrities? Or indeed even the survival of consciousness in nonmortal—or at least nonphysiological or artificial—crystallographic patterns?

Buckminster Fuller has proposed a metaphorical model of how human beings might enter into a form of space travel independent of the physiological body they happen to inhabit on earth:

> **As we get into cryogenics . . . the geometries become more regular and less asymmetric. . . . The asymmetries of kinetics progressively subside and approach, but do not quite attain, absolute cessation . . . at the equilibrium state.**
>
> **Employing a scanner of each of our atoms, this is one way humans could have been radio-transmitted and put aboard Earth from any place in Universe.**
>
> **Let us radiantly activate . . . modularly grouped local atoms of a human's physical organism. The human could [thus] be physically scanned . . . and programmed to move . . . through a high-frequency . . . light-matrix field.**
>
> **. . . We may understand how man, consisting of a vast yet always inherently orderly complex of *wave angles* and *line frequencies*, might be scanningly transmitted from *any here* to *any there* by radio. [*Synergetics*, 1975]**

I had long thought of that radiantly scanning model as a metaphor. But as is so often the case with Fuller I underestimated him. He meant it literally, like sending flowers by FTD, floral telegraphic delivery—not as a transfer of credit but as a telemetric reassembly of proteins and petals.

Cryogenics slows down atoms. Teleportation transports them. One of the doctrines of artificial intelligence (AI not science fiction) is the possibility in principle of teleportation of a person from here to there (Fuller says *any* here to *any* there) by transmitting a complete atom-for-atom description of the person's body and brain as a sort of radio template, using the description to construct a duplicate at the destination. The mind boggles. Does the procedure involve murder or autopsy or just another more complicated means of transportation?

Tardigrades seem to have solved the problem of restoring metabolism. Have the AIs? To transport a person you would have to restore not only metabolism but cerebration.

III

A NICHE FOR MAN

*N*O ONE EVER SAID IT WAS EASY TO BE *a mammal. But even artificial life will not relieve us of our mammaldom (or mammalhood!). Robots and people—automata and herds of social entities—could possibly be considered interchangeable. But no one is showing us robots with personhood: our identity, our sense of self seems inextricable from our animal nature.*

In this chapter we consider the human predicament of being the youngest of the vertebrates—risen apes rather than fallen angels. We consider the nature of individual self-consciousness and its biological abode, and why thinking appears to be a physiological phenomenon.

The genus of ants is contrasted with the genus of men, as the manifestation of pure instinct versus the human presence, where the operation of instinct is adulterated by intellect.

Is it possible to contemplate the long-range future of the biosphere, indeed the ultimate fate of the universe, without taking the effects of life and of human intelligence into the balance?

II
The zoological context
———————— ❦ ————————

*Does it make sense to posit that to know truth can arise
from dead matter?*
—*Max Delbruck,* Mind from Matter?, *1986*

THE BIOLOGICAL PREDICAMENT

A person thinking, the intellect working cold and aloof in
a dry light, is the highest-known biological function.* As
far as we know from our own experience, this kind of ra-
tiocination cannot yet manifest itself without some kind
of dependence on an organic host, a biological abode. Man's
faculty of reason is not just encapsulated in a mortal coil
of carbon imprisonment, it is peculiar to a single species.
Hence man's lodgment in the zoological hierarchy, his inescapable biological predicament, his very animality, has
served, if not as the recurring theme, at least as the source
of the limits of human action without which tragedy and
comedy are not possible . . . perhaps not even necessary.

Cerebration functions within biological constraints
that are the sources of both ecstasy and raw atrocity. If we
are to be succeeded by artificial robots, tin woodmen of our
own devising, would they—should they be—bound by the
same kind of limbic reflexes?

Many, perhaps most, life forms have individuality; only

———————

* *The ecstasy of orgasm aside, cerebration—thinking—is the highest recognizable physiological function, incomparably higher than pole vaulting, dueling, or
even landing on the moon.*

human life forms have self. Other mammals, friendly quadrupeds like dogs and horses, certainly have enough sense of self to distinguish themselves from their kennel and stable mates. But only humans are aware that they are aware, able to exercise that philosophical faculty called the doubling of consciousness. We know that we know. Cows may know, but we don't think they know they know. (This assertion is not susceptible of proof. We can't even say among humans that your awareness is like my awareness. We can only assert that it seems plausible, and get on with the matter.) The experiments of animal behaviorists have determined that only a few of our primate cousins—chimpanzees and orangutans alone—share with humans the ability to recognize themselves in mirrors, an experience on the verge of self-awareness. The youngest of human infants can smile; baby chimpanzees can only grimace.

The self or subject is the only point of departure for any kind of exploration—practical or philosophical, tangible and mundane or abstract and speculative. "Apart from self you cannot find a mind," as Fritjof Capra puts it. "When you speak of experience you mean and can only mean the experience of the self, for there is no other kind of experience. . . . Even in dreams it surveys the scene."

In our pursuit of human cognitive capabilities we may have to wait a long time for the computational neurobiologists to come up with anything useful. Meanwhile we can be artless. Max Delbruck himself characterized as naïve the question that appears as an epigraph above. But it was not his only naïve question; he had two others: "How can we construct a theory of a universe without life, and therefore without mind, and then expect [them] to evolve from this lifeless and mindless beginning?" And "How can we conceive of the evolution of organisms with mind as a strictly adaptive response to selective pressures for survival?"

We are creatures who once lived in caves. Did we really gain the capacity for speculations into cosmology and the profound insights of mathematics as a response to pressures for survival? . . . adaptive responses? . . . selective pressures?

THE ANCESTRY OF THE PRIMATES

We are vertebrates and, judging from what we see of non-vertebrates in pantry and zoo, we wouldn't want to be anything else. But we weren't always vertebrates. In the evolutionary tree shortly after organisms with bilateral symmetry broke away from the lines of molluscs and jellyfish, *We*—at least the upright ambulatory creatures we have become—evolved successively as coelemates, deuterostomes, and echinodermata (which survive today as marine organisms with tubed feet).

Theories of the ontogeny of vertebrates are still speculative, but there is general agreement that the fossil record suggests that about half a billion years ago the vertebrates arose from the neotenous larval stage of calcichordate tunicates. Tunicates are sessile (immobilized) animals lacking a brain, and they look like sponge bags attached to the seabed, but for various reasons the paleontologists confirm that these urchins, starfish, and sea cucumbers are the closest surviving relatives to the vertebrates—a distant home for our psyche.

Without a quick review of the time scale of evolution there can be no context for our biological predicament, so I offer a homemade but conscientious chronology of how the brain evolved:

Chronology from vertebrates to primates:

Age of the earth—4.5 billion years

Single-cell forms of life—3.6 billion years ago. (There is a calculated window of between 3.9 and 3.6 billion years ago for the appearance of the first prokaryotic cells.)

The first vertebrates were fishes—475 million years (myr) ago, followed by

Amphibians—350 myr ago

Reptiles—275 myr ago

Mammals—180 myr ago

Primates—40 myr ago. (Hominoids: apelike creatures with large brains, motor dexterity and superb vision. The fossil record shows a wide geographical distribution.)

Hominids—9 myr ago. (Hominids split off from hominoids and came down from the trees to become land-based bipedalists.)

[Here follows an inexplicable 5 myr of fossil blackout. It began with creatures moving on all fours, and it ended with our primate ancestors walking upright on two feet—their hands and arms free.]

Australopithecines—3.8 to 2.8 myr ago

Homo habilis—2.4 to 2.0 myr ago (increase in brain size commences).

Neandertal man—100,000 years ago. (Neandertals had not only fire and tools, but clothing and shelter of animal skins. They are a parallel line that died out: They might have become us but did not.)

Modern man (*Homo sapiens sapiens*)—40–30,000 years ago. (At this stage the species achieved—or committed—cultural evolution. A burst of symbol and ceremony, art and music ensued, followed by the rise of leaders and people of status.)

One foggy winter day in the early 1950s I was driving along the Autobahn in the industrial Ruhr Valley of northern Germany when I saw an exit sign marked "Neanderthal." I knew that *thal* was German for valley, and I saw we were crossing a little stream called the Neander, and when I got home, I looked it up in the encyclopedia to confirm that this was indeed the site where the Neandertal skeleton—the first relic of our extinct antecedents—had been found in 1856. *Homo sapiens neanderthalensis* (the latinized scientific name retains the German spelling) sounded so synthetic, so made up, a scholarly description. It was equally unnerving to discover that Cro-Magnon is not a synthetic anthropological modifier; it is likewise the name of a place, a community in the Dordogne, in southwestern France near Bordeaux. Neanderthal and Cro-Magnon are not technical terms: they are simply the names of small settlements like Podunk or Poughkeepsie.

In Darwin's time the evidence that man's ancestors were not men was virtually nonexistent. The Neandertal skull was found in 1856 but its true significance was appreciated only much later.

Few members of the 20th-century world are so jaded that they don't have some curiosity about their origins, like orphans searching for biological parents. We have learned only in this century that the earliest members of the hominid family persisted virtually unchanged for millions of years. As long as five millions years ago our primate ancestors used fires to keep warm, cook food, and prolong the working day.

The first members of our species with brain size nearly equal to ours appeared quite suddenly between 100,000 to 70,000 years ago. They were the ones found in that German valley. Modern humans of our own subspecies appeared in Europe only about 40,000 years ago. *Homo sapiens* are a phenomenon of the Pleistocene (interglacial) Epoch of the Cenozoic Era.

Since the formation of the earth's crust, the vast range of geologic time was Precambrian; it was followed by the Phanerozoic, which means "evident life." The Phanerozoic is broken down into three eras: Paleozoic (ancient life), Mesozoic (middle life), and Cenozoic (modern life). The Cenozoic in turn is broken down into seven successive epochs: Paleocene, Eocene, Oligocene, Miocene, Pliocene, Pleistocene (interglacial), and Holocene (recent).

Chronology of modern man. A chronology for language has not been established. Estimates range from 200,000 to 50,000 years ago, with the likelihood that the comprehensive linguistic capability seen in humans emerged about 100,000 years ago, just before the advent of *Homo sapiens sapiens.*

The human brain achieved its present size and complexity —about 125,000 yrs ago

Ceremonial burial of the dead—80,000 yrs ago

Formed household or family units—about 35,000 yrs ago

Primitive agriculture—18,000 yrs ago (end of the last ice age)

Social organization and armed warfare—12,000 yrs ago

Domestication of goats and barley—9,000 yrs ago

Civilization: word-signs introduced by Sumerians—6,000 yrs ago

Founding of cities—5,000 yrs ago

Phonetic alphabet replaces ideograms—3,500 yrs ago

Culture of industrial technology—200 yrs ago

Contrast this 40 millennia of human development with the time scale of dinosaurs: They ruled the earth for 165 million years, having a whole geological chapter to themselves—the Cretaceous Period of the Mesozoic Era. Theodosius Dobzhansky describes the novelty of the event: "As soon as the hominids had achieved upright posture, bipedal gait, the use of hands for manipulating, for carrying, and for manufacturing generalized tools, and language, they had become men. The human revolution was over."

There is a hypothesis that competition of humans vs. humans (rather than technological challenges) is the key to the rapidity of human evolution, the chief threats to humans being other members of their own species. Humans alone play competitively group against group.

Man in the Holocene. If you want to know how it feels to live in a geologic epoch, just bear in mind that we are creatures of the Holocene, covering the last 10,000 years of earth's history since the close of the most recent ice age. (Less time has elapsed since the last ice age than intervened between the three preceding ones.) Following the interglacial Pleistocene Epoch, the Holocene is presumably the final epoch in the Cenozoic Era. Our subspecies were hunter-gatherers in the prehistoric times of the late ice ages. History itself is relatively recent, a phenomenon of the Holocene.

To the biologist Stephen Jay Gould man is a product of historical contingency.

No law of nature decrees any particular evolutionary pathway. Humans are here because *Pikaia* (the first chordate) survived the first winnowing of the earth's first modern multicellular fauna, because one odd group of early fishes had forelimbs that could be modified to support a body under terrestrial gravity, because dinosaurs died and mammals prevailed, because ice ages never froze the entire globe, because a tiny lineage of ground-dwelling African apes did not meet the fate of most species and has managed to prevail for an uncertain geological moment.

A LITTLE HOMEWORK ON NICHES

The niche concept in ecology arose first as a rather vague metaphor for the natural community in which an organism lives and the range of resources it requires in order to survive or prevail or even flourish. Originally the concept implied the notion that interspecific competition would prevent species with similar niches from living together. But this came to be recognized as an oversimplification, in part because it fails to describe the reciprocity of niches by which organisms structure environments quite as much as environments permit organisms to live in them—not to mention the indulgence of different species for each other.

Ecological interactions are not simple chains of cause and effect; the variety of concurrent factors and conditions produces patterns too complex for easy measurement. This has so far prevented ecology from becoming a predictive science, but the introduction of sophisticated computer models gives high promise of providing new tools for complex analysis.

A niche is not an address or a place, but a dynamic role; it can be described, but not exhaustively defined. *Niche*: The range of each environmental variable, such as temperature, humidity, and food items—not to mention parasites and enemies—within which a species can exist and reproduce. A niche is abstract, in contrast to a habitat, which is a defined geographical area. The preferred niche is the one in which the species performs best, and the realized niche is the one in which it actually comes to live in a particular environment. Thus a niche is not just a biotic address, it is more of an occupation, the status of an animal in its community.

Biologists have dignified the niche with a number of theoretical concepts, such as the Principle of Competitive Exclusion (Volterra-Gause Principle, 1920), which asserts that when two species compete, one wins out, and the other is reduced to zero. Species defying the principle are called sympatric or symbionts.

The comfort of niches. The Germans have the expression *umwelt*, loosely translated as "the world around me." It suggests the total sensory input of an animal, with each species, including man, having its own distinctive umwelt. Symbionts, parasites, and commensals design their own reciprocal niches. Some niches are periodic, recurring for only a few minutes a day. The complex ecosystems of coral reefs teem with plant and animal life 24 hours a day. Species active during the day and during the night meet, dramatically, at dusk and dawn.

Niche is also used abstractly to describe the role or position of an individual in his community or in his work

or profession. There is a general rule that the more complex
the entity, the more vulnerable the niche.

Niche is widely used as an architectural term to describe a recess carved in a wall, often for the display of some
vase or object of art. Temples and cathedrals abound with
semicircular niches for urns, relics, and statues of dead
saints. (The stairways on many old narrow Baltimore row
houses were furnished with niches at the turn of steps at
the top landing, specifically to facilitate the carrying up of
a coffin—empty—to the second floor and the return of the
coffin—occupied—to the ground floor). The French word
for a dog kennel is *niche*, and to find something that has
been long displaced is to *denicher*. And publishers signing
on a new writer hope that he will find a niche in the market.

A niche for man. There are myriads of species that do
not live socially. But once human beings started to live in
groups, first family groups and then communities and tribes,
the trend was irreversible. Individuals might have been able
to compete with other individuals but not with other
groups. After the first groups established themselves, the
possibility of living nonsocially virtually disappeared.

Once man became a social animal, culture began to
affect genetic evolution as genes affected cultural evolution,
but the latter process was much more rapid, and culture
came to usurp nature as the moving force in our development. For modern man the principal habitat of the human
mind is the very culture it creates. But biospherically speaking, a cultural niche may be a very temporary affair. Nature
has not ordained civilization; quite the contrary. Humans
survive today only as members of an interacting network
of mutually dependent animal and vegetable organisms.

Man as homeotherm. Fungi and bacteria can survive
at greater extremes of temperature than other organisms.
Animals are more limited in their ability to resist extremes
of temperature. Some degenerate insects inhabit Antarctica.
Only man—among all animals—has survived the coldest

and hottest climates. This is because of two factors: (1) He is homeothermous, i.e., possessing a regulatory mechanism that maintains a constant internal temperature. Only mammals and birds are homeotherms. All other animals are poikilothermous (poikilo = variable). (2) Man carries his artificial environment with him.

The chief constraint on niches is their tendency to instability. This is illustrated by the ecologists' concept of "carrying capacity": the maximum load an environment can support permanently without reducing its ability to support future generations. One of the reasons human beings are especially likely to transgress an environment's sustainable carrying capacity is that our cultural propensities drive our desires vastly in excess of our mere physiological appetites.

The culture of human societies has introduced new constraints, indeed threats, to the environment. And politicians are compelled by the opportunistic nature of their calling to remain deaf to suggestions that growth of human activities and elevation of consumption cannot be perpetual.

A TAXONOMY FOR MAN

Children play a game of addressing a letter to a friend at apartment number so-and-so at address number such-and-such at This street in the borough of That in the city of Name in the county of Place in the State of the union of the country of the United States of America in the Western Hemisphere on the Planet Earth in the Solar System in the Milky Way Galaxy somewhere in the whole known Universe. The search for a cosmic zip code expresses an inherent impulse in all of us to establish a recognized sense of place and identity. The childrens' addresses are a response to the mystery and curiosity of geographic orientation. The attempt to establish a chronology for man—and a taxonomy for his genus—is a similar response to the mystery of time and where we belong on a geologic scale in the evolution of life.

For some such reasons I sought in vain for an exhaustive taxonomy for the human species. Failing that, I made one up as a synthesis from various textbook and reference sources in an exhaustive attempt to find every conceivable level of taxon. This is a device totally without benefit of any academic sanction. The exercise may have no more bearing to reality and may be no more useful in helping you to find your way home than the child's letter addressed from the Galaxy to his neighborhood. Such taxonomies are seldom featured in the textbooks now, possibly because they are relics from the time when biology was primarily a descriptive discipline, before the impact of molecular biology. The catalogue of classifications is totally abstract, derived by convention, and the few biologists who condone it seem to do so with reservations and solely on the grounds of some otherwise unspecified "convenience." It may tell less about man than it does about how man likes to classify.

Superkingdom: Eukaryota (nucleate cell organization)

Kingdom: Animalia or Metazoa (multicellular organisms developed from an egg with complex cells and tissues)

Subkingdom: Eumetazoa (tissues and organ systems)

Branch: Bilateralia (animals with bilateral symmetry)

Grade: Coelemata (with body cavity)

Series: Deurostoma, or

Subgrade: Enterocoela (embryological development of mouth far from gut)

Superphylum: Chordata (includes small marine invertebrates)

Phylum*: CHORDATA (single dorsal nerve with closed blood system)

Subphylum: VERTEBRATA or CRANIATA (jointed spine with brain case)

Superclass: TETRAPODA (land vertebrates—all vertebrates higher than fish; four limbs)

Class*: MAMMALIA (nourish young with milk)

Subclass: THERIA (bear young alive)

Infraclass: EUTHERIA (placental)

Cohort or Suborder: UNGUICULATA (nails and claws)

Order*: PRIMATES (monkeys, apes, and men)

Suborder: ANTHROPOIDEA (quadrupeds and bipeds)

Superfamily: HOMINOIDEA (apes, ape-men, and men)

Family*: HOMINIDAE (ape-men and men)

Subfamily: HOMININAE (men)

[Tribe: HOMINI (none described for this group)]

Genus*: HOMO (men)

Species: HOMO ERECTUS (ancient)

Species: HOMO SAPIENS (ancient and modern)

Subspecies: HOMO SAPIENS SAPIENS (all living human beings)

[Race: (avoided in taxonomic practice**)]

The first seven taxa—those above phylum—are after R. H. Whitaker and L. Margulis, 1978, as shown by Luria,

---

* *Obligate taxa in most of the literature.*
* * *The practice is a philosophical and ethical imperative, but it does not make life any easier for census takers, demographers, and market researchers.*

Gould, and Singer, 1981. Other taxa are a composite from various sources and certainly not all agreed to by all authorities.

The sequence of initial terms on the left represent abstract categorical classes. The sequence of secondary terms in small capitals represent *taxa* or *taxons* designating a set of actual organisms that may be living or extinct or some of each.

Julian Huxley proposed raising man to the rank of a separate kingdom, for which he proposed the name *Psychozoa* as a recognition of the unique capacities of man's central nervous system. (Ernst Mayr described Huxley as a nontaxonomist, perhaps for resorting to Greek roots.)

William R. Catton, Jr., a sociologist at the Washington State University, has proposed *Homo colossus* as a new ecosocial taxon for man in recognition of the fact that human society imposes a cultural superstructure as an instrument of direction and control upon the biotic substructure.

Kirtley F. Mather suggests (Mather, 1986) that it was presumptuous of Linnaeus to classify us in 1735 as *Homo sapiens* when *Homo faber*, man the maker, would have been a more appropriate "diagnostic characteristic" to distinguish human beings from other creatures.

Speaking of diagnostic characteristics—as if there were something mildly pathological about being wise or making things—would it be too late to consider another name for human beings? Adhering to the obligatory Latin, I would propose *Homo rogans*, for the only phenomenon in the known universe with the capacity to question itself—a pathological tendency that may or may not be transferrable to the eventual artificial life of computers.

NATURE'S INVESTMENT IN ORGANISMS

Life as borrowing. Human beings cannot synthesize eight of the essential amino acids that occur in the proteins in our cells. In order to live, we must consume proteins that contain these amino acids. Some of the molecules and all of the atoms of our makeup are borrowed for the briefness of a lifetime. It is a debt that we resist paying back with every ounce of energy that supports our conscious will.

In a book that is otherwise ungenerous in spirit, Jeremy Rifkin, an activist on issues of the social effects of biological research, has written:

> **We live by the grace of sacrifice. Every amplification of our being owes its existence to some diminution somewhere else. In an ultimate sense, nothing we claim as ours belongs to us, not even our fiber and sinew. Everything about us has been borrowed. We have been lent by nature. It has given over to us parts of itself, thus precluding their use for an infinite number of other things.**

Our daily life borrows also from ancient bacteria. Listen to the evocative phrases of Lewis Thomas.

> **We are shared, rented, and occupied. At the interior of our cells, driving them, providing the oxidative energy that sends us out for the improvement of each shining day, are the mitochondria, and in a strict sense they are not ours. They turn out to be little separate creatures, the colonial posterity of migrant procaryocytes, probably primitive bacteria that swam into ancestral precursors of our eukaryotic cells and stayed there. . . . They are as much symbionts as the rhizobial bacteria in the roots of beans. Without them, we would not move a muscle, drum a finger, think a thought.**

Life as robbery. Borrowings are paid back; robberies are irreversible. Here is Alfred North Whitehead (*Process and Reality*, 1929) on the subject:

> **. . . in a museum the crystals are kept under glass cases; in zoological gardens the animals are fed. Having regard to the universality of reactions with environment, the distinction is not quite absolute. It cannot, however, be ignored. The**

crystals are not agencies requiring the destruction of elaborate societies derived from the environment; a living society is such an agency. The societies which it destroys are its food. This food is destroyed by dissolving it into somewhat simpler social elements. It has been robbed of something. Thus, all societies require interplay with their environment; and in the case of living societies this interplay takes the form of robbery. The living society may, or may not, be a higher type of organism than the food which it disintegrates. But whether or no it be for the general good, life is robbery.

12
The biology of consciousness

―――――――――― ∾ ――――――――――

ENTRE NOUS

Nous is a fine old Greek word for *mind*, and, inexplicably, it is also a word for "common sense" in Anglo-Saxon vernacular. The British archaeologist Jacquetta Hawkes described one of her colleagues as someone who ". . . may be full of erudite theories but is liable to go astray from lack of ordinary sense and common nous." The word embraces the abstract and the down to earth.

Webster 3 defines the word as "Nous: an intelligent purposive principle controlling and ordering the world of matter." There cannot be many words linking intelligence on the one hand and the world of matter on the other. I liked the word *nous* so much that I thought of using it somewhere in the title of this book. But common sense is supposed to keep one from going astray, and I decided that people using words like that might end up talking only to themselves.

In Platonism, nous means the capacity for the highest intuitive and immediate insight. In Aristotelianism, nous means "mind, intellect, thought, purpose . . . to think, to see, to perceive with the mind, to understand, to consider, to apprehend, to recognize" . . . and even to connect. Nous is from the beginning intellective or cognitive, "expressive of seeing as knowing."

The Institute of Noetic Sciences (a research organization in Sausalito, California, founded by former astronaut Edgar D. Mitchell) has adopted an adjectival form of the word to describe their focus on "sciences related to consciousness." Which is what we are talking about here: the relationship—if any—of the biological sciences to consciousness.

Whether Greek or vernacular, nous = order in matter. In describing life so far, we often find that common speech hits closer home than scientific abstractions; *nous* has roots in both camps.

THE ABODE OF CONSCIOUSNESS

States of consciousness mutually exclude each other: A salmon spawning does not eat. A salmon eating does not spawn. A behaviorist in psychology does not speak about consciousness at all. He has no consciousness.
—Karl H. Pribram, 1985

Science is trying very hard, in its own way, to find an abode of consciousness ... nothing mystical, nothing occult, nothing even mental; something that can be explained by the physical activity of brain cells. Molecular biology has provided a basis for the mechanical description of much of the structure and functions of living organisms. But so far, the problem of consciousness—how the range of our mental processes can arise from purely physical operations in the brain—defies experimental, physico-chemical analysis.

All we can say as a minimum description of consciousness is that it is caused by specific but largely unknown neurobiological processes in human and some animal brains. And that description is chiefly intuitive, affording little to count or measure. The insight of evolutionary biology adds only further confusion: At one time no organisms were conscious and now some are. What happened?

By and large the neurobiologists in the vanguard of this

quest are "physicalists" who are not interested in the brain as a host to the mind unless and until all our supposed mental functions can be explained by the way the brain works. Most of the progress published in the teeming scientific journals has been made by the neurophysicists, the neural networkers, and the neural network modelers—a convenient marriage of neuroscience and computer science. If they succeed, they will reveal for us a brain that understands the brain in strictly reductionist, purely mechanical terms.

What these neuroscientists in collaboration with computer scientists regard as their conceptual breakthrough is the creation of neural networks, computer models with some of the attributes of human cerebration. It is a radically different kind of computer that can learn, that can deal with approximations and that can tolerate faults. (Some fuzziness has to be built in.) Their goal is nothing less than a new neurobiological theory to explain the physical basis of our mental lives.

Although consciousness is under widespread and continuing investigation, partly under the guise of studies in perception and cognition, there are deep conceptual conflicts among philosophers and scientists about the very nature of the beast. There is no agreement about the set of conditions for conscious functioning in general. Its definition is as elusive as that of life itself. Metaphysical concern is not a biological property.

Some philosophers tell us that the very idea of consciousness—like that of self—is merely an artifact of metaphysics, which itself is the least respectable branch of philosophy in our culture.

Physicists and metaphysicists agree that there is a reality, though they disagree about the extent to which it is knowable. Harry J. Jerison, a professor of psychiatry at UCLA, says that "the organization of events in time, which appears so natural and elementary to us, is not a simple phenomenon from a neural point of view." As we ordinarily experience it, reality is not so much a phenomenon of the outside physical world as it is a construct of the brain. In an early 19th-century essay on metaphysics, Sir William Hamilton wrote: "Consciousness cannot be defined; we may be ourselves fully aware of what consciousness is, but we cannot without confusion convey to others a definition of what we ourselves clearly apprehend. The reason is plain: consciousness lies at the root of all knowledge."

The reason was clear to Sir William perhaps, but not to me. I am interested in the kind of individual consciousness that finds its host in every human being. And what I seek is what to the philosopher and scientist is the most naïve question that can be asked. Where does consciousness reside? What is its abode? Its answer is the chief reason that the difference between life and death matters. The answer is that what preoccupies us has to be more than just an artifact of metaphysics. Once again we turn to Lewis Thomas:

> You start out as a single cell derived from the coupling of a sperm and an egg, this divides into two, then four, then eight, and so on, and at a certain stage there emerges a single cell which will have as all its progeny the human brain. The mere existence of that cell should be one of the great astonishments of the earth.
>
> One cell is switched on to become the whole trillion-cell, massive apparatus for thinking and imagining. . . . All the information needed for learning to read and write, playing the piano . . . walking across a street through traffic or the marvelous human act of putting out one hand and leaning against a tree, is contained in that first cell. All of grammar, all syntax, all arithmetic, all music.
>
> All of this information and much more is contained in every cell in the [embryo] cluster. When the stem cell for the brain emerges, it could be that the special quality of brainness is simply switched on.

The history of the universe is marked by eons for the creation of matter in space—particles, dust, planets, and galaxies, the stuff of physics and astronomy. Billions of years later self-replicating macromolecules arranged themselves as organisms in a process still only dimly understood by the disciplines of biology. Only after all of this has consciousness emerged in man "as perhaps the most remarkable of nature's products." As Colin McGinn goes on to say, however, consciousness has no discipline of its own. "Psychology sounds like a good name for such a science," but psychology "has been notably unconcerned with consciousness—its laws, functions, origins." Certainly the successes of psychology have not come from the undue preoccupation with consciousness. There is now a new discipline in the field, neurophilosophy, but its concern with consciousness is only tangential. Philosophy is the synoptic discipline with a mandate to synthesize the biological and physical sciences into a coherent account of reality. Neurophilosophers are dedicated to this cause; they tend to be philosophers who have tried to master biology rather than the other way round.

BRAIN & MIND

Living brains are actually observed in vastly greater detail by their owners than by anyone else, brain surgeons included.
  —M. J. Donald, Quantum Theory and the Brain, *1990*

In the paper cited above, Professor Donald introduces his topic with the observation that "a functioning human brain is a lump of warm wet matter of inordinate complexity . . . it carries very complex patterns of information." To say that it is warm and wet is to say that it is not thermally isolated nor is it in thermal equilibrium: In other words, unlike a computer, it is physiologically dependent on the body.

  It seems a safe generalization to say that the only thing in the universe more complicated than the brain is the universe itself. The human brain is also the only thing we know in the universe that makes an effort to understand itself. It is still too early—in the 1990s—to say if we are smart enough to figure out how it works.

A cardiac physiologist can get directly to an understanding of the heart, blood vessels, and circulatory functions—the heart of the matter—without distractions of supposed amatory impulses and affectionate sensibilities associated with that organ in our daily life and culture, especially as authenticated in literature and song. (Democritus called the heart "the queen, the nurse of anger," and the liver "the center of desire.")

The neuroscientists do not have this luxury of avoiding the intangibles—the mind-body problem, the perpetual agony of epistemology—without devising some kind of escape route, usually by means of an intense specialization of observation. There is no place for consciousness in a reductionist world. (The reductionists have no way of coping with anything that doesn't *reduce* to matter in motion.) Nevertheless, many scientists in varying degrees are in accord with our commonsense view that the brain is the organ of the mind, the seat of personality, the abode of consciousness, and the home of identity.

The human brain is the great terra incognita of our age. It is to the late 20th century what China was to the 13th century, and what America was to the 16th century.

Neurogenesis. Jean-Pierre Changeux writes that "Of all the organs of the body, the nervous system is unusual in that its total number of cells is fixed at birth. Any neurons that are destroyed are never replaced."

Neurons are nerve cells, the gray matter. (Glia are the connecting tissues.) During gestation the brain of a human fetus generates neurons at an average estimated rate of 250,000 per minute. It is an unconfirmed dogma that neurogenesis—the proliferation of new neurons—is a process that comes to an end just a few months after birth. But for the first 21 months the brain continues to grow at the very rapid fetal birth rate (cerebral tissue grows as synapses proliferate). Our brains lose nerve cells at the rate of 10,000 a day after puberty, and we have no way of replacing them. But since we have billions, we are told not to worry.

The failure of neurons to proliferate may be the secret of their immunity to cancer. Brain tumors invariably are restricted to the glia and supportive tissues. Glial cells are more abundant than neurons, but they do not transmit information by electrical impulses.

In human development during infancy the organs of sense have to become tuned to external stimuli in order to develop their mature capacities. The ear has to hear sounds to develop the right nerve connections. The eye must respond to light in order to develop the neural pathways from eye to brain. The brain is the only organ that develops by experiencing itself: by thinking. There is general agreement that whatever *mind* is, it is the brain experiencing itself.

A paper published by the National Science Foundation (Winter 1989) says that "the brain has just two jobs: to run the body and to create the mind." It runs the body by subconscious somatic regulation. But to say it *creates* the mind is hardly the word for it; it may create or become or produce or make a home for the mind, but no one verb seems able to capture all the overlapping ambiguities of the relationship.

What the brain actually senses is energy in the form of vibrations of different frequencies. Low frequencies for hearing and touch; higher frequencies for warmth; and higher still for vision. These radiations trigger neural codes which are somehow converted by the brain into a model of the external world. Thus subjective mental experience arises with no sure confirmation of an objective external world to match it. All can agree that the mind and the brain are connected, but none can yet bridge the chasm between the manner in which neurons become excited on the one hand, and the way thinking and self-awareness result on the other.

Evolutionary context of the brain. Unlike most creatures of evolution there was no gradualism in the emergence of the human brain. On the scale of geological time, its emergence is a very rapid and very recent phenomenon. The hominid brain just about tripled in size in the last three million years. The brain can be seen both as a prisoner of its evolution and as a quantum-jump vessel of intellect engaged in a runaway trajectory as if to escape from evolution itself.

The kinetics of the brain's representations of the world recapitulate its history. It has been calculated that the growth of the central nervous system of the human embryo—from the time of the appearance of the primitive streak (about 14 days)—retraces more than a century of its ancestors' evolution for every second of its early rapid growth. The brain's pictures (its mechanisms for recording sensations) encompass time scales of neural transactions ranging from tenths of a second of observation to the hundreds of millions of years it took to develop the patterns of reception.

Brain & mind. Although philosophies of the mind are old, the science of the brain is young. Scientifically, philosophically and psychologically, the question about the nature of mind and its relation to the brain remains unresolved. There is not even any agreement on how the question should be best addressed. No one has the faintest idea what is necessary for there to be a thought. No one has been able to put down a meaningful relationship between physical phenomena and what it is to compose a thought.

We know that the brain evolved; we do not know whether the mind has evolved.

Mind. The brain records; the mind connects. "There is no virgin forest, no clump of seaweed, no maze, no cellular labyrinth that is richer in connections than the domain of the mind." (Paul Valery)

The mind may be regarded as an emergent property of

brain circuits. (There is no rudiment of psyche in a crystal or in a molecule.)

Julian Huxley overleaps all the constraints of philosophy and science in a sweeping dismissal of the brain-mind duality altogether. "I believe in the unity of mind and matter," he tells us. "To my belief there are just two aspects of one reality, two abstractions made by us from the concrete ground of experience. They cannot be separated and it is false philosophy to think them apart." For him, the mind-body problem arises not from experience but from us and our predilections for undue categorization.

"Mind is like no other property of physical systems," writes the physicist Erich Harth. "It is not just that we don't know the mechanisms that give rise to it. We have difficulty seeing how *any* mechanism can give rise to it."

(By the way, the Germans have a completely different vocabulary for discussing the world of the mind. They are said to have no word for subtle, and apparently they have no word for mind. The Germans have *Seele* for soul, *Geist* for spirit, *Verstand* for intellect, *Vernunft* for reason, *Gemut* for disposition, *Gedachtnis* for memory, *Meinung* for opinion, and *Absicht* for intent . . . but they have no word that has all the shades of the meaning of mind.)

NEUROSCIENCE

The human brain is the most highly organized assembly of matter that has ever existed on earth—perhaps in the cosmos. The DNA molecule, that masterpiece of the evolution of matter, contains in its simplest form about ten billion atoms, but the mind of man is many times more complex, more detailed, more intricately wrought. Its birth initiated a vastly expedited phase of the evolution of form.
—*Louise B. Young,* The Unfinished Universe, *1986*

Neurobiology. Neurobiology at its simplest is the study of the central nervous system and how it is organized to process information and to help glands regulate our bodily functions. Nervous systems, first developed to permit animals to cope with their environment—including especially coping with other animals—have given rise in human beings to a virtuoso range of mental capacities. The goal of neuroscience is the revelation of the linkages between primitive sensory inputs and the higher levels of comprehension displayed by humans. In addition to perception (the processing of information), the brain somehow engenders a gamut of more abstruse mental functions such as self-awareness, memory, intuition, intentionality, and even possible altruistic and ethical characteristics—all capacities observed in our introvert and social experience but quite beyond the technical, even *conceptual*, competence of neuroscientists to measure and explain.

As recently as 1978 a neurophysiologist, David Hubel, wrote that "our knowledge of the brain is in a very primitive state . . . the same state of knowledge as we were with regard to the heart before we realized that it pumped blood." We have been able to do little more than study the neuron as the fundamental unit of brain functioning. John Searle in one of his Reith lectures put the matter plainly:

All of the enormous variety of inputs that the brain receives—the photons that strike the retina, the sound waves that stimulate the eardrum, the pressure on the skin that activates nerve endings for pressure, heat, cold, and pain, etc.—all of these inputs are converted into one common medium: variable rates of neuron firing. . . . The smell of a rose, the experience of the blue sky, the taste of onions, the thought of a mathematical formula: all of these are produced by variable rates of neuron-firing . . .

Nervous systems are the most complex biological structures known, and the study of the brain is biology's greatest challenge. New conceptual schemes and new tactical approaches from the computational to the endocrinological (no category of inquiry is sacrosanct) loom on the horizon with the likelihood that advances in our understanding of the nature of mind will inevitably affect the organization and structure of all the other long-established disciplines of physical science . . . perhaps even the (somehow less influential) social sciences as well.

Neurobiology is subsumed generically as neuroscience. It is a pursuit—now involving scores of subdisciplines* ranging from behaviorists to molecular biologists—that confronts the ultimate biological frontier, addressing, in the judgment of Freeman Judson, "if not the deepest, certainly the most complex problems that can be posed in science today."

The field is teeming with radical strategies for research. For Candace Pert the junction between nerve cells is a liaison between the new pharmacology and Freudian theory. Dr. Richard Bergland, a neurosurgeon, proposes that the most suitable research model of the brain is as a gland controlled by hormones. He suggests that unraveling the hormone signals between body and brain will offer the best understanding of the mysteries of behavior.

Molecular biologists and chemists study neurons as a system of interacting macromolecules. Neurobiologists and embryologists regard the neuron as a basic system from which the brain is constructed. The protean Dr. Lynn Margulis argues that neither of these approaches gives sufficient regard to the evolutionary history of the brain's development. To reduce the study of the nervous system to physics and chemistry, she says, is to overlook the microbiological evolution of the brain's axons and dendrites which, she claims, may be descended from bacteria—whiplashing spirochetes! She argues for nothing less than a comparison of human consciousness with spirochete ecology. Margulis has confronted neuroscience with a controversial new paradigm: could our brains be merely relics of archaean bacterial broth?

---

* For a description of some of the subdisciplines see Appendix: List of Disciplines, Neuroscience.

THE THREE-PART BRAIN MODEL

It has long been a staple of popular journalism that wars are inevitable due to man's innate combativeness and his inherently aggressive nature, inbred for survival in a competitive social environment. Nature red in tooth and claw. The beast in man prevails. The sanction of violence for selfish motives is a paranoid creed, uncomforting, and though it is being discredited by an increasing number of theoretical biologists, it remains at the heart of the three-part brain theory.

Some biologists assert that throughout evolutionary development the need for a function has preceded the appearance of the organ through which it is to be exercised. They say that organs develop in response to a need, and the brain is no exception.

In 1949 the neuroanatomist Paul D. MacLean first introduced the theory of the three-layer brain, in which the successive layers record its evolutionary development much like the compacted strata of an archaeological site. MacLean postulated that the brain expanded in a hierarchical fashion along the lines of three basic successive but overlapping patterns, with differing chemistry and structure, and eons apart in their separate slow development.

In his system MacLean recapitulates what he calls the *paleopsychic processes*. The oldest part—the "reptile brain"—survives and still exercises its original primitive functions from its central location at the head of the brain stem. The second brain, for which he introduced the term "limbic," consists of the central neural network of the emotions. The third is the highly convoluted outer layer, the cerebral cortex that makes *Homo sapiens* sapient.

1. *The reptilian brain*. Originated 250–280 million years (myr) ago. Its large ganglia embrace the olfactory system. It is presumed to coordinate a rich spectrum of behaviors including territoriality, ritual encounters, greeting, courtship, formation of social hierarchies, migration, and hoarding. The reptilian brain is responsible for irresistible

drives, impulses, and compulsive behavior: hunting, mating, and fighting. It appears to lack any clear learning capacity.

2. *The limbic, or paleomammalian brain.* Originated 165 myr ago. It deals with the emotions. It includes the amygdala and the hippocampus. The survival of the limbic brain in modern human beings suggests that there must be a large element of genetic programming in what is called "human nature." It harbors a reservoir of ancient emotional responses beyond the niceties of logic and reason.

3. *The neomammalian brain.* Originated perhaps 50 myr ago. We think it has the capacity to learn.

Apparently our mental evolution parallels our physical evolution in that, when new traits emerge, the earlier characteristics they replace are modified but not entirely lost. The biologist W. H. Thorpe says "We all exhibit in our behavior types of action and reaction which we share not merely with our primitive primate ancestors, but with the dog, the protozoan, and the plant." Even the most mature human personality is not innocent of atavistic reflexes and irrational impulses. For Arthur Koestler the triune brain meant that when a patient lies down on the psychiatrist's couch there are three creatures there: an alligator, a horse, and a man or woman.

The essence of the MacLean model is that while the cerebral function is highly developed and has achieved a mammal with intellect, the cerebral cortex has augmented but not entirely replaced the earlier brain mechanisms: the reptilian brain, the limbic brain, and the cerebral brain all function concurrently as hostages to each other.

It may be comforting to speculate that the cerebellum will in the course of evolution—right here and now in the Holocene Period (as the geological present is termed)—not only dominate but eventually supersede the more primitive functions, but most biologists would probably tell you that there is little other than conceit and knocking on wood to support this philanthropic view.

The human brain was formed by superimposing new

structures on old ones. The primitive and more recent evolutionary elements of the brain have not been completely integrated. The old rhinencephalon remains in charge of emotional and visceral activities. The recent neocortex controls intellectual and cognitive activity. As Francois Jacob recognizes, aggressive behavior in the modern world is a handicap.

> The old structure which, in lower mammals, was in total command, has been relegated to the department of emotions. In man, it constitutes what MacLean calls "the visceral brain." Perhaps because development is so prolonged and maturity so delayed in man, these centers maintain strong connections with lower autonomic centers and continue to coordinate such fundamental drives as obtaining food, hunting for a sexual partner, or reacting to an enemy. . . . It is somewhat like adding a jet engine to an old cart horse.

While MacLean's triune brain remains a theory—a foray into paleopsychology—it is a provocative one, stimulating the imagination of his fellow researchers in brain evolution.

13
Self

―――――――― ✲ ――――――――

SELF & EXPERIENCE

La plus grande chose du monde, c'est de savoir être à soi.
    The greatest thing in the world is to know how to belong to oneself.
                                    —Montaigne, Essays, Book II

There is no aspect of human experience more elusive than the concept of self. Though the existence of a self is inconceivable without a biological vessel for its containment, the concept of self and selfness is only marginally a topic of biology. The self is a prisoner of its organic setting. No food has taste until mixed with saliva.

In its simplest form consciousness deals with the capacity of the organism to respond to stimuli. Sensations of pain, hunger, and thirst condition behavior into patterns of search or avoidance. In social animals like ourselves, consciousness involves a whole new level of complexity: awareness of self, including the distinction between self and others.

Biologically, the self is a product of development—certainly an unpredicted and probably an unpredictable product of long evolutionary history. The development of individuality is the evolutionary outcome of an ancient transition between the cell as a unit of selection and the individual as the unit of selection.

Sir John Eccles identifies the origin of the self-awareness of the human person with ceremonial burial as practiced by Neandertal Man. (Primitive man strayed from the rest of the animal kingdom when he became the first—and still only—animal to bury its own kind.) Professor Julian Jaynes of Princeton has argued that not only does no sense of self exist in other primates but that it evolved in humans as recently as 3,000 years ago. Anthropologists tell us that we sense our belonging first to our species, second to our gender, and last to our race. But that we would give up these attributes, if we were forced to, in reverse order.

Reductionists are leery of admitting into the landscape of science any notion of *self* even as an artifact of the way our mind works. (That would be metaphysical.) The strict materialists imply that there is less involved in personhood and in our preoccupation with identity than the situation warrants. Such a deflationary stance does violence to our natural supposition that our individuality is important—in accord with an innate sense of our distinction from otherness. The commonsense view of self assumes the existence of something (accessible through introspection) that endures through change. Is it not the chief business of selfhood to know our own past and be concerned about our own future?

There is a widely held principle that mind stands higher than matter, the spirit higher than the flesh, that the mental universe stands higher than the physical universe. This principle might have its origin in human physiology and in the feeling which identifies "self" with "mind" and locates the mind in the brain. Replace an organ such as a leg or an eye with an artificial or transplanted organ, and this does not appear to alter or threaten the self. But if one imagines a brain transplant or the dumping of the content of someone else's brain into one's own, then the self seems to shriek bloody murder, it is being destroyed. [Philip J. Davis and Reuben Hersh, *The Mathematical Experience*, 1981]

Most philosophers identify selfness with such abstract concepts as religion, morality, or even language, concepts ranging from the absolute to the merely cultural, depending on your point of view. Modern materialists have nothing to offer comparable to the embrace of religion as (in Charles Taylor's words) "the act of bringing meaning outside humankind to our earthly existence."

Nietzsche has argued that "the self is an artifact of a particular grammar, a shadow cast by the network of language rather than a reality independent of it. . . . So we would be different persons if our language were different and no person at all if we had no language."

Here we have two artifacts, one of metaphysics, one of language. To see how devastating is such a rejection of *self*, you have only to consider the definition of artifact as known to the laboratory scientist; for him an artifact is "any phenomenon produced by the specific methods or apparatus used and not causally related to whatever hypothesis is being examined." In order to carry on without a notion of selfhood, philosophers have to persuade us that it is merely an accidental by-product of our metaphysical speculations or an unintended result of our acquisition of language and grammar.

The fact is that philosophers and psychologists have failed to come to grips with this introspective aspect of our common lives. The concept of self is so ambiguous that some philosophers (such as Hume) doubt its existence. Philosophers have no science of the self, only theories, one of which, phenomenology, has a whole vocabulary in which its practitioners can speak (or at least be understood) only among themselves.

Self used to be called soul, with overtones of religion; self threatens to be called identity, with overtones of Freudian analysis. The only thing that self has going for it is common sense: we know in our hearts (and we are usually quite consoled) that we are not someone else—this is an everyday phenomenon beyond the grasp of chemistry and physics. Biologists have their chief confrontation with the phenomenon of selfness in the study of immunity as the agent of organic integrity, the capacity of an organism's cells to distinguish alien from host. Biology may never acquire any better access to the concept of self.

The problem will not go away, and the accelerating introduction of computers into our culture only adds a new perspective. As young people become adept in conversing with computers they are compelled to grapple with the interface between their own sense of self and the otherness of the video screen and its responsiveness to the operator.

Unresolved questions about the role of the self remain a rich source of creativity. As William H. Gass puts it:

> **"Who am I?" is a question that has many answers, depending on what self is sought. Is it the legal self who hopes for an inheritance? Is it the tribal self whose finger will follow every vein that carries the family colors? Is it the psychological self, hoping for a harmony among its conflicting skills and feelings? Is it the cultural self, the native of a language, the exiled self who simply needs a passport and a port of entry? Or is it the self who is searching for a fresh essence, the ambitious self, the self of a better future, who shall eventually be described by his accomplishments the way Sir Walter Scott is now said to be the author of "Waverly."**

Perhaps, as John Updike has suggested that Proust has suggested, "the transformation of experience by memory into something ineffably precious is the one transcendent meaning each life wrests from death."

SELF & OTHERNESS

You do not belong to you. You belong to the Universe.
—R. Buckminster Fuller

A different view from Montaigne's. For Montaigne, belonging to oneself was simply the greatest thing in the world. And so it was to Walt Whitman: "And nothing, not God, is greater to one than one's self is."

In pagan antiquity it was taken for granted that, except for slaves, people owned themselves. Christianity changed all that. In the Christian tradition persons possess but do not own themselves. Thus suicide became not only a sin but in some societies a crime.

B. F. Skinner—the behaviorist dervish, the exorcist of free will—almost succeeded in owning the universe by reducing it to his narrow dimensions. The most influential psychologist of our generation persuaded himself that we live in a world of Roman slaves in which scientific analysis has no place for the individual as an initiator of behavior. Nevertheless, biologists are paying increasing attention to the objective evidence for the persistence of altruism in human, animal, and insect societies. This may supply reinforcement to the notion that self has no function without regard to otherness.

Biology and religion each take note of otherness and cope with it in different ways. In religions, the relationship between self and otherness is a source of meaning, as in biology it is a source of behavior. (The metaphysical sin remains pride.)

The business of religion is salvation, and salvation is not available without some compromise—some would say sacrifice—of self and selfness. A Christian can be prayerful and even worshipful without too much expense of personality, but he cannot be *devout*, truly faithful and believing, without some surrender of ego. This is why converts are so zealous: They are volunteers, they have taken the enormous risk of merging their destiny with that of other communicants in a larger cause.

Biological processes can likewise entail risk: the risk of submerging the interest of the individual for the sake of the species. But biology has no counterpart of sacrament—only risk. There is a precept in the pharmaceutical industry that *without risk there is no potency*. That dictum has been enshrined in legal cases involving commercial liabilities and consumer rights. There is an analogy between the makers of medicine and the guardians of the faith. Custodians of Christian doctrine allow to the same degree that without doubt there is no faith. Without risk and doubt life loses savor. (It is the received theological wisdom that there is no heaven without some glimpse of hell.)

The poet Diane Ackerman attributes to Simone Weil the observation that we come into this world with only one possession, the slender word "I," and to give that up—in love, in religious fervor, in a pastoral sense of belonging—is the ultimate ecstasy.

THE IMMUNITY OF BODIES

Even the most primitive organisms are able to distinguish themselves from others, and even from others of their kind, but their means of doing so are varied, and there is no single mechanism at work. Recognition of foreign-ness (and its obverse, self-recognition) may be universal among animals, and even plants, although only vertebrates possess a biochemical mechanism for immunity with a capacity for exquisite discrimination between the body's own tissues and hostile invasions of microbes. The immune system is the biological source for a claim to *selfness*. It is the physiological vessel of identity.

The body tissues of animals provide an ideal environment for the growth of microbes. That putrefaction does not occur in living things is a testament to the efficacy of the immune system.

In the complexity of its functions the immune system is comparable to the nervous system. For instance, at birth both are only partly developed; they both depend on learned behavior to achieve their fully mature effectiveness. As far as we know the immune system exists only in vertebrates; and it is perhaps the most intensively studied aspect of vertebrate physiology. It has been most exhaustively researched in the mouse, and less so in humans, rats, chickens, and toads.

In the words of Stephen Grossberg, a mathematician,

"the immune system is dependent on self-organizing bio-chemical memory that functions in unexpected environments." This is the source of its capacity to form antibodies. The surfaces of most cells are studded with antigens, convoluted proteins that act as identifying markers helping the body to distinguish self from nonself. In man the immune system consists of about two pounds of white blood cells (lymphocytes) and antibodies dispersed throughout the body with special capabilities for pattern recognition. The function of the lymphocytes is to patrol the body and ensure its integrity from alien entities. Humans and other mammals produce a vast number—perhaps as many as 100 million—of different antibodies.

Sir Peter Medawar made the most important contribution to the science of immunology when he was able to demonstrate that "the ability of the immune system to distinguish 'self' from 'nonself' is not inherent but is learnt during the system's development as a result of exposure to 'self' molecules."

The immune system has both positive and negative values. In some of its aberrations it can produce the autoimmune diseases that are destructive of the body's own tissues. Even the fetus in the mother is in a way a foreign body—a foreign graft in which the paternal proteins usually differ from the maternal ones. For immunologists the ultimate puzzle is not why women miscarry, but why most don't. Pregnancy is a physiological (as well as a psychological) paradox of selfhood.

Psychoneuroimmunology is a new discipline in which the biological manifestation of self appears in its most exquisite form. It is an attempt by science to link the psyche to not just the brain but the entire body. To its enthusiasts, psychoneuroimmunology is a therapeutic endeavor exploring "the pathways in which mind, brain and immune system interact in producing disease or well-being."

THE PSYCHE AND BIOLOGY

What would we really like to be doing? The link between the psyche and biology is a tenuous one. We can have biology without psyche, but there is no psyche without a biological abode for the ego. Molecular biology is in its heyday, but when it comes to human beings, Freud still reigns.

Some use the word *psyche* descriptively to denote self or ego; others (sometimes called therapists) use it prescriptively to indicate man's capacity to deal with the world outside himself. The mental phenomena of brain and body as regarded by neurobiology occupy a different domain from that of psychoanalysis, in which mind exercises a realm of meaning without so-far-discerned physical properties.

The Cambridge anthropologist Ernest Gellner asserts that the source of greatest anxiety and concern "for a modern Western person" is his or her relationships with other people. If psyche indicates man's capacity to deal with the world outside himself, a broad area of inquiry, and perhaps therapy, is defined. Psychoanalysis has succeeded as a respectable mode of therapy because "it offers to individuals in crisis a system of solace, support and orientation without invoking the sort of archaic transcendence that would be offensive to the modern spirit." In other words, without religion.

An American psychiatrist practicing in London, Dr. Morton Schatzman, has gotten to the core of the matter: "Like religion, psychoanalysis confronts our brutal and devious tendencies, which have obscure origins. Unlike religion, it postulates a naturalistic and quasi-biological realm—the "unconscious"—to account for them. The 'salvation' that psychoanalysis promises is the mastery of that realm."

The psychoanalytic technique addresses the patient as a single individual with a unique history. Erik H. Erikson, the author of many works in the field, may not have been the first to remark that "*We* is not a term of psychoanalysis." (For all I know he was quoting Freud.) And Erwin Schrödinger asserts that "Consciousness is never experienced in the plural, only in the singular. . . . Consciousness is a singular of which the plural is unknown." Freudian psychology provides no place for commitment, and no conceptual framework for what the therapists call interpersonal relationships.

In analysis, the psyche and biology part company; as a discipline it is a humanistic rather than scientific endeavor.

Objects unavailable for display. Even to the uninitiated, Freud commands respect as the curator of a vast and obscure museum of real objects of introspection unavailable for display in any other arena. The interplay of Freud's Id, Superego, and Ego have been described as "a fight in a coal cellar between a sex-mad gorilla and a maiden aunt referred by a rather nervous college student." The cast of characters comprises a curious agenda for research.

The Freudian system reduces consciousness to only a small part of the realm of the mind. All the rest is unconscious: involuntary and often inadmissible ideas that motivate our behavior in irrational ways. Consciousness itself is elusive enough, while the unconscious is purely intuitive—totally beyond the grasp of physical science. The philosopher Owen Flanagan describes the Freudian system in terms of an epistemological crisis:

> **Freud revolutionized . . . our philosophical conception of human nature. He created an epistemological crisis by questioning the degree to which human motives are known and knowable. He painted the selfish, aggressive, and sexual quality of human motivation more vividly than any previous thinker. He saw accidents as intentional, and dreams, not rational discourse, as reflecting our real hopes, desires, and wishes. He viewed religion as an illusion, morality as a social invention, and culture itself as the compromise that makes social life possible by keeping us busy with tasks which keep our minds off what we would really like to be doing.**

Under this prescription social life, our capacity to deal with the world outside ourselves, would be disastrous or at least impracticable if we all spent our time—perhaps vividly and certainly immorally—doing what we would really like to be doing. Freud's structure of the human psyche has been described as "a bundle of contradictions and disharmonies which at first sight seems anything but a product of adoptive evolution." To the extent that therapeutic strategies reduce the mental illness of individuals they contribute to the stability of society and thus serve as a survival factor for the species.

Freud's documentation of our brutal and devious tendencies is compelling, but trivial in relation to the more important consequences of his insight. His psychoanalytic theories acquire their chief dignity from offering a lay version of salvation independent of sacred and institutional apparatus, independent of any illusory religion. The Washington, D.C., neurologist Dr. Richard Restak states: "The goal of psychoanalysis is to 'make the unconscious conscious.' . . . In other words, the relevant factors responsible for behavior are, in principle, accessible to introspection. I think this claim is closer to a religious dogma than it is to anything approaching scientific proof." And as Freud himself wrote: "I do not think our successes can compete with those of Lourdes. There are so many more people who believe in the miracles of the Blessed Virgin than in the existence of the unconscious." It is the concern for a kind of nonreligious salvation that has given Freud and psychoanalysis its great hold in our culture. It survives as a chronic preoccupation of our artists and writers, a star boarder in our house of the arts and humanities. He has kept in business people like Eugene O'Neill and Woody Allen.

The psyche as interpreted by Freud has an enormous poetic and metaphorical appeal to "modern Western persons," a constituency which may be becoming obsolescent. For instance, neither shrinks (nor lawyers for that matter) have found a sure clientele in Tokyo. Freud's dogma still finds no comfortable niche among the disciplines of science.

It remains on the fringes of therapy as a cultural rather than a scientific concept, surviving in our public and private climate of opinion—in the bedroom and the salon—not in the laboratory.

What contributions from the biological sciences can be found to confirm or amplify the Freudian dogma? The neurophysiologists ply away at the cellular frontiers of sleep and learning and memory. We know that memory and learning occur, but we have only an inkling of the physiology that may be involved. Freud has had more to tell us about the suppression of memory than the experimentalists have had to tell us about how it may operate.

Neuroscience is not even close to identifying a biological substrate for the unconscious mind itself.* This, of course, would not have disturbed Freud, as he renounced any search for neurobiological mechanisms in favor of understanding the mind through the life story of his patient, through the intensive exploration of the personal history, of the person who has the mind. It was as simple as the slogan for the old Packard automobile: Ask the man who owns one. So far no one has found any models or language to make biology and psychoanalysis commensurate.

Some neurologists describe the mechanisms of the mind by recognizing two separate (or rather semiseparable) mechanisms: somatic and psychic. The somatic includes the sensory and motor functions; in man and other mammals they are committed as to function at birth. The hippocampus, for instance, is committed to a role in scanning the record of past experience and in memory recall. The psychic mechanism includes those of speech and memory of the past stream of consciousness, essential for the interpretation of present experience, but uncommitted as to exact function at the time of birth. (Psychoanalysis is concerned with the life of the individual in his past and his roots in a kind of group memory. It brings to mind the

* *An exception might be the triune brain theory of Paul D. MacLean. (See page 152.)*

characterization of the Germans as a people who are perpetually dissatisfied because they have a past and a future but no present.)

Molecular biology has been masterful in unraveling the secret language of the gene and revealing the immortal lifelines of genetic continuity—the mechanics of reproduction. Such explorations, however promising, could not be more remote from the problems of sex as experienced by humans. To engage in sex for its own sake is uniquely human. When James Thurber and E. B. White wrote a book in the 1930s, asking *Is Sex Necessary?*, their facetiousness failed to conceal that they really cared terribly about the problems sex brings to the lives of all of us. Thurber's drawings of middle-age, middle-class men and women in the amateur ceremonies of courtship embrace two themes: the "melancholy of sex" and the "implausibility of animals." E. B. White supplied a consummate answer to their naïve query:

Men and women have always sought, by one means and another, to be together rather than apart. At first they were together by the simple expedient of being unicellular, and there was no conflict. Later the cell separated, or began living apart, for reasons which are not clear even today, although there is considerable talk. Almost immediately the two halves of the original cell began experiencing a desire to unite again—usually with a half of some other cell. This urge has survived down to our own time. Its commonest manifestations are marriage, divorce, neuroses, and, a little less frequently, gunfire.

We are the only animal for whom sexual behavior means not just the begetting of new life but the refining and deepening of emotional bonds. Discussion of sex and concern with its raptures and torments in our daily lives is no longer taboo, and this surely beneficial advance is largely a result of what Freud—not Watson and Crick—has had to say to us. "By calling attention to the unconscious mental processes Freud gave the Western world an opportunity to improve the relations of the individual as subject to nature as object, in the daily life of ordinary people as well as in the thinking of the clinics and the academies." (L. L. Whyte, *The Unconsciousness Before Freud*, 1960.)

Biology will advance with or without the psyche; meanwhile, it is hard to see how Freud will be put out to pasture. We are still at sea and far from home.

SLEEP & DREAMS

The royal road to the unconscious—Freud's phrase—is found in the significance of dreams. But he tells us little about the mechanisms that regulate his insight that dreams are the disguised expression of suppressed desires. Sleep makes dreams possible. Sleep may help us learn. Only advanced mammals have REM (rapid eye movement) sleep, now seen to be a recent development in evolution. Although human beings spend more time dreaming than in any other single mental activity, dreams are perhaps more inaccessible to laboratory examination than any other habit of the mind.

Animal researchers claim to have determined that echidnas, the small, spiny-coated primitive mammals, have no capacity for REM sleep. Possibly their behavioral repertoire is insufficently complex to require integration over time.

The only thing we know about dreams is a fragment captured on waking. The stuff of reverie, introspection, and fantasy is not the stuff of easy scientific exploration. Laboratory conditions probably freeze spontaneity as they freeze most human attributes when submitted to measurement.

Sleep and dreams are also of concern to neurophysiology. There is a respectable hypothesis that dreaming is the bridge between brain and psyche. Dreams are among the most inaccessible of psychological phenomena, and the area is difficult to quantify. J. A. Hobson has deduced that during an average lifetime, "an individual spends at least 50,000 hours in dreaming."

Francis Crick, the codiscoverer of the structure of DNA, says that although dreams have no meaning, they have a function: They "randomly purge the brain of unneeded and overabundant associations stored in the networks of brain cells."

Buckminister Fuller says sleep is the great normalizer: that the function of sleep is to serve as a subconscious sorting process, to restore metaphysical symmetry to all the unresolved asymmetries accumulated during the waking day spent in the physical world bombarding our consciousness. *"Ceux qui ont apparie nôtre vie a un songe ont eu de la raison. . . . Nous veillons dormants et veillants dormons."* (Those who have compared our life to a dream were right. . . . We sleeping wake, and waking sleep. [Montaigne, *Essays*, Book II])

Row, row, row your boat.

PSYCHOLOGY

PACED is a mnemonic for the five goals of psychology:
    prediction
        application
            control
                explanation
                    description

But, in practice, in the attempt to analyze human and animal behavior by means of psychological techniques, the sequence of these objectives would appear to be reshuffled if not reversed.

As a discipline, psychology seems to invite an inescapable circularity of argument. There are no doubt a number of psychological theories that contribute to the goals cited above. But a psychological theory, in the words of one of its practitioners, Geoffrey Hall, can be defined as no more than "a fairly abstract specification of the mechanisms that must exist in order to generate the behavior that is observed." (Hmm.)

Predictability, the capacity to test theory by the results of experiment, is the distinguishing criterion of any science worthy of the name. Would we really want to live in a world foreshadowed by Pavlov and Skinner where human response to stimuli would be all that measurably predictable?

But there is, however, a rationale for psychology; it is more than just a body of attempts to systematize common sense. It may be in the nature of things that psychology is not reducible to neuroscience. There is an empirical possibility that mental states a priori have certain properties not explicable in terms of neurofunctional organization or neurostructural dynamics. Even the most committed of neurobiologists can concede that without the insights that psychology can provide it is unlikely that they will ever understand what brain chemistry is all about.

Psychology is both a practice and a discipline. As practitioners psychologists are concerned with counseling and mental health care; as a discipline they are focused on scientific research. For almost a century these two pursuits flourished within the same professional organization, the APA, the American Psychological Association. In 1988 those members devoted to scientific and applied psychology broke away and founded their own American Psychological Society. To further complicate the picture large areas of psychology have been cannibalized by other fields, notably cognitive science and neuroscience.

Howard Gardner of Harvard University says that

Psychology is going to flourish much more as an applied field. I think that the answer to the question of how to conceptualize a child's mind is going to be a key to all kinds of issues having to do with formal schooling, lifelong learn-

ing and things like that. The person who can take the next step beyond Piaget . . . if there were a Nobel prize for that sort of thing, that person would earn it.

Psychology, like biology itself, appears ripe for a new synthesis.

THE VOCABULARY OF SELF

It is a grievous defect of the English language that it does not have two different words to indicate a member of the human race and a member of the male gender. The historic name for our race is man, even Man. A leading journal of anthropology has been called *Man.* At Expo '67 in Montreal, Canada had its Musée de l'Homme. Only a decade or so ago, the Smithsonian Institution in Washington was contemplating the organization of a Museum of Man out of its Museum of Natural History. We can envy the Greeks, who have *anthropos*, and the Germans, who have *Mensch.*

Feminine objections to the usage of "man" in the past are legitimate and irreversible, and the word can no longer be used in the sense of human being without a heavy burden of self-consciousness if not guilt. The available alternatives are not altogether satisfactory.

Humans. Purists used to object to *human* as inherently adjectival, suitable only as a modifier, as in the phrase *human beings* to describe the genus *Homo*, and especially the species *Homo sapiens.* But *humans* has now become acceptable for general use.

People. *People* is a plural noun for which there is no singular (except as indicating a group like "the Caucasian people" or "the Jewish people.") There is no singular for people because the word specifically refers to human beings collectively, not individually known or considered as individuals.

Persons. This a term descended from the Greek word for the wearer of a mask, as in the classic theater, hence the role attributed to this mask. *Person* designates an individual and is thus the converse of people. People are abstract and statistical; persons are conscious, rational, even moral, individuals. There are many aspects of personhood. Theologically, the principal activity of a person is believing and choosing between good and evil. Philosophically, persons have moral and ethical values beyond their role as organisms in nature; such values being insusceptible to scientific scrutiny. Rationally, a person is a seeker of knowledge; politically, a person functions in the community; biologically, a person is a product of genetic coding. With the advent of artificial intelligence, the idea of personhood confronts the machine. We know that machines can process information; we do not know the extent to which they can model other aspects of personal activity. (*Persona* survives from the Latin in erudite and technical senses in literature and psychology.)

14
Observing man

MAN AS OBSERVER

Is consciousness passive or active? Are we humans visitors meandering around the museum of life? Or does our consciousness actively create experience? Ian Hacking makes this point:

> **The members of our species are five or six feet tall. We seem now to have investigated the inner constitution of matter down to 10^{-16} centimeter, a number pertaining to the W and Z [particles], where theory and experimental intervention mesh astonishingly well. There seems nothing in the theory of evolution to explain how a species our size should have acquired the ability to do that.**

In what Buckminster Fuller calls his "epistemography of generalizations," he explains that while environment plus me equals Universe, Universe minus me does not equal environment. This is because environment does not exist without the observer, because observation is prior to experience.

Of course, speculations like these hover at the margins of solipsism.

THE ANTHROPIC PRINCIPLE

In its simplest form the anthropic principle states that the conditions of the universe appear to have been specially contrived—by accident or design—to facilitate the appearance of conscious intelligence as manifest in human beings. Time and again scientists have been struck by the fact that, if given characteristics of the universe were only slightly different, life would be impossible. In other words, if the prevailing physical forces of the material world were not in such exquisitely fine balance, a planet Earth with a temperate climate and energy from the sun would not have evolved, carbonaceous life would not have arisen, human intelligence through the evolution of vertebrates would not have evolved, and no astronomer would have matured to sit at the telescope and gaze at all the wonderful stars and galaxies of the cosmos. In a metaphorical sense man appears to be the universe's instrument for observing itself.

Observer participancy. John Archibald Wheeler is the nuclear physicist who coined the term "black Hole." His boldest intuitions are so maverick that some of his colleagues say they are barely contained within the accepted paradigm of physics. It is Wheeler who tells us that "the universe is a self-excited circuit. As it expands, cools, and develops it gives rise to observer participancy."

Is the existence of observers an incidental or a fundamental feature of the universe? (If we assume an unlimited number of universes, it is of course incidental.) Heisenberg says that science reveals nature as exposed to our method of questioning. Max Planck had earlier asserted, "it is impossible to separate the law that we are seeking to discover from the methods that are being used to bring about the discovery." Albert Einstein was careful not to blame nature for the dilemma when he wrote, "The fact that in science we have to be content with an incomplete picture of the physical universe is not due to the nature of the universe itself but rather to us."

The anthropic principle is the term coined by the English cosmologist, Dr. Brandon Carter, in a paper presented to astrophysicists in 1974. He modestly proposed the term to describe a philosophical middle ground between primitive anthropocentrism and the antithetical dogma that no part of the universe is in any way privileged. (Carter has subsequently, in a 1983 paper, expressed regret that the term "anthropic" would apply only to mankind, whereas he is actually concerned with a principle of self-selection that would be applicable to any extraterrestrial civilization that might exist.)

Antecedents of the anthropic line of reasoning appeared as far back as P. A. M. Dirac's "large number hypothesis" (1937), and the Princeton physicist Robert Dicke's assertion in 1957 that the fundamental physical constants, such as the gravitational constant and the charge on the electron—which appear to be otherwise arbitrary—are "not random," but conditioned by the biological fact that organisms must exist in order for constants to be measured.

The strong anthropic principle states that any meaningful or real universe *must* evolve life. The conclusion derives primarily from the extraordinary number of coincidences that had to occur for life to exist. The coincidences are extremely fine-tuned, and the list of them is overwhelming, but there is no evidence that they are in any way ordained.

15
Ants & instinct

Ants show how much time nature spent nurturing instinct before she got around to investing in intellect.

Theriophily. In 1933 the literary critic and historian George Boas coined the term *theriophily* to express admiration for animals and their ways. In opposition to the dogma that mankind is superior to all other forms of life, theriophily advances a broad doctrine that the characteristics of animals are at least equal to, if not superior, to those of human beings. Dislodging man from his perch between beasts and angels, Boas quotes Pliny "... it is hard to tell whether nature has been a kindly parent to man or a cruel stepmother." Nature gives the animals a natural covering of shells, hulls, spines, shaggy hair, fur, feathers, scales, or fleeces, "but man [says Pliny] she casts forth on his natal day, naked upon a naked soil, casts him forth to weep and beg; and no other animal weeps from the moment of its birth."

Ants as tenacious protoplasm. While men beg and weep, ant colonies flourish in dry sandy deserts as well as the dampest of rain forests and from the Alps to Texas streams. The ant world embraces 15,000 species, with a new species being described roughly every working day. They range in size from a millimeter long to three and a half inches. Ants can be frozen for 24 hours and then thaw and survive; they can go without food for the greater part of a year; they can be submerged in cold water for eight days or be maimed to the point of decapitation—and still survive. Individual worker ants are known to live for up to seven years and queens for from 13 to 15 years, while their colonies are so stable they can outlast a generation of men. They are made of remarkably tenacious protoplasm; a paragon of social animals in their variety, number, geographical distribution, in their ubiquity and their longevity.

The animal kingdom manifests no greater exemplars of pure *instinct* than the social insects, and among the social insects none has survived longer—since the Mesozoic Epoch 200 million years ago—and under a greater variety of environments than the ant. They are the ascendant social creatures among the invertebrates just as mammals are among the vertebrates. The psychic attributes that make ants social is what make them worth comparing with *Homo sapiens* (wise man)—the biological vessels of *intellect* who suddenly appeared just 30,000 years ago. Instinct has been around for a long time; flesh has harbored intellect— through which nature has achieved humanity—only recently.

But ants live in a condition of anarchic socialism, a system of unsupervised division of labor, in which, unlike human beings, a single individual has no survival value and if left alone will perish of its own accord. (There are no Robinson Crusoes among the Formicidae.)

Colonies of ants are least like the society of humans in that the role of males is totally subordinate to that of females,* and that the specialized community roles of its members (mostly neuter workers) are fixed physiologically at the time of their hatching. But in two other respects they are most like men: the extraordinary instinctive endow-

---

* Males are created only for a brief nuptial flight with the virgin queen, often descending to earth in copula, but always dying after consummation.

ment implicit in the complexity of their society, and the fact that they have no real enemy save their own kind.

(There are of course anteaters—the Myrmecophaga— who really aren't that much of a threat; with their slothful movement and very small brains they have managed to survive only in South America. In most of the world earthworms play a vital role in aerating the soil and bringing new earth to the surface. But there are no earthworms in South America; hence the ants have such a field day to themselves. Hence also a few anteaters.)

The ants may not have many enemies but there is hardly any animal or plant that is not threatened by ants. Hence the potential victims resort to the shells, hulls, spines, hair, fur, feathers, scales, and fleeces that Pliny wrote about.

Ants in the taxonomic hierarchy. The taxonomic hierachy for ants illustrates their evolutionary remoteness from man:

> **Kingdom ANIMALIA: Kingdom METAZOA (multicellular organisms developed from an egg**
>
> **Branch EUMETAZOA (tissues and organ systems)**
>
> **Grade BILATERIA (bilateral symmetry)**
>
> *[This is the level at which ant and man part company]*
>
> **Section COELEMATA (three tissue layers; body cavity; with anus)**
>
> **Phylum ARTHROPODA (hardened exoskeleton or cuticle; segmented bodies and appendages) (Arthropoda are the largest and most diverse of all phyla, comprising 75 percent of known species.)**
>
> **Class INSECTA (having mandibles, three pairs of appendages and one pair of antennae)**
>
> **Subclass PTERYGOTA (winged or secondarily wingless)**

Division ENDOPTERYGOTA (complex metamorphosis)

Order HYMENOPTERA (membrane wings; ants, bees, wasps)

Suborder APOCRITA (abdomen and thorax separated by waist)

Superfamily SCOLIODEA (parasitic wasps and ants)

Family FORMICIDAE* (Ants; all social in habit, a few parasitic)

Subfamily (many)

Genus (hundreds)

Species (thousands)

A note on classes of ant study. Devotion to the study of animals other than man has flourished in modern times with the development of the various disciplines of zoology. *Entomology* is the scientific study of *Insecta*, the largest single class of animals. (Entomology comes from Aristotle's use of the word *entoma*, to cut from. Compare the French *entamer*, to cut into a piece of cake or venture into a new topic of conversation.) *Myrmecology* is that branch of entomology devoted to the study of ants. In 1909 William Morton Wheeler, curator of invertebrate zoology at the American Museum of Natural History, wrote a great book on ants which remains a classic today. He describes the range of myrmecology as follows:

> Ants, like other organisms, may be studied from at least three different points of view, according as the observer is most interested in their classification, or taxonomy (including geographical distribution), their morphology (anatomy

---

* *The family* Formicidae *includes all the ants. Formic acid occurs naturally in ants and it is the exudation of this acid that gives anthills their urinous smell. Hence* pismire, *an archaic English word meaning either an ant or an insignificant or contemptible person.*

and development) or their ethology, that is, their functional aspect (physiology and psychology).

The *psychology* of ants? A myrmecologist, Derek Morley, writing in 1953, hastens to reassure us that ant psychology is different from ours:

> What is important to know is the degree to which it is permissible to think of ant behavior in human terms. The answer is simple—not at all. . . . The mystery of the ants is in their empathy, the bond of nervous tension which builds so quick a response one to another that it seems more akin to a response to a nerve-carried impulse within a single individual than one involving two quite separate and recognizable characters separated by space.

Within the biological sciences, what are the specialized disciplines involved in the systematic observation and study of ants? (The breakdown of disciplines is of interest because the way biologists work reveals an explicit view of their approach to organic life in general.) *Ant taxonomists* classify specimens on the basis of their measurable visual and physical descriptions which inevitably lead to the assignment of an implicit place in the scale of evolutionary development. *Biogeographers* work on the geographical distribution of species, including ants. *Morphologists* classify ants on the basis of their structure (anatomy), their cellular characteristics (cytology), their submicroscopic tissues (histology), their embryology, and other factors both analogous and homologous. *Sociobiologists* study the biological—even the bleakly genetic—basis of the social behavior of living creatures including ants and men. The discipline focuses particularly on the mode of organization including the forms of communication, division of labor, and time budgets of both the group and its members. Some anthropologists have described six stages in the development of human societies: the hunting, pastoral, agricultural, commercial, industrial, and intellectual. Ants have been perceived as revealing stages corresponding to the first three of those categories.

Ant society: instinct and group behavior. In the Holocene epoch we live in, the evolution of ants appears to have been arrested; they seem to have reached a plateau that might give man a chance to catch up. The returns are not yet in. Instinct and intelligence each represent basic tendencies of protoplasm in the form of living organisms. Instinct has reached its most complex manifestation in the family Formicidae, intelligence in genus Homo.

We do not yet have the answer to the the question of how the phenomenon known as instinct is even acquired by organisms, much less how it is retained and passed on to successive generations. Most continuing investigations of this question assume that the information required is somehow manifest in a chemical or electrical way, with the information stored or transmitted by alterations of the shape or arrangement of complex organic molecules. Somehow the accumulated experience of the species is passed on to individuals whose behavior patterns are wired in from birth. In this hierarchy of living things, ants have a considerably more complex nervous system than more primitive creatures such as sponges, who have no nervous systems at all, while man possesses a vastly more complex nervous system than intermediate creatures such as ants, who have no intellect at all. Ants have enough nerve cells for instinct but not for intelligence, not for a capacity for learning. The fact that man has a sufficient number of nerve cells to have achieved intelligence does not mean that he has relinquished all the imperatives of instinct.

Edward O. Wilson, the founder and a chief pillar of sociobiology, has this to say about ants as a society without leaders:

> ... despite all our efforts over many years of research, those of us who study social insects have never been able to find

**a command center. No individual—not even the queen, an
oversized creature concerned mainly with reproduction—
lays plans for the colony as a whole. . . . the activity of an
ant colony . . . is the summation of a vast number of personal
decisions by individual ants.**

Ants may make personal decisions but they must be on the
level of pure reflex or instinct. The existence of social organization in insects is not dependent upon mental events.
The ants have developed their elaborate societies without
being remotely aware of the fact.

Insect societies are not so much societies as organisms.
The nest of the ant is the operative unit; the isolated ant
is not quite an abstraction but it can occur only by accident.
Philosophical biologists make an analogy between the ant
colony and the cell colony. "The queen mother of the ant
colony displays the generalized potentialities of all the individuals, just as the Metazoan egg contains *in potentia* all
the other cells of the body." Professor Wheeler defines instinct as the activity of an organism acting as a whole rather
than as a part, as representative of a species rather than an
individual—acting in response to situations where there is
no previous experience and with an end or purpose of which
the organism can have no knowledge. ". . . [It] is certain that
the man lives not who can tell where the whole begins and
the part leaves off in a living organism, or can frame a
satisfactory definition of a living individual or species; and
the intellect abdicates when it is called upon to grasp an
activity that is unconsciously purposeful." If instinct is unconsciously purposeful, can intellect be likewise?

Plasticity. The instinct of ants and the intelligence of
human beings illustrate parallel strategies of maintaining a
natural social commonwealth in the face of vastly changing
ecological conditions. Both strategies demand complex dependence on individual cooperation for group ends and for
learned behavior in adapting to environmental extremes:
This is a characteristic described by biologists as *plasticity,*

a goal-directed capacity for symbiotic accommodation with plants and with other species, and a shifting of the behavior of individuals from egocentric to altruistic proclivities.

Of all the attributes of ants, plasticity is the one most closely shared with humans. We have it on the authority of J.B.S. Haldane that man is the most plastic of all the animals with his patterns of behavior less fixed by heredity and more dependent on environment. From this he draws a comfortably unscientific conclusion: "This feature, which is so highly developed in man, and which we call plasticity of behavior when we look at it from outside, is called the freedom of the will when we look at it from inside. In any evolution which could be called progressive we are likely to develop it still further."

16
Conscious evolution

—————————◦◦◦◦◦◦—————————

A FUNCTION FOR MAN

Is there a possible function for man in the universe? Other animals have the advantage of being regulated by instinct. Nature makes all of the decisions for other animals, but only some of the decisions for us. Our intellect provides us with imagined options, a latitude—an opportunity or obligation?—to continue or complete what tasks? To what ends might we improve each shining hour?

The question is presumptuous. It is teleological, but it is also logical. Speculation on the function of humans in the scheme of things—put that way, and on the cosmic scale—lacks a rationale in the myths of our culture. The doctrine of conscious evolution arises from the brash vision of human beings controlling their own destiny—an impulse with little sanction in the learning and literature of the past. Man's fate is usually put the other way round, in terms of man's duty. Even John Milton skirted blasphemy in justifying to man the ways of God. The question of whether man has more than a transient role in the evolutionary scheme is deeply profane and subversive of religious institutions because it eschews any appeal to, or indulgence of, the supernatural.

The question is nevertheless unscientific, innately heterodox, and offensive to the content and values of established religion and even conventional fields of study. Substitutes for salvation have been the stamping ground for movers and shakers in the occult. The answer does not require a scientific endorsement, but in order to be plausible it should not be in conflict with any of the findings of science. The answer must be natural rather than supernatural.

The question of man's function in the scheme of things is at the heart of the growing school of adherents of the doctrine of conscious evolution—with its hints (*pace* such reductionists as Stephen Jay Gould and Lynn Margulis) that man is in charge of his own destiny, and that even the natural processes of evolution on earth and the course of the biosphere are somehow hostage to human folly.

The epigraph appearing as the proem for this book links the destiny of man with the destiny of atoms, with no hint of sanctity or divine intervention. Conscious evolution is unconcerned with divinity.

If the prospect were to present itself, few of us would disdain salvation—the survival after death of our individual consciousness. I harbor only the most fleeting hope that the search for a scientifically credible explanation of man's evolutionary function would afford any personal advantage to the seeker in avoiding the effects of sin. Grace—unmerited favor—abounds not here.

THE DOCTRINE OF CONSCIOUS EVOLUTION

Everything evolves. For men and women concerned about our fate in the world, but jaded with the excesses of nationalism, the tediousness of politics and the quaintness of patriotism, evolution provides the most appealing context for a kind of secular salvation. Evolution has to be considered in all its overlapping aspects. Not just biological evolution but the evolution of our galaxy and the solar system in the universe. Not just cosmic evolution but the evolution of the interaction of life and the environment on our planet. Up until now man has shared biological evolution with the rest of the animal kingdom. His achievement of cultural evolution is an apparently irreversible trait that makes him unique among species.

Culture makes human beings unique but it by no means ensures their dominion on earth. The hegemony of humans over the rest of the animal kingdom seems irreversibly established. But in the other kingdoms of plants, fungi, monera, and protists, we have barely left a mark, and they give every evidence of continuing to flourish with very little threat from us.

The net context is that the big bang was about 15 billion years ago; the solar system almost 5 billion years ago; and life on earth about 3.5 billion years ago. The sequence and ratio of those numbers is very significant, and the time values they represent remained undiscovered until the 20th century.

Can it be that the whole of evolution with which Darwin was concerned is only a local phenomenon? It depends on the context. We can posit protoevolution, or at least a protouniverse before there was any kind of evolution, and that time—preceding the familiar universe—could have been infinite. The length of physical evolution forming all the now identified elements and galaxies is about 15 billion years.

There is now a new vision of evolution in the land, though it has not yet won the support of much of a political constituency. Politics and the free market—the preoccupations of contemporary Western civilization—are unprepared for the didactic, occasionally hortatory, view that propounds a new evolutionary function for genus Homo. The doctrine focuses on the inseparability of organism— particularly the human organism—and its environment. By taking the whole biosphere for their province, the conscious evolutionists change the rules of evolutionary nature, not just for our own species but for all other species as well, as documented by the exponential growth of domestication or extinction of animals depending on their short-term utility for man.

Not since the first plants poisoned the atmosphere with oxygen has a single species had such power. We have in a few hundred years changed the biosphere to an extent that it took the plants a few million years. Involuntarily we have become agents of change, and human history is utterly superseded by planetary evolution.

The doctrine of conscious evolution comes in a number of varieties of which the most conservative calls itself directed evolution.

Directed evolution. Some philosophers of biology have proposed the term *directed evolution* for the current stage of development of life in the cosmos—an evolutionary bridge from protobiology to postbiology. There is a sequence in which physical evolution leads to biological evolution; biological evolution leads to cultural evolution; and cultural evolution leads to directed evolution, in which life evolves through human intervention rather than random mutation. In a recent article, Dr. Edward Rubenstein has formulated the stages of evolution and their mechanisms of communication:

> **The messengers of physical evolution are the intermediary subatomic particles belonging to the class of bosons.**
>
> **The messengers of biological evolution are the molecules of messenger RNA.**
>
> **The messengers of cultural evolution are the symbols of acoustic, graphic and body language.**
>
> **The epochs of evolution telescope ever more quickly . . . that of biological evolution about three billion years and that of cultural evolution about 50,000 years. Although directed evolution has just begun, extrapolation suggests its span will be brief, and so it is not too soon to wonder what will succeed it.**

Tripartite evolution. Eugene Mallove in *The Quickening Universe* describes a tripartite evolution in which the first stage is *genetic*, the familiar evolutionary development as described in biology textbooks. The second form of evolution, which currently engulfs us, is *cultural*, an extragenetic and extrasomatic process that evolves far faster than biological evolution. He sees human beings now at the brink of the third stage a *technological* evolution, which anticipates the quickening of self-replicating computers begetting mechanisms increasingly more talented than the originals and eventually our symbiotic counterparts in the stewardship of terrestrial life.

Ecological evolution. Fritjof Capra in *The Turning Point* envisions "a passage to the solar age" in which shallow environmentalism (efficient control and management of earth resources for the benefit of man) will be superseded by a "deep ecology" movement based on profound changes in our perception of the role of human beings in the planetary ecosystem. He maintains that our entire culture is witnessing a shift from the mechanistic to the ecological paradigm. "Self organizing systems in continual interaction with their environment are capable of tremendously increasing their complexity by abandoning structural stability in favor of flexibility and open-ended evolution."

Cosmic evolution. In his book *Cosmic Dawn: The Origins of Matter and Life*, Eric Chaisson, a physicist with the Smithsonian–Harvard Center for Astrophysics, in Cambridge, Massachusetts, adopts the term *cosmic evolution* for "the study of change through time." It deals with nothing less than the changes in the composition of (1) energy, (2) matter, and (3) life—in that order of progression. Developmental change is the hallmark of what we see in the universe. Evolution is the broadest of concepts; it includes the evolution of both animate and inanimate systems—and there is even a distant prospect of such a thing as an evolution of ethics.

First there was energy. Then there is the era where energy is dominated by matter. Now we are at the point where

intelligent technology is manipulating matter. Even evolution evolves. Life may have an impact on the fate of the Universe. . . . It is as though the Universe waited to produce Us—not so much us as a species but us as a civilization.

Cosmic ecology. This is Freeman Dyson's term for the science of life in interaction with the cosmos as a whole. His argument is based on "a fundamental assumption concerning the nature of life, that life resides in organization rather than in substance. If this assumption is true . . . then it makes sense to imagine life detached from flesh and blood and embodied in networks of superconducting circuitry or in interstellar dust clouds."

Are you beginning to see the range? We are putting all the old paradigms out of business.

Evolutionary governance. This version is also known by its chief proponent, Walter Truett Anderson, as "creeping evolution." I would also call it commonsense evolution, or human intervention in evolution by default. Our political leaders may fear creeping socialism or creeping capitalism . . . but they often do not seem to be aware of creeping globalism. The biosphere has already become globalized by anthrogenic causes with no regard for national boundaries. Like it or not, we are governing evolution *now*.

There is no hint of destiny in Anderson's prescription:

I am not here to argue that the human species ought to take responsibility for the evolution of the planet. If that were the question to be decided, I would advocate that we put it off for a few centuries or more—let things run themselves while we get accustomed to the idea, develop the appropriate ethics and myths and political structures, and perhaps mature a bit. However . . . the threshold is not out there ahead of us somewhere, a line from which we might conceivably draw back. We are well across it. To say we are not ready for evolutionary governance is equivalent to saying that a teenage child is not ready for puberty; the statement may be true but it is not much help.

THE PROSPECTS FOR CATASTROPHE

The Second International Conference on the Environmental Future was convened in Reykjavík, Iceland, in June of 1977 under the sponsorship of the world's leading conservation organization, the IUCN (the International Union for the Conservation of Nature and Natural Resources). The mood of the conference was one of informed pessimism. Dr. R. Fosberg, a delegate from the Smithsonian Institution, raised the question of whether man could overcome the cyclic nature of his past cultural development—whether man could learn to behave as a climax species rather than a pioneer species.

When the conference issued its final report, *The Reykjavík Imperative on the Environment and the Future of Mankind*, it deplored that "Governments, as well as people, tend to concentrate on immediate problems. It is unusual for a country to develop a 10 year plan, and unheard of to have a 100 year plan." Yet the conference delegates unanimously concluded that "there is ... a high probability, almost a certainty, that the greatest human catastrophe of recorded history will occur in the lifetime of most of us."

Theologically, eschatology is the dogma of last things, namely, death, judgment, heaven and hell. Philosophically, it is concerned with theories about the ultimate end of mankind and the final stages of the physical cosmos. Maybe Chicken Little was right.

A NICHE FOR MAN: AN ARRAIGNMENT

There is nothing in the evolution of the universe or the laws of nature or the imperatives of genetics that ordains that there should be a humanly intelligent species. Biologically, we are what happens to have turned up. There is no scientific evidence that we have anything to do with what the universe might have been aiming at from the beginning.

(Religion and artistic bravura subsist on our penchant for wondering what could have been aimed at.)

The universe by assumption has no intrinsic property beyond existence. Science has had only a few centuries to ponder the advent of human beings. Science—evolutionary biologists—are preoccupied with survival values. In evolutionary terms, the salvation of *Homo sapiens* means the preservation of the hominid taxon from extinction. What we know of biology would thus permit a kind of secular salvation in which man could preserve his niche by means of his own devising, by works indeed rather than by faith.

That branch of theology dealing with last things: death, judgment, heaven and hell, is called *eschatology* (Greek *eschata* = death). This is the rubric for religious theories of the fate of mankind and even the final stages of the physical cosmos—the end of the world. This is where the intense increase in attention to environmental issues in the last decades of the 20th century (properly understood) is an affront to the church, the mosque, and the synagogue in diverting us from the spiritual drama of the struggle for men's souls. In the words of Edward Norman, Dean of Chapel, Christ Church College, Canterbury, England, "environmental issues . . . are ideally suited to all those who need some kind of secular eschatology," because environmentalism actually operates to reinforce materialism.

It is a consequence of our *biological arraignment* that we human beings have to make our own history, though not in circumstances of our own choosing. That's what makes it a predicament. Evolution has its own imperatives in which natural selection supersedes any legal cause for merits of survival. Ecological concerns with global change provide only a theater, not a court for resolution of the issue on the merits.

What makes it more of a predicament is that we are the first creatures to be prisoners—eager prisoners though we be—of culture. Cultural evolution is a new kind of process analogous to physical evolution, but taking place at an explosively faster rate. The situation has made man a special phenomenon. And surely it is not perverse or antis-cientific to insist on this.

Man makes his own history. That is our destiny. But there's no guarantee that we will be nearly as successful as the 200-million-year history of dinosaurs, who weren't even aware at the time that they were residents of a niche. Could dinosaurs have had bliss if they were innocent of context? (It's like cows . . . cows know, but they don't know that they know.)

What is the moral? Don't rattle my cage? Don't mess with my niche? Biology has made us comfortable. Intellect has endowed us with a capacity for tragedy. We are indeed special. Isn't that enough?

IV

ARTIFICIAL LIFE VS. NATURAL LIFE

———————⌇———————

*M*ATTER AND ENERGY POSSESS AN IN-*nate ability to self-organize. In the natural world this happens spontaneously; in the mechanical world it can be triggered by human intervention. The distinction between artificial and natural may be bred of cultural bias—discounting human agency as somehow unnatural.*

The advent of artificial life suggests that while humankind may not become obsolete, our breed will be confronted with an inevitable symbiosis with biomechanical creatures of our own devising. The transfer of our individual psyches from mammalian to robotic vessels comes within the realm of speculation, and suggests the vista of a kind of mechanical immortality.

17
Self-organization

―――――――⟋⟍――――――――

SELF-ORGANIZATION IN THE NATURAL WORLD

The spontaneous emergence of order is a chief characteristic of life at all scales. Without some self-organizing principle it would take many times the age of the universe for chance alone to bring together the amino acids of our genetic machinery, let alone the hierarchies of higher plants and animals that amino acids' interaction with environment has produced. Self-organizing processes manifest themselves in virtually every aspect of nature and every branch of science. Snowflakes are spontaneously self-organized. Tropical storms and hurricanes are spontaneously self-organized. The organizing tendencies arising in complexity are easy to recognize and have a powerful intuitive appeal, but they represent phenomena that have been systematically studied only in recent years in terms of chaotic and feedback models. The recent recognition of the phenomenon of self-organization suggests we have ignored an important avenue to the nature of the physical world.

Living organisms depend on chemical organization, and the higher and more complex their organization, the lower is their entropy or tendency to equilibrium. In recent years more and more attention is being paid to recognition that chemical systems can spontaneously evolve to organized states.

Over time, natural systems tend to become, in varying degrees, more complicated and larger in size, scope, or throughput. To the degree that *self-organization* is predictable, it involves *development*, to the degree that it is not, it involves *evolution* or *individuation*. Importantly, some of the drive to change must come from within the system itself, so this is not a Newtonian idea. Since individuation is important, such systems can acquire agency, the capacity to act on their own.

Self-organization also appears to contradict the spirit if not the letter of the second law of thermodynamics. The second law describes entropy, the tendency of atoms and molecules to randomize themselves into a state of maximum disorder.

There are a number of human impulses that make the notion of self-organization attractive or disturbing, depending on your point of view. The idea that matter possesses an innate potential for pattern seeking—if it takes hold—might lead to a view of religion that would change the nature of Christian apologetics. (There is nothing about self-organization in Genesis.) For order to arise spontaneously out of chaos appears to contradict not only the second law but scripture, a potential challenge to the function of divinity and the nature of salvation.

Self-organization in evolutionary theory. The doctrine of natural selection describes one method of introducing order by the sifting out of rare useful mutations from myriads of useless mutations. There may be other self-ordering imperatives at work, such as what population biologists call genetic drift. There is a thesis that the complexity of organic systems arises not at the expense of increasing entropy, but because of it. Somehow in natural processes order emerges from randomness, a phenomenon by which —in the shadow of Darwin—other disciplines are momentarily transfixed.

In evolutionary theory natural selection produces myriads of genetic mutations, most of which are useless. The survival of the rare successful mutations generates a major—some would say the sole—source of order in biological systems. In a book on the physical basis of intelligent life, Dean E. Wooldridge has written:

> Relatively large organic molecules—carbohydrates, oils, nucleic acids—aggregated to form the first droplets in the primordial seas. The amount of high-molecular-weight material available for the formation of droplets was only a tiny fraction of the partially processed ingredients. [Sooner or later the process of *autocatalysis* appeared.] One of the products of the reaction stimulated by the catalyst is more of the catalyst itself ... droplets that started as inert bags of chemicals could slowly lead to structures with properties of growth, metabolism, and reproduction at least crudely similar to those exhibited by modern single-celled organisms. ... Some metabolic cycles must have been more efficient than others ... in the formation of catalytic molecules, accidental changes in their structure, or *mutations*, must subsequently have occurred. ... There is a name that is commonly applied to such a competition for a single source of raw materials among a number of self-aggrandizing chemical systems each of which is subject to small random changes affecting its rate of activity—it is called *evolution*.

Systems. If you want to believe in self-organization it helps to have a penchant for systems and systems thinking. Systems may be defined, according to von Bertalanffy (who, as the founder of systems theory, should know), as "a complex of interacting elements." The elements may be objects or processes operating at any level from the components of a chemical reaction, the arrangement of macromolecules in the organelle of a cell, the configuration of cells in an embryo, the organization of individuals in society, or the clustering of stars in a galaxy.

Systems theory. This theory holds that it is possible to reduce everything that occurs in natural or man-made worlds to certain mathematical properties common to every system. Biological systems are open systems, that is, they maintain themselves in a continuous exchange of matter with the environment. Some of the early impetus for systems theory came from attempts to establish parallels between physiological systems in biology and social systems in the social sciences. The self-regulating machine is the central metaphor in much systems thinking.

Dissipative structures. The work of Ilya Prigogine and others has led to a common language for the description of both living and nonliving systems. Dissipative structures are complex physical or chemical structures because, compared with the simpler structures they replace, they require more energy to sustain them.

PATTERNS OF ORGANIZATION

Artificial life is the study of quasi-biological systems including their construction and classification. Both natural life and artificial life are characterized by some degree of self-organization. In natural systems, matter apparently organizes itself; in artificial systems, matter organizes itself at the instigation of human agency.

The academic pursuit of the processes of self-organization—as manifest in either natural or robotic systems—is not sufficiently mature to tell us whether organizational patterns in the two are different or similar. Students of spontaneous organization are somewhat removed from the mainstream of biology. They derive their arguments from abstract mathematics and computer models with little claim to support from empirical data or laboratory experiment.

It is always the hope of proponents of artificial intelligence (AI) and artificial life (AL) that the development of quasi-biological systems will shed light—either by emulation or contrast—on our natural human capacities.

The primitive and spontaneous manifestation of order seems to be triggered implausibly without positing a self. The apostles of self-organization (whether natural or artificial) are oblivious of psyche.

18
Artificial life

————⌾————

MACHINES AS ORGANISMS

Artificial life is the study of man-made systems that exhibit behaviors characteristic of natural living systems. Artificial life uses computer technology to explore the dynamics of interacting information structures. The information structures explored may be biomechanical or nanotechnological (submicroscopic) or a combination of the two.

Artificial lifers assume implicitly that a pattern or logic of life can be abstracted within the computer. They conjecture that one way to study life is to try to make some of their own. The pursuit of this impulse flourishes at the Center for Nonlinear Studies at Los Alamos National Laboratory, where, at a recent conference, computer-automated life forms simulated flocking birds, schooling fish, and budding flowers. They found lifelike qualities emerging spontaneously—complexity arising unpredictably from simpler systems—arranging themselves in unprogrammed hierarchies. As a dedicated conference organizer put it, they found "essence arising out of matter but independent of it—the ghost in the machine."

Nonlinearity. As the title of the Los Alamos institute suggests, nonlinearity is a crucial feature of self-organizing systems. Nonlinearity is a mathematical term. Nonlinear equations express relations that are not strictly proportional. Linear equations are finite and can be illustrated on a straight line on a graph. Nonlinear equations are so complex and difficult that generally they cannot be solved; they cannot even be added together. Even the keenest proponents of artificial life concede that the difficulty of nonlinear mathematics provides an insight into why the mechanisms of life are so elusive.

Linear systems can be broken down into their component parts and subjected to separate analysis. Piecemeal solutions of the parts can be reassembled with no loss of integrity and provide a basis for the solution of the reassembled whole system. Nonlinear systems are not susceptible of analysis. They require the reverse of analysis, which is synthesis. Nonlinear parts are not susceptible to treatment in isolation. "The key feature of nonlinear systems is that their primary behaviors of interest are properties of the *interactions between parts*, rather than being properties of the parts themselves, and these interaction-based properties necessarily disappear when the parts are studied independently."

This is a phenomenon that can be expressed mathematically, albeit only with great difficulty. It is the property that R. Buckminster Fuller had in mind as the crucial feature of his system of geometry:

> **Synergy means behavior of integral, aggregate, whole systems unpredicted by behaviors of their components or any subassemblies of their components taken separately from the whole.**
>
> **Intuition and mind apprehend that which is comprehensively between, and not of, the parts.**

For Fuller, human access to the performance of wholes rather than parts is not available through physical models; such access requires the employment of the metaphysical instruments of intuition and mind. Practitioners of artificial life seek to employ nonlinear models and computer techniques in the study of the behaviors of whole organized systems. The pursuit of artificial life is inherently synergetic; it would be as misleading to consider artificial life studies as a branch of computer science as it would be to consider molecular biology as a branch of microscopy.

At the beginning of the 20th century biological processes were described exclusively in terms of exchanges involving matter and energy. By the end of the century a new element, *information*, was introduced into the equation. One cell of an organism recognizes another cell by reading the molecular signatures on membranes of adjacent cells. This is the essence of the immune process, the source of biological identity. The difference between being dead and being alive is coming increasingly to be seen as the ability to process information, a capacity that may no longer be the monopoly of biological systems. (One of the arguments that computers are like organisms arises from their apparent susceptibility to illness. Viruses can invade a community of computers in direct analogy to the viral plagues of humans.)

ARTIFICIALITY

Mechanics is the paradise of the mathematical sciences.
— *Leonardo da Vinci*, Notebooks

In our culture the word *artificial* tends to be pejorative. For Buckminster Fuller the term was not just distasteful but positively misleading.

> In my view there is no meaning to the word *artificial*. Man can only do what nature permits him to do. Man does not invent anything. He makes discoveries of principles operative in nature and often finds ways of generalizing those principles and reapplying them in surprise directions. That is called *invention*. But he does not do anything artificial. Nature has to permit it, and if nature permits it, it is natural.

There is naught which is unnatural. [*Education Automation*, 1961]

Even today, despite interim knowledge of fundamental development to the contrary, we speak erroneously of *artificial* materials, *synthetics* and so forth. The basis for this erroneous terminology is the notion that nature has certain things which we call natural, and everything else is "man-made," ergo artificial. But what one learns in chemistry is that nature wrote all the rules of structuring; man does not invent chemical structuring rules; he only discovers the rules. All the chemist can do is to find out what nature permits, and any substances that are thus developed or discovered are inherently *natural*. It is very important to remember that. [*Ideas and Integrities*, 1959]

I suspect that most practitioners of artificial life would not agree that the notion of synthetics is erroneous. For them, artificial life is life made by man rather than by nature. I think Fuller would resolve the apparent contradiction by merely restating the formula as: Artificial life is just another form of natural life permitted by nature through the agency of man. Fuller simply enlarged the definition of nature to include biochemical, biogenetic, and biomechanical artifacts of human manufacture.

ORGANIZING MATTER.

Induced complexity. The idea of artificial life seems so improbable, so oxymoronic, that it runs counter to all our intuitive notions of how life manifests itself physically. In real living creatures the atoms and molecules are organized in evolutionary patterns inherited from previous living complexes: they are made of soft squishy stuff, fluids, and colloids and membranes and cells articulating in physiological ensemble. Whereas the induced complexity of machinery employs the clamp and release of ratchets, the meshing of gears and cogs, the coil of springs and the trigger of escapements—all designed by human inventors to modulate and transmit energy with a minimum of lubrication. Electronic and computer devices are even more dehydrated, simulating lifelike complexity through relays and switches and hard dry communicating chips and disk drives, with subvisible electrical connections from one module to the next, and without benefit of physical muscles, nerves, gristle, or tendons . . . no flesh, no ichor, no serum, no lymph fluids, and no nourishing blood plasma.

Induced complexity aims at the articulation of energy and information—even cerebration—by mechanical devices designed by people. That the pursuit of artificial life is serious business is attested to by the fact that the U. S. Government is involved, most directly in laboratory programs at the Los Alamos National Laboratory, which was once the home of the Manhattan Project that created the A bomb, now operated by the Department of Energy as an arm of the government.

Artificial lifers start out with a working definition of life that may or may not be adequate. They posit an organized complex with the capacities to process matter and energy (i.e., to metabolize), to create replicas of themselves (i.e., reproduction), and to improve or at least modify their complex models (i.e., evolution). The literature in this field documents a variety of computer models that have simulated a combination of at least some of these capacities in a superficial way.

One of the problems with such model-making is how does the process arrive at autonomy? What is the robotic equivalent of a umbilical cord? Devotees of artificial life are confident that their inventions will develop independent integrities, eventually able to function without further human intervention . . . putting Faust and Frankenstein altogether out of business.

Spontaneous complexity. Other approaches start with a suspected tendency of matter to organize complexity by means of chemical and physical processes that remain to be discovered. This would be spontaneous complexity. Contemporary developments in chemistry and physics reveal increasing attention to an apparently inherent capacity of matter to organize itself: Hence, the new frontiers of fractals and chaos.

Von Neuman machines. That systems require a certain minimum degree of complexity in order to reproduce themselves is a principle introduced by the mathematical theorist John von Neuman with regard to computers. (The term *systems* in this case subsumes organisms and machinery under the same caption.) Von Neuman's principle with regard to computers seems equally apposite for organisms. But this usage proposes *reproduction* as the distinguishing characteristic of living organisms. Metabolism is the conversion of energy from the environment to preserve the integrity and growth of the organism. It is an equally important attribute of living creatures.

Up until now the dictum has been: "Machines produce; organisms reproduce." The time may come, in the not very distant future, when computers will exquisitely reproduce themselves—with error-correcting mechanisms comparable to the function of genes in the world of nature. They may even metabolize, drawing their own energy and information from the environment.

HUMAN INITIATION OF ARTIFICIAL LIFE

The prospect of artificial life lurks in the emerging technological landscape of the 21st century; it is the chief threat to the collective psyche of those of us who will be surviving from the 20th. Artificial intelligence, of sorts, is already here. The time scale for the appearance of artificial life is uncertain. When it comes, it may first appear as a toy or pet or slave; as it develops it may be symbiotic or commensal. If global climatic change makes life uncongenial for mammals, mechanical life may become the successor to organic life: the very vessels of our destiny—lifeboats of the *Titanic*—in an earthly scene reduced to artifacts and minerals and microbes. (With perhaps a few vestigial human beings reduced in turn to toys or pets or slaves?)

We have no idea how natural life originated. If artificial life is invented we will, for the first time, know how at least one kind of life can originate. (Not even the wildest science fiction suggests that artificial life could create itself—*ab initio* and in the first instance, making a gorgeous assembly from off-the-shelf components.) Artificial life is not inevitable; what is inevitable is that, if it occurs, it will do so only as a relic of human civilization.

For my generation it is much too early to speculate. We do not yet know whether there are aspects of human intelligence beyond the grasp of a computer. John Searle of the University of California at Berkeley stresses that computation does not equate with consciousness. No one has the slightest idea how electronic circuitry could evoke self-awareness. Searle argues that no computer has given rise to such mental phenomena as awareness, hope, pain, understanding, or intentionality. *Intentionality*—that's the ethical and psychological fly in the biomechanical ointment of artificial life.

Farewell, liquid carbon dreams: Hello, clanky silicon dreams. The essence of life is behavior, nature's way of knowing itself. Are we witnesses here to this ancient burden, the burden of knowing, being transferred from the animal kingdom to the mineral? Will sentient computers of the future summon symposia to consider that curious period in earth's history when information was stored on carbon molecules in a form of life called "real"?

What will be the destiny of computer beings? In the evolutionary context, natural selection has been a relentless—albeit ruthless—agency for directing the destiny of the creatures of earth.

In *Mind Children: The Future of Robot and Human Intelligence,* Hans Moravec documents his vision of the obsolescence of mankind. As computers become self-improving thinking machines, they will transform our world suddenly in an almost instantaneous revolution, producing a new generation of artificial minds comparable in scope to the billion-year evolution of human minds.

Fastened to a dying animal. Such is the human initiative: We are becoming the agents of our future irrelevance. The metaphor of the machine has a long history. The disappearence of human beings—superseded by computers— can be heralded as the birth of new kinds of awareness. William Butler Yeats foreshadowed that eternal life might come not through religious salvation but through man-made artifacts. Is this not what he is saying in "Sailing to Byzantium"?

> *. . . sick with desire*
> *And fastened to a dying animal*
> *. . . gather me*
> *Into the artifice of eternity.*
>
> *Once out of nature, I shall never take*
> *My bodily form from any natural thing . . .*

COGNITIVE SCIENCE

Human beings have a mental life. We don't know yet what kind of mental life computers might have. How is mental life to be explained? What is the best way to understand how we think, and how computers may come to think?

Psychology was invented to answer the question of how human intelligence can be measured and described, but it no longer searches alone. It has been joined, if not pushed out of the bed, by cognitive science, a term introduced in the late 1960s by H. Christopher Longuet-Higgins, who abandoned theoretical chemistry for the new field he christened. (Paternity for the discipline is also accorded to George Miller, who founded the Center for Cognitive Studies at

Harvard, bringing mathematics, linguistics, and engineering into consort with his initial career as a psychologist.)

Cognitive science is not a cohesive theory but a collection of related investigations into the human mind subsuming the following disciplines.

artifical intelligence (as a branch of computer science)
cognitive anthropology
linguistics
philosophy of mind
psychology

And some would add neuroscience or neurophysiology.

Two of the most common aspects of intelligence are also the most beyond the grasp of the disciplines most concerned. The terms *common sense* and *intuition* make psychologists as uncomfortable as philosophers. Neither function can be programmed into a computer. Common sense is as uncongenial to mechanical manipulations as simple motor-sensory activities such as grasping objects: It is easier to teach a computer to play expert chess than it is to teach it to move the pieces on the board. It took millions of years for us to learn how to see and hear and touch; we learned how to play chess only just yesterday.

19
Postbiology

———— ～ ————

Our old symbiosis with cereals will go on, and our new symbiosis with computers will develop.
—*L. Kowarski, 1966*

BIOMECHANICAL PROCESSES

Biological processes are enormously faster, more economical, and more versatile than mechanical ones. As Freeman Dyson describes it:

> **A skunk dies in a forest; within a few days an army of ants and beetles and bacteria goes to work, and after a few weeks barely a bone remains. An automobile dies and is taken to a junk yard; after ten years it is still there. Consider anything that our industrial machines can do, whether it is mining, chemical refining, material processing, building or scavenging; biological processes in the natural world do the same thing more efficiently, more quietly and usually more quickly.**

What Dyson says of biological processes in the physical—especially physiological—world applies quite differently to the world of mental processes. Some computer mechanical capacities are already greatly superior to human biological capacities. Human intelligence performs things computers can't do. Not just with intuition, common sense, imagination, and metaphor, but in intentionality and consciousness. Proponents of artificial intelligence say that computers can acquire these capacities or their virtual equivalents. Virtual mechanical equivalences of our mortal impulses? There is no question about the future more critical to human destiny.

John Searle holds that cognition is a biological phenomenon. For him thinking is practically a blood sport that can be engaged in only by a brain made of protoplasm and nourished by a respiring animal.

Wheels. Organic life at the macroscale does not roll, while in the mechanical realm wheels are ubiquitous. Buckminster Fuller muses that when the wheel really came into its own with the assembly lines of Detroit, most people did not recognize the other half of the invention. The other half of the invention was the road—the ratchet for the cogs—the highways built by politicians in response to popular pressures so that the conversion to an automotive era could become complete ... with trucks, vans, and mobile homes eventually being extruded by bridges and overpasses.

So far wheels have appeared in the physical world of our experience only through the indirect cultural evolution of nature through the agency of humans. The general superiority of wheels is overrated; in the narrow, winding streets of the casbah cars and wagons are no match for camels, burros, and porters. When we see life on other planets will there be wheels in the picture? And will they have evolved directly through chemical and organic evolution, or indirectly through some kind of deliberate and cultural manufacture? What is there about wheelness that seems uncongenial to organic processes?

Artificial photosynthesis. The presence of photosynthesis as a certain condition for the foundation of organic processes has already been compromised by advances on the biosynthetic frontier. Chemists at Arizona State University in Tempe have assembled a five-component molecular machine, or pentad, that harvests light energy and uses it to segregate positive and negative charges on opposite ends of the molecule. What they have done is to refine zinc-centered, electron-hungry molecules similar to those found in natural photosynthetic processes. They have the same capacity to store a large fraction of the light energy from the sun. They are an energy source to drive virtually any kind of chemical reaction. Future Popeyes may no longer have to eat spinach to get proteins.

THE TECHNOLOGICAL IMPERATIVE

So far, most of the complexities with which molecules are arranged in living organisms seem to be beyond simulation in the metal and silicon apparatus of today's computers. Even so, computers remain the heralds of artificial life. That science is on the verge of achieving protean transfers of capabilities from the natural world to an artificial one is a proposition that has advanced from conjecture to plausibility. Miniaturization, nanotechnology, and ephemeralization are already at hand; vulgar self-assembly, rude diversity, and even some kind of techno-evolution may be expected to follow.

Computers and information technology are inextricable. Together they have compromised the function of boundaries between nations. The piratability of software subverts our familiar, property-based economy of scarcity.

The French president François Mitterand has already confronted the trend in an arresting premonition, at a conference of 67 Nobel laureates at Elysée Palace January 18, 1988:

"Politicians should be modest when faced with the man of knowledge. Tomorrow will be less like today, because we are seeing a transfer of power from politics to science."

I think President Mitterand and I (and Buckminster

Fuller) are the only kids on the block who really believe that gradual transformation of our technological environment will make politics if not irrelevant at least less important, less all-consuming of good talent. Imperatives are not the sole prerogatives of natural evolution or cultural evolution. Ever since the Stone Age, we may have been, all along, captives, even happy captives, of the relentless pattern of improvements in technology.*

If we really entertain a technological imperative, if—God forbid—history ever becomes a scientific discipline, it will have to be something along these lines.

A POSTBIOLOGICAL WORLD?

Who is in charge in a postbiological world? "Plants don't really need brains," Margulis and Sagan tell us, "they borrow ours . . . We behave for them." Plants have been around on land longer than animals have, and they have tricked animals, especially mammals, into doing the one thing they cannot do for themselves: move. The central nervous systems of mammals have developed in ways to ensure the propagation of plants and the success of the botanicals. Will computer organisms ever co-opt human beings, in similar fashion, into doing those tasks they cannot do for themselves?

It is certain that computers will rapidly become ever more exquisite tools for the evolution of human life and society, and their advent will drastically affect the way humans behave. The present state of the literature on artificial life provides little more than a few hints on where the functions of intellect may find their ultimate home. This is a quite unpredictable process with its own imperatives for which the term "artificial intelligence" is totally inadequate.

* *The Neanderthals made beautiful tools stupidly almost without change for more than 60,000 years, but since then the rate of refinement of artifacts has increased by orders of magnitude.*

Lifelike computers may become independent beings with the prospect of a symbiosis between natural and artificial life in which computer beings and human beings might reciprocate with each other—no longer as tools but as symbionts—admitting computers into an irreversible dependence in the same way that plants (and animals that eat plants) have been admitted. Mammals, birds, and insects gave plants a new kind of interconnectedness; computers bring to human society an even more radical kind of interconnectedness. The question is not: Will computers ever think? In a postbiological world the question is: Will computers behave for us or will we behave for them?

Early zealots of AI have speculated that we would have to make computers sentimental about the past so they would retain us as interesting pets.

There is no doctrine relating to evolutionary biology—not even the anthropic principle—which suggests that we humans are the end product of evolution. Even though *Homo sapiens* has apparently evolved without a final cause or goal in view, the results are more than simply accidental; the range of genetic possibilities is not unlimited. Our development may have been improbable, but it occurred within limits of the possible.

The question of postbiology becomes not whether life can be reinvented, but whether life can be transferred to complex mechanical systems. The keenest of AI adherents, in anticipating that machines might take over as one of the vessels of evolution, do not appear to be proposing that the machines could have initiated the process without human intervention. If AI systems employ new life forms embodying chemical and mechanical interactions, biological paradigms would continue to apply even though drastically altered from the animal kingdom as we know it. If AI systems develop into purely electronic and mechanical complexes, drawing on energy sources without chemical interactions at the molecular level, then the term postbiology would seem to apply. Since we do not know how organic life began—either spontaneously or from galactic intervention—who can say that machine life is really dependent on human intervention? Human beings did not invent viruses, but we had a hand in the invention of computer viruses.

V

A FUNCTION FOR DEATH

———————❦———————

*H*ERE WE EXAMINE THE ROLE OF DEATH
in the cycles of nature and its reciprocity with the process
of birth. Logic but little solace is found in the view that a
world without death might be intolerable. A deathless
world would inhibit evolution, affront society, and un-
bearably strain the psyche of the individual.

We briefly consider the mechanics of the immortality
of the species and the ephemerality of the individual; the
near-death experience; the secularity of life, and the fragile
nature of dignity. The technological perpetuity of postbiology suggests a kind of sterile immortality.

20

Birth & death

———————— ❧ ————————

BIRTH & DEATH

The opposite of death is not life but birth.

To define death as the absence of life is simplistic, a failure to recognize death as an act and a process. The preponderance of the physical material world is not alive and is too remote from biological processes for life and death to have left their pattern of involvement. Death is not life's absence; it is life's price.

Birth is the antonym of death as the beginning is always prior to the end. The design is the substrate for the material. To put the matter more abstractly, conceptuality is prior to realization; the entity precedes annihilation. In evolutionary terms, genesis is prior to doomsday. Speaking psychologically, I the observer am prior to you the observed. (We may not know all that much about *me*, but we know even less about *you*.)

Dead means much more than inert and lifeless. Dead means *having lived*; it means having been born, having been conceived in seed or womb. In the remains of death survive traces of structure and arrangement, the mineral debris of the once lively patterns of former organic excitement. The entropy and disorder of death echo the syntropy and order of life. Birth and death are complementary, since one does not occur without the inevitable involvement of the other; they are opposite functions unified through reciprocity.

Visceral functions are intimately involved in birth as they are in death. The life of human beings begins in the bursting of membranes, and as many a firsthand witness can attest, life ends with a relaxation of the sphincters. But birth is more of an event *in life* than is death; in birth awareness is congruent with the visceral, but death is beyond that, not lived through, a facet of our experience that lies in principle beyond our reach. Thus it is infelicitous that there is only a passive predicate for birth: *being born*, while there is an active verb, a gerund, *dying*, for death. Dynamic processes deserve a wider verbal range than stasis.

The loam and compost of death beget life. Aging and death here engender birth and growth elsewhere.

Although most of the matter in the world is inanimate, much of it may have been transformed or modified by organic processes in the past. The deposits of iron in the earth were driven there by bacteria; the seams of coal were laid there by vegetation. Death is meaningless except in reference to an organism that was recently or patently alive. A dead moon is one thing, a dead Caesar another. Lifelessness has no nuances; death has many.

Death makes it possible for life to feed furiously on life. The importance of death is that it takes living things and puts the valuable material of their bodies where it can become part of other animals. Of course the most efficient way of doing this is to be devoured. Joseph G. Hoffman explains:

> **The intense craving for living matter gives one answer to the question: What is life? It is: Life is recurrent; it comes and goes rapidly.**
>
> **Living things have an enormous capacity for taking up organic material and with it renewing their living bodies. The cells of the body individually take up the special molecules they need to grow and multiply fast. To offset the shortness of life, living matter grows furiously.**

The definition of death involves as many elements of conjecture—even to philosophers and theologians—as does the definition of life at the occasion of birth. (See Chapter 8, "Quickening.") The doctrine of metempsychosis includes the argument that life before birth is quite as valid as life after death. It is attractive to consider death as the opposite of birth, for having been born is the only sure prerequisite for dying.

The birth process. In all primate species females experience pain during the birth process. But human mothers labor longer than other female primates and virtually always require assistance during delivery. Human infants are less fully developed and therefore more physically dependent than other primate infants. In the evolution of the species *Homo sapiens* the advent of bipedalism reduced the size and elasticity of the human pelvis; this and the greater encephalization of the infant combined to make delivery more difficult. Birth and death are both ordeals; they are concomitants, equally necessary for the fulfillment of life.

Though birth and its indicators come as a surprise, the prospect is usually a welcome one. Not so with death; the concession that death is necessary for fulfillment is more than disagreeable, it is a notion dismissed by the healthy psyche. Hints of mortality are a hovering burden on the dailiness of life. Where is the consolation in the view that death is an inherent consequence of propagation? The dilemma may be what Søren Kierkegaard was hinting at in his pronouncement that "Life can only be understood backwards but it must be lived forwards."

There exists in classic mythology a view that man's destiny requires more than a guardian of birth and death; it enshrines the idea of a custodian of the span of life measuring the interval in which our consciousness is embodied as persons. One Fate for birth and one for death is augmented by a third Fate, Lachesis, presiding over that brief time between our baptism and our obituary. In the three-fate system of the Greeks and Romans—the Moirae and Parcae—lifespan was admitted as part of a triad of which birth and death were the anchors. They are all old women spinning. Clotho presiding over birth draws from her distaff the thread of life. Lachesis is the Fate who spins its thread and determines its length. It is the duty of Atropos, the eldest of the three, to sever the thread. Even in this system life is not the antonym of death: The role of Lachesis is reduced to an actuarial one, that of referee and timekeeper.

Every individual person feels that his or her *self* had a start in time—whether the moment of fertilization, conception, first movement of the fetus, or some other equally arbitrary point. So it is also inconceivable (*le mot juste*) that the individual shall not also have a stop in time. There is as much uncertainty about the moment of personal death as there is about the moment of personal birth. There are unresolved ambiguities at both terminals of a lifespan. Many of the arguments advanced for therapeutic abortion apply also to euthanasia.

Discontinuity. Our conscious and unconscious mental life is bracketed by various kinds of discontinuity. The discontinuity between life and death is the only break that is ultimate, irrevocable—a disconnection beyond all mendability. The other mental fractures work at the threshold of consciousness. That between our prenatal and our postnatal existence is an irreversible event occurring only once in a lifetime. Less traumatic are the recurrent interruptions between sleeping and waking. (Dreams were for Byron the heralds of eternity.) Most benign of all are the overlapping phases of forgetfulness and remembering. And yet, forgetting and sleeping and prenatal intuitions may afford us the best hints we have, the only glimpses accessible, of what it was like before we were born and of what it will be like to be dead.

EVOLUTIONARY ROLE OF DEATH

Old men must die, or the world would grow mouldy.
—Tennyson

A species whose individuals were immortal would exhaust its possibilities for future evolution as soon as its numbers saturated all the ecological niches suitable for its way of life. Death is a necessary condition for the trying out of new genetic combinations in later generations.

The total genetic constitution of an organism is called the *genotype*. The totality of characteristics of an individual is called the *phenotype*. Phenotypic features develop under the combined influences of the genetic constitution of the individual and its environment. The proteins form the phenotype of an organism. Clearly, aging and death are a property of the phenotype. The genotype and germ line cells are in principle immortal.

Life is continuous; life does not begin anew with each generation; it is only the identity of the individual that begins with birth and ends with death. According to Clifford Grobstein, an authority on human fertilization:

> ... there is no question that life is continuous between generations and does not begin anew in each. Egg and sperm are alive, as is their fusion product. New life out of nonlife has not been created on earth for at least some three billion years. All organisms are continuous living descendants from earlier ones. It is not life that begins in each human generation, it is self.

Old worn-out citizens. Almost all organisms die without having reproduced. They may not bear but they were born. Fecundity is not guaranteed, only death is. Rodney Cotterill gives us a picture of social discards:

> There are ... similarities in the way societies and multicellular organisms subordinate the individual to the point

of dispensability. A nation survives the death of any citizen, however prominent, and a mature organism hardly seems to notice the replacement of its individual cells. Moreover, it now appears that the collective structure has a vested interest in the mortality of its members; the multicellular organism follows a policy of programmed death, and a steady turnover increases the chance of a favorable mutation. This too might have its social counterpart; what happens to individual members after they have procreated is of minor importance, and old worn-out citizens are replaced by young individuals.

The phrase *old worn-out citizens* encapsulates our unrelenting biological predicament. We feel with confidence that our mental life would flourish indefinitely if it were not for the capricious physiology of its containment. Proteins perish; only the genes survive.

For the individual human being, life starts at awareness and stops at the loss of self. Life does not begin at conception; it does not begin at any particular level of cell division; it does not begin at forty; it may have its first intimations of awareness in utero. Life does not start or stop; individuals capture a fragment of the ensemble to hold in custody for a generation. The particular generation is not even of one's own choosing: it is ordained by others in loving trust or wanton rape.

Illness diminishes our sense of person, and with death that sense is lost altogether. Life ends when all the biological organization to supply blood to the brain disintegrates. Thus commences the irrevocable loss of self. Nothing survives of self except in memory of friends and overlapping contemporaries—and the occasional legacy of one's acts to posterity.

When the body dies the living processes at the gross level of the person disintegrate and transform as the living processes of bacterial and fungal microorganisms take over. The putrefaction—the decomposition of all the beautifully folded proteins—that ensues is very much a living process, sometimes only deferred by embalming or other conventions of burial.

21
Proclivities of death
———————— ❧ ————————

Et in Circadia ego
> *—adopted from a classic tomb inscription:
> not just in Arcadia, but even in life's dai-
> liness, there am I, Death*

The most universal and mundane of all human crises is
death, known to be inevitable, and yet infrequent enough
in the average face-to-face community to be a shock when
it does happen. Life identifies with motion and dynamics;
death with stillness and stasis. But dying is a process of
gradual transition, not a quantum fault line: As death approaches, ". . . enzymes cease to function, the high-velocity,
specifically biological processes slow down and become submerged in the sea of background chemistry, and the system
loses its kinetic identity."

A loss of kinetic identity in a sea of background chemistry. Can a kinetic identity—what Buckminster Fuller calls
a pattern integrity—survive if it is no longer physically
manifest? Did a pattern integrity come into existence independent of the atoms and molecules that become its scaffold? We can be preoccupied with such questions, if we want
to, as the survival of consciousness after death, but in the
present state of affairs we have no reason to look to science
for an answer.

The cold gradations of decay. The legal and medical
aspects of the subject do not afford a basis for satisfactory
philosophical definitions; they are arbitrary determinations

that attempt to reconcile pragmatic questions of everyday living with an intractable and elusive continuum of an ever-receding physical threshold into sleep, syncope, and death.

> **To the eye of science, nature is a continuum, and man, like everything else, is part of a process. . . . and we have lately become aware that death is a process too. The medical difficulty of deciding whether a person is dead has long been known; what has more recently become appreciated is that the problem lies not merely in the interpretation of symptoms, but in deciding what we mean by death. It is said that an animal begins to die when it begins to live, because its recuperative power dwindles gradually with age. But the problem of drawing a line in 'the cold gradations of decay' appears in cruder form when medical means are used to revive the heart.**
>
> **Is it death in law when the heart stops beating? If so, there can be life on this earth after death. But perhaps death is only when the heart stops beating beyond the known limit of medical recall. On this view, we cannot tell whether a man is dead or merely in a state of suspended animation, until such time has elapsed as puts revivification out of the question. But such a definition would introduce some indeterminacy into the time of death. [Glanville Williams, *The Sanctity of Life and the Criminal Law*, 1957]**

Every human being has a unique genome—the sum of all the different genes in an organism (a cell's compendium of genetic information). But the structure of that genome does not disintegrate when a person stops breathing or when brain activity ceases. The molecules of an individual's DNA can be extricated from a no-longer-living body, and under certain conditions they can be replicated. Not just immediately after death, but successful cloning has been effected from DNA relics extracted from an Egyptian mummy. If this surviving DNA is not alive, it is at least a persistent structure of information—an instruction, a pattern integrity?—with some important attributes of life. This whole phenomenon, in fact, has prompted some reexamination of the practice of cremation, with the thought that the procedure might perhaps be supplemented with a sample of the individual's DNA sealed in a test tube, as a hostage to some future time when biotechnology may permit the laboratory resurrection of at least a certain prototype of an individual's traits.

Here is Friedrich Cramer's description of the death function in genetic terms:

> **I shall speak about death as an inherent limitation to the system life. . . .**
>
> **The role of errors in protein synthesis is [not] obvious. . . . Death is a catastrophic event in a network system in which a limit cycle or the system of limit cycles can no longer be kept up. . . . Death and life are symmetrical. . . .**
>
> **Death is a final consequence of the limitation to chemistry which in its more complicated structures is not error free. These limitations of the chemistry of life can be corrected by input of energy in principle. Death could be postponed with a large input of energy, immortality be reached through infinite input of energy. This, however, would not be in the interest of life so far as the genotype is concerned. What must be preserved is not the phenotype but the genotype. The genotype must be propagated.**
>
> **Therefore, for the required continuation of the genotype the phenotype must be sacrificed sooner or later and it depends on the living conditions of the particular species what is the most advantageous life span for that purpose.**

What happens to us, as individuals, when we die? Does our consciousness in any way survive? (This is the central problem at the heart of all religions.) There are, according to Dr. Arthur S. Berger, Director of the International Institute for the Study of Death (Pembroke Pines, Florida), three commonly held views of what happens at death. His formulation is clinically objective, and purged of philosophical or ethical bias. None of the three views is easy to embrace, because all of them involve confronting the meaning of life. Most normal people do not welcome confrontations in general, and they usually have a series of infallible stratagems to ensure serenity by avoiding this confrontation in particular.

The first has been called the finalistic view. "When you're dead, you're dead." Death is as final as the decomposition of our physical body. Consciousness cannot survive independently of the brain and nervous system in which it dwelt. This purely physiological consideration is reinforced by a philosophical one: How could a postmortem person without a physical body and without sense organs reacting to the environment be anything but radically different from the antemortem person we think we are? The finalistic view invites personal reactions ranging from courage to stoicism to repression of all idea of death. (If you prefer to believe in survival, you have two choices, as follows.)

Second is the natural continuance view, which adopts the hope for endurance beyond the grave. In its weakest form this view entertains at least some kind of psychological continuance, as in the surviving artifacts of our diaries, the art we may have created, videotapes, life insurance and photographs, not to mention good works and the fond regard of survivors. If we have children, there is a survival of the characteristics of our genes in our descendants. In its strongest form the view considers the psychic evidence of near-death and out-of-body experiences, and even sustains the hope that death may be just a springboard for another kind of abstract noncorporeal survival.

Third is what Dr. Berger calls belief in personal continuance, belief in a soul, belief that the individual personally survives physical death either indefinitely or for an infinite time, with all its memories and intellectual capacities intact. The argument was put forward by Plato in *Phaedo*: The soul is freed by death and exists by itself apart—like a tune that exists after the harp and the strings on which it is played have been destroyed. In religious terms, the notion of personal continuance could take the discarnate form of Buddhism, the reincarnation of Hindu philosophy or the resurrection of Christian doctrine. Many liberal Christians do not believe that their physical bodies will literally be raised from the dead, but that their souls will enjoy a disembodied state to be called back at some future time in a resurrected life of the spirit.

It is a modern paradox that death is more mysterious in a scientific age than ever before.

It is our common modern belief that life is separated from death by a one-way bridge. Our most sentimental playwright, J.M. Barrie, must have been trying to put the best possible face on the matter when he had Wendy tell Peter Pan the way to get to Neverland—"Second to the right and straight on till morning."

CELL DEATH: HOW DOES THE CELL KNOW?

Apoptosis: falling leaves in autumn. When a tiny embryo first develops feet and hands they start out like little paddles and later differentiate into fingers and toes. As the digits begin to develop the cells that were between them die off; they are deleted by a process called *apoptosis*. It describes the elimination of superfluous tissue or neurons during early stages of development. Almost everywhere that cell growth takes place, so too does cell death. Apoptosis comes from the Greek word for the falling away of leaves and it is applied in cell biology to the falling away of cells from the organism when their time is up.

Chlorophyll is the agent of photosynthesis; it traps the energy of sunlight, and its pigment makes the tree leaves green. Every autumn this chlorophyll rapidly degrades itself as the tree leaves slowly wither and fall to the ground. It produces one of the most spectacular displays of color in nature. Orbiting satellites record and advancing wave of green turning to yellow, gold, and red, dramatically changing the appearance of the planet from outer space. Once the process starts it advances from the polar regions to the temperate zones at a rate of about 50 miles a day. In two to three weeks the destruction is complete. Globally, over a billion tons of chlorophyll destroys itself to make way for new seasons and new generations.

Programmed cell death. In mammals nearly all normal cells seem to cease dividing after a certain finite number of divisions. Cells taken from a mature animal and grown in a laboratory will divide a fewer number of times in a culture than the same cells taken from a younger animal. Individual cells will also take progressively longer to go through the cycle of divisions until eventually the entire population stops dividing and dies. This phenomenon is known as *programmed cell death*, and it is seen as a possible safeguard against unbridled cell proliferation if cells should escape from the normal constraints on cell division. The programming of cells to die appears to be crucial to the normal development of the organism

The definition of death at the level of the cell is probably as obscure and elusive as the definition of death of the organism as a whole. Cells may die because they are damaged, infected, or old. What triggers destruction rather than repair? Is cell death suicide or murder? There are scavenger cells that police the communal existence among body cells. And there may be also triggers for cell death by chemical signals from the internal environment of the body. But many cells seem to bear directions, ancient inherited signals, for their death when their continued survival no longer bears a useful purpose for the organism as a whole.

In the tissues of complex animals like mammals the multitudinous teeming activity of cells is dominated by death. One of the reasons that the brain generates such a huge number of nerve cells during gestation and infancy is because such a huge number of them—up to 70 percent—die during development. New cells are made each day in an orderly way because others die at their appointed time. There is no mutual destruction according to the law of the jungle. The organism would self-destruct if cell death were not the normal course of events. The absolute certainty of cell death is as important as life itself. On the whole, cells seem to perish more by suicide than by defeat in combat.

Is it not paradoxical that cancer cells and germ cells are the only two mammalian cell types known that avoid the inevitability of death? The biologist Joseph G. Hoffman explains:

> **Organisms exhibit the stochastic probability of spontaneous death when the normalizing tendencies fail. In fact, spontaneous death is completely explicable by the laws of physics and nature; while the spontaneous origin of life—the opposite confluence of improbabilities—has so far proved completely contrary to the laws of physics and nature.**

Parts of us begin to die long before we are born. Gills and tails and body fur are unassembled. Cells and tissues replace one another in a sustained dynamic process.

Marantology. Dr. William D. Poe of Duke University has proposed a new medical specialty to be called *marantology*. It is from the Greek word *marantos*, meaning "withered, faded, turned, as leaves become withered in autumn." The purpose of this medical specialty would be to provide peace, comfort, and relief rather than heroic measures to prolong the lives of medically hopeless patients. There is an analogy to the harvest.

PROXIMATE CAUSES OF DEATH

No dog likes to die in the presence of human beings or under anybody's bed. It is a profound instinct which makes it just want to die alone and not with all its relatives around the bed. It is probable that a dog would kill itself to avoid the kind of death it abhors.
—James Thurber, Selected Letters

The literature of death, thanatology, asserts that human beings alone among all living creatures know that they have to die. But ask any dog owner: the dog may not be aware of his ultimate fate, but when his time comes he usually betrays more than an inkling. Most mammals, indeed most vertebrates, get gradually weaker as they get older and they get killed. Only people, pets, and creatures in zoos die natural deaths. What man calls natural death seldom occurs in nature.

Death always catches us by surprise. Even when we are participants in the certain doom of the terminally ill, even if the doctor has said two days at most or 20 minutes, we are still shocked.

The proximate causes of death are the nearest and most immediate occasions that prevent the organism from continuing to function. In the days before antibiotics pneumonia was the old patient's friend ... an opportunist infection seizing on debility. Cigarette smoking and lung cancer may be the ultimate causes of a demise; but suffocation (lack of a sufficient supply of air to the lungs) is the proximate cause as the inevitable course of illness plays itself out. In AIDS it is often the scourge of Kaposi's sarcoma, a cancer rarely acquired until the epidemic of immune deficiency. Ultimate causes of death are as manifold as the variety of individuals. But the proximate causes are critical interventions, much more limited in range, and they appear to be integral aspects of the life process itself.

Proximate causes. Death in its proximate occurrence has only three possible causes:

- respiratory failure or asphyxia (as in choking, strangulation, or paralysis);
- circulatory failure or syncope (from shock, hemorrhage, or heart failure);
- breakdown of the nervous system or coma (due to brain injury, poisons, or drugs).

And none of the three causes has any immediately apparent or characteristic external symptoms. This is what brings suspense to postmortems. (The word autopsy comes as a crazy misnomer; from its derivation it means "seen by oneself," while it describes a situation in which observation is uniquely dependent on others.)

Death also presents itself in a matter of degree. Clinical death occurs with the cessation of vital functions, the brain and the eyes deteriorate in a matter of minutes while hair and nails continue to grow and the liver can go on making glucose for up to three days. Absolute death comes only with the breakdown of the cells producing those functions. The act of cremation converts clinical death to absolute death with all loss of cellular or genetic individuality.

Natural causes. In summary, there are five main causes of natural death:

- disease;
- devouring (being eaten by predators);
- inadvertent genetic mistakes (misfits, deformities, and cancerous malignancies);
- senescence (rare in the animal world except in zoos; rare among men until the age of modern medicine);
- accidents (floods, storms, falling off cliffs, and automobile accidents).

There is a fallacy in dividing the causes of death between the natural and the unnatural. Coroner's offices and medical examiners deal with unnatural death. But in fact violent death, predatory death—even cannibalism—are natural in their social and evolutionary context. If nature permits it and society allows for it, it is natural.

Considering all organisms in the gross, the desire of life to feed on life is the main cause of death in the living world. For modern human beings, accidents and the vulnerability of the body at the cellular level are the main causes of death

Cancer research continues to shed an indirect light on the process of cell death, but the underlying processes still remain a mystery. Among the mechanisms suggested by recent research are an accumulation of epigenetic error; that is, errors in the control of gene expression, "silent epigenetic defects" that appear only after a given period of time or a given number of cell divisions.

Illness in the form of heart disease, pneumonia, or cancer is the main cause of death in the elderly. And when the aging don't die of heart disease or infection, it simply means that they have lived long enough to get cancer—not an infectious disease, but a form of misgrowth—commonly of the generative organs in women and the prostate in men.

If we cured all disease and malignancy, would we be prepared for the concomitant increase in death by accident, drug abuse, and suicide? It could be argued that in a world without disease the options for the individual would marginally improve. Nevertheless, at any given time quite a few of us are waiting for some close friend or relative to be released by death from a situation in which illness has a much more likely incidence than accident, drug abuse, or suicide.

Sudden death. The certificates of death issued by the Chief Medical Examiner of New York City provide for only three forms of unnatural death: suicide, homicide, or accident. The police formula fails to cover:

- capital punishment; execution; death penalty;
- abortion at full term;
- euthanasia (induced termination of life);
- cannibalism.

Premeditation. In a recent homicide case handled by the Prince William County prosecutor Paul B. Ebert, the northern Virginia medical examiner, James C. Beyer, estimated that the victim took three to five minutes to die as she was being strangled. The defendant in the trial said that the murder was not premeditated. The prosecutor gave this account of his address to the jury: "I stopped my final argument and let the jury look at the clock for three minutes . . . It seemed an eternity, I think it helped get first degree murder . . . the defendant had enough time to stop and think about what he was doing."

SENESCENCE & AGING

Senility, like drunkenness, bothers beholders more than the possessor.
                    —John Updike, Self-Consciousness, 1989

Of course, you and I are merely senescent. Only *they* are senile. You and I may forget names; they forget who they are.

Senescence is a complex biological process, a reduction in the body's capacity for self-maintenance and self-repair, that begins even before birth; the *Encyclopaedia Britannica* makes the arresting assertion that senescence begins with conception . . . a stark way of saying that faculties deteriorate inexorably with age. Physiological aging is such a systematic and predictable process that it appears as deeply programmatic in character as physiological development . . . manifesting concurrent and overlapping patterns framed by birth and death.

As it gets older the human body tires more easily. In an aperçu delivered when he had reached the age of 80, West German Chancellor Konrad Adenauer said, "all parts of the human body get tired eventually—except the tongue." I am sure he was being more then facetious; the observation seems literally true.

Senescence is the condition of a system that has come to rely more on habits than on random impulse or open inquiry. As a consequence one's overt behavior tends to become more disorderly and less appropriate to external conditions. Both physiologically and psychologically senescence is characterized by a decrease in redundancy and an increase in vulnerability; every source of deterioration increases the likelihood of dying. The individual, however, is somewhat insulated from the bleakness of the situation because he knows that the incidence of vulnerability is statistical in character and not predictable for any particular person in the dailiness of life. Inside every fat man lives a thin one: Inside every old man lives a young one.

Time, as individually experienced, varies with a person's age. After the age of 40 the years go by a little faster, in the 50s they begin to zip along, and in the 60s they accelerate even more. After the age of 70, years seem as ephemeral as months; days seem to fill themselves with routine; between brushing the teeth in the morning and putting the cat out at night there's barely time for events to register and accumulate. I thought it was a very modern sentiment to say that 40 is the old age of youth, and 50 the youth of old age. I guess it is fairly modern—it's from Victor Hugo.*

The well-written obituary is one of the few art forms that flourish in the shadow of aging and death. Most of us as adults read only the occasional obituary of a friend or relative. But in middle age, and especially after a severe or life-threatening illness, a morbid interest in the genre sometimes takes over, and some of us read all obituaries everywhere with a relish known only to survivors.

W. H. Thorpe in his book *Biology and the Nature of Man* recalls Lear's lament that ripeness is all.

It is common knowledge that in some physical and physiological respects man is at his peak of performance in his twenties or early thirties and that by that time the deterioration of senescence has already begun. So it is with some mental qualities; mathematical genius is often at its highest at about the same age, reaching a peak which can never later be surpassed or even equalled. Other mental qualities may,

---

* Victor Hugo had a feeling for time even at the cosmic scale. He once wrote: "Where the telescope ends, the microscope begins. Who is to say of the two, which is the grander view?"

of course, mature much later. But it remains a fact that, in some respects, we can be said to be dying slowly from the age of 30. And this senescence affects the same qualities which seem to be the very core of the personality, creating a problem in connection with the belief in immortality which the theologian should not ignore.

The twilight years. After three score years and ten people are, actuarially speaking, living on borrowed time. People from 70 to 90 years old have peculiar dreams and vigors. In the increasing shadow of death many of them can muster a capacity for living with a renewed intensity. In the words of a medical school professor:

> Every aging person experiences, sooner or later, at least some decline in some of his powers. But the subject is a touchy one, and those who speak of it openly are not likely to win any popularity contests. It is an unhappy fact that the elderly are an increasing burden on society, as people live longer and as the aged constitute an ever-larger proportion of the population. The problem is psychological as well as economic; as the elderly require, through no fault of their own, a growing share of society's resources, they draw down on themselves an inevitable, if sometimes camouflaged, resentment.

Between 1900 and 1990, due to dramatic improvements in living conditions in the United States, life expectancy at birth rose from 47.9 years to 74.9 years. Life expectancy has now reached an apparent plateau at 75 years. Geriatricians tell us that even the conquest of cancer and heart disease would increase average life expectancy by no more than five years. We have it on the authority of the executive director of the American Aging Association that: "Conventional billion-dollar disease research to further decrease premature deaths is becoming progressively more futile, thanks to limits imposed not by disease, but by the mysterious, inexorable, universal, and subtle phenomenon we call aging."

The functional life span. Whatever its biological causes, senescence is innately a part of the natural order of things. We should think twice before seeking a cure for aging. There is no cure, but perhaps advances in medical research may lead to some retardation of the aging process and a consequent extension of our functional life span, "functional" meaning the capacity to live active and productive lives. Mere extension of life span is without merit unless accompanied by a deferment of impairment and deterioration, what doctors call deficits. For biotechnology to extend the traditional life span beyond 70 years promises a cure that might be worse than the disease.

DISEASE

Disease may not be as final and quantifiable as death in the evolutionary scheme, but it still has its uses. The history of medical progress shows that we understand how the healthy body works only, or at least chiefly, from studying its pathologies. Some leading biologists suggest that disease may have a larger destiny than just providing an avenue to understanding of physiological processes. Disease may have its own imperatives at the cellular and molecular levels. "The upsurge of molecular diseases, whether cellular, subviral, or viral, is apparently the consequence of a molecular tendency toward an escape from cellular control, toward autonomy." (André Lwoff, *Biological Order*, 1968.)

Molecular biologists provide us with an unexpected scientific rationale for the brash suggestion that life is a disease of matter (see page 69). Contagious diseases are strictly another phase of the general form of death, which follows from the desire of life to prey on life.

Disease is the failure of the normal physiological systems due to external factors or breakdown. The major categories of diseases are:

genetic	traumatic
infectious	degenerative
allergic	cancerous
nutritional	mental

Affliction. Beckett in his book on Proust, where the themes are time, repetition, and habit, invokes "the poisonous ingenuity of time in the science of affliction." For Bertolt Brecht also, the protraction of disease is worse than quick death, and so it was logical for Brecht to ask: "Why murder a man, when you can employ him?"

Brain damage. There are degrees of brain damage. A *coma* is a sleeplike state in which breathing is impaired and many reflexes are absent; it usually lasts only a matter of weeks. In *brain death*, the brain stem cannot function, so that the body cannot regulate the heart, kidneys, lungs, or intestines. Machines can continue those functions for a varying but limited period of time. *A persistent vegetative state* is a condition of permanent brain damage, a more severe neurological disability than brain death or coma.

Hospitals. The hospital is the one place where it is most difficult to pretend anymore; the hospital is the place where life most cruelly falls short of its ideal. "Dying is a misunderstanding you have to get straightened out before you go," in the words penned by the literary critic Anatole Broyard from his confinement in a hospital bed with cancer of the prostate: "It may not be dying we fear so much," he adds "but the diminished self."

EXTINCTION

If an intelligent being had been able to study the world of, say, the Jurassic or Cretaceous without knowledge of what was to follow, he would have had as much reason as we have now to think that evolution had exhausted all possibilities.

—*George Gaylord Simpson,*
The Meaning of Evolution, *1949*

Furbish's lousewort. This is an herb that grows along the banks of rivers; it is dependent for its nutriment on the roots of other plants, making it technically an obligate hemiparasite, and practically difficult to cultivate in the home garden. Its seeds are not produced until the plants are at least three years old. Though there are over 500 species of lousewort throughout the Northern Hemisphere—they obviously thrive—their processes of pollination and germination are far from well understood. Their survival appears to depend on the steepness of the riverbanks and their progress seems to depend on recurrent bank cave-ins caused by the periodic scouring of river ice. They are among the large number of plants facing extinction, but to dig up specimens and grow them in botanical gardens would require the most elaborate mechanisms to duplicate the conditions of their natural habitat.

The point is that it would be simpler to protect the natural habitat than to attempt to re-create it. However useful botanic gardens are for research and education, their potential as a strategy for preserving endangered species is very limited. And the same is true of zoos; according to a recent report of the New York Zoological Society, if zoos were expected to maintain viable populations of the animals they keep, existing worldwide capacity of zoos would allow for maintenance of no more than 900 species. And there are an estimated 5 to 10 million animal species on earth.

Rates of extinction. There are more extinct species than there are species that survive today. All the extinct species number perhaps 1,000 times all those alive today. Extinction is the eventual destiny of all species.

The familiar evolutionary concept to the layman is that organisms undergo gradual modification into ever more successful forms until the species succumbs to (1) competition from another species; (2) environmental disaster; or (3) some unspecified form of "racial senescence," diminution of the species from some kind of internal imperatives. It is the last alternative that has only recently come into recognition.

Extinction is the motor of species evolution. Without it, there could be no development. To take one of the most spectacular examples, had it not been for the disappearance of the dinosaurs, mammals would not have been able to inherit the earth. Dinosaurs were not inherently inferior to mammals, losing out in evolutionary competition; they were simply less lucky in being able to avoid extinction.

A fisheries expert recently pointed out that fish are the only wild animals that are caught commercially for food because all the other animals have been domesticated. . . . commercial exploitation of wild fish will have vanished by the year 2020 . . . it is said that all seafood will be grown in mariculture.

By saying that all other animals except fish have been domesticated, I don't mean that they are all captured by husbandry or battery processes. Animals preserved for game or for sentimental reasons or even as specimens of diversity (in the wild or in zoos) are effectively domesticated when they are protected from unregulated exploitation. For instance, in such big horse-breeding states as Florida, there are many more horses now than there were at the peak of their employment in agriculture and transportation.

SEX & DEATH

Consider Sexual Organization and hide thee in the dust.
—*William Blake,* Jerusalem

That epigraph from Blake is a puritanical one, and it is not clear whether thee or Thee should hide in the dust. Whether the blame attaches to us or the Deity, the link between sex and shame is inescapable. The link between sex and death is less so, but also as a macabre inevitability.

From the point of view of guaranteeing the success of evolutionary processes, the two most important inventions of nature are sex and death. The rationale for sex is found in the origin of species. By introducing randomness into the process of reproduction, sex makes speciation possible. About 1,000 million years ago the first eukaryotic (nucleated) cells adapted by gathering into one bound package (the nucleus) as much DNA as possible. They abandoned the self-dividing tactics of their prokaryotic ancestors, which survive today as one-celled bacteria.

Sex means having a meiotic reproductive system in which each parent donates a cell containing half a set of chromosomes. The alternative is to reproduce by dividing: it is an alternative that ordains immortality. The obverse side of the coin is that sex means death. As soon as sexuality arises death becomes obligatory.

Francois Jacob gives us this picture of the reciprocity of sex and death:

The other necessary condition for the very possibility of evolution is death. Not death from without, as the result of some accident; but death from within, as a necessity prescribed from the egg onward by the genetic program itself.

[There is] an equilibrium between sexual effectiveness on one hand, with its cortege of gestation, care and training; and the disappearance of the generation that has completed its role in reproduction on the other.

Most single-celled creatures are never born, and they neither age nor die in the usual sense. When it is ready, an amoeba simply splits in two. One half turns right and the other half left, and soon the halves are fully grown and ready to split in two again. Living in near solitude, the prokaryotic bacteria resort to the various techniques of transduction, lysogenation, or conjugation. The price they pay is the absence of identity, but as compensation the single-cell creature attains a kind of immortality. There is never a moment at which one can say that the first amoeba has passed away. In a sense, the original amoeba, the Adam of the amoebae, though billions of years old is among us still.

Birds and bees do not have it so easy. For them, reproduction can be life's most difficult mission. Sex requires two unions, one right after the other. First a male and female must meet. Then a sperm and an egg must meet. Neither rendezvous is easy to arrange. Nevertheless, creatures of the multinucleated eukaryotic superkingdom, having once tasted the pleasures of individuality, pursue it feverishly unto this day.

For the biologist sex is technically nothing more than the recombination of separate sets of genes. But the story of the pain and extravagance involved in the origin of sex and its maintenance in animal societies causes few of its beneficiaries to question that the game is more than worth the candle and more than adequate compensation for the amoeba's complacency.

ORGANIC DEBRIS

Photosynthesis is generally considered the most important chemical reaction on earth. It is the chief biological regulator of the effect of sunlight on the atmosphere—a process in which the oxygen and carbon cycles intersect. The agent of photosynthesis is chlorophyll, the substance that makes leaves green, that captures solar energy and stores it in the form of chemical bonds in sugar molecules, and that thus becomes directly or indirectly the source of energy for almost all living things. As preprogrammed leaves disassemble, their chlorophyll machinery, seeds, roots, and tubers salvage and store still useful carbohydrates. Rancidity, decay, and entropy are all pathways to the destruction that breaks down the bonds of chlorophyll and degrades them into LMWCCs—low-molecular-weight colorless compounds. Chlorophylls thus have an inherent and programmed instability. The same process occurs in the oceans, where algae and other zooplankton undergo a comparable seasonal metamorphosis.

Fragments of life. The varying remnants of life discerned in the geological debris of nature illustrate how the organic merges into the inorganic in an almost imperceptibly fading continuum, from fossil skeleton and fly in amber to the faintest traces of pollen in seams of coal. Materials that once were living show that these fragments were a part of life. There are, among the igneous and sedimentary and composite mineral deposits, certain biological artifacts— such as perhaps a diamond—in which the carbon constituents might be too remote to trace as to their organic or interstellar origins. But vast amounts of once-organic matter on the earth can be considered a rich and unique testament to life, beyond the reach of archaeobiology. The debris and excrement and waste of living things provide nourishment, and the fragments of life in middens are not irreversibly defunct.

No single species could persist alone on the planet. It would eventually exhaust all the nutrients and have no way of converting its waste products into food; it would die. One species subsists on the detritus and excreta of the next. There is no such thing as waste in nature. Even those acres of seagull-haunted garbage landfills in the Jersey flats succumb in time to organic processes. Everything is eventually recycled.

The living process of cells does something to matter. . . . In practically every aspect of the world, new growth is enhanced by the presence of any former part of a living being. François Jacob describes the process as a continuum:

Whether born of a seed or a foetus, each living body has once been part of a similar body. Before acquiring autonomy, be-

fore becoming in its turn the seat of an independent life, each organism has first shared the life of another organism from which it has subsequently become detached.

Autumn and spring. Speaking ecologically, autumn may be less celebrated but just as essential to the biotic drama as spring. The importance of marshes—wetlands in the terminology of the nature conservation movements— is suggested in an arresting passage of an epidemiologist's otherwise so often tedious book:

With us, in the same modern world in which we cultivate what we call art and science, our almost ultimate ancestors, the Protozoa and bacteria, have survived. The bacteria particularly (nearest of all recognizable cells to the stem of living things) are still more important than we. Omnipresent in infinite varieties, they perform fermentations and putrefactions by which they release the carbon and nitrogen held in the dead bodies of plants and animals which would—without bacteria and yeasts—remain locked up forever in useless combinations, removed forever as further sources of energy and synthesis. Incessantly busy in swamp and field, these minute benefactors release the frozen elements and return them to the common stock, so that they may pass through other cycles as parts of other living bodies. Some of them correct the excessive enthusiasms of their too thorough brethren, which break down nitrogenous substances to free nitrogen. In the soil and in the root tubercles of clover, peas, and other legumes, bacteria are busy fixing into complexes ready for revitalization. Without the bacteria to maintain the continuities of the cycles of carbon and nitrogen between plants and animals, all life would eventually cease, plants would have no nitrates and no carbon dioxide with which to grow, cows would have no clover to eat, men would have no beef and vegetables. Without them, the physical world would become a storehouse of well-preserved dead specimens of its

past flora and fauna. [Hans Zinsser, *Rats, Lice, and History*, 1934]

As Robert Burns once celebrated lice, we need more poets to celebrate fermentations and putrefactions. Tidings of compost and joy.

22

Immortality

To dwell on the presumed bliss of immortality has always been the chief solace for the bleak prospect of death's inevitability. Immortality is the doctrine that our soul or personality survives the death of the body. It can take two forms: in temporal immortality the individual mind continues after death indefinitely; in eternal immortality the soul ascends to a higher plane of timelessness.

But the concept of personal immortality is rife with contradictions and philosophical absurdities. The Struldbrugs in Swift's *Gulliver's Travels* could not die; they just went on getting weaker, despised, and ignored. The Wandering Jew was unable to grow old and die. Ludwig Wittgenstein gives us the suggestion that the only way in which the notion of immortality can acquire a meaning is through one's feeling that one has duties from which one cannot be released even by death. This is a theme that persists in novels, theater, and opera, particularly as the maternal imperative.

Immortality can bring no solace without meaning. For Heidegger, the essence of being human was the capacity of the individual consciousness to integrate past, present, and future in a single unity. For Oswald Spengler, in *Decline of the West*, centuries of European civilization were authenticated by the clock towers of their churches, but Heidegger rejects that image, asserting that the public time of clocks on towers is possessed by no man, and is therefore meaningless. Only the life span of a single individual with a sense of beginning and an end can have meaning. Man is above all a creature of possibilities, and the future is the direction in which all possibility lies. And since the future, for Heidegger, is wholly an invention of the individual mind, there can be no sense of an immortality beyond an individual's life span.

Heidegger was an apostle of the sterile cause of existentialism. But he provided us with a rationale for the view that endless being, like endless time, would eliminate meaning and purpose.

W. H. Thorpe, a professor of animal behavior at Cambridge University, presents another sombre aspect of immortality:

> **Now man's mind as studied by the biologist and the psychologist is essentially anticipatory. As a corollary of this it becomes quickly habituated to the familiar. Hence in this aspect mind is conceivable only in a temporal world. So if eternity were attained where all knowledge and all beings simultaneously are present, where—to quote Boethius— "unending life is possessed all at once in its completeness," nothing could be left for the mind of man save pure ecstasy of contemplation. . . .**

With or without the vision of immortality, I have never been able in thinking about death to muster any hint of ecstasy. Nor have I ever had a friend who evinced the remotest vocation for death. Resignation yes; vocation no. Such solaces appear only in literature. Thoreau tried to teach us to see "human existence as the finding of ecstasy in the knowledge of loss." Where are his companions in that vista?

The *Nunc Dimittus* is one of the most dramatic elements in the liturgy of Christian worship. The words that Simeon speaks to Jesus (Luke 2:29) are "Now lettest Thou (thy servant) depart." Simeon was privileged; unlike most of the rest of us, he was satisfied that he had finally seen the Messiah and therefore he could depart in peace. To "sing *nunc dimittus*" is to express a readiness to depart or die. The grave awakens no terror for those who have the certainty of eternal life. Hope is not enough; *nunc dimittus* is no comfort to the skeptic.

For those of us who are not Simeons, for those of us preoccupied with the *self*, death is a finite, an irreversible quantum event, indeed a catastrophe at the brink of doom and the abyss of perdition. For the species, however, the death of the individual is an insignificant event in the continuum of life. Try as I might, I have found no way to reword this sentiment—*nunc dimittus*: the species survives—so it might become a comforting inscription on a wall of the waiting room at New York's Memorial Sloan-Kettering Cancer Center, often a refuge of last resort for those of us stricken with irreversible malignancies.

A secular alternative to *nunc dimittus* is *taedium vitae*, nowhere more poignantly expressed than by Schopenhauer. In his pessimistic thesis of the boredom of life he cited card-playing as a kill-time device. To one of his austere temperament, pastimes were "quite peculiarly an indication of the miserable side of humanity." That mortals should desire immortality, and yet find difficulty in passing an afternoon—well, if you have a fancy for paradoxes, there's a pretty one.

When the holy fathers of the Church promised immortality it became the chief currency of the Church in commanding a following among the faithful. If the Christian doctrine of eternal life means anything it means that every individual human being is going to live forever. But what the founders did not know—what Byzantium did not know, what the medieval scholastics did not know—is the modern view that *infinity is the enemy of any system*. Absolute symmetry is ideal—beyond the grasp of any physically realized body.

In the world of nature, only the genotype and germ line are in principle immortal. Postbiology is technological. Technology flourishes only in a finite universe. The prospective transformation of consciousness from the vessel of the organic human body to the computer program of organometallic artifice renders immortality of the individual irrelevant ... poignant, but irrelevant. On the day when man makes himself immortal he makes himself extinct.

The metaphysical poet had it all wrong. "One short sleep past, we wake eternally, / And death shall be no more; death, thou shalt die." (John Donne, *Divine Poems X*.) The only way for death to die is for birth to die first.

Einstein, writing in his 1931 essay "The World as I see It," said, "I cannot conceive of a God who rewards and punishes its creatures, or has a will of the kind we experience in ourselves. Neither can I nor would I want to conceive of an individual that survives his physical death." When Einstein died on 18 April 1955, he mumbled his final words in German to an uncomprehending attendant ... "Is there not a certain satisfaction in the fact that natural limits are set to the life of the individual, so that at its conclusion it may appear as a work of art?"

At the age of 90 Will Durant, the most popular American philosopher and historian of his time, completed (with his wife Ariel) the eleventh volume of his monumental *Story of Civilization*. Two years before his death at the age of 96 he made a statement about death and how close it seemed to him:

Life might be unforgiveable if it were not for death. Suppose you live forever. Not only would you be useless to everyone around you but you'd be sick and tired of being what you are. The thought you'd not be allowed to die would be a horrible thought. Has it ever occurred to you that death is a blessing?

It must be a lot easier to feel that way after you've hit 90.

NEAR-DEATH EXPERIENCES

There is a continuing serious interest, by no means all occult or fringy, in the study of what is called the near-death experience or NDE: a person's vivid memory of sights, sounds, and sensations when he or she is clinically dying or very close to the point of no return. It is a temporary exiting of the self from the body, a period of disembodied hovering about.

People who have been revived from apparent death report a structured set of experiences. The accumulation of these documentary accounts provides some remarkable indications of what may lie beyond the grave, though they are not quantifiably measurable in any scientific way. There is no easy methodology of observation at hand, but the recurring patterns common to so many reports of firsthand recollections at the threshold of death suggest a universal pattern that may provide some kind of insight, if not to salvation, at least to some unrecognized capacities of consciousness and the brain.

Those who have testified on the NDE experience claim that it is *not* dreamlike and *not* fantasizing; rather it is hyper-real. NDE phenomena include what is called "the out-of-body experience," an apparent return from beyond.

Dr. Kenneth Ring, a professor of psychology at the University of Connecticut, on the basis of interviews with more than 100 cases of people who had come close to death through accidents or illness or attempts at suicide, has identified five phases of NDE:

- an unexpected feeling of peace;
- a sense of separation from the body;
- an entrance into darkness (sometimes experienced as a tunnel);
- entering into the area of lightness; and
- a return (often with reluctance) to the body.

Note that those five phases may permit but *do not require* an ultimate destination outside the body. Heaven may or may not be involved.

Those who have studied NDE maintain that it is relevant to but not proof of life after death or the survival of consciousness. Most of those who have experienced NDE attest that it is accompanied by a riveting, pervading sense of personal identity. And some who have undergone the NDE say that they have as a result lost all fear of death.

The NDE also invokes a vision of the reciprocity of birth and death. An almost universal aspect of the NDE— the "tunnel experience"—calls up the one experience we all share, birth. The coincidence of the tunnel and the birth canal suggest to many observers the reliving of one's birth. In fact, Carol Zaleski in her book *Otherworld Journeys* describes parturition as the converse of the NDE: "Being born is like dying from a previous existence—for the child and the mother too."

There exists a *Journal of Near-Death Studies,* which is the official organ of the Institute for the Advancement of Near-Death Studies (IANDS). It is devoted to study of the empirical effects and theoretical implications of such phenomena as the tunnel experience (reality or hallucination?), the out-of-body experience, and the deathbed visions of dying persons.

23
The secularity of life &
death

———————⟨≈⟩———————

SECULARITY OF LIFE

We live in a culture that all too easily invokes the sanctity
of life and all too easily vilifies anything violating that doctrine from capital punishment to vivisection. The trouble
with the notion of *sanctity* is that it has no familiar opposite, no easy antithesis. Certainly not diabolic, not an
atrocity, but the simple notion of the laic or secular seems
insufficient to the occasion. The bureaucrats can anticipate
age-adjusted genocide.

Sanctity & profanity. A belief in the sanctity of life is
deeply embedded in our culture and system of law. It is
violently defended by the right-to-lifers—so much so that
opponents of abortion have been maneuvered (sometimes
to their dismay) into opposition to capital punishment—if
only to demonstrate the purity of their view that all human
life is sacred. Anthony Dyson, a professor of theology at the
University of Manchester, suggests that many Christians
are so threatened by the increasing incursions of the secular
world on things sacred that they feel "an overwhelming
compulsion to identify *one* position . . . at which the believers can stand firm and which opponents cannot seize."
Thus, "the coming together of sperm and ovum is main-

tained as a point of indecipherable mystery, overriding any kind of scientific account or any kind of . . . philosophical objections."

In 1984—the year of George Orwell's portentous rendezvous with destiny—Governor Richard D. Lamm of Colorado in the heat of a televised debate pronounced an extraordinary program of nothing less than geriatricide. What he said was that people who are old and sick "have a duty to die and get out of the way." He was making respectable in human society a practice familiar in animal husbandry: culling the herd so the species can flourish. Governor Lamm was 48 years old at the time.

In view of the earth's population explosion, writes Lewis Thomas, "We will have to give up the notion that death is a catastrophe, or avoidable, or even strange. We will need to learn more about the cycling of life into the rest of the system. . . ."

As the 20th century draws to a close, environmental (economic and social) factors will cause the sanctity doctrines to be reexamined. When the nation has over 90 million people above the age of 65, the drain on our resources will become so apparent that no remedy will remain unexplored. The opposite of sanctity is profanity. May we not anticipate that, on the purely pragmatic grounds of managing a society with shrinking resources and according equity to the working generation, sheer pragmatism may invoke a doctrine of the Profanity or Disposability of life. That life—human life—is not sacred introduces a secularity as profound as that introduced by Darwin in evolution's challenge to the certainties of God.

Life can be sacred; being alive—at the brink of moldiness—is not necessarily so. Dignity attaches not to the body but to the mind.

Longevity & ephemerality. May flies (*Drosophila melanogaster*) live only four hours, which is one reason they are so coveted for laboratory experimentation: generations can be crowded into a single weekend. But how much difference would it really make to the fly if its career were to be curtailed at three hours or extended to five?

Neither should human life expectancy—or at least the psychological consequences—be reckoned in arbitrary decades. What is one decade more or less—calculated at the particle or cosmic scale? When I go to the dentist to get a tooth filled, I try to persuade myself that the pain is small because my tooth is a small part of a small creature on a small planet in a small solar system in a small galaxy in the edge of one of many Milky Ways, and so on. This strategy is only partly successful in anodyne effect: it is mostly just a distraction, but I go through with it anyway.

Seen from the minuscule rather than the cosmic, we glimpse at the elemental level another vista of our life span that equally boggles the mind. Consider for instance the innate resonance of a two-atom molecule of iodine. Typically it vibrates at 10^{-13} seconds and rotates at 10^{-10} seconds. (These are fundamental motions that characterize chemical reaction and bonding.) With femtosecond laser techniques it is now possible to freeze-frame these motions (the vibrations are a thousand times faster than the rotations) in real time. Consider also that a photographer has to use a shutter speed of one-thousandth of a second or less to snap a clear picture of a sprinter in a 100-yard dash, whereas our laser is acting at 10-quadrillionths of a second. A femtosecond is to a second as a second is to roughly 32 million years.

Worrying about whether we are going to live for a life span of 45 years or 75 years seems terribly important at our particular temporal niche. But, measured in multiples of laser-pulsed femtoseconds or in fractions of astronomical light-years, the biblical allotment of three score years and ten becomes devoid of all significance.

The role of medicine. It is an agreeable prospect in our society that the individual has not only a claim to life but an obligation to live out his normal span of the days that nature allots him. All cultures concede that life has its natural limit, say three score years and ten, or longer for those endowed with exceptional good health. Once a natural limit has been reached, the individual's claim to life is diminished, as is also his obligation to acquit himself for the allotted number of days. Death can take more than one form—natural or unnatural—and it is in society's interest to foster the former and avoid the latter.

This kind of rational view of death as a release, however, is not easily accommodated within the institutions of medical care, geared as they are to regard death as an implacable and dangerous foe: death not as friend but as enemy. In the United States medical priorities, at the expenses of such social needs as education and housing, have commanded more research and institutional resources than should rationally be spent. Our health care system should be directed more to preventive medicine and caring than to curing at all cost.

In a bureaucracy seeking to conquer all disease, what role is left for *dignity?*

VI

THE RANGE OF
BIOLOGY

*T*HE CHEMISTRY OF LIFE IS IN APPARENT
*harmony with the material and energetic composition of
the rest of the universe. Although most elements play no
role in plant and animal species, those few that do seem
to get recirculated in organic systems once they have been
caught up in them.*

*In Part VI, after discussing the circulation of atoms in
the natural world, we consider the tiny cell and the vast
biosphere as polar paradigms of the unity of life. Hierarchical organizations are innate in the world of nature,
whereas names and classifications appear to be imposed
by man. This is the given background in which the disciplines and doctrines of biological science are discussed—
without neglecting their ambiguities and limitations.*

*A brief review of research frontiers in biology con-
cludes with some tentative speculations of what new
knowledge natural science might bring to bear on the perennial questions about the evolution of life and in particular the extent to which biology can be expected to shed
light on man's destiny.*

24
The abundance of the elements

━━━━━━━━━━━━⟋⟍⟍⟋━━━━━━━━━━━━

Living in a material world
And I'm a material girl. . . .

—*Pop star Madonna*

WE ARE STARDUST

The history of astrophysics and of particle physics attests that every atom in our body—as indeed every atom on earth—has already passed through particle, galactic, stellar, planetary, and chemical evolution. It is not just galaxies, stars, and planets, but subatomic *particles* that have all evolved. It is not us but the matter we are made of that has come from so far away and so long ago. The scientific name for the process is *stellar nucleosynthesis*.

The analysis of high-energy radiations from supernova 1987A confirms the theory of stellar nucleosynthesis: that exploding stars do indeed synthesize new atoms of the higher elements, generating their energy by fusing lighter elements into heavier ones, hydrogen into helium, helium into carbon and oxygen, which are further fused into the heavier elements magnesium, silicon, sulfur, and calcium, with the cycle normally ending with iron. As William Fowler, a physicist studying supernova 1987A, put it, "Each one of us and all of us are truly and literally a little bit of star dust."

So much for the atoms themselves; but there is no such accounting for how the atoms have managed to arrange themselves into molecules and the complex patterns that trap matter in living organisms.

Unexplained origins. These series of galactic and stellar evolutions do nothing to explain how life arose: they account only for the existence of a material world as science knows it—a material world in which life arose as an apparently uninvited guest. Attempts to explain how living organisms arose spontaneously from nonliving matter are called theories of *abiogenesis* or *biopoiesis*, but they are only theories. The only thing we know for sure is the limited and not very useful doctrine of *biogenesis*—that the living organisms we have been able to observe appear to have arisen from previous organisms. Hmm.

The enormous advances of biological science in this century have shed little light on the question of how the primordial elements arranged themselves into their concurrent botanical and zoological patterns of organization. Ninety-four percent of the weight of our bodies, including the iron in our blood and the calcium in our bones, is constituted of just four atoms: oxygen, silicon, aluminum, and iron. We know only that none of the atoms man is made of originated here on earth, that all of them were created by the nuclear explosions within stars, and that they arrived on earth from elsewhere in the cosmos.

CIRCULATION OF ATOMS AND MOLECULES AMONG THE KINGDOMS

There are some facts thrust upon us that, no matter how true, nevertheless register in our consciousness as bizarre. Most of us are just as happy not knowing, for instance, about the concentrations of bacteria at either end of our alimentary canal. What is it? . . . something like a million bacteria, or a million bacteria per square centimeter, in our mouth?

And a similar concentration of *Escherichia coli* at the other end? For normal people these facts cause no undue preoccupation. We read about them from time to time—as in old Listerine ads—but we soon forget. We put morbidity out of business by making certain kinds of unpleasant knowledge a minuscule fraction of our waking consciousness.

A couple of decades ago I read an item about the migration of atoms in the earth's atmosphere, more specifically the provenance of the atoms in the next breath you take, that I still find fascinating but disturbing and difficult to accept at face value. I don't think about it all the time, but I have hung on all these years to the clipped quotation from an article in *Scientific American* of September 1970:

> **the earth's atmosphere is so thoroughly mixed and so rapidly recycled through the biosphere that the next breath you inhale will contain atoms exhaled by Jesus at Gethsemane and by Adolf Hitler at Munich. It will also contain atoms of radioactive strontium 90 and iodine 131 from atomic explosions and gases from the chimneys and exhaust pipes of the world.**

Why do they tell me this about my *next* breath and not my last one? (I would rather have just expelled an atom associated with Hitler than just be anticipating its ingestion.) One of the authors of that statement, Dr. Preston Cloud, is a leading paleontologist, a founder of the discipline of geobiology, and the man who wrote the article on the atmosphere in the *Encyclopaedia Britannica*. He would not lie to us; he would not even exaggerate.

But the bald statement still seems implausible; so much so that I have never been able to quote it convincingly from memory; I could never look someone in the eye and muster to the assertion any tone of conviction. It makes human beings out to be just so many random processors of the atmosphere. This must have been what Walt Whitman was anticipating in the strained syntax of "Leaves of

Grass.": "for every atom belonging to me as good belongs to you."

What we are dealing with here is not an analogy or a metaphor, but an explicit statement of fact. So savor your next breath, and remember that atoms from those radioactive gases are not lethal if they are insufficiently concentrated, and dwell on those atoms that might have been exhaled by Joan of Arc and Charles Lindbergh rather than by Nero and Spiro Agnew.

The biologist Joseph G. Hoffman observes that once matter falls into the organic trap it tends to stay there:

> **The preying of life on life leads to a cyclic effect in that the atoms that make up a particular piece of living matter may find themselves going from one animal to another continuously. . . . Once caught up in the network of living matter, atoms are apt to find themselves within living things for a long time. It can readily be calculated that many atoms today became enmeshed in living matter many hundreds of years ago, and may stay there for many more years.**

Turnover of molecules. Every cubic centimeter of air contains some 10^{19} molecules. Here is their pattern of circulation as described by a chemist, Dr. William F. Kieffer:

> **Imagine . . . that you could take a glass full of water from the ocean, and by some means paint the molecules purple so that they could be identified if you found them again. Then toss your glass full of purple molecules back into the ocean and allow them to mix completely with all the waters of the globe. Then take a second glass full of water from the ocean and look for purple molecules. You would find about 200! There are 200 times as many molecules in a glass of water as there are glasses of water in the world! Another analogy is this. If each molecule of water in a typical snowball were magnified to be the size of a pea, there would be enough snow to blanket the whole surface of the earth to a depth about equal to the height of the Eiffel Tower.**

The time span of our human memory is often a matter of years or tens of years. But whatever molecular mechanism is involved in memory, the molecules themselves are ephemeral—only the patterns persist. We have it on the authority of Francis Crick that, with the exception of DNA, almost all the molecules in our bodies turn over in a matter of days, weeks, or at the most a few months.

BIOMASS

Wordsworth told us an awful lot about nature but he didn't know a thing about biomass. The England of his generation simply did not have the statistical tools to measure our environment in a manner at once more subtle and more gross than those accessible to the poet. *Biomass* is a synthetic word conjured up by ecologists who apparently could find for their macro abstractions no better roots in the Indo-European tongue.

Biomass is our home away from home, the niche we share willy-nilly with other creatures and vegetation in that fragile envelope of earth's thin atmosphere. Statistical incursions into this realm rob us of the kind of access poets have to nature through naïveté and intuition. Statistics may not rob us of such feelings, but they at least tend to compromise them. We turn again to our chemist friend William F. Kieffer:

> Living matter is a specialized form of matter. There is much less of it. An estimate is that the mass of living organisms is about one-billionth of the entire mass of the earth, about 7×10^{21} tons.
>
> Just how small a part of the whole system is represented by living things is revealed by the estimate that the total mass of things alive in this world is about 10^{19} grams. . . . The fraction of the total life on the planet that is *human* life is even more minuscule.

The soil and rocks of the earth have accumulated a mass of formerly living sedimentary compounds. All the oil and coal and many minerals came indirectly from photosynthetic and chemosynthetic (largely bacterial) processes. These rich soils and rocks contain the debris of organic matter, or formerly organic matter, and they are orders of magnitude larger by volume and weight than the total mass of living biota at any given moment.

Considerations of biomass are not directly available to our senses; they are abstract constructs of sophisticated ecological measurement. Such large-scale observations confront us with dizzying statistics and ratios unfamiliar in the dailiness of our lives. For instance, we have in this book discussed human beings and we have discussed ants, and some temperamental and social comparisons between the two. But consider ants and people in terms of biomass—as the weight of organisms per unit of volume in a given habitat. Traditionally one-third of the biomass has been in the form of social insects. The sociobiologist E. O. Wilson tells us that now that there are over five billion humans, the total weight of humans on earth equals the total weight of ants for the first time in history. (And he thinks that's a big mistake for the prospects of human survival.)

Here are some other gross figures, most of them in one way or another disturbing to Wordsworth's still, sad music of humanity, and our natural sense of the fitness of things:

- An ecologist at the National Center for Atmospheric Research in Boulder gives us a picture of how many termites there are in the world—he estimates perhaps as many as half a ton's worth for every human being on earth.
- Microbiologists estimate that 20 times the present biomass exists in the form of bacteria as exists in the form of animals.
- Each of our intestinal tracts contains more *Escherichia coli* bacteria than the earth houses people.

- From whales weighing up to 150 tons to microscopic plankton, the biomass of the oceans is thought to exceed that of the whole human race.
- Almost all biomass is made up of six elements: carbon, hydrogen, nitrogen, oxygen, phosphorus, and sulfur.
- Over 90 percent of the earth's biomass is contributed by plants.
- Wood fuel is the main source of domestic energy for half the world's population.
- Throughout history a total of 7,000 kinds of plants have been grown or gathered as food. Of these, 20 species provide 90 percent of the world's food, and just three species—wheat, maize, and rice—supply more than half.
- Bacteria in the guts of cows and termites are the chief source of methane in the world's atmosphere. (James Lovelock tells us that termites and trees—generating oxygen and carbon dioxide—together help keep the world just right for the maintenance of life.)
- 65–90 percent of all living matter is water.
- It takes about 108,000 cattle a day to supply the grocery stores and restaurants of the United States.
- It has been calculated that the combined weight of earth's insects is 12 times greater than that of its human population.
- Current population of earth: There are now more people alive than all those who have lived before added together.

And two observations having as much to do with species classification as with biomass:

- In terms of the number of species they comprise, vertebrates are only about 5 percent of the animal kingdom. The remaining 95 percent consists of animals without backbones.
- As much as one-third of tropical biomass circulates through ants and termites, but there are only six people [taxonomists] in the world capable of classifying them.

25
The cell as a unit of life

PROTOPLASM

The theory of protoplasm was a 19th-century concept. In 1861 Max Schultze revived the Greek word for "first created thing" and employed it to designate what we now call *cytoplasm*, that part of the cell outside of the nucleus. That Thomas Huxley celebrated protoplasm as "the physical basis of life" is a textbook cliché. Ernst Haeckel, in his search for a bridge between inorganic and organic nature, speculated about the properties of the primitive slime— *Urschleim*—as "naked protoplasm." The interest in protoplasm as a colloidal gel was reinforced by optical illusions resulting from the light microscope, but this was only the last gasp of a tendency "to identify life with a particular substance as the locus of a vital activity."

The introduction of the electron microscope and the application of X-ray crystallography to the mysteries of cellular organization revealed a kind of structural orderliness of metabolic processes far removed from primordial slime and colloidal associations with water. The term *protoplasm* refers now only to the gel-like sap of cells, and textbooks now refer to it as cytoplasm. For the past few decades the extraordinary attention paid to the genetic modeling of

RNA and DNA molecules has focused popular interest in their residence in the nucleus with a tendency to dismiss the rest of the cell as so much boring irrelevance. This is far from the case; the entire cell structure including its organelles and membrane contribute in complex but essential ways to its metabolic functioning.

Nucleus and membrane. The physicist Lancelot Law Whyte asserted in 1947 that "the nucleus is the region of undifferentiated multiplication characteristic only of the species, the membrane is the differentiated boundary linking the cell with other differentiated cells and with the environment, and the cytoplasm is the field of interplay of hereditary and environmental factors." That is an arresting paradigm, but—except for the crystallographer Cyril Stanley Smith—I cannot find that it has been much dwelt upon by later authorities. Smith wrote of nucleus and membrane in an even higher level of generalization:

> **Everything in the universe consists of something surrounded by a boundary and the conditions of the boundary determine whether or not the organism inside will thrive. If its boundary is too rigid and impermeable, the organism can't feed or breathe or excrete wastes—can't communicate effectively with the rest of the universe to function—it loses its identity. With amoebas and human beings, with stars and nation-states, even with atoms, boundary conditions are crucial.**

Limit cases. The cell appears to be the minimum and maximum theater in which the functions of life perform at the endosomatic level within living bodies and their parts. But cells and bodies don't function in isolation. The internal landscape depends upon an external one. The biosphere is likewise a minimum and maximum theater congenial to the manifestation of life in the gross at the exosomatic level of the environment.

CELL AS THE UNIT OF LIFE

Oversimplifications are inherently vulgar. The notion of the cell as a unit of life—like that of the word as a unit of thought—is an attempt to introduce units and unity into areas of consideration that have so far proved too complex and untidy to sustain them. Nevertheless, biological study has to begin at some point, and postulating the cell as a "unit of life" has attractions that are both logical and pedagogical, and there is a large body of literature (both textbooks and learned journals) and institutes of advanced research that employ the cell as the ultimate biological paradigm.

The analogy of cell and word has further resonances: They are alike in their awesome diversity. Cells are the fruition of millions of years of biological evolution; words are the instrument of a few thousands of years of cultural evolution. And while cells, some of them, can survive independently, as a single word can communicate without context (like the old IBM motto *Think*), neither cells nor words can acquire much meaning until associated in complex patterns with others of their kind. The British crystallographer Alan L. Mackay has come up with a powerful analogy of word and cell: "Words and meanings evolve together like DNA and proteins, and Grimm's law in linguistics has its molecular parallels." But the similarity is not without limits. We can discern certain processes of the mind and modes of speech that seem beyond the reach of words, but in the physical world of nature we know of no life without cells.

The starkest argument for considering the cell as an absolute limit case of organized matter comes to us from the physicist Lancelot Law Whyte, writing in 1949:

> The cell is . . . the only unit of biological organization which can multiply itself. No smaller unit can do so without the aid of a cell, and no more complex multicellular systems can do so, other than through single cells specially adapted

to this function. **No simpler and no more complex form of organization can multiply itself, because only the constituents of a single cell can spontaneously organize themselves. . . .**

The role of cells. The cell is a physical unit of life. We can even say that it is the primary unit of life. Under the right conditions cells are capable of independent reproduction—the smallest such capacity in nature. Cells can be produced only by other cells. *Omnis cellula e cellula.* ("Every cell from a cell" is the dictum.) We have no idea how the first cell was produced, and it appears quite possible that we never will.

All animals and plants are made up of cells. There are no exceptions. Some forms of life like bacteria may be nothing more than a single cell able to reproduce itself and metabolize. (Bacteria = germs = microbes = prokaryotes = Monera—in that they are all independent, single-celled organisms.) Animals and plants are built up of structural aggregations of specialized cells, but the cell itself remains the lowest common denominator of all forms of life.

The business of cells is the transformation of energy and the transmission of genetic instructions. Cells translate the information in the genes into biologically active molecules. Cells convert energy from the environment in order to survive, and they encode information in order to reproduce and regulate the design of the tissues and organs that they manufacture to become their host.

Cells have only two strategies available to maintain themselves: either the single-celled organism or the cooperative aggregation of a multicelled organism. Either way, they develop in accordance with the genetic blueprints each cell harbors within it. But cellular organelles and cilia exhibit remarkable capacities for regeneration and pattern regulation—even a capacity for structural inheritance—appearing to transcend strictly molecular (or genetic) instruction. A London anatomist, Dr. Lewis Wolpert, has even gone so far as to suggest that "underlying patterning in the single cell is a fundamental biological mechanism that has been taken over by multicellular organisms."

The growth of most organisms is caused not by the enlargement of their constituent cells but by the increase in their number. Each cell may be said to have a life of its own but only as a hostage to its role in the organism. The average cell in the pancreas is replaced every 24 hours; cells in the gut may be sloughed off to die after only a day or two; white blood cells stick around for a couple of weeks and red blood cells survive up to several months, while nerve cells may stay alive for a lifetime. Millions of cells die every day in the typical animal, but with a reproduction rate that results in no net loss in the cell population.

CELL THEORY

Except for the theory of evolution, biology is hard up for generalized laws, and the few others that it has (like the cell theory and central dogma of the sequence from genes to protein) do not sound very dramatic. The "cell theory" simply states that *all tissues are composed of cells*. There it is, stark and unvarnished; in its most expanded formulation one can say that a cell with its nucleus, cytoplasm, and cell membrane is the microscopic unit of which all plants and animals are composed.

That simple cell theory proposition is the basis for some of the most spectacular developments in modern biology. The theory forced the recognition that even the nervous system is cellular in nature. Cell theory alone has provided the insights for how organisms grow and develop, how diseases plague man, and how heredity perpetuates him. Before the cell theory it was thought that bodily structures simply grew like crystals or taffy or Topsy. The concept of the body as a multicellular organism provided the scientists with very fruitful access to the mechanics of life processes.

Conceptually the cell is the unit of two distinctly different categories of living systems: (1) it is the independent unicellular organism of the prokaryote kingdom of monera, and (2) it is the integral dependent unit of the multicellular world of the rest of the natural kingdoms including metazoa and man. "Long ago it became evident that the key to every biological problem must finally be sought in the cell, for every living organism is, or at some time has been, a cell."

Whole biological disciplines have grown up from devotion to different aspects of the cell as a unit of structure, or as a unit of function, or of development, or of physiology, or of heredity, or of disease or pathology, or of organization. Cells also possess duality; that is, their independent lives exist only within a higher form of life.

Among the consequences of the cell theory are the following propositions:

- Cells reproduce by division, or mitosis.
- Chromosomes double their number and segregate before mitosis.
- In complex organisms, sperm and egg fuse into one cell, the zygote.
- That complex zygote divides into 2, 4, 8, 16 cells and so on, so that each of the cells in the new organism bears the same genetic endowment.
- Though cells specialize to make up different tissues and perform different functions, they all carry out the same metabolic processes.
- They break down molecules to release energy and assemble more complex molecules like proteins.
- Cell membranes are not just barriers but play a dynamic role in the metabolic process.

Shelves groan with the volumes of all the hard-earned knowledge that has been recorded by cell biologists on every clause in the above catalogue of functions. High-technology enterprises engaged in genetic engineering abound along the freeways of our cities. With such accomplishments in mind it is hard to see why the proposition that tissues are made up of cells remains only a theory.

THE CENTRAL DOGMA

DNA is a strand of chemistry (a spiral of nucleic acid) designed to store information. It consists of a pair of long
chains of smaller molecules in an arrangement known as a
double helix. It is the master molecule of life because the
information in DNA tells each cell what features to develop
and what processes to engage in. The inescapable principle
involved is that *information has shape.* Information is not
a prisoner of the alphabet or mathematical notation or the
binary code. Biological information is inherent in the linear
sequence of aperiodic polymers (deoxyribonucleotides, ri-
bonucleotides, or amino acids).

Genetics—the mechanics of reproduction—involves
an additional type of nucleic acid called RNA. The development of biological organisms requires the translation of
genetic information stored in DNA through templates of
RNA into the creation of complex, three-dimensional protein molecules. The process is universally applicable to all
organisms from the humble *Escherichia coli* to people like
us.

In its simplest formulation: DNA makes RNA and
RNA makes protein. The transfer is not of substance but
only of information. And when James D. Watson and Francis Crick formulated these general principles in the years
1953–1955, they prescribed that the flow of information
was in one direction only from gene to protein: Once information has passed into protein it cannot get out again.
This is the *central dogma.*

I do not know enough chemistry to understand the
beautiful graphic depictions of nucleotide sequences in the
textbooks. Suffice it to say that somehow they manage to
achieve morphogenesis, the translation from a three-letter
genetic code to a three-dimensional organism. The mechanisms of genetics also give the central dogma its meaning
and resonance, as anticipated in the germ-plasm theory or
the Weissman hypothesis.

August Weismann was a professor of zoology at the

University of Freiburg in 1885 when he was among the first to conclude that Lamarck was wrong—that acquired characteristics are not transmitted to progeny after all. He proposed that organisms have two basically different parts. One part is the stuff of heredity and survives from generation to generation; the other part makes up the main body of the individual organism and is destined to die. What makes up the body of an organism he called the *soma* or *somatoplasm*, while the property of inheritance resides in the *germ cells* or *germ plasm*. Although he knew nothing of DNA, Weismann located the germ plasm in the nucleus of the cell.

This theory prevails today except we use the terms *chromosomes*, *genes*, and *DNA* to refer to the hereditary material that Weismann called germ plasm. The division of the organism into two parts is the essence of the central dogma: Information flows from the hereditary material to the body, but no instructions for adaptation, no information, flows back into the DNA in the germ cells to affect the design of the next generation. This prohibition is known as Weismann's barrier.

The central dogma continues to flourish as the arena for the increasing scientific insight into the role of the nucleic acids in the life processes.

SOME CELLULAR ANOMALIES

Perhaps the cell paradigm remains only a theory because there are so many exceptions and variations from the standard model. The first great exception is that not all cells contain nuclei. The oldest cells, the *prokaryotes*, constitute a whole family of their own and are nonnuclear by definition—although they contain nuclear material. In the human body red blood cells start out with a nucleus, which disintegrates after they are formed. And some fungi at a stage in their life cycle present two distinct nuclei in their cells.

Nor are all cells microscopic. Nerve cells in the giant

squid grow to six feet, while even a few neural cells in man grow to three feet. The eggs of birds are familiar giant cells. Think of the ostrich egg, the largest single cell extant, though only the embryo is considered a single cell. And among marine alga Acetabularia is a seawood with giant cells about a half an inch in radius and easily visible to the naked eye.

Most distressing of all—after my exposure to the charms of cell theory—was the discovery that most of human flesh consists of bundles of skeletal muscle fibers, not of conventional tissue but of an unfamiliar material called *syncytium*, a multinucleate mass of protoplasm with no clear cell boundaries at all. In syncytium many nuclei share the same cytoplasm.

End cells. Just as the skin is an important organ of the human body, the membranes of cells are critical to cell performance and constitute a separate discipline of biological inquiry. "End cells" can no longer divide and carry on the lineage. Nerve cells, red blood cells, and the cells that make up chitin, fingernails, and skin epithelium are examples. They are the final product of differentiation.

Complexity of cells. Even the simplest cell contains at least several hundred different types of molecules. A typical cell in the human body contains at least a thousand different types of protein molecules alone. The cell is immensely complex because of the enormously large number of ways in which its constituent atoms and molecules can be arranged. The number of permutations and combinations is enormously greater than the number of particles in the universe. In fact the complexity is "transcalculational," that is, too complicated to solve exactly by any imaginable device designed by human beings. Here is how Frederick Seitz, a physicist, put the matter in his plenary address to a recent International Conference on the Unity of the Sciences:

> **Of the immensely large number of ways of arranging the atoms in a cell, regarded as a physical ensemble of atoms or**

> molecules, it is evident that only an immensely small fraction can represent viable living systems. The vast majority of arrangements correspond to non-living states of the aggregate. The probability that we could accidentally assemble a living configuration from inert ingredients is immensely improbable.

Standard chess games that involve only 64 pieces can be calculated by computers very successfully, but only for a few steps ahead, not for the entire game. The mechanics of the atoms or molecules of a cell are transcalculational at a much higher level.

SWISS FAMILY E. COLI

Cells come to our attention in myriad forms, and there is no generic "cell" except in the hypothetical diagrams of their minimal components in elementary textbooks. We have been speaking of cells as a unit of life and as common constituents of multicellular organisms. But cells prevail also in a prodigal array of independent forms and behaviors, including cooperative aggregates of single cells in communities (algae and sponges) and free-living unicellular organisms (bacteria). Microbes and protists are surviving first animals; among the most familiar is the bacterium *Escherichia coli*.

    E. coli is a primitive but very hardy organism—older than humans and mammals and vertebrates by an order of magnitude. It is the creature that finds its inevitable and prolific home in the human gut where its dominion is largely, but not entirely, benign. It is a member of the family Enterobacteriaceae of coliforms (residents of the intestines of people and other animals). Most of us carry about two pounds of bacteria in our intestinal tracts. There are more *E. coli* in one person's guts than the earth houses people.

    Though an *E. coli* cell is about 500 times smaller than an average eukaryote cell, it is still 6×10^{10} the mass of a water molecule, which suggests its imperviousness to direct chemical analysis. But it is highly discriminatory of its chemical environment; it has something akin to memory. And it functions like a "biochip" with the capacity to store the equivalent of 200 billion bits of information, not in the binary form of computer programs, but in the quaternary scheme of the A-C-G-T chemical base coding of its DNA structure.

E. coli is now the most intensely studied organism on earth, and more is known about its gene regulation, structure, and metabolism than any other single species—more than is known about the physiology of human beings. The concentration of attention on the bacterium *Escherichia coli* came about more or less by accident, as a result of laboratory convenience as much as anything else. *E. coli* is to the molecular biologist what the hydrogen atom is to the chemist and physicist—the most common and convenient unit of study, the site, host, and armature of the most exquisite laboratory concentration.

Of all the possible chemical reactions within the living factory of this microbe, somewhere between one-sixth to one-third of all the total possible molecular arrangements have already been identified and described. Since there is good reason to assume a finite number of possible chemical combinations, the microbiologists now feel they have the tools to describe completely and exhaustively all the features of *E. coli* life by the end of the century. The molecular biology of *E. coli* is practically synonymous with cancer research.

Our concentrated investigation of *E. coli* was a chief arena for the greatest evolutionary discovery of our century: that nature is dialectical. The accumulated literature—the definitive biography—of this microbe provides us the most accurate laboratory picture of how the proteins and enzymes that make up the metabolic pathways of all living matter contain an information system, like a word processor or a library catalog, describing their functions and structure in the discrete language of DNA.

Through *E. coli* we have a mirror into our own human bodies to demonstrate how an informational structure can be subject directly to the laws of chemistry—how patterns at the molecular level can design and control the transformation of organs and organisms from one phase of transition to another.

GENETIC CODING

To say that DNA transmits information is not an analogy. It is literally true. But the information transmitted is not graphic but coded; it is more like a recipe than a blueprint. The genetic code is contained in a molecule, but that molecule does not exist by itself, it is part of a cell. The cell is a complex of elaborate molecular mechanisms for self-replication and differentiation. The organism, and the cells and molecules that compose it, cannot be thought of separately from their environments since each evolved in a series of previous environments.

Genetic coding functions at the exact threshold between the animate and the inanimate. The threshold is exquisitely chemical. The molecules of the cell are themselves inanimate; it is the genetic program that organizes them in such a way as to produce a living entity. The program directs highly specific chemical reactions whose interactions produce proteins, which produce life. (This must have been at least part of what Buckminster Fuller had in mind when he said, "I am not a thing—a noun. I seem to be a verb.") Life is a property of certain chemical ways of organizing matter; the genetic programs permitting all biological phenomena have evolved in the earth's evolution over three billion years.

The direct function of DNA is to specify chemical structure. Its indirect function is to generate form. The net function of DNA is to provide a mechanism for accelerating higher levels of organization. As far as we know, DNA is the only molecule replete with—certainly a biological, and perhaps a cosmic—destiny: the vessel and instrument for the continuity of life.

The Nobel laureate Renato Dulbecco advances the premise that DNA is the instructional basis of life but that through evolution DNA has relinquished some of its control to the brain.

> **The study of life shows that in advanced creatures DNA is not the sole ruler. In them the autocracy of DNA, almost absolute in simple creatures, is mitigated. Instead DNA acts as a benevolent dictator that has relinquished some of its powers to the organisms themselves, allowing them to determine their own fate within some rigidly determined boundaries.**

How DNA translates the linear specifications of chemical information into instructions for the development of three-dimensional forms remains a mystery.

26

The biosphere as a unit of life

————— ⌁ —————

THE MINIMUM & MAXIMUM UNIT OF LIFE

It was not until we had science fiction and space exploration that the biosphere of the earth came dramatically into its own as a proper subject for comprehensive scientific attention. In 1966, when we had the first pictures of the earth from the moon, when we saw ourselves drifting serenely through the wastes of space, the biosphere replaced the ark as a metaphor for escape from extinction. The biosphere as a complex is the largest living ensemble in the solar system.

Its ordination as a "unit of life" was celebrated in a collaborative work by Robert A. Shapiro, a professor of chemistry, and Gerald Feinberg, a professor of physics. In their zeal they had it set in italics: *"Life is fundamentally the activity of a biosphere. A biosphere is a highly ordered system of matter and energy characterized by complex cycles that maintain or gradually increase the order of the system through an exchange of energy with its environment."* The biosphere is at once the minimum and the maximum unit of life. Whether or not the biosphere is the exclusive unit of life depends on returns from SETI explorations and galaxies still unheard from. The biosphere shares minimality with the cell because cells cannot flourish without their ambient environment. Reciprocally, the ambient environment is the handiwork of bacterial and other organic industry. Increments or niches of the ambient environment can be isolated only momentarily—at least in the geological time frame—from the entire evolution of earth's atmosphere, oceans, and crustal rocks.

The science fiction writer Arthur C. Clarke is at home among the planets, and he offers us a radical perspective: "how inappropriate it is to call this planet Earth when clearly it is Ocean." The sea is not just a home for the largest of living creatures, the whales; it is also a vast petri dish, a culture medium in which every teaspoonful of seawater harbors more than a billion viruses. According to *The Faber Book of the Sea*, there are 329 million cubic miles of sea water, 3.5 percent of which is solid matter. By comparison, the land above sea level is a puny 30 million cubic miles.

THE GAIA HYPOTHESIS

This is the proposition that the forms of life have coevolved with their environment; that the climate, geology, and biota of earth function as a concerted whole. Organisms and the elements have not only evolved together, they also assert a continuing homeostatic relationship—a biotic to abiotic feedback—between the animate and the inanimate worlds.

It is an attractive view: organisms do not simply exist in the environment, they determine it. Plants turn carbon dioxide into oxygen while animals do the reverse. The balance that exists suits both as it slowly evolves. Life regulates the environment on a global scale. The earth, considered together with its integral biomass, demonstrates an enhanced stability of behavior similar to that of a living organism. The relationship between life and the geophysical earth is more than coincidental; it is apparently also more than platonic: It makes plausible the notion of a kind of a superorganism regulating itself as a body does.

The scum of the planet. Since the earth was born, atmospheric methane and carbon dioxide have decreased, while oxygen has increased. The ratios changed as life evolved. Life interacts physically, chemically, and ecologically with the air, the waters, and the crustal rocks. From the point of view of skeptics, life has no choice but to adapt to geophysical constraints; from the point of view of Gaians, life is the dynamic element maintaining optimum conditions for itself. The most conspicuous difference between the earth and the other planets is the thin layer of biota visible from space, the phenomenon that the founders of the theory called "ubiquitous scum" and rechristened Gaia (for the Greek goddess of the earth).

When in 1974 James Lovelock and Lynn Margulis published their second paper on the Gaia hypothesis, they made no claim that the self-regulation of the planet is purposeful. The Gaia paradigm—that life keeps the environment suitable for the continuance of life—is presented as a hypothesis of a coupled feedback system of climatic and chemical interactions as emergent properties of the system. There is no teleology, expressed or implied. The hypothesis has already generated testable predictions and has thus been admitted into scientific orthodoxy. Lovelock has said he is quite content with the suspicion that the chief attraction of his thesis is that it has compelled geophysicists, biologists, and other specialists to address the whole-system model. It is said that Lovelock is to science what Gandhi was to politics.

The Gaia effect is often summoned as a metaphor—a prey of charlatans and mystics—by New Age activists and Jeremiahs of anthrogenesis. Dorion Sagan goes so far as to posit that "human beings are 'genitals' ... the planetary counterpart to reproductive organs, and says that they have become "incestuously involved" with Mother Earth through industrial technology. Well, the relationship between nature and culture may be more than platonic, but that does not mean it is incestuous. These extreme visions are abuses of what is at core a scientific proposition.

Following are some examples of the Gaia effect:

Temperature. Without the moderating effect of millions of years of life on earth, temperatures might rise up to 80°F. hotter than today; a climate in which only the most primitive microbes could survive. For the past 3.3 billion years the temperature of the earth's atmosphere has remained constant within fairly narrow limits, even though the energy output from the sun has more than doubled in that period. (Even the ice ages did not lower tropical temperatures more than about 8°C.)

Cosmic thermostat. It is a cosmic condition that the temperature of the earth (as an average velocity of all its atoms) is a median between the heat of the sun and the cold of outer space.

Glaciers. From the local point of view, residents of Europe and North America tend to view glaciations as a disaster, but on a planetary scale glaciers may serve as a preferred state, a spur to evolutionary vigor. The atmosphere as an equilibrium system will resist perturbation; an excess of pollutants may accelerate the new ice age. Glaciers have been called living ice. (Bogs are ecological dead ends. Glaciers unbog bogs.)

Plankton vs. gasoline. The Gaia effect has led to identification of dimethyl sulfide emissions from the oceans as a climate regulator comparable to the greenhouse effect of carbon dioxide and methane in the atmosphere. Plankton from the sea *may* actually compensate for the carbon dioxide buildup from automobile exhausts.

Population growth. There is a direct correlation between the growth in the atmospheric carbon dioxide and the growth of the world's human population for the last 25 years. In fact, the correlation is so statistically exact that it could supplant census estimates for world population growth.

Oxygen. All of the oxygen in the atmosphere, were it not replenished by plants, bacteria, and algae, would be totally exhausted in under 20 years. Oxygen, primarily in its molecular form, was to the early biosphere what, by analogy, nuclear power is to the biosphere of today: "pregnant with potentialities and cursed with contradictions" in the words of Preston Cloud.

Inquiries anticipating the Gaia paradigm:

Anthrozoos. This is a word (a pretentious word) for a multidisciplinary inquiry into the relationships between humans and the living environment. Early works in the field include George P. Marsh's *The Earth as Modified by Human Action* (New York, 1877), which asserted that the making of the Panama Canal was impossible. When I was stationed in Germany in 1949, I found in a British YMCA bookstore R. L. Sherlock's *Man's Influence on the Earth* (London, 1931), which was an early attempt to document the notion that man's interference with nature is more than trivial. Sherlock employs, but does not claim priority for, the term anthropogeography (not in the *Oxford English Dictionary*) for the study of a converse effect, "the effect on Man of local characteristics of the earth's surface." That's the kind of thing that could keep poets in business till the cock crows.

BIODIVERSITY

Biodiversity has been identified most prominently with E. O. Wilson's doctrine of human dependence on biological diversity and its importance in a global exchange economy: "The pool of species diversity . . . comprises a vast reservoir of potential new crops, pharmaceuticals, and restorers of depleted soils." One of the chief disciplines on which it depends—indeed which it would even subsume—is systematics (taxonomy), which aims at nothing less than a categorical description of all life on earth. In the neglect of biological research on species diversity, Wilson argues, the economic costs in terms of lost opportunities are very high.

At the present time the total number of scientific names assigned to plants, animals, and organisms under the system Linnaeus gave us is about 1.4 million species, but estimates of the actual number of species that exist range between 5 million and 30 million. "We don't know to the nearest order of magnitude how many species there are on the planet. And . . . we don't know why there are that number of species and we don't really understand fully why there are more species in certain parts of the world such as the tropics."

"Biodiversity" is the general caption for legislation being generated in recent years in the Subcommittee on Natural Resources, Agriculture Research, and Environment of the House Committee on Science, Space, and Technology. The legislation is designed to embrace a national policy statement toward biological diversity; management of biological conservation; increased coordination, direction, and emphasis on biotic inventories; and research in conservation biology.

THE TRAGEDY OF THE COMMONS

The commons, in Anglo-American property law, is an area of land set aside for public use—especially for pasture. The concept of the commons has been applied by analogy to dispel the notion of earth as a cornucopia, and to recognize that natural resources, both within and beyond the realms of private property, are a hostage to the collective greed of nations.

Two decades ago Garrett Hardin, a professor of biology at the University of California, Santa Barbara, delivered an address to the Pacific Division of the American Association of the Advancement of Science that was published as "The Tragedy of the Commons," and that since has become one of the sacred texts of ecological writing. That speech became a catchphrase for the idea that self-interest would inevitably destroy shared and freely available natural resources. The *tragedy* derives from the remorseless, inherent logic of a situation where resources held in common will invariably be overexploited; the essence of the tragedy being not unhappiness but, in A. N. Whitehead's words, "the solemnity of the remorseless working of things."

Hardin's paper is a classic rationale for the ethical problems in conservation in general and the problem of overpopulation in particular. Based on a rigorously logical analysis of population constraints, he concludes that "The only way we can preserve and nurture other more precious freedoms is by relinquishing the freedom to breed."

The critical ratio of food to population in an ecosystem is called its *carrying capacity*. In a publication contemporary to Hardin's, the ecologist P. A. Colinvaux forecast that "the time is already on us when . . . the carrying capacity of our living space is not enough to provide a broadened niche for all men who now exist." (That was written in 1973.) The curse of too many people is not a biological imperative, merely a misfortunate side effect of our culture. In the most cynical view, "politicians are professionally compelled to remain deaf to suggestions that growth of human activities and elevation of consumption cannot be perpetual." It could even be argued that vote-seeking governments make up the chief environmental hazard of all.

Hardin's position is that the population problem has no technical solution, and that it can be resolved only by what he calls "a fundamental extension in morality," by applying mutual coercion to abandon the commons in breeding.

Hardin is not without his detractors, some of whom brand his viewpoint as ecofascist. Sociobiologists and others are paying increasing attention to a contrary hypothesis: that group self-governance and the exclusion of outsiders can form the basis for the maintenance of benign and stable harvested ecosystems. The arena for these conflicting impulses is the real world.

27
Hierarchy & classification

———————— ❧ ————————

TWENTY QUESTIONS

When I was in high school in the days before television and even before cars had radios, people actually amused themselves by playing games such as Animal, Vegetable or Mineral?—or Twenty Questions, as it was also called (at least since the time of Victorian England). You could pick anything in the world, any object you could think of, and once you declared its kingdom (mineral is a kingdom like animal and vegetable), the other players had twenty questions, phrased so they could be answered by *yes* or *no*, to narrow the categories of time, place, size, shape, function, or smell in order to home in on the particular item in question by a process of elimination and intuition. With experienced players twenty questions was usually more than enough to get the answer, to dismiss irrelevancies and to get *it* into a corner—be it even the feather of a dove that flew from Noah's Ark.

Aggressive players would make sure that the last winner, who got to choose the next "thing," would write it down on a piece of paper and put it face down on the dashboard or mantelpiece, just to keep everything honest.

There was a variant of the game that admitted a fourth major category, Abstract. This would provide for such items as "the crack of doom" or "an idea in the mind of God." These four categories were regarded as surely embracing every aspect of our culture and every conceivable item of our experience (or, as a philosopher might put it, *every thing that is the case*.) This made for a comfortable world, since human nature takes solace in pigeonholes and abhors the unclassifiable.

When I started to use the wood-shingled public library in Newport News where I grew up, I soon mastered the Dewey Decimal system in which every book was classified. I was consoled to note that its nine general classes (broken down into 999 specifics) were compatible with the system of kingdoms with which I was already familiar. Thus I had an easy extension of identity with the world around me. Just imagine knowing that no matter what happened to me or how long I might live I would never have to face any event not anticipated by one of Mr. Dewey's numbers— give or take a few decimals.

Once while playing Twenty Questions I remember picking an artifact from my infrequent experiences with restaurants, and I thought I had a sure winner: I picked the paper doily with six oval holes covering the ice on a plate serving a half-dozen oysters on the half shell. I didn't even know if it had a name, but I said that what I had in mind was a *mineral*—on the simple notion that anything living had to be animal or vegetable and everything else was mineral. To my dismay, the other players guessed it at about question number fifteen.

But one of them demurred: Even by these simple rules there was a problem. Was the paper mineral, being made up of synthetic materials and dead rags—or was paper vegetable, consisting of recently living, processed cellulose fibers? Since I'd lost the game, the point was moot, but the blurring of what I had thought was two neat categorical pigeonholes still rankles. Does organic matter become mineral when it ceases to grow? Is an aborted foetus or a hanged man instant mineral?*

* Even a dead bee can sting, and the reflex of a dead snake can release its venom.

I have since come to see that most of the feathers of birds, once they have grown to their full extent, are devoid of nervous or cellular input and thus are virtually mineral or inanimate, or at least deader than our fingernails, whose chitin still grows. Conversely, are not the synthetic materials and dead fibers, being man-made, also products of life?

The paper oyster doily was a harbinger of that philosophical dilemma—still unresolved by religion or science or the law—the dilemma of the threshold between the animate and the inanimate, between the organic and the inorganic, between the quick and the dead, in the littered biological landscape from which the inquiries in this book arise. How do we define life? How do we define death? What is the vital threshold between protoplasm and dust?

In playing Twenty Questions, tracing the provenance of *paper* blurred the divide between vegetable and mineral. This was hard to live with, but I took some comfort from the thought that always and everywhere one could tell, intuitively, the difference between an animal and a vegetable, between a cow and a cowslip. All forms of life had to be one or the other, and their difference was self-evident. This commonsense notion is reinforced by the authority of a distinguished biologist and Nobel medalist, Sir Peter Medawar, the author of a dictionary entry on *biosystematics*, the classification of living things, also known as *taxonomy*: "The most majestic of taxonomic distinctions is into plant and animal kingdoms (the subject-matters of botany and zoology respectively)." It is just as well that I had not looked the matter up in the encyclopedia back when I was in grade school. This is what I would have found: "The actual boundaries between animals and plants are artificial and are solely [. . . *solely*] due to the ingenious analysis of the systematist." (*Encyclopaedia Britannica*, 14th Edition, 1929.)

So much for majesty; let's hear it for ingenuity.

ORGANIC HIERARCHY

In the world of nature, hierarchies evolve spontaneously and irrevocably with the introduction of complexity. The inanimate world has its material hierarchy of elementary particles, atoms, molecules, and crystals. Living systems have their own hierarches, all of which are compatible with those of the rest of the physical world. Consideration of hierarchy provides an escape from the ambiguities of attempts to define the "fundamental units of life."

There are two principal kinds of hierarchy in living systems: functional and systematic. The functional progression describes the internal attributes of organisms, from macromolecule to cellular organelle to cell to tissue to organ to individual organism.

The systematic hierarchy is a taxonomic progression of classification from lower to higher levels, as from species to genus to family. Despite the fact that members of the lower levels are descended from the higher levels, the most devoted systematists insist that the sequence has no philosophical significance and that their method of classification is merely a convenient tool. Nevertheless, the method does invite generalizations suggesting the existence of evolutionary patterns.

There is a standard irreducible sequence of the textbooks: atom; molecule; organelle; cell; tissue; organ; organism. And above that: population; community; ecosystem; biosphere.

There is a reciprocity between hierarchy and complexity that the analysts have not yet exhausted. Eugene Mallove proposes an operational definition of complexity as "the quality of having a significant *functional* intricacy on distance scales very small compared to overall size." Such a criterion would admit animals and human beings into an organic hierarchy but would exclude crystal minerals as having insufficient complexity of components. (Compare pages 47–49.)

TAXONOMIC HIERARCHY

Seeing that the human race falls into the same classification as the feathered creatures, we must divide the biped class into featherless and feathered.
—Plato, The Statesman

Man is by nature a classifying animal. To the four elements of the classic Greek cosmology (fire, earth, air, and water) the Chinese added a fifth, wood. . . . Jorge Luis Borges claims that "a certain Chinese encyclopedia" divided animals into such categories as

belonging to the emperor;
embalmed;
tame;
mermaids;
fabulous;
apt to wave their limbs like madmen;
drawn with a fine camel hair brush;
looking from a distance like flies.

That dictionary is otherwise unspecified, but it had obviously found some lodgment between Borges' ears if not in the Ming Dynasty.

Classification systems are inherently cultural, reflecting abstract patterns as well as descriptive facts. Taxonomy is no exception, but it is primarily a descriptive discipline. Unlike other physical sciences, taxonomy is not subject to demonstrability by laboratory experiment, although, since the middle of this century, its hypotheses have enjoyed general reinforcement by evolutionary genetics. It is the task of taxonomy to bring some kind of objective order to the description of nature's relentless diversification.

The chief divisions in the taxonomic hierarchy are

Phylum
Class

Order
Genus
Species

Taxonomy is fundamental to all the other disciplines of biology from the first naming of newly discovered variations to the incorporation of all knowledge into a system. It is also being revitalized by new techniques of analysis such as phenetics, cladistics and numerical taxonomy. The conventional system of classification as inherited from Linnaeus is based upon evolutionary development: descriptions of organisms in terms of their *phyletic* relationship. The phyletic taxonomists used to have the field to themselves, but the advent of the computer with its capacity for much more complex forms of analysis has introduced the newer—and controversial—phenetic and cladistic approaches. *Phenetic* relationships refer to measurable visual and physical description; *cladistic* relationships are based on "branching" characteristics with other relations and species.

A proposal for domains. In recent years advances in gene sequencing have put in jeopardy all classification systems derived from phylogeny alone, i.e., systems based on simple descriptions of physical characteristics of organisms. Dr. Carl R. Woese, a microbiologist at the University of Illinois, Urbana, asserts that "the basis for the definition of taxa has progressively shifted from the organismal to the cellular to the molecular level." He maintains that molecular structures and genetic sequences are much more revealing of evolutionary relationships than is the gross physiology of the resulting organisms. Molecular comparisons reveal dissimilarities much more profound than those between the existing kingdoms, such as animals and plants. His analysis supports the establishment of a new level of taxon above that of kingdom—to be called a *domain*. To reflect widely dissimilar evolutionary patterns at the microscopic level, he makes a radical proposal for a new tree of life based on the sequencing of nucleotides in the ribosomal RNA found in every cell. They reveal a pattern of metabolic pathways and evolutionary development quite different from taxonomies of the past. The three new domains emerging from the molecular point of view are to be called Archaea, Bacteria, and Eucarya.

In evolutionary terms, plants and animals are mere survival machines occupying no position of privileged importance. In the taxonomy proposed by Dr. Woese, Animalia and Plantae would be relegated to one of six kingdoms in the domain Eucarya, one of 14 or more in the entire domain system. Thus have the ever more exquisite instruments of microscopy and the inexorable sequencing of genes in our common RNA removed human beings even further from their ancestral home, their preferred niche, their claim on taxonomic dignity—lost in the rampant diversity of 14 kingdoms.

Taxons. Taxons are static takeouts from the dynamic manifestations of life. They are abstract freeze frames of living organisms as found by naturalists in the landscape and microbiologists in the laboratory and are employed as orderly descriptions of classes of plants and animals, with the recognition that few species appear to be permanent (maybe some ants and redwood trees come close) and that the majority of species that ever existed are already extinct.

The word *taxon* itself is not in the *Oxford English Dictionary*, perhaps because it is a back-formation from *taxonomy*. It means the name assigned to any group or entity in a formal system of hierarchical—especially biological—nomenclature. Man's proclivity for names and labels flourishes under academic and scientific convention. Taxonomic terms attempt to accommodate the general and the specific, or, you might say the genera and the species with their many other supervening and intervening layers in the hierarchy.

As always in the process of assigning names to objects (ask any museum curator), there is some risk of stressing the container at the expense of the thing contained. Taxonomy is a purely descriptive pursuit, a totally nonexperimental science. Hence it is incurably subjective.

In 1908 Henri Bergson recognized that the employment of labels and names and signs, however great their utility, entails a certain conceptual and philosophic price. What he has to say about the vulnerability of *signs* is relevant to the fragility of *taxa*.

> **Modern science, no less than ancient science, proceeds according to the cinematic method. It cannot do otherwise; all science is subject to this law. It is in fact, of the essence of science, to manipulate *signs*, which it substitutes for the objects themselves. These signs undoubtedly differ from those of languages in their greater precision and higher efficacity, but they ... denote a fixed aspect of reality under an arrested form. In order to think movement, an incessantly renewed effort of the mind is necessary. Signs are made for the purpose of dispensing with this effort by substituting for the moving continuity of things an artificial recomposition which is their equivalent in practice and has the advantage of being easily manipulated.**

Two years after Bergson wrote that, William Morton Wheeler quoted it in his book *Ants* in a footnote explaining, as only an evolutionary biologist could, that the intellect "was evolved as an instrument of action and fabrication, and not for the purpose of understanding or explaining an inorganic flux or movement . . . like that which we call life." So the intellect did not arise in order to explain life. The intellect serves just to fabricate names. Okay, but isn't all that pretty heavy freight for a footnote?

Since 1910 the further adventures of the structuralists and the semioticians, talking to each other in increasingly technical language, have only made matters worse. The Bergson formula is a wholesome antidote for the excesses of the semanticists.

Semantic traps aside, taxonomy has an innate intellectual and esthetic appeal. Some taxons are poetic in their Latinate economy:

Chaos chaos . . . amoeba*
Didus ineptus . . . dodo
Indicator indicator . . . the honey guide bird who leads the badger to the honeybee nest
Kalmia latifolia . . . mountain laurel
Magnolia grandiflora . . . magnolia
Mimosa pudica . . . sensitive plant (*pudic* = to be ashamed)
Quelea quelea . . . African weaverbird pest; the most numerous bird on earth
Solanum tuberosum . . . potato

Prokaryotes & eukaryotes: the great dichotomy. When it comes to trying to place where man belongs in the great scheme of the natural world, there are a great many divisions and vistas that have become part of our common imagination. We are all comfortable in the distinction between men and apes, between mammals and other vertebrates, between vertebrates and all other animals, and above all between animal and vegetable life. But none of these distinctions is as significant, none has a hint of the resonance, as that between two different kinds of cells: old cells without a nucleus and new cells with a nucleus: prokaryotes and eukaryotes. The old cells still flourish as protozoa (microbes), and the newer nucleated cells are the constituents of the Metazoa—multicellular animal life.

The endosymbiosis theory. The great chasm between those two types of cells is where any thought of biological classification has to begin. There are only two types of cells on earth. One type has a nucleus. The other type does not.

---

* *According to Professor Harold Morowitz, Linnaeus' description of the amoeba is the first appearance in biology of the term* chaos. *He says that if you have looked at an amoeba under the microscope, you can see what he meant. The modern meaning of the term* chaos *in physics and biology is a child of the computer.*

Animals and plants are made of nucleated cells. Most microbes are made of nonnucleated cells. During the Precambrian period more than a billion years ago the earth was inhabited only by the old cells. In fact, for more than half the total span of life on earth the only life for which a fossil record exists was prokaryotic bacteria. The evidence is now clear that the organelles of cells survive as prokaryote vestiges in a eukaryotic world. That view was once regarded as heresy, but it has only recently become recognized by mainstream biologists as the *serial endosymbiosis theory* (SET for short).

Symbiosis is the living together of two or more organisms in close association. It differs from parasitism in that it applies only to relationships that are mutually advantageous to the partners concerned. Endosymbiosis is a process like swallowing without digesting, like the engulfing of one organism by another. Such was the origin of cell organelles like chloroplasts and mitochondria. The result is that each cell in our body has the evolutionary status of a former colony.

Eukaryotic cells of higher plants and animals have specialized organelles such as chloroplasts and mitochondria. The mitochondria have their own DNA unrelated to the DNA of the cell nucleus. The mitochondria—and other groups of organelles—were once free-living bacteria.

The most effective advocate for the endosymbiotic theory is the virtuoso Dr. Lynn Margulis of the University of Massachusetts. She is an ecologist, a microbiologist, a daring theorist and a splendid writer. Early in her career she committed herself to the notion that parasitism and symbiosis were the driving forces in the evolution of cells. The internal structure of most cells did not originate within the cells but are relics of independent bacteria who invaded the complex from outside like carriers of an infectious disease. Over the millennia the invaders turned from parasites to symbionts to mutually dependent hostages.

At a time when most of her colleagues were preoccupied with the role of competition in evolution, Margulis was constructing theories about the role of symbiosis. It was her theory that cells with nuclei evolved from the merger of two or more different bacterial cells without nuclei in the theater of the eukaryotic cell. It started out as parasitism and ended up as symbiosis. From that vision she has advanced a number of striking new paradigms of which endosymbiosis is only one. As an intuitive theorist she knows no restraint: she proposes that the sperm in our gonads and the neurons in our brain are, quite literally, remnants of free-living microbial spirochetes.

SOME OF THE LURES AND LIMITS OF CLASSIFICATION

There is no unique, essential, natural, or a priori system of classification that is alone adequate to the nature of reality.
—W. Stanley Jevons, Principles of Science, 1874

The man who wrote the first modern book about classification put the matter that way, and he has not since been gainsaid. He prescribed a limit to the impulse to classify, but he did not dispel its lure.

That word *reality* brings a certain number of problems with it. There is no discipline or system to confirm that what we see "out there" is mirrored by mental representations "in here." Objective reality refers not only to the totality of things that exist (or things that would be included in a description of all the facts about the world), but it accords to the objects of man's knowledge an existence independent of whether an observer is perceiving or thinking about them. Thus classification systems do more than just serve as a framework for practical activities, they involve the structure of reality on a metaphysical level. The librarian Mary Midgely allows that there is no neutral terminology. So there really are no wholly neutral facts. All describing is classifying according to some conceptual scheme or other.

We are stuck with the unhappy condition that all attempts at classification are inherently subjective. All observation is contextual, and just as there are no neutral facts there is no wholly neutral terminology. Librarians cannot permit themselves to be discouraged by the subjective limitations noted by Mary Midgely or the philosophic reservations of Professor Jevons.

Classification and theories of classification may or may not conform to an "objective real world" as permitted by some philosophers. The one certain thing about classification is that it reveals aspects of how our minds work in preferred ways of recording experience . . . how our minds work, sometimes deliberately or sometimes reflexively, in filing the facts, observations, remembered events, and abstract thoughts of our daily round of work and play under the labels and categories and myths—the verbal and ideographic and alphanumeric matrixes—of whatever particular culture we live, think, and talk in. A good filing system is like a conversation with your own mind.

A practical function of classification is to make diversity intelligible and manageable. Classification in biology and in anthropology is as indispensable, and for the same reason, as in a large library; a book misplaced may be as useless as a book lost.

Homo sapiens seems to have an innate tendency to seek order, to recognize common elements in objects and events, and to find patterns in the multifarious sensations that bombard us in every waking moment. Some people are indifferent to order in such matters as housekeeping or paying bills or changing the oil and rotating the tires, but almost everyone is orderly about a few things of personal or professional interest, be it baseball or ballet, while there is nothing under the sun that isn't of exhaustive and systematic interest to at least a few people who seek for their specialty common names and descriptions in order to communicate . . . in order to communicate and indeed in order to possess their own minds. This applies to a wide range of commitment from collectors of bottle caps and matchboxes to entire academic disciplines. Only professional librarians and indexers try to classify everything. (Zealous computer networkers have often not reckoned the hazards.)

Our classification systems appear to be culture-specific. The Chinese have their mouse operas. Borges has his labyrinths. The windscales of Beaufort prevail, as do the earthquake scales of Richter. Dog fanciers have their Westminster championship ratings. Accountants and money men derive vast satisfaction and even profit from such concepts as price-earnings ratios and profit-and-loss statements and bottom lines. For the baseball fan statistics on earned run averages and runs batted in are essential to savoring the sport.

28
Disciplines

SPECIALIZATION VS. INTEGRATION

To some people discipline is a matter of early rising and hard work. To others, it is the flogging of schoolboys or the charm of the drill sergeant. Havelock Ellis said that the most austere of disciplines was dancing. Institutions are ordained by good order and discipline.

Academic disciplines are created to insure that research and inquiry into new objects of study are pursued in a systematic, conventional manner with adherence to commonly accepted standards of procedure and reporting—indeed, *disciplined* rather than impulsive or extemporaneous or self-indulgent. Disciplines exist to curb, if not purge, excesses of zeal.

A professor of social science and policy studies, Kenneth P. Ruscio, explains that disciplines arise from "the natural tendency of educated groups with common interests to band together, create a technical language, form a status hierarchy, and restrict entrance into its ranks. Disciplines serve a purpose. They simplify the storage of acquired knowledge; they categorize knowledge and those who seek it in a manner convenient for academic institutions and the reporting of research. Disciplines, as suggested by the word itself, facilitate disciplined inquiry." . . . Endemic to discipline, however, is the occupational disease of hypertrophy, the excessive development of attention to one area to the detriment of others. (A classic biological example of hypertophy is the outsized growth of antlers in the Irish elk, an indulgence thought to be the cause of its extinction.)

Disciplines invoke a dismissal of irrelevancies, the kind of concentration that insures against distraction. Buckminster Fuller, a devout advocate of the unity of all science, nevertheless described the process of thinking as "a dismissal of irrelevancies." So the procedure of specialization is all well and good but it has a concomitant penalty in the loss of context. To guard against this tendency Fuller was always careful to prescribe only a *momentary* dismissal of irrelevancies and consideration of parts, while holding the full context of the whole in only temporary suspension, a sort of holding pattern, of consideration. (*Synergetics*, 509.06.)

One of the functions of a discipline is to provide specialists with a context for their inquiry as well as a license to rigidly dismiss all matters irrelevant to their chief concern. It is the function of discipline, says Freeman Dyson, to "submerge the individual fantasy in a greater whole." Perversely, almost all biologists have difficulty in keeping up with the literature, and for many it is a temptation (some say a chief strategy) to do so by redefining their field.

With the possible exception of the printing trades, no other pursuit is so finely subdivided into distinct specialties as science. It is widely regarded that the end of the 17th century marks the last chapter of Western civilization in which an educated man could master or be well versed in all the major ideas of his time. Leibnitz is the archetype of the last polymath. A generation before Leibnitz, John Milton is believed to be the last person to have read every book published in his lifetime. Since their time, specialism in intellectual inquiry has prevailed, and today the only licensed generalists are called journalists. Some readers grant the same license to poets.

The big picture. As you stand in line for the next event at the McLaughlin Planetarium in Toronto, you have plenty of time to scrutinize an epigraph inscribed in gilt and neon on marble:

The highest wisdom has but one science—the science of the whole—the science of explaining the whole creation and man's place in it.
                                   —Leo Tolstoy, War and Peace, *1869*

For Tolstoy, it is not just the humanities that are anthropocentric. The central role of man pervades the universe and provides a rationale for all the physical sciences; it endows even inorganic chemistry with meaning.

Interdisciplines. *Interdisciplinary* is the current buzz-word for the big picture that Tolstoy invoked. I say buzz-word because the term has yet to achieve respectability. It has even been dismissed as a synonym for sloppy. Once you add *inter* it stops being a discipline. Enterprises known as "information science" and the "knowledge industry" hover at its brink. Fritz Machlup was the first to attempt a systematic study of the role of the knowledge industries in the economies of the United States. The exposition of his abstract findings is projected in ten erudite volumes of a work still in progress. They are said to exemplify the principle that "the best interdisciplinary work is that carried on within the confines of a single brain." Is it not comforting that academic curricula can only crudely approach the mental model?

The innovative Dr. Alan Mackay of Birkbeck College, University of London, whose discipline is crystallography, has proposed the word "polytropic" as an alternative for "interdisciplinary," which he finds inappropriate and awkward. Polytropic is the idiom applied to Odysseus in the opening line of the Odyssey and is often translated as "resourceful," "versatile," or "much traveled." Pope's translation says Odysseus was a "man of many wiles," while a later Victorian translator said he was "a man of many devices." Devices may have heraldic overtones, but both devices and wiles suggest something short of trustworthiness. Mackay says that the modern usage derives from the Oxford English Dictionary definition of "tropism" as the turning of an organism in a particular direction in response to some special external stimulus. Anyway, departing from a single discipline invites hazards.

Interdisciplinary studies address great themes or styles of thought or methods of investigation with no vocabulary adequate to the new categories that transcend recognized concepts of scientific language. The metallurgist Cyril Stanley Smith has this to say as an Institute Professor Emeritus of MIT:

> **I predict the development of some new principles of hierarchy that will enable the effective resonance between molecule and organism to be explored. . . .**
>
> **Human capacities are such that most must specialize, and the liaison man will be far more important than he has been in the past when the greatest intellectual opportunities lay at the frontier.**

Real world problems have little regard for the convenience of academics. They refuse to fall neatly into our preformed categories. Lines of inquiry at the frontiers of biological research find that the conjoining of various disciplines has an almost irresistible imperative.

In 1988 the University of Southern California reorganized the research programs of its professional schools in a radical departure from the long-established departments. Up to 100 faculty members ranging from linguistics to electrical engineering, but focusing on computational neurobiology, have been reorganized under the acronym NIBS for Neural, Informational, and Behavioral Sciences. With comparable aplomb the University of Illinois, Urbana, has established a Department of Ecology, Ethology and Evolution.

The ambition and academic authority behind arrangements suggest that interdisciplinary programs may have achieved at least a de facto recognition if not a rationale.

The limits of generality. On 27 November 1987, when the International Conference on the Unity of the Sciences convened for its XVIth session in Atlanta, Georgia, it was expecting a ritual opening address offering the usual praise for the cause of scientific unity and a summons to dissolve the barriers between disciplines. Instead, the Chicago sociologist Edward A. Shils of the Committee on Social Thought at the University of Chicago and a fellow of Peterhouse College, Cambridge, told the plenary session of the conference that they could just about forget that noble impulse. "The unifiability of all knowledge exists in the mind of God. It is not given to us mortals to know the unity of knowledge," he said. Since "there is something esthetically pleasing about a unitary theory . . . why is science so specialized? Because knowledge could not progress without specialized investigation." Shils goes on to say:

> **There is too much produced in the world to permit any living human being, however capacious his mind, however long his life, however good his memory, however diligent he may be, to master the literature produced by scholars and scientists in any but a few specialized fields. . . . Specialization is prized because it's the only way one can get new knowledge. Specialization is inherent in the scientific method. . . . The natural theology in the human mind is gratified by the unity of science . . . but the disciplines are here to stay. And even if you unified all the physical sciences you would still have to reconcile them with philosophy, metaphysics and theology.**

In the words of William Blake: "He who would do good to another must do it in Minute Particulars. General Good is the plea of the scoundrel, hypocrite and flatterer; for Art and Science cannot exist but in minutely organized Particulars." . . . Even art.

THE AMBIGUITY OF BIOLOGY

There may be a few scientists somewhere who are just plain *biologists*, studying the whole range of life; but those who take the whole range for their province are more apt to be people like high school teachers or writers of books like the present one, with no more claim to being biologists than someone with a butterfly net from the attic can claim to be a naturalist. Most biologists are specialists because it is not the normal method of biology to advance by propounding dogmas, and because biological organisms are so complex that by trying to understand everything, one ends up learning little that is solid. Molecular biology especially has thrived on the tradition of meticulous inquiry into narrow, well-defined problems.

The grammatical element *bio* lends itself to easy association with so many other roots that any practitioner in the field can make up his own terms to describe his particular frontier of concentration. Dr. Robert M. Yerkes, an experimenter in primate behavior and comparative animal psychology, called himself a *psychobiologist*. R. Freitas has proposed *xenobiology* for extraterrestrial forms of life. . . . You see the range.

Perhaps a word count of the most common *bio* words in everyday speech would single out *biography*, as the most familiar. But biography is an art, not a science, although it is a *discipline* in the field of the humanities. (Virginia Woolf regarded biography as more of a craft than an art due to the obligation to adhere to the facts of the case.) Biography is an extremely popular and often dramatic form of literature. The lengthened shadow of a man or woman is history (as Emerson half-said), and—happily for the human condition—any attempt to make a science of biography is as doomed as the impulse to make a science of history. A biography accounts the development, maturity, and impact of organized consciousness as uniquely manifest in an individual human being. After all, the study of behavior is a recent, though increasingly respectable, discipline in the biological sciences, and one of its fundamental assumptions is that the lives of animals, including people, are as significant an object of study as the lives of cells.

What biography reveals is how a preoccupation not with evolution, not with the species, but with the record of an individual human life in all its rich complexity can reveal biological limitations and potentials in their most exquisite form. One could argue analogically that cultural ventures such as pro football and opera—comparable manifests of organized and cooperative consciousness—are also not fully accountable without some recourse to biological constraints.

Biological disciplines. A list of documented and recognized biological disciplines appears at at the end of this book, not so much for practical reference as for the unique window it provides into the complex ramifications of biological studies and their insusceptibility to easy categorization. Long as the list is, it remains illustrative rather than exhaustive, for there is no consensus in the naming of biological specializations.

Administrators of graduate level research institutes attest that when biologists make a new discovery, they tend to want to break off from the pack and establish a new field of inquiry with its own terminology and apparatus and lines of communication. Real world problems are impervious to the institutional departments established for the convenience of academic administrators. The tendency of pioneers to arrive at a mutually agreed vocabulary and agreed-upon techniques of investigation is understandable. (The concomitant status hierarchy and exclusiveness is not altogether uncongenial to the parties at interest.)

It is the ambivalent nature of the life sciences that they are at once the most integrative of disciplines and the most self-fragmenting. The list of hybrid fields of study in the appendix document biological allegiances with almost every other field of scientific exploration.

An autonomous science. Biology is what chemistry does, says Frederick Turner, when given a volatile cesspool like the planet Earth and some billions of years to play around with . . . billions of years and a narrow stable range of ambient temperature somewhere between absolute zero and 3000°C.

In its broadest sense, biology accounts for diversity, the causes of differences between objects. As a descriptive science it is in fact the very study of betweenness: between organisms, like that between bird and blossom, between animate and inanimate, like that between algae and coal, and even betweenness within species themselves. In the realm of organisms biology describes the differences; its integral subdiscipline, genetics, describes the mechanisms.

If the world described by biology can successfully be reduced to physics, then biology is a science like all the other hard sciences. If it cannot, if it has too much complexity, too much contingency, then it is autonomous.

Ernst Mayr, the most influential commentator on biology of his generation, divided the study of biology into evolutionary and functional patterns, the latter being concerned only with how organisms, cells, and biological molecules work. He felt that the functional part of biology is reducible to physics while the evolutionary aspect is not. Biology is probably destined always to remain something of an anomaly in contrast to the hard sciences of physics and chemistry.

Here is a concise statement by Gairdner B. Moment of where the role of biology rests within the whole range of scientific endeavor:

> **Within biology, DNA speaks a universal language, the same for bacteria, oak trees, and the human race. DNA is the creator of diversity, without which there would be no evolution, indeed no life. It plays opposite natural selection, which is the censor determining what survives and what perishes. Together they form the evolutionary dialogue that is ecology.**

BIOLOGY AND THE PHYSICAL SCIENCES

There is a hierarchy of intellectual pursuits ranging from the abstract to the most concrete, and in which successive categories of increasing density embrace the simpler concepts of the previous ones.

The first and most abstract branch of investigation would be mathematics, which invents rules for the game. Mathematics is the science of pattern, and, according to Rudy Rucker, there are five sorts of patterns dealt with: number, space, logic, infinity, and information. Most university faculties deal with mathematics apart from the physical sciences because it is a product of human thought independent of experience. (It has never been an experimental discipline, although the computer may yet drag mathematics into the laboratory.) In the last analysis mathematics relates to biology because, in Einstein's words, "it is so admirably adapted to the objects of reality." (From a philosophical point of view, we have discovered no necessary reason why mathematical abstraction should be useful in accounting physical processes: We really cannot be sure whether this is because of the way the world works or because of the way our mind works.)

Next comes physics, which uses mathematics as a tool to interpret the physical world. Physics deals with the internal world of the atom and the cosmic environment of the universe. Physics is involved with biology only through the mediation of chemistry. Chemistry is a special case of physics because it had to wait until the earth cooled before the phenomena it studies—stable molecules—could come into being. Chemistry flourishes in the middle ground of molecules and macromolecules.

Chemical concepts had to be developed to address the phenomenon of chemical reactions at the molecular level. Chemical reactions are interpreted in the language of physics, in which the one hundred varieties of atoms combine chemically in myriad unique molecular arrangements, but all in strict conformance with physical concepts of energy, electrons, and forces. Chemistry invades the world of the nucleus and that of the galaxies in only tentative forays; it operates in the middle range of the physical world. But there is a corollary threshold between chemistry and physics; physics operates at any temperature this side of singularity, chemistry only between zero and 3000°F.

Intervening in the hierarchy of pursuits between chemistry and biology is the special case of geology, in which time operates on a completely different level of magnitude from that ordinarily encountered in physics and chemistry. Geology provides the context not for cosmic evolution but for local biological evolution.

As biology introduces the concept of living matter, we arrive at a big step up in the level of complexity and down in the level of abstraction. The complexity of life involves such organic patterns and functions as metabolism, locomotion, and reproduction, far more elaborate than the sequence of individual chemical reactions upon which the living creature depends. As William F. Kieffer wrote in a 1971 textbook of chemistry, "as one science uses more fully the conceptual tools provided it by another [as for instance, genetics involves chemical bonding] the dividing line between them blurs. More and more is this becoming true for biology and chemistry." The microstructure of biology appears to be completely susceptible to chemical analysis; the macrostructures of evolutionary biology may still be awaiting their appropriate disciplines. J. G. Kemeny, a philosopher of science, offers this prospect:

The most likely solution of the question of the reduction of biology to physics is that a new theory will be found, covering both fields in new terms. Inanimate nature will appear as the simplest extreme case of this theory. In that case, one would say that physics was reduced to biology and not biology to physics.

Biology is on the verge of overtaking physics in not only reshaping science, but in reshaping philosophy and religion as well.

IS THE SCIENCE OF HUMAN BEINGS THE PARAMOUNT SCIENCE?

Educators have a tendency to believe that the academic curricula of universities reflect a conception of the shape of the world, a sense of cognitive unity from which our values unfold and therefore a manner for introducing students to it. For educators, in fact, the curriculum dominates the scene, hovering between truth and error . . . salvation or enormity.

It is a common form of rationalization for any discipline to make itself the centerpiece of scholarship, with all the other vocations arrayed around it supporting the central sanctioned effort of inquiry and research in varying degrees.

One of the most radical proposals for a new curriculum for biology—indeed, superseding biology—has come from outside the scientific community, from Frederick Turner, a professor of arts and the humanities at the University of Texas at Dallas. He begins his argument with the question of whether it is appropriate to confuse the study of human beings with the study of animal species. He concludes that it is totally valid to do so; in fact, human beings cannot be properly studied in any other way. This judgment causes him to reverse the normal hierarchy of the disciplines, placing anthropology at the top.

Turner sees the crucial role of anthropology as a convergence of "paleoanthropology, sociobiology, human ethology (the study of human behavior as one kind of animal behavior), neurology, psychophysics, linguistics, genetic archaeology, and archaeology." This convergence, he says, may lead—indeed, *will* lead–to a collapse of the old boundary separating the study of humankind from the rest of nature. Anthropology should be the dominant roof science providing a framework for all the other disciplines in simple recognition of the fact that "the evolutionary later always subsumes the evolutionarily earlier." (But, I wonder, where do we stop? Do we look at the world anew with each new tool of investigation? Do we look at the world anew through holographs?)

Turner summons the prospect of a "full mutual engagement of all fields of study, physics as well as poetry." Just as chemistry validates itself by physics, and physics validates itself by mathematics, so will the arts and the humanities have to revalidate themselves by reference to the broad range of physical and cultural anthropology. "To put this in an even more radical way: the arts and humanities *are* higher physics."

If the arts and humanities are the higher physics, they are also the higher biology.

And, on a purely churlish note, I add a few descriptions of anthropology as provided (with the majestic collegial detachment of a fellow social scientist) by one of its most distinguished observers, Professor Clifford Geertz of the Institute of Advanced Studies in Princeton:

> **Anthropology—long one of the most homespun of disciplines, hostile to anything smacking of intellectual pretension and unnaturally proud of an outdoorsman image.**
>
> **All ethnography is part philosophy, and a good deal of the rest is confession.**
>
> **One of the advantages of anthropology as a scholarly enterprise is that no one, including its own practitioners, quite knows exactly what it is ... a collection of quite differently conceived sciences rather accidentally thrown together ... a triumph of life over logic ... [with] paradigmlessness a permanent affliction.**

THE LIMITS OF BIOLOGY

It is no accident that biology, particularly molecular biology, has made its greatest strides in research related to medicine. The relief of pain and suffering, and the search for the causes of disease in humans, have been the rationale for the massive funding for the programs of the National Institutes of Health, where pure research is accomplished under the umbrella, and often urgency, of practical applications. But it is not just political imperatives that are operating here; there are other factors, both practical and conceptual.

For the laboratory scientist, nature becomes, if not what can always be measured, at least what can be examined, with increasingly exquisite instruments. The laboratory can cope only with those physiological functions of the organs and tissues and cells. Wetware indeed. Biology has becomed focused on the animal nature of our bodies; and the resulting advances in scientific medicine have been magnificent. Biology, however, is not equipped to study those adjuncts of our bodies that make humans human. The layman cannot help thinking that the essence of life is never recovered by biology.

What is the role for other animals? Our culture has never totally accommodated itself to the differences between nonhuman animals and human animals. To the laboratory technician, animal specimens are unique examples of apparently immortal and certainly manipulatable genetic cultures. To the ecologist, animals are fauna—part of the environment. Domesticated animals, in the name of husbandry, have become artifacts for human consumption, and undomesticated animals are becoming redundant if not superfluous. The rationale for zoos is being continually reformulated. Animals as game to be hunted are an indulgence of human societies. Not to mention sports: there are more horses now in Florida—none of them working—than at any time in history. Pets are something else again: they are surrogates for friends.

ARCANE FIELDS

Human curiosity and new tools of investigation rapidly find their institutional expression in academic departments and frontiers of commercial research. The life sciences burgeon with new fields of specialization to engage the most jaded of scholars. This list of arcane fields of study suggests only the range of interdisciplinary pursuits. None of them have I made up, and all of them flourish with literature, specialized journals, and annual meetings of their own:

anthropogeography
behavioral neurogenetics
behavior-neuroethology
biomolecular stereodynamics
biotech intellectual–property law (dollars and genes)
comparative vertebrate endocrinology
correlative biological microscopy
developmental psychobiology
electromagnetoelasticity
endocytobiology
ethnomethodology
fish population dynamics
genetic psychology
mathematical biology
molecular psychiatry
neuroimmunomodulation (NIM)
paleoagrostology
pharmacolinguistics (coined at UCLA)
plant behavior (indeed)
psychoneuroimmunology (PNI—a major new frontier)
zoosemiotics

29
The nature of biological doctrines

Biology has its laws such as those of Mendelian genetics, but they are often only broad generalizations with significant exceptions. The laws of physics are believed to be the same everywhere in the universe. This is unlikely to be true of biology. The living systems we know are local, apparently endemic to our own planetary environment. Furthermore, complex factors are at work in matter organized as plants and animals: They are not as susceptible of precise measurement as is matter in motion in the form of stars and atoms—the stuff of physics.

We have it on the authority of Max Planck that "the microscopic method of research is very much more difficult to carry out in physiology than in physics. For this . . . reason the majority of physiological laws are of a statistical character and are called rules."

Take, for example, some adaptation rules:

Allen's rule: concerns the protruding body parts (extremities, ears, tails, etc.), which tend to be shorter relative to body size in colder parts of the species range.
Bergmann's rule: races which inhabit the warmer parts of the geographic range of a species tend to be smaller in body size than races living in colder parts.
Farenholz's rule: postulates that parasites and their hosts

"speciate in sychrony," i.e., they evolve together, and as hostage to each other.

And some evolutionary principles:

Bionomogenesis: The doctrine that evolution is a process governed by causal and logical laws.

Competitive exclusion: That in competition between species that seek the same ecological niche, one species survives while the other expires.

Dollo's law: Evolution does not repeat itself or go backward. There is greater evidence for this view than for any other conclusion about the course of terrestrial evolution.

And a few broader paradigms:

Biodiversity: The doctrine of human dependence on diversity of natural life.

Endosymbiosis, the endosymbionic theory: It is basically a theory of the origin of organelles within the eukaryotic cell (see page 297). For Lynn Margulis, a corollary of the endosymbiotic theory is that *all organisms today are equally evolved*. There are no contemporary ancestors.

Holism: For some, holism is not so much a doctrine as it is a strategy of analysis that attempts to explain complex phenomena by laws operating at the level of the phenomena themselves, and not by the reduction to laws regulating the behavior of component parts. Compare synergy, emergentism, and hierarchies. Holism is the recognition and study of emergent properties; it flourished in the earlier part of this century until eclipsed by the reductionism of molecular biology. It still survives, albeit in a more quantitative than intuitive mode.

Mutation: It is a principle of modern biology that mutations arise at random. An organism cannot specifically produce mutations that are advantageous. Chance mutations that happen to be beneficial have a better chance of surviving.

Neoteny: The varying rates of development of the various

parts of the body, especially the gonads, whereby organisms become sexually mature at a relatively juvenile stage, including the retention of juvenile, even larval, characteristics in adult life. Under this concept we regard the especially helpless state of newborn human infants and its effect in establishing the nuclear family as a unit of social structure.

Recapitulation theory: The famous biogenetic law postulated by Ernst Haeckel that the development of the animal embryo traces the evolutionary development of the species. Also known as "ontogeny recapitulates phylogeny" —hence gills in two-month-old human embryos. Once it was a staple and metaphorically powerful revelation to sophomores; now a largely discredited oversimplification.

Variation: The observation that individuals of any species (except identical twins) differ from one another, and that such genetic variation is one of the sources of evolutionary change.

BIOLOGICAL CONTROL

The concept of biological control had its beginnings in practical tactics to limit the spread of pests and weeds. The term was introduced in 1919 by Harry Scott Smith, who was to define it in the applied sense as the suppression of a pest by means of the introduction, propagation, and dissemination of the predators, the parasites, and the diseases by which it is attacked. The University of California at Berkeley maintains a Division of Biological Control with emphasis on entomological research.

Biological control invokes the antagonistic interaction of species, and their manipulation for practical purposes in horticulture and husbandry. Human intervention in large-scale natural processes inevitably has ecological impacts that are too complicated for all their consequences—benign or adverse—to be anticipated in advance. Biological methods, which often began as simple augmentation of host plant resistance to natural enemies, came to be supplemented by chemical means (such as application of toxins) and cultural strategies (such as crop rotation, tillage, and sanitation). Thus the concept grew from simple pest control to the dynamic manipulation of a growing number of complex ecological factors.

The array of control methods was further complicated by the availability of gene products and genetic techniques for the modification of organisms. Thus in 1987 the National Academy of Sciences broadened the definition of biological control to add to the already recognized chemical, cultural, and conservation techniques the full range of genetic intervention. Some entomologists fear that this broadened inclusion of genetic factors only clouds the issue, making it more difficult to anticipate and resolve the economic, sociological, and ecological consequences of what began as a simple program to dust pests and weeds with poison.

The president of the World Resources Institute has put the matter in a most positive light:

> **The emerging biotech industry has great potential for cutting pollution. New microbial and other bioengineered products, for example, can substitute for chemical pesticides and fertilizer, help treat effluent and other waste, promote vegetation growth on impoverished soils, increase the potential of biological sources of energy, and improve human health and contraception, thus reducing population pressures.**

30
Research frontiers in biology

———————— ❧ ————————

As 20th-century science approaches the turn of the millennium, three basic areas of ignorance preoccupy us and remain as intractable as they were at mid-century:

- a grand unified theory for particle physics;
- the character of biological organization;
- the structure of the brain-mind processes.

That formulation was advanced by Lancelot Law Whyte in 1965. He further speculated that any theoretical or mathematical method found appropriate to one of them may aid the solution of the others.

More recently Freeman Dyson has selected the three most likely areas for technological progress through the middle of the next century. In his formulation they are:

- molecular biology and cellular physiology at the molecular level, manifest as genetic engineering;
- neurophysiology and the science of complex information-processing networks and brains, manifest as artificial intelligence;
- space physics, the exploration of the solar system and the physical environment of the earth, manifest as space colonization.

All aspects of the remaining challenges to biology have been summarized by Joseph G. Gall, a professor of developmental genetics, in one simple sentence: "Since the end of the 19th century biologists have sought a unified theory explaining what is special about the organization of living matter, how the organization is inherited, how it develops within the individual and how it evolves with time." There you have it all: what is life? How does genetics work? How do embryos and organisms develop? How is evolution governed?

SOME PROGRAMS AND PRIORITIES OF RESEARCH

Institutional priorities. At the top of the nation's scientific research program are the megascience projects in the multibillion-dollar-budget range in response to an active political constituency. Chief among these in the field of biology are AIDS research and the human genome project. A little further down in the hierarchy are the programs of professional interest to the American Association for the Advancement of Science, whose panel on "Frontiers in the Life Sciences" at their 1988 convention featured:

cancer ontogeny
neural basis of memory
plant resistance mechanisms
genetic basis of biological rhythms
protein folding problem

The AAAS areas of concentration are closer to fields of practical application than the large nets cast by the megascience projects. As research moves from large national goals to the more focused issues in the laboratory they seem to gain in intellectual appeal. The following checklist of frontiers illustrates lines of inquiry most irresistible to human curiosity. Few can say which of them will prove tractable to human ingenuity or even which are most relevant to human survival.

The following list of projects and objectives is illustrative, but far from exhaustive.

Biosphere II: (II because the Earth is I.) An experimental self-contained ecosystem where eight people will live for two years. It will not only test models for space settlements but aims to improve the stewardship of Biosphere I. Established at a site north of Tucson, Arizona, it is under the direction of the London-based Institute of Ecotechnics and Space Ventures. (It is financed in part by Edward Bass of Fort Worth, Texas.)

Brain-mind puzzle: Research on the higher nervous system remains the most intractable of biological problems. It is the unique attribute of the brain that it endows its possessor with self-awareness. The quest for a physical explanation of consciousness involves paradoxes that, without doing violence to the laws of physics, bring us uncomfortably to the limits of human understanding. It is not at all certain that the brain is capable of providing an explanation of itself.

Cancer ontogeny: How does a healthy cell turn into a cancer tumor?

Ecology: an ecological survey: Dr. Jonathan Roughgarden of Stanford University has proposed that Congress should create a U.S. Ecological Survey along the lines of the U.S. Geological Survey. He submits that pronouncing the acronym USES as "uses" would emphasize that it has applications transcending its scientific discipline. He further submits that ecology is an earth science, "as much as or more so than a biological science." (An active constituency is urging the U.S. Congress to charter and fund an agency to be called the National Institutes for the Environment— NIE—to be broadly modeled on the National Institutes of Health.)

Ecotechnology: A concept introduced by the Japanese Professor Aida (and underwritten by the Honda Foundation) to address the long-term effects of *eco*logical, *techno*logical and *eco*nomic systems, including nothing less than the evolutionary processes underlying biological and socio-cultural change.

Embryology and developmental biology: In spite of all the successes of genetics, molecular biology, and neurophysiology, biologists have still not managed to explain the genetic mechanisms for the development of embryos or the inheritance of instincts. Rupert Sheldrake writes:

How does the inheritance of a certain set of chemical genes and the synthesis of certain proteins make swallows, for example, migrate from a certain part of England to Southern Africa before the English winter begins, and then make the same birds migrate back to the same place in England in the spring? No one knows. No one knows how embryos progressively take up their forms or how instincts are inherited or how habits develop or how memories work.

Evolution: For many if not most people today, the outstanding question about evolution remains the same as it did in Darwin's day—given descent from a common ancestor, how did the extraordinary diversity of life in space and time come about?

Human genome sequencing project: Although ultimately aimed at constructing a complete sequence of the 3,000 million nucleotide base pairs that make up the human genome, the controversial project would have many useful concurrent spinoffs such as genetic linkage maps, clone repositories, and genetic databases. The controversy arises from its implications for public policy and from the thorny problem of how to administer a project involving private laboratories, public funding, patents, copyright, technology transfer, and foreign governments. Many biologists deplore the headlong rush to sequence the human genome as a diversion of academic resources. Even a layman can question whether such an exhaustive description of living flesh will afford any clues to what it is to be human.

Human Frontiers Science Program: Advanced by the

Japanese government in 1986 as an internationally coordinated program to demonstrate a commitment to academic rather than commercial investment in basic interdisciplinary research. The initial focus of HFSP is into basic research in neuroscience and the molecular mechanisms of biological functions.

Human protein index: Nothing less than an inventory of the the estimated 30,000 to 50,000 different kinds of proteins that make up the human body. Computer technology and the technique of two-dimensional electrophoresis would be combined to rewrite the description of pathology at the molecular level.

International Geosphere Biosphere Program (IGBP): The long-term study of global change from the interior of the earth to the interior of the sun, concentrating on the chemistry of biogeographical cycles. The goals are comparable in scope to the landmark IGY (International Geophysical Year) of 1957–58. In September 1986 the International Council of Scientific Unions (ICSU) endorsed the IGBP, designed to: "describe and understand the interactive physical, chemical, and biological processes that regulate the total Earth system, the unique environment it provides for life, the changes that are occurring in that system, and the manner by which these changes are influenced by human actions." Advances in interdisciplinary concern have forced the enlargement of the geophysical paradigm— to include a grand survey of how organisms and the material world settle their accounts with each other. The program is scheduled to come into full effect in the late 1990s.

Joint Global Ocean Flux Study (JGOFS): To study how carbon is cycled through the oceans, particularly its effect on the scale of global warming.

Last common ancestor: What are the date, identity, and characteristics of the last common ancestor of all living species?

Molecular biology: A discipline in which there are vast strides in the accumulation of data, but as a special case of physical chemistry—with which it has not yet quite come to terms—it is a pursuit still devoid of a conceptual framework. John Maddox, the editor of *Nature* magazine, predicts that "Molecular biology will soon move beyond its present preoccupation with the naming of the molecular parts of which organisms are made to search for the dynamic relationships between them."

National Institute for Global Environmental Change: The University of California and the U.S. Department of Energy have jointly launched the NIGEC to fund and coordinate interdisciplinary research in universities throughout the nation, covering such concerns as the greenhouse effect, ozone depletion, and energy use and pollution. The NIGEC program may or may not come up with some technological fixes, but it does not address policy issues at the roots of the problem: namely the short-term accounting practices of industrial societies involving economic, political, and moral questions beyond the range of environmental sciences per se.

Ontogenetic coding: The problem of how the unidimensional genetic information encoded in the DNA of a single cell becomes transformed into a four-dimensional human being [organism], a creature heterogeneous in time and space, the individual that grows, matures, and dies. Cancer, disease and aging are epiphenomena of ontogenetic coding. . . . The egg-to-adult transformation is essentially similar, and similarly mysterious, in humans and other mammals.

Origin of life: Not a pressing concern to most biologists.

Plant molecular biology: For the past fifty years crop yields and productivity in the United States have risen on an average of somewhere between 1 and 2 percent a year, with about three-quarters of the increase being due to genetic improvement from selective breeding. It is the goal of plant molecular biology to provide seeds to produce plants resistant both to pests and viral diseases, with greater nutritional value, and able to grow in marginal inhospitable soil. (Petunias—related to tobacco and tomatoes—are the white mice of plant biology.)

Protein-folding problem: The prediction of the three-dimensional structure of a protein from its amino-acid sequence remains one of the fundamental unsolved problems in molecular biology.

Space—Biological applications in space exploration: Freeman Dyson has proposed that space exploration in the 21st century will require a combination of technologies from three different disciplines: genetic engineering, artificial intelligence, and solar-electric propulsion. But note that the latest report on enabling technologies issued by the Aerospace Industrial Association of America (1987) surveys the entire field of technologies relating to space exploration with no mention of *any* biological techniques, strategies, or applications.

PROSPECTS FOR NEW PARADIGMS IN BIOLOGY

Advances in biological knowledge have been magnificently well served by two grand paradigms, the evolutionary model of Darwin and the genetic code of Watson and Crick. Nevertheless, further progress in biology still awaits an overdue conceptual breakthrough—particularly with regard to the central nervous system.

Biological organisms as relics of their past. All biological organisms are prisoners of historicity, the inability to escape from the stream of their historical past. Every species is the terminus of an ancient lineage hammered and shaped into its present form by a complex interplay of genetic recombination and natural selection. Understanding organisms at any level involves the ubiquitous cliché of their previous condition: *What was there before?*

Karl Popper put the matter starkly in the first Medawar lecture to the Royal Society: He declaimed that biology is irreducible to physics because biochemistry is irreducible to chemistry. Popper argues that an understanding of biological systems requires a knowledge of function and history that chemistry cannot provide. Molecular biology is still incapable of predicting what three-dimensional molecular structure will arise from a given sequence of amino acids. Where are we to find the biologist—or chemist—who will propose a strategy to resolve the dilemma?

The historicity of biological phenomena. From the outset, biology has particularly lent itself to historical and descriptive approaches. The success of molecular biology brought a prospect of reducing all biology to the first principles of atomic and molecular physics, but to date there has been no success in attempts to apply chemistry and physics to make biology a predictive science. According to E. O. Wilson,

> New general principles, the grail of biology, are becoming ever more elusive ... while factual knowledge grows exponentially, with a doubling time of perhaps 10 to 20 years, the number of broadly applicable discoveries made per investigator per year is declining steeply. A large part of the reason is the historicity of biological phenomena, which generates special cases and crumbles generality in direct proportion to the depth of understanding.

Even the computer has not—or at least not yet—rescued biology from its historical and descriptive restraints. Dr. Harold Morowitz tells us not to expect relief soon:

> The space of possibilities [of molecular biology] is too large and too multidimensional for existing computational principles to indicate the actual pathway taken. After the encoding of genetic information in molecules, the historical aspects of the subject, including random mutations, so dominate that they preclude predicting biology from the first principles of physics. Thus it seems highly unlikely that we will ever have a grand unified theory of biology.

Everything interesting happens only once. Biological organisms are not only complex, they are historical accidents. This poses a problem for physicists, who are accustomed to generalizations, to rules of regularity and order. It was left to a physicist, Max Delbruck, to explain that "there are no absolute phenomena in biology. Everything is time-bound and space-bound." It is asking too much for the functional to explain the historical, to ask the parts to explain the whole. Max Delbruck wrote, "If it be true, that the essence of life is the accumulation of experience through the generations, then, one may perhaps suspect that the key problem of biology, from the physicist's point of view, is how living matter manages to record and perpetuate experience." Stephen Jay Gould says that evolutionary biologists "work . . . more as historians than as guardians of 'the scientific method' . . . because our empirical world is a temporal sequence of complex events, so unrepeatable by the laws of probability and so irreversible by the principles of thermodynamics, that *everything interesting happens only once in its meaningful details.*" (The italics are mine.) Biologists do not attempt to predict, although, after the fact, they can explain with confidence.

Homeostatic systems of molecules. Noting that Erwin Schrödinger had in 1944 first proposed to biologists that they should investigate the molecular structure of the gene, Freeman Dyson now suggests, in *Infinite in All Directions*, that biologists might find it comparably rewarding if they could at the present time concentrate their experimental energies on investigation of the population structure of homeostatic systems of molecules.

Topobiology attempts to answer the problems of development from the bottom up, starting with molecules and cell interactions—the properties that arise not from individual cells but from interactions among them. The term was introduced by Dr. Gerald M. Edelman, the director of the Neurosciences Institute at Rockefeller University, to describe his particular brand of molecular embryology. His hypothesis addresses the chief remaining mystery of embryology and morphogenesis: How does the one-dimensional genetic code translate into a three-dimensional organism?

The lure of hierarchies. Biological paradigms never stray far from a hierarchical context. Cyril Stanley Smith writes:

> Hesitantly, in my ignorance, I predict the development of some new principles of hierarchy that will enable the effective resonance between molecule and organism to be explored: possibly the way to this may be pointed by the emerging science of materials, so incredibly simple beside biology but complex enough to demonstrate a kind of symbiosis between scales, the interwoven importance of both atoms and aggregates. . . . A few men will be in touch with both levels, but human capacities are such that most must specialize, and the liaison man will be far more important than he has been in the past when the greatest intellectual opportunities lay at the frontier.

31
Prospects for a scientific explanation of life

─────────── ❦ ───────────

WHAT SOME PHYSICISTS SAY

Some of the most eloquent writing about the nature of life has come to us not from biologists but from physicists. Niels Bohr, Erwin Schrödinger, Werner Heisenberg, Max Delbruck, Francis Crick, Victor Weisskopf, Gerald Feinberg, and Philip Morrison have all made stimulating comments on the application of physics to biology.

A philosopher, Patricia Smith Churchland, has complained about the curious fact that while physicists often become biologists (for instance, Lancelot Law Whyte, Schrödinger, Crick, and Delbruck), biologists rarely become physicists. One of the factors is said to be that the research environment in physics is dominated by group effort, while in biology it is still possible to work alone.

Here in chronological order is a recapitulation:

Niels Bohr, (1885–1962), to whose temperament indeterminacy was most congenial, believed that life was just an elementary fact that cannot be explained. This doesn't mean he cared more about science—its methods and its results—than he did about life; just that the former was susceptible to human understanding while the latter is not. "Only by renouncing an explanation about life in the ordinary sense do we gain the possibility of accounting for its characteristics." (*Atomic Physics and Human Knowledge,* 1958.)

From Erwin Schrödinger (1887–1961) we have an intuitive anticipation of the hologram. "This life of yours which you are living is not merely a piece of the entire existence, but is in a certain sense the *whole;* only this whole is not so constituted that it can be surveyed in one single glance." (*My View of the World,* 1925.)

The world makes no sense by itself; it is left to us to make sense of the world. The advent of intelligence in the universe poses a dilemma which Werner Heisenberg (1901–1976) has formulated in an item of particular philosophical daring: "Natural science does not simply describe and explain nature; it is part of the interplay between nature and ourselves; it describes nature as exposed to our method of questioning." (*Physics and Philosophy,* 1959.)

While the aim of physics is to discover universal laws, the complex phenomena of biology do not lend themselves easily to such generalizations. Max Delbruck (1906–1981):

> **Any one cell, embodying as it does the record of a billion years of evolution, represents more a historical than a physical event ... You cannot expect to explain so wise an old bird in a few simple words. ... If it be true, that the essence of life is the accumulation of experience through the generations, then, one may perhaps suspect that the key problem of biology, from the physicist's point of view, is how living matter manages to record and perpetuate experience. [1949 Lecture: "A Physicist Looks at Biology"]**

Francis H.C. Crick (1916–), the man who discovered the molecular strucure of DNA, can bring a peculiar authority to this prognosis: "Only if life was *very* easy to start, because there is in fact some rather direct pathway through the maze of possibilities, are we likely to be able to reproduce it in the laboratories, at least in the immediate future." (*Life Itself: Its Origin and Nature,* 1981.)

Notwithstanding the title of the work cited, Lancelot

Law Whyte (1896–1974) was a mathematician and theoretical physicist. (He had studied at Cambridge under Ruth-
erford.)

> **The kind of order in most chemical molecules, in crystals,
> and in the solar system is known; that in atomic nuclei, in
> living systems, and in brain-minds is not. Temporal succes-
> sion illustrates one type of order; regular spatial patterns
> another . . . The two great tendencies in the universe: toward
> order and toward disorder, seem to be locked in cosmic op-
> position, perhaps because we view them wrongly. [*The Un-
> consciousness Before Freud*, 1960]**

And from Philip Morrison, an MIT physics teacher,
widely revered on television, and for many years a book
reviewer for *Scientific American*: "I would bet right now
that matter, like logic, is destined to remain forever in part
within, and in part without, the reach of any closed form."

THE COMFORTS OF SKEPTICISM

Each discovery of science seems to create in the long run
more mystery than it solves. We say the light always gleams
ahead at the end of the tunnel but maybe we should not be
so sure that the tunnel has an end. Almost every Sunday
newspaper encourages us in the overwhelming belief that
we are rapidly filling in the details of the cosmic picture.

Here is what three scholars from completely different
walks of life have had to say about access to scientific truth.
The astronomer, Edward Harrison, says that Stone Age people were no smarter or better off then we are. The engineer-
poet, Fuller, says truth is unrealizable as pure metaphysics.
The philosopher Wittgenstein says we should stop worrying
about explanations of life.

> **Dare I say—contrary to popular belief—that secure knowl-
> edge can never be found? . . . That each discovery creates in**

the long run more mystery than it solves? That we stand no closer to the ultimate "truths" than did our forebears? And that we are no better intellectually and morally than the people who lived a thousand and even ten thousand years ago?

We have this overwhelming belief that we are rapidly filling in the detail of the cosmic picture. Unfortunately, the picture keeps changing. One landscape with figures melts away and a new landscape with figures emerges requiring fresh paintwork. The picture keeps growing bigger and we cannot help occasionally noticing how gaps on the canvas are spreading faster than dabs of paint. [Edward Harrison, professor of physics and astronomy, University of Massachusetts]

We may say that thinking about the truth alters truth, but only to the extent of defining it. We always clarify and re-define the truth by making it more comprehensively considerate and more incisively exquisite. Truth alters truth only by refining the definition. The substance of the sensing and instrumental control of the physical means of communication is always refinable and tends toward the ephemeralization of doing ever more with ever less, but you can never get to the exact, most economical statement of the truth, for the very communication will have ephemeralized to pure metaphysics. [R. Buckminster Fuller]

When science has answered all its last questions—and solved all its problems—life will still be unexplained. [Ludwig Wittgenstein]

So what are we worrying about? Cannot we take their advice? If you really want to know that kind of fixed, unerring truth seek for it not in science but in revelation.

PROSPECTS FOR A SCIENTIFIC EXPLANATION OF LIFE

Most scientists express litle confidence that life—the mechanics of living organisms, the full range of their capacities and interdependence—will ever be explained within the reach of their investigative methods and to the complete satisfaction of their rigorous standards of measurement. Whereas some say, especially in the light of the spectacular progress of molecular biology in the last half of this century, a complete explanation is close at hand. Others are certain that the more we learn, the more elusive will the target become.

In a middle path are those who see no contradiction between reductionism (the molecule explains everything in terms of chemistry and physics) and holism. Reductionism is the view that the parts account for the whole, that the protein molecules of organisms can explain everything in terms of chemistry and physics. Holism is the philosophy that attempts to explain complex phenomena by laws operating at a level above the component parts—emergent evolution, explanations in terms of the organism or larger system. Those in the middle path argue that the two concepts are interdependent and complementary. As Paul A. Weiss of Rockefeller University puts it, "there is no phenomenon in a living system that is *not* molecular, but there is none that is *only* molecular, either." We cannot be sure of the capacity of science to deal with what may be a nonscientific question.

The art of the soluble. To say that scientists have left life unexplained is perhaps more an appreciation than a condemnation of their vocation. Science is by its nature inexhaustible. Peter Medawar advanced the concept that science is "the art of the soluble." Here there seems to be a resonance between the two senses of the word: soluble as tractable to laboratory techniques (susceptible of being dissolved in a fluid); and soluble as the correct answer to an exercise or proposition. Life remains complex and difficult to describe, and may well remain outside "the soluble" for science for some time to come.

The mind-matter mystery. The most remote and complex manifestation of how animate matter differs from inanimate matter is the unfathomable functioning of the human mind. Here is how the situation looks to the molecular biologist Gunther S. Stent:

> **Increasing numbers of veteran molecular geneticists are now turning their attention to the higher nervous system in the hope of finding relief from jejune genetic investigations along more or less clearly established lines. They have good reason to hope that, unlike the quest for fathoming the gene, the quest for understanding the brain will not soon reach a disappointingly workaday denouement. For since the mind-matter mystery is not likely to be amenable to scientific analysis, the most interesting attribute of life may never be explained.**

It has been proved easier to study life than to define it. Atoms, for instance, are neither dead nor alive. Atoms *are*, they can be split, and they may decay, or they can persist in an orderly molecular arrangements of energy and matter. As the crudest of starting points we may say that atoms can exist without life but life cannot manifest itself in the physical world of nature without atoms. All matter, even inorganic matter, shares the kinds of mysteries associated with life. An endless regression of intricacy applies to the inorganic as well as the organic. Somehow, the organic contains the inorganic, but not the reverse. To quote P. C. W. Davies again:

> **. . . if mind is *pattern* rather than *substance*, then it is capable of many different representations. . . . Insofar as human beings are concerned, mind is a product of matter, or put more accurately, mind finds expression through matter. . . .The lesson of the quantum is that the link works the other way too: Matter can only achieve concrete, well-defined existence in conjunction with mind.**

A catechism on teleology. In a 1990 symposium at Georgetown University commemorating Teilhard de Chardin, Dr. Harold J. Morowitz, the perennial essayist and biochemist of George Mason University, submitted himself to a question period from the audience. In a symposium not devoid of Jesuit scholars, the following dialogue ensued:

Q. Do the fundamental physical constants (and perhaps their large-number coincidences) imply a teleology in the world of nature?

A. The nontheological way of answering this is to say that the universe works better than we have any right to expect.

Q. As a biologist what future do you see for us humans?

A. The evolving universe is not in any way predictable. One single atomic event in a single strand of DNA could kill a whale. Reductionists like Stephen Jay Gould, however, fail to appreciate the envelope of possibility within which the random events take place.

Q. What makes teleology respectable?

A. In 1960 I asked myself: What is the smallest single, autonomous, self-replicating entity? (I ruled out viruses because of their dependence on the chemistry of their host to replicate.) The answer is mycoplasma: the smallest single cell. Even mycoplasmas require 400 different enzymatic reactions. But 400 is a finite number, and this means that life can be reduced to a finite system.

Q. Can you create life in the laboratory from nonlife?

A. What we do experimentally is to try to replicate a sequence of polar lipid molecules into membranous vesicles. Such a structure could become a site of catalysis leading to further energy processing. All of our efforts in this century have left us very, very far from anything as complex as the simplest cells.

Dualities of biology. Meanwhile, the most comprehensive generalization of the process of life comes to us not from a scientist but from the polymath literary critic, George Steiner:

All we can guess is that the capacity of living things to alter while retaining their identity seems to depend on a subtle interplay between indeterminacy in the small and determinacy in the gross.

There it is, much better said than textbook talk of phylogeny and ontogeny. The world of biology, the world of things that are born and die, is pervaded by dualities. The classic antitheses of the one and the many, and identity and change, are manifest organically in living matter. Ambivalence and ambiguity prevail.

Paradise mislaid. What all this means is that we might as well get used to our mortality. Where is the prospect of life everlasting in a world where the true dynamics of history are biological and ecological? If immortality has some cosmic niche it is not within the grasp of the individual nor is it within the province of the species; and even the evolutionary process itself is, as far as we know, finite. We can still contemplate—and some may find comfort—in a prospect of the mind's postmortem survival in a realm where consciousness may be divorced from nature as so far revealed. Is there a next world and what is it like? We have no better sense of it than the proverbial dialogue between the twins in utero about what *their* next world will be like.

Many of the voices we have listened to in these pages have linked the destiny of man with the destiny of the atom. As Dobhzhansky foretold in the epigraph at the beginning of this book, Darwin was the keystone of the arch, linking not only our kinship with apes, grasses, and amoebas but our further kinship with molecules, stones, and stars. Whether we find these affinities alien or congenial, they are inescapable. Our window of survival on this planet maybe as brief as a few hundred months, but certainly not much longer than that of the dinosaurs—a few hundred million years. We can conjecture that our children may acquire a surer grasp of the matter. There seems to be plenty of room for further happy exploration by all of the biological disciplines involved—cognitive science, artificial intelligence, neurobiology—and none of them will soon exhaust themselves.

Our friendly biologists with all their overgrown vines and laboratory broth and neural network models have provided us with only the dimmest view of where our *we* and our *I* may be embedded in that luxuriance. What we are left with is the role of observers instead of believers. The itch to believe still lingers; the fact that we observe has to be its own reward.

APPENDIX: BIOLOGICAL DISCIPLINES

AN ANNOTATED SURVEY, EXCLUSIVE OF THE AGRICULTURAL AND MEDICAL SCIENCES

As an area of scientific inquiry and as a field of professional practice, biology is barely contained within an established academy. It is so broad a field that, like the legal profession, it is not totally able to police its membership and discourage uninvited adherents. Lawyers at least have state bar examinations, though they still have to let many into the tent.

Since I could find no satisfactory reference work that described the various disciplines of biology in more than a single phrase, and since the subject is so inherently interesting, I created a list of my own, making no claim to academic rigor. I found a range of everything from bioaesthetics to xenobiosis. You can put *bio* in front of almost any word in English; it is the most protean of prefixes.

My goal was to include any serious effort at investigation or practical application, rejecting only the trivial. I have tried to describe each discipline as a composite of how the specialists themselves describe what they do. When you think how long the list is, with all its overlapping hierarchies and wealth of hyphenated hybrid enterprises—a survey of what those who profess biology are doing all day on any given day—it suggests a remarkably synoptic takeout, a sort of freeze-frame picture of how biology flourishes in the last decade of the 20th century. The field is so dynamic that some of its specialties were unheard of a decade ago; others will be superseded—or transformed—a decade hence.

They are listed in alphabetical order for convenience, not just for reference, not just as an isolated appendix, but to be perused as a text for its comprehensive survey of the range of biology. (Some of the relevance of disciplines to conceptual problems in biology is discussed in Part VI.)

aging—see gerontology.

anatomy—study of the structural makeup of an organism and its parts. It has been traditionally concerned with structure that can be observed with the naked eye—a primitive constraint that had brought it to be regarded as one of the mature disciplines (like, for instance, acoustics), from which no great new discoveries would be expected. Now, however, with the introduction of supercomputational scanning, anatomy has been rescued from the brink of moribundity. Computational anatomy with its employment of computer graphics is resurrecting the cadaver as a renewed object of scientific regard.

Anatomy is one of the two oldest formal disciplines of biology (the other is systematics).

> **comparative anatomy**—"Comparative anatomy does not evoke a natural fondness among most working biologists," says Henry Gee, one of their number. "To many, the smell of formalin means mustiness more generally. Yet to work on a living organism without sound knowledge of what it is, and how it is put together, diminishes the worth of what results emerge."

anthropogeography—see biogeography.

anthropology—the study of human beings, their evolutionary history and their cultural diversity. Like other social sciences it derives as much from humanistic as scientific impulses. Its admission to the academy of American science was accelerated in the mid-1850s by the practical need to understand aboriginal native American culture. In treating cultural characteristics—man *and* his works—anthropology goes beyond strictly biological concerns. See paleontology, and see text discussion of anthropology on pages 312–313.

> **biological anthropology**—an offshoot spearheaded by the very articulate Melvin Konner of Harvard University. In *The Tangled Web* (1983) he applies findings from molecular biology, neurobiology, and genetics to augment conventional anthropology in its efforts to explain human behavior.
>
> **molecular anthropology**—concerned with genetic aspects of human and animal evolution.

anthrozoos—see ecology.

artificial intelligence—a computer-based discipline (known as AI) aimed at understanding human intelligence and developing machines capable of intelligent problem solving.

artificial life—this burgeoning field of study (known as AL) has many definitions suggesting that it is unlimited in scope and ambitious in its future prospects, as it attempts to synthesize biological behaviors beyond carbon-chain life as it has evolved on earth. The most modest definition that I could find is at once the most comprehensive: Artificial life is a speculative discipline exploring the use of the computer and other modeling techniques to provide new ways of thinking about the universal principles of life.

bacteriology—study of bacteria, especially in relation to medicine and agriculture. Bacteria that cause diseases are known as *germs*, and their study appears to evoke particular passions. In *Rats, Lice and History* Hans Zinsser wrote of the history of the bacillus that causes typhus fever:

> **We have chosen to write the biography of our disease because we love it platonically—as Amy Lowell loved Keats—and have sought its acquaintance wherever we could find it. And in this growing intimacy we have become increasingly im-**

pressed with the influence that this and other infectious diseases, which span—in their protoplasmic continuities— the entire history of mankind, have had upon the fates of men.

behavioral biology—see behavioral ecology at ecology, ethology, psychobiology.

behavioral and social sciences—The predicament within the academy of this broad field of the so-called soft sciences has tended to place them in a defensive posture. A high-level committee of the U.S. National Research Council has come up with a definition that—without putting religion and philosophy altogether out of business— lends a certain nobility to the calling:

The behavioral and social sciences strive to understand the conduct of human beings and animals, singly and in groups, from the moments of their birth to the moments of their death. The subject matter . . . ranges from global commerce and conflict to the neurochemical substrates of memory and motivation. The interests of research carry from the origins of species to forecasts of political, economic, and techno-logical behavior and events. [Dean R. Gerstein et al., eds, *The Behavioral and Social Sciences Achievements and Opportunities*, 1988]

bioacoustics—(1) the study and measurement of the interaction of sound waves—from the infrasound through audible and ultrasound ranges—with biological systems, especially human beings, for diagnostic and therapeutic purposes. (2) the study of echolocation as employed by bats and porpoises.

bioarchitecture—a special group within the Japanese MITI organization aimed at developing new algorithms and simulations for neurocomputing through the study of living organisms.

bioassay—determination of the relative effective strengths of organic substances such as vitamins and hormones, using living organisms.

bioastronomy—see exobiology.

biocentrism—the doctrine that nature has its own rights. It is opposed to an anthropocentric view, in asserting that the human species has no implicit authority over other species, or indeed other natural elements, e.g., rivers.

biochemistry—the study of the chemical reactions within living tissue. It is at the summit of an implicit hierarchy: chemistry, organic chemistry, biochemistry. Biochemistry—virtually synonymous with "molecular life sciences"—is a young and aggressive discipline, studying how cells manage to produce and transform biologically useful chemicals. It derives its force from the assumption that there is no fundamental difference between chemical reactions that take place in the test tube and the laboratory and those that occur in a bacterium or a human being. It is nothing less than an attempt to provide a consistent system of explanation for all processes occurring in living matter in terms of chemical events. It appears on the verge of becoming a mature discipline with predictive powers.

A specialist in gene transduction at NIH,[*] with a penchant for sweeping generalizations, describes biochemistry as nothing less than "the name for things that change." There you have it all: things that change on their own account, the processes of anabolism, catabolism, and metabolism in general—all the patterns of organized energy that distinguish life from the inertia of dead matter.

One of the first departments of biochemistry in the American university system was established in the college of agriculture at the University of Wisconsin in the 1930s; it was initially preoccupied with practical—not to say mundane—applications, the blood testing and urinalysis of farm mammals domesticated for commercial purposes.

More philosophically, note the subjunctive observation that: "The range of constants that permit chemistry may well also permit biochemistry." (Dr. Virginia Trimble, ICUS

[*] *Dr. Paul Goldsmith of the Metabolic Diseases Branch, National Institute of Diabetes and Digestive and Kidney Diseases, National Institutes of Health, Bethesda, Maryland.*

paper, 1987.) The point is not trivial. When Karl Popper delivered the first Medawar lecture to the Royal Society, he declared that biochemistry was irreducible to chemistry because an understanding of biological systems requires a knowledge of function and history which chemistry cannot provide.

biochemical engineering—see bioengineering.

bioconjugate chemistry—concern for the joining of two different molecular functions by chemical or biological means, including, for instance, antibodies and their fragments, and nucleic acids and their analogs.

biochronology—the study of (1) biological periodicities. (2) the time-keeping devices in living organisms. See chronobiology.

bioclimatology—study of the effects of the physical environment on living organisms, particularly the effect of climatic conditions on human habitation. See ecology.

biocracy—a nonce word introduced by W. B. Cannon to attempt to encompass the influence of biological science on society and public policy.

biocybernetics—(1) the mathematics of control systems in living organisms. (2) the attempt to quantify—indeed to apply differential equations to—emotions such as love and and anger.

biodiversity—See conservation biology.

bioeconomics—a name chosen by its exponents as analogous to biophysics and biochemistry. Its ultimate goal is nothing less than achieving a synthesis of evolutionary and economic theory. One of its chief proponents, Dr. Michael T. Ghiselin of the California Academy of Sciences, Golden Gate Park, San Francisco, California, says that "In biology and economics alike . . . an excessive confidence in the optimal character of the world has lead to serious misconceptions." The remedy proposed is empirical research, which might result in the discovery of generalized laws and principles applicable to both biology and economics.

bioelectricity—study of the generation or action of electric current or voltage in the biological processes.

bioelectrochemistry—combines two very potent disciplines: the study of microorganisms and electrochemistry. As versatile biocatalysts microorganisms have industrial potentials, as, for example, in the treatment of effluents. Electrochemistry offers the prospect of converting matter into energy through microbial fuel cells, which may obviate high operating temperature.

bioelectromagnetics—study of the interaction of electromagnetic radiation—infra and ultra frequencies—with biological systems.

bioenergetics—(1) The study of the energetics of basic metabolic processes; the study of "vitality, the coupling of energy: the physical and chemical mechanisms by which organisms capture energy and transduce it into useful forms." (2) The attempt to enhance natural healing processes by bringing body rhythms into harmony—no kidding—with the natural environment. (3) a technique of psychology introduced by Wilhelm Reich that seeks to modify emotional patterns by means of physiological manipulations.

bioengineering—another science of interface, a hybrid of independent pursuits. Bioengineering subsumes, among other things, biology, mechanics, and information theory. Compare biomechanics and biotechnology. Bioengineering ventures into an untravelled twilight region where organisms and machines seem to resemble each other; and it does so on purely pragmatic grounds and with little regard for inescapable philosophic implications. Thus for some of us it presents an aggressive and even threatening presumption about the nature of life.

> **biocatalysis**—the industrial application of organisms or parts of organisms that function as catalysts (enzymes). (See same term under biotechnology.)
>
> **biochemical engineering**—the translation of basic biological functions such as fermentation and tissue culture into large-scale industrial processes.

bionics—(1) The construction of mechanical systems or instruments modeled after organisms. (2) The adoption of biological structures to problems in engineering, electronics, or computer design. (3) The application of electronic devices—such as computers and solid state circuitry—to medical problems. Its most familiar exemplar is the *pacemaker*, which corrects abnormal heart rhythms. The Division of Research Services (NIH) has under development a *prosthetic urethral valve.*

protein engineering—requires expertise in two distinct disciplines, molecular genetics and structural biophysics.

bioethics—In its most abstract sense, bioethics deals with the effect of biology on human values. (Not just biology, but our increasing *knowledge* of biology: the scientific command of biological processes.)

More specifically, it is involved with concern for the inescapable ethical problems involved in such applications as organ transplant, the use of patients in medical research, experimentation on human embryos and fetuses, artificial insemination, *in vitro* fertilization, genetic engineering, the use of life-prolonging medical technology, physician-patient relations, euthanasia, and the allocation of finite medical resources.

Since it involves contributions from specialists in philosophy, theology, law, sociology, economics, and medicine and other health sciences, it is perhaps more a program than a discipline. (A current bibliography of bioethics, including legal decisions of courts, runs to thirteen volumes.) Compare genethics.

bio-forensics—see forensic biology.

biofouling—study of microbial, plant, or animal fouling on natural or man-made surfaces in the environment.

biogeochemistry—various usages occur: (1) The study of the origin of forces and matter at the dawn of time, and the way they evolved to the complexity of the system earth. (2) The study of the circulation of those chemical elements—approximately 40—absorbed by plants and animals as metabolized and finally returned to the inorganic world. (3) The chemistry of the biosphere, principally the behavior of inorganic elements in geological and biological systems. (4) The interaction of chemical elements in ecological systems as a basis for intervention to modify such adverse reactions as erosion and pollution.

    biogeochemical dynamics—term adopted by the National Science Foundation for the large-scale computer modeling of its "interagency initiative for a global environmental change research program." Although it's called a foundation, the NSF is a federal government agency with its own bureaucratic way of putting things.

In 1987 the American Geophysical Union inaugurated a new quarterly journal entitled *Global Biogeochemical Cycles.*

    biogeography—the study of the geographic distribution of plants and animals and the search for an explanation of distribution patterns. More than a descriptive science, it is a critical study of the behavior and ecology of organisms as factors of distribution. (Mayr, 1988). In the past two decades, aspects of floristic and faunal distribution have been illuminated by the advent of the geological concept of plate tectonics.

    Biogeography embraces two overlapping objectives: (1) the geographer's concern with biomes, community structure, and climax theory; and (2) the aim of explaining the the distribution of organisms on all time scales, past and present. "A key problem . . . throughout biogeography," says Eugene P. Odum, "is the dearth of specific predictions for each of many possible hypotheses."

    anthropogeography—the study of the effect on human beings of local characteristics of the earth's surface.

    areography—study of the form and size of the geographic ranges of a particular species or other taxa.

    island biogeography—study of immigration, extinction, and attainment of equilibrium of numbers of species inhabiting islands or isolated habitats.

phytogeography—study of plant distribution in the larger geographic divisions of the earth.

zoogeography—study of animal distribution in the larger geographic divisions of the earth.

biogeology—description of the biotic distribution of earth's boundaries and regions, delineating the average compositions of flora and fauna. Compare geobiology.

biogeomorphology—study of the effect of land forms on living organisms as well as the effect of organisms on geomorphic processes, including the interface between the biosphere and geosphere.

biohistory—a polemical discipline proposed by Stephen Boyden to study the interplay of cultural and biological processes in the development of civilizations, as well as the undesirable effects of culturally induced changes in biological systems.

bioinorganic chemistry—aka inorganic biochemistry—although most biochemistry involves carbon and carbon compounds with hydrogen, oxygen, nitrogen, phosphorus and sulfur, organisms also require other elements from the realm of inorganic chemistry, such as sulfur and trace amounts of copper. Bioinorganic chemistry deals chiefly with metallic and nonmetallic structures in organisms (coenzymes). Compare bioorganic chemistry.

organometallics—The chemistry of organotransition metal complexes; an arcane consideration of main group and transition elements.

biology—biology embraces the most intimate of scientific disciplines. It is the science of life and life processes including their origin, evolution and development; the study of anything that is or has been alive. Several major sciences are concerned with living things but not considered parts of biology: agriculture, medicine, anthropology, psychology, and sociology. There are other sciences that belong equally to biology and to medicine: bacteriology, physiology, and anatomy.

It is a relatively new term in the language: the *Oxford English Dictionary* records its first use in English in 1813.

Biological studies may be divided into a range of broad programs as follows:

molecular biology
cell biology
developmental biology
organismal biology
evolutionary biology

Or an Aristotelian breakdown into

morphology
systematics
physiology
embryology
ethology

biological control—see page 318.

biologism—a nonce word for the erroneous belief that all human behavior may be traced to biology.

biology of metals—a multidisciplinary study of the function of metal ions and biominerals involved in the cellular metabolism of microbes, plants, animals, and humans.

experimental biology—certain biologists organize themselves under this rubric as FASEB, the Federation of American Societies for Experimental Biology.

functional biology—term employed by Ernst Mayr for isolated study of organic functions through physical or chemical experiment without regard to their evolutionary context.

whole organism biology—a term adopted within the American Institute of Biological Sciences to recognize the de facto separation of molecular biology, cell biology, and biochemistry from the rest of the field, which they call whole organism biology. Whole organism biologists seem to have trouble convincing their colleagues that the study of the lives of animals is as significant as the study of the lives of cells. Also known as organismic biology.

bioluminescence—study of the emission of light from living organisms. The phenomenon involves a surprisingly disparate range of creatures in addition to fireflies and jellyfish—insects, deep sea fishes, marine invertebrates, and many types of bacteria.

biomagnetism—the study of the interaction of organisms and magnetism: (1) magnetoreception and magnetic minerals in living organisms. (2) the observation of magnetic fields produced by a living object, especially the human body, for diagnostic and possibly therapeutic purposes—also the organisms' response to magnetic fields. (3) biogenic magnetite in the fossil record; and (4) magnetotropism in plants. . . . You see the range.

There has been no proof developed for the widespread belief that pigeons find their way home by employing the earth's magnetic field. Only for bacteria is there unambiguous evidence of an ability to sense magnetic fields.

biomaterials science—research on the interaction between biomaterials, particularly those of polymeric nature, and living tissue.

biomechanics—(1) the study of biological form from the functional viewpoint, an examination of the principles of engineering design as implemented in living organisms. (2) as comparative biomechanics, study of how the form and functions of plants and animals evolved in the context of physical environment. (3) as clinical biomechanics, it is concerned with prosthetic compensation for dysfunctions of the musculoskeletal system. (Also (4) an avant-garde school of dramatic production in the Soviet Union of the 1920s in which the actors' role was totally subordinated to the director's will.)

As (1) and (2) biomechanics thrives in describing some of the limits of biological design. The evolutionary process cannot alter the earth's gravity, the properties of water, the compressibility of air, or the behavior of diffusing molecules.

biomedicine, biomedical research—a term sometimes resorted to by institutions seeking funds by stressing the practical benefits of research. For instance, the famous Marine Biological Laboratory in Woods Hole, Massachusetts —long dedicated to basic research—established the Marine Biomedical Institute for Advanced Studies to expand its endowment by focusing on the medical spin-offs of basic research. The term *biomedicine* is still problematical; it obscures a basic difference in the pace of basic science, such as molecular biology, and its application to human problems, such as the therapy of lung cancer.

biometeorology—see ecology.

biometry—the application of statistical and mathematical methods to the study of biological phenomena.

> **computational biology**—an interdisciplinary approach involving biologists, computer scientists and mathematicians in pursuit of mathematical models of the nonlinear phenomena that emerge in broad areas of biology ranging from the properties of DNA to those of human cultures. Computational biology finds a spiritual home at the Santa Fe Institute among their Studies in the Sciences of Complexity.
>
> **computational molecular biology**—methods for sequence analysis of nucleic acids and their inferred proteins.

biomineralization, biomineralogy—study of the mineralization of biological tissues, including the ability of organisms to mold the form of minerals coming out of solution. See also biology of metals.

bionics—see bioengineering.

bioorganic chemistry—the NIH maintains, with no apparent concern for the tautology involved, a laboratory of bioorganic chemistry concerned with the synthesis of organic medicinal compounds and natural product chemistry.

biophilosophy—addresses the conceptual implications of evolutionary theory, including even the question of whether biology is an autonomous discipline susceptible to reduction to physicochemical terms. (There is a note of desperation here verging on nihilism.) See dialectical biology, neurophilosophy, philosophy of biology and theoretical biology.

biophysics—(1) The study of the physical forces and phenomena involved in living organisms. (2) the application of physical methods such as ultracentrifugation, electrophoresis, ultrasonics, and tracer techniques in biological studies. (3) study of the structure and interaction of biologically important macromolecules and the changes in their physical and chemical properties (National Science Foundation usage). (4) molecular biophysics, a more specific term.

In the broadest sense modern biology depends heavily on physics. John Maynard Smith reminds us that "there would be no molecular biology without isotopes, and no neurobiology without electronics."

biopoiesis—the exploration of how life began, how to make living organisms from nonliving replicating molecules. See biogenesis; ecopoiesis.

biopolitics—a nonce word which may yet acquire respectability. (1) proposed in 1971 by J. P. Miller, a columnist for the defunct New York Herald Tribune, for "the science of proving that what must be done for political reasons is biologically safe for the human race." (2) seriously proposed by a political scientist, Walter Truett Anderson, to introduce the concept of "a shift from environmentalism to biopolitics—to a larger frame of reference that includes such concerns as the general problem of extinction (not just the loss of certain species), genetic erosion, and regulation of the new biotechnologies." (Anderson, 1987.) (3) a discipline proposed by Roger D. Masters emphasizing human nature as the foundation of politics, a synthesis of biology and politics as a branch of the life sciences.

biopsychology—term proposed by Dr. Leonard A. Wisneski as an alternative to psychoneuroimmunoendocrinology. But his holistic definition subsumes medicine with sociology. "The study of the interaction of the psyche with the physiologic systems. This field emphasizes the relationship of the individual to the environment, and incorporates the interaction of social systems is it applies to the health of the individual and of society." See psychobiology.

biorheology—the study of flow and deformation in biological fluids, such as blood and mucus.

bioscience—an umbrella term to embrace a multitude of disciplines. When Dr. Peter Gray compiled for the American Institute of Biological Sciences his directory of "Bioscience Departments and Faculties in the United States and Canada" in 1976 he encountered more than 200 different names for faculty departments . . . from Acarology (mites and ticks) to Zymology (fermentation).

The National Science Foundation, a U.S. Government agency, for the purposes of its research programs recognizes two broad divisions of cellular biosciences and molecular biosciences.

biosensory monitoring—(1) A technology that began with canaries in coal mines has expanded through the use of electrochemical, acoustic, calorimetric, and photometric instrumentation, to applications ranging from battlefield early warning systems to industrial process controls. (Compare biotelemetry.) (2) The development of sensors between biologically active substances and electronic materials; these will augment the world of semiconductors in permitting the transfer of information between the electronic and biological worlds.

biospherics research—(1) Conceptually, investigation of self-sustaining living systems that are closed to matter but open to energy. (2) Programmatically, interdisciplinary study of living organisms together with their total environment in parts of the lithosphere, hydrosphere, and atmosphere. (In 1990 the Philecology Trust of the Bass Family in Fort Worth, Texas, gave $20 million to Yale University for a program in biospheric studies.)

biostatistics—see biometry.

biostitutes—harsh journalese to describe professional biologists who will interpret the results of their field work or laboratory analyses with less concern for good science than for what pleases their clients.

biosynthesis—(1) the study of the production of chemical compounds by a living organism through either synthesis or degradation. (2) the use of living organisms to produce complex substances from simple ones.

biotechnology—manifest variously as (1) the application of biological knowledge to practical or industrial purposes; the technology of exploiting the growth, metabolism, or chemistry of living organisms to produce food, medicine, or other useful products. (2) the interaction of biology with technology. (3) bioprocess engineering. (4) industrial microbiology; and sometimes archly as (5) the university-industrial complex (which is contentious in part because of the effect of commercial factors, such as the shared ownership of patents, on academic research agendas). Biotechnology also has alternate meaning as (6) the study of the relationships between man and machines. (7) technology and the problem of maintaining the quality of the human species (compare eugenics); and (8) ergonomics, which see.

Biotechnology is not so much a discipline as a broad field of applications to which many disciplines contribute; it is, for instance, currently served by more than 250 specialized technical periodicals.

The pharmaceutical and related industries underwrite much of the current biotechnological revolution—particularly in recombinant DNA technology—in a system where industry looks to the universities for talent and academics look to the corporations for funding. In much journalistic usage biotechnology is practically synonymous with genetic engineering, which see. See also space biotechnology.

Even though plant sciences are traditionally accorded a lower priority than the other life sciences, biotechnology is well into the process of converting agriculture from a resource-based endeavor to a science-based one.

    biocatalysis—study of the kinetics and thermodynamics of biological catalysts and their manipulation by genetics and protein engineering, particularly in industrial applications. (See same term under bioengineering.)

    bioremediation—the application of biotechnological techniques (such as the use of oil-eating bacteria at the site of oil spills) to enhance nature's own methods of alleviating pollution.

biotelemetry—monitoring the vital functions of the body for transmission to distant points for interpretation. (Compare biosensory monitoring.)

biotherapy—the use of natural agents in the treatment of disease. See phytotherapy.

biotoxicology—study of poisons produced by living things.

biotropic universe—see exobiology.

botany—the study of plants, the vegetable kingdom. See ethnobotany, paleobotany, plant growth, and vegetation science.

There is a stereotype of botanists "hiding behind herbarium cases and hating one another." Outsiders wonder what there is in the type of work involved that makes it so absorbing. (It is one of my disappointments in writing this book that I have been unable to muster much zeal for the vegetable kingdom. Has botany engendered an entirely different kind of literature—an entirely different constituency—from zoology, or indeed from biology in general?)

agrostology—branch of botany concerned with grasses.

batology—brambles.

bryology—mosses and liverworts.

dendrology—trees, including woody plants and shrubs.

lichenology—lichens.

mycology—fungi.

palynology—pollen and spores.

phyllotaxis—strictly, the study of the arrangement of leaves on a stem and their relation to one another; more broadly, the study of spiral patterns on plants and inside their buds.

phytogeography—see biogeography.

phytopathology—plant diseases.

phytotherapy—therapeutic use of plants as remedies for animal and human diseases.

pteridology—ferns.

brain and cognitive sciences—see neurobiology.

cell biology, cell physiology—the molecular biology of the cell has been the chief business of 20th-century biology. See molecular biology and cytology.
> **cell membrane biology**—a roof term for a large area of experimental and theoretical work relating to membranes at the molecular and cellular levels.

chronobiology—the study of the timing, rhythms, and periodicities of biological systems.
> **circadian periodicity**—study of the basic mechanisms of biological rhythmicity on or about a daily (24-hour) basis.
> **ultradian periodicity**—study of rhythms operating on a cycle of less than 24 hours, such as heart rate and respiration.

cognitive sciences—see neurobiology.
comparative anatomy—see anatomy.
comparative biology—in any division of biological science comparative studies are an investigative approach that focuses attention on a limited subject such as anatomy or aspects of anatomy, but considers data drawn from many species.

computational biology—see biometry, computational neurobiology, and computational molecular biology.

conservation biology—narrowly, it concerns the captured breeding of endangered species. But more broadly, gains wide allegiance as the science of scarcity and diversity; an applied—indeed, programmatic—discipline burgeoning under the societal implications of threats of escalating rates of man-made extinctions. The Society for Conservation Biology is now drafting a sort of recipe for an epidemiology of the planetary environment; it seeks to arrive at descriptions of such matters as the minimum critical size of ecosystems.
See also biopolitics, ecology, and population biology.
> **biodiversity**—the study of the total diversity of life: the flora and fauna of the world, where they came from, how they

are maintained, and how they can be managed, preserved and put to use for human benefit (E. O. Wilson).

conservation—the worldwide conservation movement is spearheaded by the IUCN, the International Union for the Conservation of Nature and Natural Resources, founded in 1948 as the premier program organization to promote scientifically based action that will ensure the perpetuation of man's natural environment.

wildlife biology—the management of game, fish, fowl, fur-bearing animals, or any type of wildlife.

cosmobiology—term proposed by Arnold Lieber (*The Lunar Effect*, 1985) for "a new field of science evolving before our very eyes . . . that will clarify the relationship of man to the universe." Our culture seems to be still adjusting to this late-20th-century paradigm. (For further discussion see Chapter 16.)

cryobiology—the freezing of living cells, tissues, organs, and conceivably even whole organisms, with the goal of holding their life in suspension for varying periods.

cryptobiosis—study of suspended animation, the "hidden life," in the deathlike state of certain primitive organisms that have become almost completely dehydrated.

cybersymbiosis—a presumptuous enterprise that envisions the commingling of human and manufactured parts in new life forms with the ultimate goal of evolutionary modification of the species. As if eugenics wasn't bad enough.

cytology—study of cells and their origin adopting the methods of physics and chemistry.

cytomechanics—the mechanical basis of cell form and structure.

endocytobiology—a branch of cell biology concerned with the origin by symbiosis of a variety of organelles in the eukaryotic cell. It is a new term coined by two German scientists (H. E. A. Schenk and Werner Schwemmler) who organized the first international colloquium on the subject in 1980. Endocytobiology is the haven for a major new biological paradigm: the serial endosymbiosis theory, or SET for short. SET holds that symbionticism—the permanent symbiotic association of organelles within the eukaryotic cell—is the fundamental factor in the origin of species. (See page 297.)

developmental biology—two quite different ideas—or are they? (1) The sequential changes that continuously transform any biological system or relatively simple organization into one of increasing complexity and differentiation until a final stable stage is reached. (2) The attempt to discover how a single cell can develop into organs and organisms made of billions of cells with different shapes and actions. At the level of the individual organism developmental biology deals with the morphogenetic changes that take place during the formation of tissues and organs.

Development has been defined as predictable, irreversible change.

Developmental biology is not strictly a scientific discipline, but it does provide a context for those versed in its contributory specialties—biochemistry, genetics, cell biology, and immunology. Compare embryology.

    developmental neurobiology—which studies, for instance, how the fetal brain grows from a simple cluster of cells into a complex, precisely wired information processor.

    developmental psychology—study of mental activity and cognition in children; the field now includes such developments in later stages of life as well.

dialectical biology—a school of biological thought that seeks to apply some of the methodologies of Marx and Engels to overcome the shortcomings of Cartesian reductionism. Among its chief proponents are Richard Levins and Richard Lewontin. (See page 46.)

ecology—study of the relationship between organisms and their environment. It includes the relationship of plants and animals to each other as well as their relations with the environment. Ecology concerns the interrelations of the biosphere, the interplay between living matter and nonliving matter.

When Haeckel proposed the term *ecology* in 1866 he described it as the science to deal with "the household of nature." Ecology is diverse in its objects of study and disparate in its objectives. Its complexities range from the food web of a salt marsh to theoretical population studies. Ecology is a discipline, if ever there was one, that had to wait for the computer to come into its own.

Ecology, as a program of conservation, has many keepers of the flame. The *Worldwatch Institute* maintains an annual inventory of the earth's vital signs and indices of extinction and population trends. Its current reports document even a little good news: (1) the gradual emergence of the Soviet Union as a more willing cooperating partner in addressing environmental problems; and (2) an implicit extension of the notion of military security to include the goal of environmental stability—the theme that there's little point in defending national boundaries at the price of ignoring the threat of avoidable global disasters.

See conservation biology, natural history, and population biology.

> **anthrozoos**—a multidisciplinary inquiry into the relationships between humans, animals and the environment.
>
> **applied ecology**—applies the theoretical concerns of academic ecology to problems in environmental management, such as fisheries science, pest control, land reclamation, and range management.
>
> **autecology**—interrelations of a particular species or population with its environment.
>
> **behavioral ecology**—a pursuit whose goal is ultimately to explain why there are so many different organizations in the animal world, and why each species structures itself in the way it does.
>
> **biocenology**—study of natural communities and interactions of members of communities.
>
> **biometeorology**—that branch of ecology dealing with the

effects of the atmosphere on humans, animals, and plants —and vice versa.

clinical ecology—the application of clinical medical methodology to "diagnose, examine, and treat" environmental problems, mainly in "agroecosystems."

community ecology—explores patterns of community activity to discern whether they are closely linked groups of interacting species or merely unstructured assemblages.

ecological economics—a recent journal of this title celebrates the need for such a subdiscipline.

ecological restoration—a new discipline devoted to the repair of damaged environments. See conservation biology.

ecophysics—the application of physics to ecology.

ecosynthesis—a term introduced by NASA for the design and build-up of habitable atmospheric environments capable of life support in space or on other planets. Also called *terraforming* when conducted on an interplanetary scale.

ecotechnology—a term used by Ilya Prigogine for "the study of the harmonious positioning of technology in nature."

ecotoxicology—considered narrowly as dealing with pollutants in ecosystems, or broadly as the description and prediction of ecological changes resulting from a variety of human activities involving release of xenobiotic and other chemicals into the environment. (Compare anthrozoos and xenobiosis.)

experimental ecology—the creation of artificial closed-system ecologies for research and heuristic purposes.

microbial ecology—a discipline without a mature methodology bent on understanding how microbes work as societies, performing such functions as geochemical recycling. Much of the potential for biotechnology in agriculture lies in genetically engineering the microorganisms that live on, in, and around plants.

statistical ecology—application of statistical techniques to the exploration of patterns and relationships in biotic communities, including spatial pattern analysis, species abundance relations, overlap models, and community classification.

synecology—structure, development, and distribution of ecological communities (populations) in an ecosystem.

embryology—study of embryo development in animals *and plants* from the fertilization of the egg to the completion of the body structure. Basically, embryology is concerned with the origin of form, the process of morphogenesis, the translation from a genetic code to a three-dimensional organism.

The central problem of embryology is to discover the means by which cells differentiate in response to the program carried in a primordial cell's DNA.

> **embryogeny**—the problem of embryonic development has been described as the problem of how heterogeneity arises from homogeneity.
>
> **positional embryology**—study of the response of a cell to its location within the environment as a determinant of the function the cell may ultimately perform. See molecular embryology and topobiology.

endocytobiology—see cytology.

entomology—the study of insects, the most numerous and varied of all many-celled animals. Insects have exploited every environmental niche except the sea. These creatures, like all arthropods, have bodies divided into three distinct parts: head, chest, and abdomen, and they have three pairs of feet. Insects that have become pests get much more attention in research funding than their benign relatives. In fact, many entomologists have become devoted to agricultural concerns with pest control—kill rates and percent survival. Researchers concerned with classic laboratory techniques and genetic probes sometimes call themselves insect scientists to distinguish themselves from the practical and applied concerns of their colleagues. Entomology includes the study of relations between insects and other plant and animal life. Insects are only one class of the phylum Arthropoda, and departments of entomology often include spiders, centipedes, butterflies, and so on among their concerns.

enzymology—study of enzymes, that large group of proteins that accelerate or catalyze the biochemical reactions at the heart of metabolism.

eobiology—term employed by Joshua Lederburg for studies of the origins of life.

ergonomics—term employed to describe (among other things) the study of the work, performance, and efficiency of organized societies—particularly human and insect societies.

ethnobiology—study of the relation between human societies—usually primitive—and the animals and plants of their environment.

ethnobotany—study of the relation of culture, usually primitive culture, to plants; includes the use of plants as food, medicine, and clothing in human societies.

ethnozoology—the animal lore of a race or people.

ethology—study of patterns of animal behavior in natural environments, stressing the adaptation and evolution of such patterns. (From the Greek ethos, in the sense of "custom".) In the view of ethologists the behavioral repertory of animal species can be established with as much reliability as their anatomical characteristics. Compare sociobiology.

> **behavioral biology**—studies such matters as the relevance of vertebrate social development to the evolution of human behavior.

> **human ethology**—an effort to enlist the disciplines of social behavior to answer the question posed by George Bernard Shaw: "Is human nature incurably depraved?" An optimistic answer has been proposed by the Australian ethologist S. A. Barnett: "Reductionism and determinism fail as methods of understanding the human condition because in considerable measure our future is undetermined—we make our own history, though in circumstances not of our own choosing. Human beings are playful animals, curious animals, animals

who make music, animals for whom work is not necessarily labor but can be liberating. . . ."

neuroethology—a marriage of neurobiology and ethology that attempts to describe the neural basis of animal behavior patterns.

eugenics—As the study of genetic qualities in the human population, eugenics is a legitimate discipline. As the attempt to achieve human improvement by selective breeding and genetic manipulation, eugenics is not a science. Its disreputable program has been embraced or at least condoned by some prominent scientists, for whom it remains a serious pursuit, but one that barely survives the grave moral, political, humanitarian, religious, and genetic objections to it. Eugenics is objectionable when it is politically imposed. In daily life individual eugenic decisions from abortion to marriage are widely accepted. In *Mankind Evolving*, Theodosius Dobzhansky tells us that

the race and class distortions of eugenics must certainly be rejected as a travesty of science. . . . Yet the opposite extreme, the notion that all men are born not only equal but also biologically alike, is likewise a fallacy . . . the mighty vision of human equality belongs to the realms of ethics and politics, not to that of biology. To be equal before the law people need not be identical twins.

euphenics—the program of modification of human genes through techniques controlling genetic expression.

evolutionary biology—the attempt to explain the appearance of life on earth and the forms in which living things have developed.

Evolution remains a theory, a scientifically acceptable hypothesis still awaiting proof of its precise mechanisms.

cultural evolution—nongenetic change produced by the transmission of information and learned behavior, especially language, from one generation to the next through such cultural agencies as teaching, writing, and technology. Also known as exosomatic evolution (Medawar), a much more rapid agency of change in human populations than ordinary organic endosomatic evolution.

evolutionary genetics—a field established by Theodosius Dobzhansky as a synthesis of Darwinian evolution and Mendelian genetics.

evolutionary psychology—just as human physiological characteristics are the products of the evolutionary process, that process has analogous implications for human psychological characteristics. Or at least that is an assumption of this approach.

macroevolution—Evolution above the species level: a synthesis of disciplines from paleontology to genetics. Jeffrey Levinton, one of its exponents, defines macroevolution as "the sum of those processes that explain the character-state transitions that diagnose evolutionary differences of major taxonomic rank." Just think of the level of abstraction . . . "diagnosis by character-state transitions."

macroevolutionary dynamics—name adopted by Niles Eldredge for his large-scale evolutionary theory focusing on species, niches, and their adaptive peaks.

molecular evolution—concerned with, among other things, archaebacteria.

ontogeny—the development of an individual organism through the course of its life history; the study of the process by which an adult organism develops from a fertilized egg (including oogenesis and embryogenesis.)

phylogeny—the study of the historic development of a species of plant or animal.

exobiology—the search for life beyond earth.

bioastronomy—that branch of astronomy that searches for evidence of life in the universe.

biotropic universe—the pursuit of the possibility that life may exist independent of the carbon-based chemistries of terrestrial organisms.

high-altitude biology—at the threshold of the biosphere and the heavens.

xenobiology—term proposed by R. Freitas as alternative to exobiology.

forensic biology—"fingerprinting" the DNA of an individual to identify him or her for forensic purposes.

forestry—see plant sciences.

genethics—a neologism combining Greek and Roman roots, advanced by David Suzuki and Peter Knudtson in a 1989 book of that title. They justify the term genethics on the dubious assertion that ethical problems raised by genetic manipulation are greater in kind and degree than those in other areas of medical ethics.

genetics—the science concerned with the the transmission and expression of characteristics from living organisms to descendants. It is the study of inheritance and variation in organisms; including the mechanisms and controls of the processes of heredity—what carries inherited information; how information is passed from one generation to another and from one population to another; and how it is organized to produce its effects.

As a laboratory science it is a branch of cell physiology. Genetics is the youngest of the main biological sciences, coming into its own since 1900.

behavioral genetics—studies, for instance, the contrast of social and inherited factors in identical twins.

biochemical genetics—a laboratory of the National Institutes of Health Heart, Lung, and Blood Institute. One of its chief techniques is nucleic acid and protein sequence analysis.

cytogenetics—study of chromosomes within the cell.

ecogenetics—the study of genetic variations in susceptibility to disease.

evolutionary genetics—see evolutionary biology.

genetic engineering—at its current art state, genetic engineering is the practice of taking a gene from one creature and inserting it in another creature. It results in the modification of the genetic information in a living cell to reprogram it for a particular purpose: for example, putting human genes in bacteria can manufacture proteins to be used as drugs, such as insulin. Genetic engineering is the art of making DNA do what man wants it to do. Genetic engineering is a powerful tool for exploring correlations between structure and function in proteins, but as yet we are unable to use it for effective protein design. To some extreme adherents it is, in the form of recombinant DNA technology, the panacea for all biological problems. It has potentially unlimited applications in industry, agricultural, and environmental sciences, and medical and veterinary practice, not to mention an unsought capacity for fragmenting our common view of the nature of life.

genetic epidemiology—research on the inherited causes of disease in populations.

genomics—analysis of the hierarchical organization of genomes, including gene mapping and nucleotide sequencing.

gnomics—compilation of the four-character language (A-C-G-T) of the nucleotide sequences in the DNA molecules of a cell.

immunogenetics—a laboratory of the National Institutes of Health Institute of Allergy and Infectious Diseases. See immunology.

microbial genetics—the study of the structure of genes, the nature of genetic variation and the intricacies of gene regulation in single-celled organisms; its work is the forerunner of genetic engineering.

molecular genetics—an alternate term for the above studies. Specifically, it explains how genes control the activities of cells. In its broadest formulation molecular genetics explains in terms of common chemical reactions one of the most profound mysteries of life: how like begets like.

molecular evolutionary genetics—an attempt to unify molecular biology with the discipline of population genetics. (See entry on latter at population biology.)

neurogenetics—see neuro entries.

pharmacogenetics—study of inherited dispositions and allergies to drugs.

quantitative behavioral genetics—application of statistical analyses to explore the development of individuality during infancy and early childhood.

geobiology—see paleontology and biogeology.

geophysiology—James Lovelock's term for the discipline predicated upon the Gaia hypothesis: that life sustains habitable conditions on earth by actively regulating its environment on a global scale.

gerontology—the scientific study of the phenomena of aging. Dr. Joshua Lederburg, the president of The Rockefeller University in New York, says that scientists have not yet established a consensus on the phenomenon that gerontologists are investigating, and he proposes a strategy for the explanation of aging: "I suggest we use as a standard the difference in lifespan between human and mouse: Are there any cellular attributes that can be correlated with that outcome?" (Geriatrics is a branch of medicine dealing with the problems and diseases of old age.)

glycobiology—study of the role of sugar in biological organisms.

gnotobiology—the study of organisms in isolation from bacteria. In gnotobiosis organisms are secured and maintained in germ-free conditions of both internal and external sterility. The first astronauts returned from the moon were kept in sealed gnotobiotic quarantine to protect us from their moon dust.

histology—study of the microscopic structure of animal and plant tissues.

historical biology—concerned with the history of life through geological time and the biology of extinct organisms. See paleontology.

human biology—one of many fields of concentration devoted to a single species, in this case *Homo sapiens,*— and spawning its own journal.

immunology—described by its foremost practitioner, P. B. Medawar, as "the biology of self-recognition, the molecular basis of specificity and the process of information transfer in biological systems." A far cry from its original consideration as an appendage to bacteriology, before its deep theoretical foundations were recognized. (See page 160.)

> **complementology, complement biochemistry**—a subdiscipline of immunology studying the complement system, which has been described as "a complex cascade of proteins . . . uninterpretable except by practitioners after many years of study."
>
> **immunobiology**—a laboratory of the National Institutes of Health division of cancer biology.
>
> **immunocytochemistry**—a technique for identifying the constituents of tissues by using labeled immune reagents to exploit reactions between antigens and antibodies.
>
> **immunogenetics**—employs immunological tools to locate and describe the genes of each chromosome, their nucleotide sequence and expression.
>
> **immunopharmacology**—the paradigm of a field of inquiry that started out as a narrow specialty and expanded to interdisciplinary dimensions.
>
> **neuroimmunomodulation**—study of the psychological factors affecting the physiological processes of immunity.
>
> **psychoimmunology**—concern with the effect of stress on the immune system (see further entry under psychobiology).
>
> **psychoneuroimmunology (PNI)**—an interdisciplinary field dedicated to the study of the interactions between the brain and the nervous, endocrine and immune systems of the body. "The scientific basis of psychoneuroimmunology rests on the facts that there are receptors for neurotransmitters and hormones on lymphocytes, the nervous system and the endocrine system; that changes in nervous system electrical activity have been associated with immunological events; and that organs of the immune system have been innervated by the nervous system." (Dr. Howard R. Weiner, Harvard Medical School.) Psychoneuroimmunology is also popularly understood as a technique of affirmation: a process in which a positive attitude toward illness can affect the immune system and thus help in healing.

life sciences—a general roof phraseology for all the sciences concerned with the structure, behavior, and interactions of living organisms. The term is useful—to a diminishing constituency—in subsuming agriculture, biochemistry, biology, and psychology in one embracing concept. Also considered in teaching medical institutions as health sciences.

marine biology.
benthology—life at the sea bottom and in ocean depths.
limnology—freshwater organisms.
meiobenthology—the study of meiofauna (*meio* from Greek for diminution), applied to benthic animal organisms that pass through a one-millimeter mesh sieve. A young discipline, born in the 1920s.

mathematical biology—the application of mathematical models to a broad array of phenomena cutting across the traditional divisions in biology. (A laboratory of the National Institutes of Health division of cancer biology.)

membrane biology—see cell membrane biology.

metabolic biology—study of the molecular mechanisms of regulation of biochemical pathways by which plants, microbes, and animals assimilate and transform metabolites, to provide energy for vital functions, and to respond to environmental conditions and stresses. (National Science Foundation usage.)

metals—see biology of metals.

microbiology—(1) A generic description embracing many specialties, perhaps defined not so much by its subject matter as by its techniques for the study of structures and quantities of invisible organisms. A frontier of research denied to all those not versed in the burgeoning new techniques of microscopy. One wonders whether the regressing smallness of the cutting edges in physics and biology will end in some limit to the process of ephemerality. (2) The study of microorganisms including bacteria, viruses, molds, algae, yeasts, and other organisms of microscopic or submicroscopic dimensions; i.e., too small to be seen by the naked eye.

microbiotechnology—use of microbes in industrial processes, such as brewing and baking.

molecular biology—the study of the genetic and biochemical processes—the metabolic pathways—of organic molecules. More specifically, it is the study of the very large protein molecules, the *macromolecules*, which distinguish animal and plant life from most of the rest of the material world. Molecular biology represents a shift in research emphasis from the cell to the molecule, a paradigm shift representing perhaps the ultimate reductionist approach.

Historically, Paul A. Weiss of Rockefeller University claims credit for introducing the term to his profession (concurrently with Astbury) in 1951. His objective was to restructure the conduct of biological investigation from a structure based on forms of life (botany, zoology, bacteriology, etc.) or methods of study (anatomy, biochemistry, etc.) to a hierarchical system of order according to functional principles of living organisms (molecular, cellular, genetic, developmental, etc.). Molecular biology was to indicate, on the scale of orders of magnitude, the lowest level of investigation relevant to the advancement of biological knowledge.

The shift in emphasis on the protein molecule as the object of biological study occurred during the middle half of the current century, after the discoveries of Crick and Watson in the 1950s and after the introduction of such laboratory techniques as ultracentrifugation and electrophoresis (which separate individual protein molecules) and X-ray diffraction and chromatography (which permit exploration of the interior details of molecular structure and arrangement).

Molecular biology arose in the synthesis of five distinct disciplines: physical chemistry, genetics, X-ray crystallography, microbiology, and biochemistry.

While basically reductionist, it is multidisciplinary in

its ramifications. Its spectacular achievements have provided a new scientific basis for the profession and practice of medicine. It represents the greatest success story in the history of biology since the pronouncement of the theory of evolution. In the words of Eric Lax:

Molecular biologists are the astronomers of cells. They peer into our physical universe, sorting through the maze of genes (there are between 50,000 and 100,000 of them—no one knows exactly how many—in a single human cell), guided primarily not by what is seen directly but by what is detected in autoradiographs. Yet despite the seemingly infinite complexity of genes, molecular biologists, like Orwellian census takers, are learning their addresses—their structural positions on the 23 matched pairs of chromosomes every person has—and what each member of that crowded household is up to.

This is not work for hobbyists.

C. P. Snow said that molecular biology is "likely to affect the way in which men think of themselves more profoundly than any scientific advance since Darwin's." (*The Two Cultures: A Second Look*, 1963.)

See molecular genetics, molecular neurobiology, and molecular psychology.

computational molecular biology—applies computer techniques to the analysis of protein and nucleic acid sequences. The cumulation of DNA sequence data in various central data banks is such that only computers can deal with such massive amounts of information.

informational molecular biology—the study of the communication of genetic information in the nucleus of the germ cell from one generation to the next.

molecular embryology—study of cell development in relation to neighboring cells, linking the form and function of embryonic tissues to evolution and genetics. A branch of this field has been labeled *topobiology* by Gerald M. Edelman.

molecular recognition—study of the molecular mediation

of information storage, replication, and transfer in all biological systems.

structural molecular biology—the application of crystallographic techniques to predict the shape of molecular constituents of substances of the living world, especially proteins, and the three-dimensional aspects of protein-folding. A field of investigation increasingly dependent on computers, its goal is nothing less than determining the position of each atom in every biological molecule—even when the molecule has tens of thousands of atoms.

morphogenesis—study of the evolution and development of structural characteristics of organisms.

morphology—the science of animal and plant form. The study of the different kinds of characteristics that organisms have together with theorizing about the reasons for such characteristics (Rosenberg, 1985, p. 130). Morphology is the study of shape while physiology is the study of function. For aspects of this abstract approach see anatomy, cytology, embryology, histology, and physiology.

mycology—study of fungi, a kingdom of an estimated 100,000 species. Not just mushrooms, molds, and mildews, but study of a wide range of fungal diseases in plants and animals, including humans. In the words of the mycologist Alan Rayner:

Fungi probably rival flowering plants in their species diversity, and outweigh the animal kingdom. Whilst wielding great destructive power as the agents of disease and decay, they drive the global carbon cycle, sustain our forests and grasslands via mycorrhizal associations, and clothe, as lichens, what would otherwise be bare parts of the planet. Their developmentally versatile body forms provide immense scope for industrial exploitation as well as experimentally accessible systems for studying fundamental biological issues. Yet most people's appreciation of fungi stops at mushrooms, mouldy food and fairy tales.

natural history—focuses on where organisms are and what they do in their environments, including the chronologies of reproductive events. See ecology.

naturalists—a naturalist is a field biologist as opposed to a laboratory worker. Binoculars and butterfly nets rather than pyrex flasks.

neurobiology: neuroscience—Neuroscience is the study of the brain and the central nervous system. Compare two allied but different strategies: theoretical psychology, the study of mental processes; and psychobiology, the study of the anatomical processes of perception. (Note that investigation of vision has preempted the term *psychobiology*, despite its broader connotations.)

Before the electron microscope introduced, in the 1960s, the capacity for examining synapses and the chemical signals between individual cells, neurology consisted mainly of neuroanatomy, neurochemistry, and neurophysiology (see below). A recently founded interdisciplinary journal, *neuroscience*, casts a very much larger net indeed, embracing the entire field of the relationships between nerve tissue and behavior. (See page 145.)

biological psychiatry—relates psychiatric phenomena to biochemical and structural constitution of brain and nervous system. (A branch of NIMH, the National Institute of Mental Health.)

brain and cognitive sciences—terminology adopted by MIT (1988) for their new program integrating neurobiologists, computational theorists, and psychologists in a single academic department.

cognitive neurochemistry—a multidisciplinary approach to understanding the pharmacological basis of human psychology in various clinical dementias.

cognitive neuropsychology—explores brain function in such areas as how acquired brain damage can selectively impair knowledge within specific conceptual categories.

cognitive neuroscience—term of choice for brain research in general, more specifically, the interaction of brain and behavior: how brain processes generate cognitive processes.

cognitive psychology—another term for the attempt to achieve a coherent synthesis between serial vs. parallel processing, on the one hand, and nature vs. nurture, on the other. Returns not yet in.

cognitive science—a committee of practitioners in search of an interdisciplinary synthesis. It proposes to account for mental activity in terms of computational processes—with or without reference to neurophysiology.

Undeterred by our ignorance of neurons themselves, some researchers start from the other end, trying to observe how neurons work in ensemble. Overlapping areas of study at this frontier are known as connectionism, neural network modeling, and parallel distributed processing.

computational neurobiology—an interdisciplinary program at the heart of NIBS (Neural, Informational and Behavioral Sciences, as now flourishing at USC.)

computational neuroscience—an approach to understanding information processing in the brain by modeling the nervous system at many different levels, including the biophysical, the circuit, and the system levels. One group of practitioners uses the term neural computation to describe research applying both scientific and engineering techniques to parallel exploration of brain modeling and the design of neurally inspired computers. George Johnson writes of computational neuroscience that "the chemistry of a single neuron is so complex that it continues to defy complete understanding. In the last few years, however, a group of researchers, many of them young immigrants from physics, computer science, and other fields, have come to neuroscience with a grand vision of how to cut through the tangle of details and lay bare the essence of the mind. Using computers, these researchers simulate artificial networks of simplified neurons, getting them to exhibit rudimentary forms of learning, pattern recognition, and other cognitive skills. Then they analyze these models for general principles of intelligence. . . . The hope is that most of the chemical reactions within each cell are irrelevant to an understanding of thinking. . . . Many experimenters, however, dismiss the network modelers as interlopers . . . and exercises in electrical engineering."

developmental neurobiology—study of how the fetal brain cell grows from a small cluster of cells into the complex information-processing mechanism of the brain.

molecular neurobiology—term introduced at Cold Spring Harbor Symposium of 1983 to recognize the increasing emphasis on molecular genetics and molecular techniques in the hybrid field of neurobiology.

neuroanatomy—the attempt to trace the manner in which neurons are connected to form the circuitry of the brain.

neurocomputing—another term for neural networks. See computational neuroscience.

neuroendocrinology—integrates endocrinology and neuroscience.

neurogenetics—the application of genetic research techniques to the complexities of brain function at the cellular and molecular level; particularly the study of the genetic basis by which organisms respond to stimuli—especially the neurological processes of learning, sensory perception, and reflex action.

neuroimmunology—study of how the nervous and immune systems interact.

neurolinguistics—study of brain function in language behavior and experience.

neuromagnetism—study of how certain brain functions— thoughts, emotions, dreams, and other mental activities— create detectable magnetic fields around the head. Used as a research tool for the mapping of higher levels of brain function as well as possible clinical applications.

neurophilosophy—a field pioneered by Patricia Smith Churchland that explores how scientists and philosophers together might develop explanatory theories of brain functioning. Dr. Churchland has long been an exponent of the concern that brain researchers will become engulfed in data unless they begin devising grand general theories of the brain.

neurophysiology—study of the physiological processes of the nervous system.

neuropsychology—a field of study that emerged in the second half of the twentieth century, in part as a reaction to behaviorism. It has sought relations between mental processes and brain function at a relatively gross level, such as trying to discover which functions are associated with which hemisphere of the brain.

psychoneuroimmunology—see immunology.

ontogeny—see text discussion of recapitulation theory on page 318.

organometallics—see bioinorganic chemistry.

paleontology—study of life as it existed in past geological times. There are probably one billion extinct species, roughly ten times as many as survive today. (Paleontology belongs equally to the physical and biological sciences.) The single most important fact that paleontology has contributed to evolutionary biology is that the history of life has witnessed a reduction of body-plan diversity and a stabilization of form. Some of the patterns of evolution can be seen only through paleontological spectacles.

biostratigraphy—the classification and interpretation of stratified rocks on the basis of their fossil contents.

geobiology—term adopted by Preston Cloud for the study of life on a geological scale of time; he proposes it as an analogy to geochemistry and geophysics.

paleobiology—concerned with fossils as organisms rather than as features of historical geology.

paleoanthropology—the search for human origins; possibly the most contentious of all scientific disciplines. Anthropologists inevitably compete for the most promising archeological sites available to their generation, and in the process they–the sites and the diggers—become something of hostages to one another.

paleobotany—fossil plants, including fossil pollen.

paleopalynology—study of fossil pollen grains and spores.

paleotaxonomy—classification of fossils.

taphonomy—the study of what happens to animal remains from the time the animal dies to the time its remains become fossils (including a comparison of the postmortem remains of modern animals and the fossil remains of their counterparts).

parasitology—the study of parasites, plants or animals that obtain their nutriment by living in or upon other living bodies.

pathology—study of disease, with the implicit assumption that disease is inherently abnormal.

pharmacology—the study of the effect of drugs on bodily functions, including toxicology and therapeutics.

phenology—literally "the science of appearances" (from the Greek *phanein*); the study of cycles in biological events and how they respond to climate. "The science of phenology can be used for both botany and zoology. . . . When the bluebells are flowering in my region, I can always find a parula warbler. Or when the days get shorter in fall, the violets usually bloom again because they respond to the day length." (Dr. Stanwyn G. Shetler, assistant director, National Museum of Natural History.)

philosophy of biology—the philosophy of science has historically tended to view physics as the paradigmatic science. Only in recent years have philosophers of science come to recognize that biology is just as scientific as physics and raises just as many, if not more, philosophical issues. On questions of ethics and epistemology, evolutionary biology has more relevance than any other science. See biophilosophy, neurophilosophy, and theoretical biology.

photobiology—study of the interactions of organisms with light, including photosynthesis, photomorphogenesis, photoperiodism, phototaxis, and the biological effect of such phenomena as ultraviolet radiation.

phycology—see protistology.

phylogeny—see text discussion of recapitulation theory, page 318.

physiology—in the narrowest clinical sense, physiology is the study of organisms and the functions of the cells, tissues, and organs of which they are composed. Since it embraces both the physics and chemistry of biological systems, it is a field that overlaps those of molecular biology and biochemistry.

Physiology was one of the first big words we learned in grade school; to us it meant explaining how the body worked (colored fold-out charts of ribs and liver and lungs, that sort of thing).

Physiology is actually a synoptic discipline, viewing the complete system rather than a mere assembly of its parts. Some observers predict that physiology will radically change from its present emphasis on structure and local mechanism to a more complex appreciation of behavior in an interacting dynamical system—a holistic approach to all the vital processes of an organism. Thus the Gaia hypothesis (page 283) is essentially *physiological* in its nature.

phyto entries—see botany.

plant sciences, plant cultivation.—See also vegetation science and biotechnology. Includes such specialties as:

    forestry
    poultry science
    weed science

population biology—a discipline presuming that populations are more rewarding than species as targets for biological concern. Its purest adherents would have us become blind to the artificial constructs and fragmented terminologies of taxonomy, genetics, and ecology.

Applied population biology includes ecosystem studies of such questions as maximum sustainable yields for fisheries, control of agricultural pests, and containment of epidemics. As Professor Robert May of Princeton (a physicist turned zoologist) has put it, "the basic task for population biologists is to try to disentangle from the superimposed environmental noise and spacial heterogeneity the underlying dynamical mechanisms that regulate natural populations of plants and animals." See also conservation biology and ecology.

One of the chief apostles of this new discipline, Paul R. Ehrlich, Bing Professor of Population Studies at Stanford University, even subsumes ecology, evolutionary biology, behavior, and systematics as subdisciplines of population biology. He says population ecology has uncovered new modes of dynamic behavior where mathematics and physics—particularly chaos theory—can be applied to biological models. In his many books and lectures Ehrlich argues eloquently for the importance of popular understanding that "nonhuman organisms are crucial to supplying civilization with essential and irreplaceable ecosystem services."

> **demography**—study of quantitative properties of populations, such as birth rates, mortality, and age distribution.
>
> **human biology**—human population biology.
>
> **population genetics**—study of the genetic structure of populations, the way heritable variations are transmitted from one generation of a population to the next. It is concerned more with the mechanics of gene frequencies than with historical perspectives. (Compare evolutionary genetics.)
>
> **population science**—perhaps more of a program than a science, it is concerned with developing technology for fertility regulation as well as policies for assistance to overpopulated countries.

postbiology—not a discipline, but a vision—profane or utopian, according to your point of view—of a world where human intelligence has been transferred to mechanical computers, making up a world of inorganic life where mortality has given way to an immortality of automatism. (See Chapter 19).

protistology—a kingdom of life, *protista*, defined by exclusion including everything except animals, plants, fungi, and bacteria (microbes). (Some authorities have adopted the term *protoctista* for this family, as proposed by

H. F. Copeland in 1956.) The study of microscopic protists and related eukaryotic organisms.

algology-phycology—the study of algae, an extremely diverse group of a dozen different phyla and 25,000 species surviving at greater climatic extremes than land plants and and ranging in size from 3 microns to 200 feet.

applied phycology—a rapidly expanding interest in the commercial applications of algae.

protobiology—term proposed by Koichiro Matsuno, professor of biophysics at the University of Nagaoka, Japan, for the reassessment of biological concepts in the light of modern physics and physical conservation laws.

psychobiology—(1) Study of the biological basis of behavior. An effort to provide psychiatry with an objective basis in the hard sciences of metabolism and biochemistry. (2) A general term for concern with the relationship of physical processes to mental events. (3) A controversial method of therapy, employing the techniques of hypnosis, to use the mind to heal body illness.

In the late 19th century William James argued that a philosophy of "healthy-mindedness" could bring practical consequences to the physical well-being of individual human beings. Since that time it has been observed that while the French still blame all their maladies on the liver and the English on their bowels, Americans tend to blame everything bad on stress.

Psychobiology is placed in the unique position of bringing about unity in brain research and our highest humanistic and cultural aspirations. "For the first time in history," says Dr. Richard Restak, "the interest of science and the interest of the humanities coincide."

behavioral psychology—a laboratory approach that stresses learning, rewards, and punishment, ignoring entities that cannot be observed and measured. As propounded by B. F. Skinner, it is an increasingly discredited venture.

computational psychology—an attempt to use concepts drawn from computer science to explain how the mind works. The opening sentence of a recent book on the subject tells us that "computational psychology today is rather like the dragon in earlier times: of the people who are seeking it, not all agree on what they expect to find—while many others doubt that it exists to be found at all."

molecular psychology—study of brain chemicals released by neurons in communication with other neurons.

psychochemistry—study of the relation of brain chemistry to mental illness, exploring the notion that hormones may be "the stuff of thought"—an alternative approach to that of psychotherapy.

psychoimmunology—term proposed by Dr. George Solomon to indicate how the emotions interact with the immune system. A recent issue of the *Journal of Psychosomatic Research* describes psychoimmunology as a nascent science of potentially far-reaching importance, linking mental and personality factors with vulnerability to infection.

psychometabolism—subject of a paper by Sir Julian Huxley.

psychophysics—study of the anatomical processes of perception. To the layman this term might appear hifalutin and broadly interdisciplinary, but by long-established academic practice it describes a most reductionist approach to laboratory research in perception and sensorimotor systems.

theoretical psychology—the science of mental processes. Compare neuroscience.

psychoneuroimmunology—see immunology.

psychophysics—see psychobiology.

radiation biology—study of the chemical effects of ionizing radiation on biological molecules.

radiobiology—application of pulsed-wave and other radiation techniques to biological research.

reproductive biology—studies in the field of reproduction, fertility, and sterility.

social sciences—the hard sciences tend to disdain soft sciences like the behavioral and social sciences. But the social sciences get back their own by adopting science as one of their subjects of study.

sociobiology—is really more of an *approach* than it is a discipline. Its brilliant founder, E. O. Wilson, describes it as the systematic study of the biological basis of social behavior; thus it is an outgrowth of ethology. It proposes nothing less than a genetic basis for all animal behavior. It focuses on the population structures of animal societies, including the social behavior of early man and contemporary primitive societies. Sociobiology differs from sociology in that the latter is largely structuralist in its approach and makes no reference to genetic aspects of human evolution. In Wilson's words: "It may not be too much to say that sociology and the other social sciences, *as well as the humanities* [italics mine—e.j.a.], are the last branches of biology waiting to be included in the Modern Synthesis [of evolutionary biology]. Whether the social sciences can be truly biologicized [sic] in this manner remains to be seen." The emphasis in sociobiology on genetic determinism has led to implications that are politically controversial. Wilson seems to be meeting this in part by allowing in his recent writings a larger role for cultural influences. But Dr. Richard Restak observes that

> **At its simplest, sociobiology seeks to discover the biologic basis for human behavior. Sociology, psychology, and even history are all right as far as they go, but, according to Wilson, they don't go far enough because they have never been integrated into the modern synthesis—the neo-Darwinian theory that seeks explanations for behavior in terms of its adaptive evolutionary value over millions of years.**

space biology—this field covers much more than just the logistical problems of colonizing outer space. It explores the many uncertainties of microgravity, including gravitropism, sensorimotor integration, space anemia and human behavior. See biotropic universe; ecopoiesis.

> **space biotechnology**—proposes protein crystallization and the design of fermenters and bioreactors to operate under conditions of microgravity.

structural biology—means lots of different things from the simplistic to the recondite: (1) Term adopted for the broad application of techniques and theories developed in molecular physics and chemistry to the study of protein structure. See molecular structural biology. (2)Featured in the National Academy of Sciences report on "Research Opportunities in Biology," 1989, as a catchword for the unifying principles of biology. (Simplistic.) (3) The search for a hidden set of mechanisms that control development. Taking their aim from the kind of structural analysis of Lévi-Strauss and Piaget, the *biological structuralists* seek an unknown set of rules that govern form (rules that Princeton biologist John Tyler Bonner says may not exist), while they reject the answers provided by natural selection and developmental genetics. (This is recondite stuff.)

symbiosis—the study of the association of organisms that are members of different species of all five kingdoms.

synecology—see ecology.

systematics—the science of classifying living things. It aims at the description of organic diversity, a complete catalog of all life on earth. Its ultimate (and possibly unattainable) goal would provide biology a "periodic table" as exact and predictive as Mendeleyev provided for chemistry. In the inclusion of both micro- and macroevolution it is broader than the descriptive discipline of taxonomy. The primary divisions of the field are botany and zoology, with the more recent addition of protistology.

Systematics is one of the two oldest formal disciplines of biology (the other is anatomy). Systematics is central to all of biology . . . because of its employment of the findings and theories of every other compartment of biological science in the establishment of the types, kinds, and units required for scientific description. Systematics encompasses the characteristics, genetic status, and evolutionary history of organisms. Once simply the description of obvious phenotypic variation and the application of formal names, systematics now uses a variety of molecular biological, multivariate statistical, and other sophisticated approaches in explicit analytical frameworks.

According to E. O. Wilson, "No one but the systematist can reveal the particular and extraordinary value of the alcyonacean corals, chytrid fungi, anthribid weevils, sclerogibbid wasps, melostomes, ricinuleids, elephant fish, and so on down the long enchanted roster."

taphonomy—see paleontology.

taxonomy—the classification and identification—the naming—of all living things. Though it is the most venerable of biological disciplines, it is still far from an exhausted field, there being far fewer named than unnamed species.

>**cladistics**—classifying organisms by their evolutionary branching on the basis of shared derived characters. Its adherents purport to deal with "homology, its evaluation and parsimonious interpretation . . . without regard to authority, tradition, idiosyncrasy or irrational criteria."

>**numerical taxonomy**—classifying organisms by their similarity as measured by a variety of quantifiable characteristics.

>**phenetics**—classifying organisms by similarities in the external manifestations of their genetic constitution focusing on discrete characteristics of populations of plants and animals without regard to their pattern of evolutionary branching.

teratology—(1) the study of grossly abnormal organisms (monsters, malformed fetuses and other terata). (2) the study of abnormalities, particularly in recent years with respect to harmful environmental influences.

theoretical biology—Roughly speaking, in physics 50 percent are theoretical physicists and 50 percent are experimental physicists devoted to measurement and laboratory testing. In chemistry, 90 percent work in the laboratory while about 10 percent are engaged in theoretical chemistry. In biology, almost all are engaged in descriptive, experimental, or laboratory explorations with less than 1 percent committed to theoretical studies.

There is a *Journal for Theoretical Biology*, but it has less than a thousand contributors. One area of theoretical biology focuses on mathematical models—which may range from the subcellular to population levels.

thermobiology—animal thermobiology treats with temperature effects on and of animal processes ranging, in the words of a recent text on the subject, from "molecules to the organism and from physiology to behavior," as well as considerations of phenomena ranging from photoperiodism to scale effect. A discussion of periodic endothermy describes the shivering employed by dung beetles, honeybees, hawk moths, and tuna to keep their locomotory muscles warm.

topobiology—a name introduced by Gerald M. Edelman for the study of "place-dependent cellular regulation." Topobiology is concerned with "that part of developmental biology dedicated to the understanding of animal form and to the related subject of morphologic evolution." It uniquely introduces *behavior* as a factor linking development and evolution. (See page 328.) See molecular embryology.

toxicology—study of poisons and their effects on living organisms. The Food and Drug Administration maintains a national research center in Jefferson, Arkansas, focusing on the use of biomarkers in risk assessment research. Biomarkers are designed to provide quantitative indicators of toxicant exposures in populations and individuals.

> **ecotoxicology**—the study of toxic effects on the scale of whole ecosystems.

toxinology—study of the natural toxins occurring in plants, animals, and microbes, including the chemical effects of poisons on humans and domestic livestock, the chemistry of the metabolism of toxins, the effects of toxins on cells and tissues, and the treatment of natural poisoning.

vegetation science—Botanists engaged in the description and mapping of plants have no general agreement on what is the proper unit of vegetation. (The complexity of the ecological pie makes it difficult to slice.) The main debate has to do with whether plant species behave in an independent, individualistic way, each distributed according to its own particular environmental limits of tolerance, or whether a process of coevolution has resulted in the development of distinct units of vegetation, each unit being made up of a coadapted assemblage of mutually tolerant, or even dependent, plant species.

virology—study of viruses and such viroid phenomena as virinos, plasmids, PPLOs (Pleuropneumonia-Like Organisms), and prions.

wildlife biology—see conservation.

xenobiosis—(1) study of food, drugs and poisons in the human body. (2) study of the mechanics of insecticide, fungicide, and herbicide resistance.

zoogeography—see biogeography.

zoology—animals; the animal kingdom.

> **cryptozoology**—a fringe pursuit of hidden, undiscovered, and mythical animals, and the search for same through native reports and legend.

> **protozoology**—unicellular animals.

invertebrates: Invertebrates fascinate because they are so different from us. Each of the 30 phyla describe body plans quite different from each other: Some have no guts, some have no legs, some have no heart, and some have virtually no brain, but each of them manifests some effective strategy for survival.

> **crustaceology**—study of a class of Arthropoda including shrimps, lobsters, crabs, and water fleas.

> **helminthology**—parasitic worms.

> **malacology**—mollusks.

> **nematology**—worms.

> **acarology**—mites and ticks.

> **entomology**—which see.

vertebrates:
>**herpetology**—reptiles and amphibians.
>**squamatology**—snakes and lizards.
>**ichthyology**—fishes.
>**mammology**—study of all members of the Class Mammalia.
>**ornithology**—birds.
>**primatology**—primates.

NOTES

Quotations in the text are supplied with the name of the author and publication in cases where they are deemed to be of interest to the general reader, usually because of the familiarity or authority of the person quoted.

All other quotations and paraphrased material from specialist and technical sources are credited in the following listing, identified by page number and brief excerpt in lieu of footnotes.

1. No agreed definitions

8–9, *we are ignorant about how we work . . . two centuries ago we could explain everything about everything*   Dr. Lewis Thomas, address to American Association for the Advancement of Science, 1977.

9–10, *data galore had been accumulated on every conceivable aspect of living species . . . but . . . the crux of the matter, life itself, was almost totally ignored*   Lovelock 1979, pp 3–4.

11, *living processes . . . do not exist . . . save as parts of single whole organisms.*   J. Shaxel: Jena: Fischer quoted in Augros & Stanciu 1988, p 29.

12, *life is process, not substance.*   Paul Weiss: quoted in Koestler & Smythies 1969, pp 7–8.

12, *the cellular polyphasic system of integrated macromolecules*   Florkin 1972, p 316.

12, *the eternal present in the temporal* Fuller 1975, sec 531.01.

12, *a system of integrated, cooperating enzyme reactions.* Borek 1980, p 19.

12, *a property of very special molecular arrangements called cells.* Harold Morowitz, *Science 84*, Jan–Feb, p 21.

12, *unachieved equilibrium can be taken as an essential premise, even an operational definition, of all life.* Chaisson 1987, p. 171.

12, *coded instructions contained in a chemical present in all living organisms: DNA.* Dulbecco 1987, p vii.

12, *life as a geological cosmic force* Gerard Piel, *BioScience* 38, April 1988.

12, *life is a property of form, not matter* Christopher Langton 1989, ARTIFICIAL LIFE: SFI STUDIES IN THE SCIENCES OF COMPLEXITY, p 41.

12, *whether life is a property of the organism or . . . a manifestation of life* Lwoff 1968, p 3.

13, *complexity, regulation, and metabolism, the three fundamental characteristics of life.* Henderson quoted by Harold J. Morowitz, "The search for 'fitness' in nature," *The Scientist*, 19 October 1987.

13, *life is a system that has three properties* Monod 1971, pp 3–22.

14, *living organisms are characterized by five properties.* Lewontin, "The science of metamorphoses," *The New York Review of Books*, 27 April 1989.

14, *seven physiological functions* ENCYCLOPAEDIA BRITANNICA 3, vol. 10, p 893.

14, *ten important features of living things.* Paul Davies 1989, pp 94–95.

16, *there is no true meaning . . . there is a usage that serves the purposes of the working biologists* P. B. and J. S. Medawar 1983, pp 66–67.

16, *life is difficult to define . . . Szent-Gyorgi writes: . . . the noun "life" has no sense.* André Lwoff 1968, p 3.

16, *life, . . . is an attitude of mind toward what is being observed.* N. W. Pirie in "The origin of life," *Discovery*, vol 114, 1953, quoted in Beck 1957, pp 184–85.

18, *life does not evolve, but complex populations of living organisms do.* Professor H. Sandon, *New Scientist*, 31 March 1966.

19, *biology is not the science of life. Science is not about the study of abstract nouns.* Hogben quoted by Savory in PRINCIPLES OF MECHANISTIC BIOLOGY. Timothy Dickenson to EJA, 14 September 1990.

19, *my mentor . . . admonished me . . . not to hope to 'discover the difference between living and nonliving things.'* Hall 1969, p viii.

20, *fuzz—the stuff of meaning.* Colin Tudge, *New Scientist*, 4 March 1989.

2. Describing life

24, *more than nine-tenths of all . . . chemical compounds contain carbon.* A. T. Balaban in SYMMETRY 2, 1989, p 397.

24–25, *solid as we may seem, . . . water is the universal medium for all biological activity* Walter Drost-Hansen and J. Lin Singleton in "Liquid Asset," *The Sciences*, Sept–Oct 1989.

25, *the most important properties of water are its polarity and cohesiveness; water solvates polar molecules.* Stryer 1989.

26, *the eye . . . developed independently in different species at least 40 times.* V. Salvini-Plawen and E. Mayr 1978, in *Evolutionary Biology* 10:207–63, quoted by J. A. Wheeler, 1986.

27, *consciousness has no access to the raw data.* Delbruck 1986, p 7.

27, *photoperiodism provides the seasonal schedule for the flowering . . . pupation . . . and nesting* This summary is derived from Sterling B. Hendricks, "How light interacts with living matter," in Hanawalt, ed., 1973, p 19.

28, *. . . while Life [sic] is continuous, radiation is intermittent and the possibilities of storing high-energy electrons are very limited.* Szent-Gyorgi quoted in McElroy and Glass, eds. 1961, p 7.

28, *"life is powered by proton batteries that are ultimately energized by the sun."* Stryer 1989, p 13.

29, *radiation bathes our earth, yet most of this is of no avail to life.* Bentley Glass, Symposium on Light and Life, 1961.

29, *the human species will, by 2050, be using as much energy as all land animals and plants put together.* Crispin Tickell, "Outgrowing the biosphere," *New Scientist*, 16 October 1988.

29–30, *these hydrothermal vents . . . appear to support compact ecosystems* Boyce Rensberger in *The Washington Post*, 24 March 1986.

30–31, *every individual now alive embodies the past experience of his ancestors.* Gunther S. Stent, review in *The New York Times Book Review*, 8 September 1974.

31, *the historical uniqueness of living systems . . . the concrete content of biological information . . . cannot be deduced from the laws of physics and chemistry* paraphrased from Bernd-Olaf Kuppers 1990, INFORMATION AND THE ORIGIN OF LIFE, Cambridge: MIT Press.

32, *truly biological entities ... have ancestors, and they beget progeny.*　　Michael J. Katz, neuroanatomist, Case Western Reserve University, in Davis & Park 1987, pp 24–26.

32, *echolocation, for example, has evolved independently in bats, birds, dolphins and whales;*　　paraphrased from Ed Regis in *The New York Times Book Review*, 9 April 1989.

33, *biomolecules are like meaningful sentences*　　from EJA notes of Ilya Prigogine's remarks in talk at National Science Foundation boardroom, 11 October 1989.

35, *parallel to the structure of proteins ... there is an information system made of the same atoms*　　Alan Mackay in review article on "The grammar of the genes" in *Times Literary Supplement* (London), 15 April 1983, p 381.

36, *the reality is that genes are only part of a system where information flows both ways*　　Bruce Charlton, "Falling asleep over the book of life," *New Scientist*, 11 February 1989.

36, *ants and mammals employ chemical signals; in human societies communication is uniquely characterized by language*　　John Maynard Smith, "Triumphs of Colonialism," *The New York Review of Books*, 27 September 1990.

37, *the difference between*　　Huxley, 1944, p 145.

38, *the possession of an intrinsic program*　　Luria, Gould, Singer 1981, pp vii, 6.

38, *the concept of self-assembly ... is crucial to understanding how life works.*　　Boyce Rensberger, *The Washington Post*, 18 December 1988.

39, *living organisms ... preserve their order in spite of*

continuous irreversible processes Ludwig von Berta-lanffy, GENERAL SYSTEMS THEORY, 1968, New York: George Braziller, p 159.

41, *life is, in general, an improbable state of matter.* Dob-zhansky 1967, p 41.

43, *a complex molecular ensemble all of which must be in place and functioning for the production of stuff of which bodies are made.* summarized from R. C. Lewontin, "The Corpse in the Elevator," *The New York Review of Books*, 20 January 1983, p 35.

43, *if this were produced by chance alone . . . it would be . . . infinitely improbable.* Crick 1988.

44, *warmth is required by a fetus long before it registers any other sensory stimuli* von Baeyer 1984, pp 160–61.

44, *the temperature range within which life is permitted corresponds with that within which water is a liquid* from Speakman 1966, p 126.

45, *the evolution of biological process is not the infusion of motion into a static system . . . but the modulation of chaotic motion* Levins & Lewontin 1985, p 49.

45, *in common opinion it is to living things only that belongs the power of movement* from Bernard Dixon 1937, pp 354–55.

45, *one of the most striking features of living systems is their cyclic nature . . . on a shorter time scale there are the periodicities of experimental physiology* summary from Arun V. Holden "What makes them tick?" *Nature* 336, 10 November 1988.

45, *purposeful motion . . . ultimately impelled organisms toward culture.* paraphrase of Robert Wright 1988, p 156.

46, *the organism, and the cells . . . each evolved in a series of previous environments.* Salk 1972, p 2.

46, *what dialectical biology attempts to do is to break down the alienation of subject and object*   R. C. Lewontin, "The Corpse in the Elevator," *The New York Review of Books*, 20 January 1983, p 37.

46, *organisms . . . evolve their environment*   from Howard Pattee quoted in *Nature*, 4 February 1988.

46, *epigenetic effects are . . . environmental . . . rather than built-in programming in the cell.*   from Comfort 1984, p 258.

47, *an environment which is predominantly built rather than given*   Rosalind Williams 1990, NOTES ON THE UNDERGROUND: AN ESSAY ON TECHNOLOGY, SOCIETY, AND THE IMAGINATION, Cambridge: MIT Press.

47, *on the verge of all the interesting questions.*   Barrows, "From the tiny world to the big one," *Times Literary Supplement* (London), 29 September 1989.

48, *plectics"—the study of simplicity and complexity*   Murray Gell-Mann, "A Personal Statement," *Bulletin of the Santa Fe Institute*, Summer–Fall 1989.

48, *the study of complexity offers the most serious and persuasive challenge to the reductionist view in biology.*   Careri & Nicolis 1987.

48, *"Biology and Complexity."*   The preamble to its report *Biology International*, International Union of Biological Sciences news magazine, special issue 15, 1987.

49, *the genetic system is a form of memory registering the past of the species*   Jacob, *La jeu des possibles* (Paris: Fayard), 1981, quoted in *Biology International* above.

49, *the robustness of complexity*   Hoffman 1957, pp 270, 286–87.

3. Life as the chemical interaction of macromolecules

51, *the goal of biochemistry is to discover the patterns and regularities by which matter . . . interacts with energy in its many forms to produce organic life.* from Kieffer 1971, p 2.

51, *In biology there are two main languages, molecular and electrical.* from Testa 1982.

51, *in its simplest form the DNA molecule contains about 10 billion atoms.* Young 1986, p 165ff.

52, *life is a function . . . of flows of electrons as currents in microcircuits* Dwight H. Bulkely, "Electromagnetic Theory of Life," *The Scientist*, 13 November 1989.

53, *the components of living cells that seemed to be most lifelike in their properties were found to have molecules containing thousands or tens of thousands of atoms.* from Wooldridge 1968.

53, *molecular combinations are not linear but three-dimensional.* Cotterill 1985, p 3.

53, *CHONPS . . . catchily sums up all the atomic constituents of the decisive polymers of life* Philip Morrison 1984.

54, *no organism is known that does not contain enzymes and all known enzymes are special forms of protein.* Barrow & Tipler 1986, p 317.

54, *a single cell in the human body has been estimated to contain 100,000 enzyme molecules.* Dennis Flanagan 1988, p 134.

54, *the specific nature of the interaction implies a complementarity between stimulus and response.* Medawar 1983, p 244.

54, *the enzyme binds the substrate molecule at a far higher rate of chemical reaction than is achieved by any man-made catalysis.* paraphrase of Albert et al. 1983, p 129.

55, *an enzyme . . . would be alive . . . though soluble and not organized in cellular form.* Hans Zinsser 1934, p 38.

55, *in my marriage to enzymes, I have found a level of complexity that suits me.* Arthur Kornberg article in the *Annual Review of Biochemistry,* vol 58, 1989, reprinted in *The Scientist,* 4 September 1989, p 13.

55, *if I can demonstrate a replicating molecule, I'll die a happy man.* Cyril Ponnamperuma, "Seeds of Life," *Omni* 1980, quoted in Casti 1989, p 509.

4. Erwin Schrödinger: *What is life?*

57, *the chromosome is a message written in code* John Gribbin, "What is Schrödinger?" *New Scientist,* 13 January 1990.

58, *this book very elegantly propounded the belief that . . . , to understand what life is, we must know how genes act.* James D. Watson 1969, THE DOUBLE HELIX: A PERSONAL ACCOUNT OF THE DISCOVERY OF THE STRUCTURE OF DNA, p 18.

5. Life as the impulse to replicate

62, *a hen is only an egg's way of making another egg.* Samuel Butler 1877, chapter 8.

62, *a physicist is an atom's way of knowing about atoms.* George Wald quoted in Barrow & Tipler 1986, p 510.

66, *deoxyribonucleic acid is simply a mechanism to save time in reaching higher levels of organization.* "Matter versus Materials: A Historical View," *Science* 162, 8 November 1968, p 644.

67, *when the human brain studies the human brain* The *Washington Post*, 2 November 1986, p C3.

6. Metaphoric approaches

68, *the whole of nature is a metaphor of the human mind.* Emerson quoted by the poet, Geoffrey Hill, in a review of THE OXFORD ENGLISH DICTIONARY, SECOND EDITION, *Times Literary Supplement* (London) 21 April 1989.

70, *life is a disease* George Bernard Shaw 1928, BACK TO METHUSELAH.

70, *cancer results when genetic instructions from space. . . , are received accidentally by animal or plant cells.* Robert Shapiro 1986, p 243.

71, *possibly the only way a cell of a mammal or bird can acquire immortality—is for it to become malignant or cancerous.* Arthur C. Giese 1973, p 555.

72, *a molecular disease that turned out to be evolution.* From E. Zuckerkandl and L. Pauling in HORIZONS IN BIOCHEMISTRY, M. Kasha and B. Pullman, eds. Academic Press, 1964. (quoted in Stryer 1988, p 171).

72, *[oncogenes] are very highly conserved over long, long, distances in evolution* Vogt quoted in article by Susan Okie in *The Washington Post*, 10 October 1989.

73, *species selection has favored those species in which individual self-interest is best served by their own apparent altruism.* Dawkins 1986, p 268.

73, *the pattern integrity of the human individual is evolutionary and not static.* Fuller 1975, sec 505.201.

74, *every individual is an evolutionary pattern integrity.* Fuller 1975, sec 264.15.

74, *the principles of pattern formation . . . illuminate physics on the one hand and geological, biological, and social history on the other*   C. S. Smith 1981, pp ix–x. See also pp 66–67.

75, *life . . . depends on . . . patterns which amount to infinitely more order than matter usually tolerates.*   Dr. George E. Palade, "The Organization of Living Matter" in THE SCIENTIFIC ENDEAVOR, 1964, pp 179–180.

75, *it does not at present look as though Nature had designed the Universe primarily for life*   Sir James Jeans, THE WILDER ASPECTS OF COSMOGONY, 1928.

7. The very threshold

80, *some of the animal's molecules were still alive when the beast was found*   Tom Zito, *The Washington Post,* 9 January 1980.

81, *the word life is simply not encompassed by a molecule.*   René DuBos quoted in *The Washington Post,* 6 January 1980.

82, *Life can only be the appanage of the organism as a whole.*   André Lwoff 1968, p 100.

85, *an aphorism of Linnaeus . . . he must have had crystals in mind* from A TREASURY OF SCIENCE, Harlow Shapley et al., eds. 1958, New York: Harper & Row, p 281.

85–86, *crystals in their paracrystalline or liquid crystal form . . . approach most closely the realm of the living.*   from Needham 1976, pp 132–33.

86, *they cannot be ultimately described in terms of the ordinary laws of chemical and physical science*   from Wooldridge 1968, p 17.

86, *the replication of the genome and the reproduction of the organism are mutually dependent processes.*   Brian Goodwin 1988.

86, *the living world is essentially a vast number of templates* Hoffman 1957, pp 327–28.

87, *in these terms the period of reasonable certainty that no semblance of self exists ends with the appearance of spontaneous and responsive behavior."* Grobstein 1981, p 100.

88, *Simpson 1965, footnote p 69.*

88–89, *living systems are distinguished from nonliving systems only by degrees. There is no metaphysical gap to be bridged* Paul M. Churchland 1985, p 153.

89, *it is debatable whether there are certain boundaries, or only uncertainties, around life* Secretary Robert Adams, "Smithsonian Horizons," *Smithsonian* magazine, October 1986.

8. Quickening

90, *when life commenced. Aristotle said about 40 days after conception and Hippocrates said 30* Williams 1957.

90, *life begins in contemplation of law as soon as the infant is able to stir in the mother's womb.* Blackstone, *Commentaries*, quoted in Williams 1957.

92, *the laws of physics are literally pregnant with life—complexity* Mallove 1987.

94, *embryogenesis must rank as one of the three great integrative systems underlying the multicellular mode of life.* Jonathan Cooke, "The early embryo and formation of body pattern," *American Scientist* Jan–Feb 1988, p 35.

95, *the smaller and less mature a life is the greater its value* Hardin 1985.

98–99, *on a worldwide basis somewhere between 65% to 75% of all children born were not deliberately planned.* According to remarks by Dr. Claude A. Villee, Jr., professor of biological chemistry at Harvard Medical School at the XVI ICUS Conference, Atlanta, Georgia, 29 November 1987.

99, *life in early infancy is very close to non-existence*   Millard S. Everett 1954, IDEALS OF LIFE, p 347; quoted by Williams 1957, in footnote at p 349.

104, *my emergence as a unique individual . . . began back in the ovaries and testes of my parents*   "Did I Begin?" Martin Johnson, *New Scientist*, 9 December 1989.

105, *we are standing and walking with parts of our body which we could have used for thinking if they had been developed in another position in the embryo.*   from Hans Speman, FORSCHUNG UND LEBEN, 1943.

105, *better than one trillion trillion people are conceivable . . . only a minute fraction . . . are born*   from Vale, ed. 1986, p 31.

106, *all religious and philosophical systems are . . . primarily antidotes to the terrifying certainty of death.* Schopenhauer, THE WORLD AS WILL AND IDEA, 1928 ed., New York: The Modern Library III, ch 16.

107, *R. D. Laing has produced the startling hypothesis that conscious life might begin with the "primal relationship" between the fetus and the placenta*   R. D. Laing 1982, THE VOICE OF EXPERIENCE, London: Allen Lane, quoted in review by David Ingleby, *Times Literary Supplement* (London), 3 September 1982.

108, *a fetus is just physical life, a bundle of reflexes*   R. Buckminster Fuller to E.J.A., Aspen, Colorado, 13 June 1974.

109, *the individual life does not exist until the umbilical cord is cut*   Fuller 1979, sec 1005.614.

109, *to count pregnant women twice in our censuses would instantly increase our population by about three million.*   from Vale, ed. 1986, p 31.

111, *men and women become more concerned with the idiosyncratic character of sexuality*   from Jean-Marc Samson 1973.

9. Viruses

113, *viruses . . . embody all the information needed for their own reproduction.*   R. W. Horne, "The Structure of Viruses," *Scientific American*, January 1963.

113, *viruses are more closely related to their host cells . . . than they are to each other*   from Margulis 1970.

113, *no antiviral drugs are yet available*   Handler 1968.

114, *viruses came to serve a role for the biologist that the hydrogen atom had long done for the physicist*   Darius 1984.

114, *The bacteriophage is an ideal experimental tool.* Dyson 1982.

114, *one of the oldest domesticated organisms we know*   Morrison 1949.

115, *viruses [are] a living dead thing which our language is not yet rich enough to classify*   Gardner 1969.

10. Tardigrades

116, *springtimes such as these were all the Bedu ever knew of the gentleness of life.*   Thesiger 1959, London: Longmans, p 239.

119, *David Keilin, proposed the term* cryptobiosis   from Crowe 1972.

120, *cryptobiosis will require us to redefine life in terms of the continuity of organized structural integrity.*   from Crowe 1988.

120, *an individual . . . might extend its life for as long as 60 years.* from Crowe and Cooper 1972.

121, *cryptobiotic process becomes rarer as one ascends the evolutionary ladder* from Stephen Young 1985.

121, *we may understand how man . . . might be scanningly transmitted from any here to any there by radio.* Fuller 1975, secs 427.12, 427.15 and 515.13n.

11. The zoological context

126, *does it make sense to posit that to know truth can arise from dead matter?* Max Delbruck 1986, p 22.

127, *apart from self you cannot find a mind* Capra 1987, p 380.

127, *how can we construct a theory of a universe without life, and therefore without mind* Delbruck 1986, p 22.

128, *between 3.9 and 3.6 billion years ago for the appearance of the first prokaryotic cells.* from Harold Morowitz to Georgetown University Symposium, 1 May 1990.

129, *the species became twice as smart, introducing cultural evolution.* John Pfeiffer, "The emergence of modern humans,"*Mosaic*, Spring 1990.

131, *comprehensive linguistic capability seen in human populations emerged . . . 100,000 yrs ago.* From Colin Renfrew in *Scientific American*, October 1989, p 114.

131, *the human brain achieved its present size and complexity—about 125,000 yrs ago* Cesare Emiliani 1988, THE SCIENTIFIC COMPANION, New York: John Wiley & Sons.

131, *humans alone play competitively group against group.* Richard Alexander quoted by Roger Lewin in "The origin of the human mind," *Science* 236, 8 May 1987, p 669.

131, *as soon as the hominids had achieved upright posture, bipedal gait, the use of hands . . . and language. . . . The human revolution was over.*   Dobzhansky 1967, p 58.

132, *no law of nature decrees any particular evolutionary pathway.*   Stephen Jay Gould, review of Freeman Dyson's INFINITE IN ALL DIRECTIONS in *The New York Review of Books*, 27 October 1988.

133, *the range of each environmental variable . . . within which a species can exist*   Wilson 1975, glossary.

133, *umwelt, loosely translated as "the world around me."*   Wilson 1975.

133, *ecosystems of coral reefs teem with plant and animal life 24 hours a day*   from F. H. Talbot, "Day and night on a coral reef," *Pacific Discovery*, Spring 1988, pp 217–219.

134, *the principal habitat of the human mind is the very culture it creates.*   from E. O. Wilson and Lumsden 1983.

135, *only mammals and birds are homeotherms.*   from Koob 1972, p 58.

135, *human beings are "especially likely to transgress an environment's sustainable carrying capacity"*   from William R. Catton, Jr. "The world's most polymorphic species," *BioScience*, June 1987, p 413ff.

135, *politicians are professionally compelled to remain deaf to suggestions that . . . elevation of consumption cannot be perpetual.*   from Catton, op. cit., p 413.

138, *Julian Huxley proposed raising man to the rank of . . .*   Mayr, PSYCHOZOA, 1982, p 240.

138, *[Catton] has proposed Homo colossus as a new eco-social taxon*   Catton, *BioScience*, June 1987.

138, *it was presumptuous of Linnaeus to classify us as Homo sapiens*   Mather 1986, p 91.

138, *human beings cannot synthesize eight of the essential amino acids that occur in the proteins in our cells.* from Gerald Feinberg, 1985, p. 212.

139, *we have been lent by nature.* Jeremy Rifkin, AL-GENY, 1983.

139, *we are shared, rented, and occupied* Lewis Thomas 1974, pp 3–4.

12. The biology of consciousness

141, *nous means "mind . . . to think, to see, to perceive with the mind* Pandora Campbell note to EJA.

141, *nous is from the beginning intellective or cognitive,* article by James Philip on Pythagorean doctrines in DICTIONARY OF HISTORY OF IDEAS, vol IV, p 32.

142, *a behaviorist in psychology does not speak about consciousness* Karl H. Pribram 1985, Professor of Psychology, Stanford University.

142, *unknown neurobiological processes in human and some animal brains* from John R. Searle letter in *The New York Review of Books*, 14 June 1990.

142, *at one time no organisms were conscious and now some are.* from J. Maynard Smith letter in *The New York Review of Books*, 14 June 1990.

143, *metaphysical concern is not a biological property.* Simon 1971, p 213.

143, *the organization of events in time . . . is not a simple phenomenon from a neural point of view."* Harry J. Jerison, "The evolution of consciousness" in Eccles, ed. 1985, pp 208–209.

144, *consciousness cannot be defined* Sir William Hamilton (1788–1856), "The Philosophy of the Unconditioned," 1829, p 191.

144, *it could be that the special quality of brainness is simply switched on*   Lewis Thomas 1979, pp 156–57.

145, *psychology . . . has been notably unconcerned with consciousness*   Colin McGinn, "The language of awareness," *Times Literary Supplement* (London), 14 April 1989.

145, *living brains are actually observed in vastly greater detail by their owners*   M. J. Donald, "Quantum theory and the brain," *Proc. Royal Soc. Lond.* A **427**, 1990, pp 43–93.

146, *the only thing in the universe that makes an effort to understand itself.*   adapted from Gerald Jonas, "Into the brain," *The New Yorker*, 1 July 1974.

146, *Democritus called the heart "the queen, the nurse of anger," and the liver "the center of desire."*   Quoted in Changeux 1986, p 5.

146, *the human brain is . . . to the late 20th century what . . . America was to the 16th century.*   E. Fuller Torrey, a Washington psychiatrist.

146, *the nervous system . . . its total number of cells is fixed at birth*   Changeux 1986, p 282.

147, *the failure of neurons to proliferate may be the secret of their immunity*   Scientific American, May 1985.

147, *the brain has just two jobs: to run the body and to create the mind*   Ann K. Finkbeiner, *Mosaic*, Winter 1989.

147, *what the brain actually senses is energy in the form of vibrations*   from Peter Fenwick and David Lorimer, "Can brains be conscious?" *New Scientist*, 5 August 1989.

148, *there was no gradualism in the emergence of the human brain.*   from Borek 1980, p 225.

148, *the hominid brain just about tripled in size in the last three million years.*   from Asimov 1960, p 819.

148, *the human embryo . . . retraces more than a century of its ancestors' evolution for every second of its early rapid growth.*   from Murchie 1978, p 261.

148, *the brain's pictures "encompass time scales ranging from tenths of a second to hundreds of millions of years."*   Changeux 1986, p 277.

148, *no one has the faintest idea what is necessary for there to be a thought.*   Dr. William Sweet, Massachusetts General in Boston quoted by Blaine Harden in *The Washington Post*, 21 February 1982.

148, *no virgin forest . . . richer than . . . the domain of the mind*   Paul Valery quoted at Changeux 1986, p 275.

148–149, *the mind may be regarded as an emergent property of brain circuits*   from Campbell 1987, p 352.

149, *there is no rudiment of psyche in a crystal*   P. B. Medawar and J. S. Medawar 1983, p 231.

149, *I believe in the unity of mind and matter.*   Julian Huxley: WITHOUT REVELATION, in Thomas H. Middleton acrostic puzzle, *The New York Times*, 26 November 1989.

149, *mind is like no other property of physical systems.*   Harth 1982, pp 15–16.

149, *the Germans have Seele for soul . . . but no word has all the shades of the meaning of mind.*   This list is from Harth 1982, p 235.

149, *the most highly organized assembly of matter that has ever existed on earth*   Young 1986, p 166.

150, *the same state of knowledge as we were with regard to the heart before we realized that it pumped blood.*   Hubel quoted in Searle 1984, p 8.

150, *inputs that the brain receives . . . are produced by variable rates of neuron-firing . . .*   Searle 1984, p 9.

151, *the most complex problems that can be posed in science today*   Judson 1980, p. 203.

151, *a liaison between the new pharmacology and Freudian theory.*   Hooper & Teresi 1987, p 72.

151, *a comparison of human consciousness with spirochete ecology.*   Jeanne McDermott, "A biologist whose heresy redraws Earth's tree of life," *Smithsonian*, August 1989, p 72.

152, *MacLean introduced the theory of the three-layer brain*   Paul D. MacLean 1973, A TRIUNE CONCEPT OF THE BRAIN AND BEHAVIOR, Toronto: University of Toronto Press.

152, *the brain expanded in a hierarchical fashion*   Quoted in Restak 1979, p 51.

153, *action and reaction which we share . . . with the dog, the protozoan, and the plant.*   Thorpe 1962, p 28.

154, *the visceral brain . . . like adding a jet engine to an old cart horse.*   François Jacob in *Science*, vol 196, 10 June 1977, p 1166.

13. Self

155–156, *an ancient transition between the cell as a unit of selection and the individual as the unit of selection.*   Leo W. Buss 1989, THE EVOLUTION OF INDIVIDUALITY, Princeton University Press.

156, *identifies . . . self-awareness . . . with ceremonial burial*   Eccles 1989.

156, *no sense of self exists in other primates*   Julian Jaynes, address to New York Academy of Sciences, 9 December 1985.

156, *we sense our belonging first to our species, . . . and last to our race.*   Zelda Fichandler, *The Washington Post*, 22 November 1987.

157, *bringing meaning outside humankind to our earthly existence*   Charles Taylor 1989, SOURCES OF THE SELF: THE MAKING OF THE MODERN IDENTITY, Cambridge: Harvard University Press.

157, *an artifact of a particular grammar*   Arthur C. Danto, "You are what you say," *The New York Times Book Review*, 29 July 1984.

157, *any phenomenon produced by the specific methods or apparatus used*   Stuart Sutherland, *Times Literary Supplement* (London), 9 August 1985.

158, *"Who am I?" is a question that has many answers*   William H. Gass, "Family and Fable in Galilee," *The New York Times Book Review*, 17 April 1988.

158, *as Proust has suggested . . . the transformation of experience by memory*   John Updike, "A cloud of witnesses," *The New Yorker*, 7 April 1980.

158, *you do not belong to you.*   R. Buckminster Fuller quoted in *Cleveland Plain Dealer*, 4 July 1972.

158, *and nothing, not God, is greater to one than one's self is.*   Whitman, *Leaves of Grass: Song of Myself* [48].

159, *it was taken for granted that, except for slaves, people own themselves*   Ernest van den Haag, *National Review*, 22 December 1989.

160, *we come into this world with only one possession, the slender word "I"*   Attributed to Simone Weill by Diane Ackerman in *The New York Times Book Review*, 13 May 1990.

160, *recognition of foreign-ness . . . may in fact be universal*   H. S. Micklem, "Immunology," in Duncan and Weston-Smith, eds. 1978, pp 305–310.

161, *the immune system is dependent on . . . memory*   Stephen Grossberg at Boston University Science Symposium, 15 March 1989.

161, *humans produce . . . many as 100 million different antibodies.*   John Newell "Enzymes a la Carte," *New Scientist*, 24 March 1990.

161, *mind, brain and immune system interact*   Brendan O'Regan, *Investigations, a bulletin of the Institute of Noetic Sciences*, vol 1, no. 2, p 1.

162, *psychoanalysis has succeeded . . . because it offers . . . a system of solace*   Dr. Ernest Gellner, contribution to FREUD IN EXILE, Edward Timms and Naomi Segal, eds. 1988, New Haven: Yale University Press [quoted by Schatzman below].

162, *psychoanalysis confronts our brutal and devious tendencies . . .*   Morton Schatzman, "Psychoanalysis and its vicissitudes," *New Scientist*, 9 June 1988.

163, *consciousness is a singular of which the plural is unknown.*   Erwin Schrödinger 1944, pp 94–95.

163, *Freudian psychology provides no place for . . . interpersonal relationships*   Danah Zohar 1990.

163, *Id, Superego and Ego . . . described as a fight in a coal cellar*   Roland Littlewood, "The theoretical self," *Times Literary Supplement* (London), 6 April 1984.

163, *Freud . . . questioning the degree to which human motives are . . . knowable*   Owen Flanagan 1984, p 55.

164, *the goal of psychoanalysis is to make the unconscious conscious*   Restak 1979, pp 316, 359.

164, *I do not think our successes can compete with those of Lourdes.*   Sigmund Freud 1932, NEW INTRODUCTORY LETTERS ON PSYCHOANALYSIS.

165, *psychic mechanisms . . . of speech and memory . . . are uncommitted.*   Penfield 1975, p 17.

167, *laboratory conditions probably freeze spontaneity*

from Rosemary Dinnage "Fragments of a remade world," *Times Literary Supplement* (London), 22 December 1989.

168, *an individual spends at least 50,000 hours in dreaming.* J. Allan Hobson 1988, THE DREAMING BRAIN, New York, Basic Books.

168, *dreams have no meaning . . . they randomly purge the brain.* Francis Crick in *Science News*, 29 March 1986, p 197.

168, *the function of sleep is . . . to restore . . . symmetry* R. B. Fuller to E.J.A., Santa Barbara, California, 11 February 1973.

169, *the mechanisms that must exist in order to generate the behavior that is observed,"* Geoffrey Hall in *Nature* review of 1 December 1988.

169, *mental states . . . not explicable in terms of neurofunctional organization* Bishop 1988, p 390.

169, *if we ignore the insights psychology . . . we will never understand what brain chemistry is all about.* Israel Rosenfield, *The New York Review of Books*, "The New Brain," 14 March 1985.

170, *the next step beyond Piaget . . . if there were a Nobel prize for that sort of thing.* Howard Gardner of Harvard University quoted in *The New York Times*, 23 October 1988.

170, *Greeks who have "anthropos" and the Germans who have "Mensch."* From Anthony Kenny, "Are you a person," review in *The New York Times Book Review*, 27 August 1989.

171, *in the philosophy of mind there are many aspects of personhood.* This analysis is derived from Amelie Oksenberg Rorty 1989, MIND IN ACTION: ESSAYS IN THE PHILOSOPHY OF MIND, Boston: Beacon Press.

171, *persons have moral and ethical values . . . insuscep-*

tible to scientific scrutiny. Adapted from Gunther Stent, "The Poverty of Neurophilosophy," in *The Journal of Medicine and Philosophy* 15: 539–537, 1990.

14. Observing man

172, *the members of our species are five or six feet tall. We seem now to have investigated the inner constitution of matter* Ian Hacking. "When the atom broke down," *The New York Review of Books*, 26 February 1987, p 19.

172, *environment does not exist without the observer* Fuller 1978, sec 264.10.

173, *it is Wheeler who tells us that the universe . . . gives rise to observer participancy.* William H. Press in review of BETWEEN QUANTUM AND COSMOS, *American Scientist*, Jan–Feb 1990.

173, *an incomplete picture of the physical universe is not due to the nature of the universe* letters to *Nature*, 4 January 1988.

15. Ants & instinct

178, *ants . . . may be studied from at least three different points of view . . . their classification . . . their morphology . . . or their ethology* W. M. Wheeler 1910, p 124.

179, *the degree to which it is permissible to think of ant behavior in human terms* Derek Wragge Morley 1953, THE ANT WORLD.

180–181, *those of us who study social insects have never been able to find a command center.* Edward O. Wilson, "Altruism and Ants," in *Discover*, August 1985.

181, *the existence of social organization . . . is not dependent upon mental events.* Davies 1988, p 194.

181, *who can tell where the whole begins and the part*

leaves off in a living organism.   W. M. Wheeler 1910, p 518.

182, *This feature, which . . . we call plasticity of behavior.*   J. B. S. Haldane 1947, "Human evolution; Past and future," address delivered in London, January 1947 cite to Jepsen, ed. 1963.

16. Conscious evolution

186, *we have in a few hundred years changed the biosphere to an extent that it took the plants a few million years to do.*   Alison Jolly. "We are the world," *New Scientist*, 21 May 1987.

186, *the messengers of biological evolution are the molecules of messenger RNA.*   Dr. Edward Rubenstein, "Stages of evolution and their messengers," *Scientific American*, June 1989.

186–187, *evolution in which the first stage is genetic . . . the second . . . is cultural . . . the third stage, a technological*   Mallove 1987, p 130.

187–188, *where intelligent technology is manipulating matter . . . life may have an impact on the fate of the Universe.*   Eric Chaisson, Lecture at Smithsonian Institution, 23 January 1989.

188, *life resides in organization rather than in substance . . .*   Dyson 1988, p 107.

188, *our political leaders . . . do not seem to be aware of creeping globalism.*   Alison Jolly, "We are the world," *New Scientist*, 21 May 1987.

188, *I am not here to argue that the human species ought to take responsibility for the evolution of the planet.*   Walter Truett Anderson 1987, To GOVERN EVOLUTION, New York: Harcourt Brace Jovanovich.

189, *that the greatest human catastrophe of recorded his-*

tory will occur in the lifetime of most of us. Report of Second International Conference on the Environmental Future, quoted by John Ekington in *New Scientist*, 23 June 1977.

189, *we are . . . not what the universe was aiming at from the beginning.* Stephen R. L. Clark in "With rationality and love," *Times Literary Supplement* (London), 26 September 1986.

190, *salvation . . . means the preservation of the hominid taxon from extinction* Mather 1986, p 178.

190, *environmental issues . . . are . . . some kind of secular eschatology* Edward Norman in "Not fearing to tread," *Times Literary Supplement* (London), 1 June 1990.

17. Self-organization

196, *it would take many times the age of the universe for chance alone to bring together the amino acids* James Glueck, "Artificial Life: can computers discern the soul?" *The New York Times Magazine*, 29 September 1987.

197, *individuation is important, such systems can acquire agency.* Salthe 1989.

198, *there is a name that is commonly applied to such a competition for a single source of raw materials . . . it is called evolution.* Dean E. Wooldridge 1968, MECHANICAL MAN: THE PHYSICAL BASIS OF INTELLIGENT LIFE, 25.

198, *a complex of interacting elements.* Bertalanffy 1968, GENERAL SYSTEM THEORY, New York: Braziller, p 55.

198, *the elements may be objects or processes operating at any level* Engel 1984.

199, *the self-regulating machine is the central metaphor in much systems thinking.* Sheldrake 1988.

199, *the study of quasi-biological systems including their construction and classification.* Langton, ed. 1989, p 355.

199, *abstract mathematics and computer models* M. Mitchell Waldrop, "Spontaneous Order, Evolution and Life," *Science* 247, 30 March 1990.

18. Artificial life

201, *the study of man-made systems that exhibit behaviors characteristic of natural living systems.* Langton, ed. 1989, p 1.

202, *the key feature of nonlinear systems is . . . the inter-actions between parts* Langton 1989, p 41.

202, *synergy means behavior of integral, aggregate, whole systems* Fuller 1975, sec 102.00.

202, *intuition and mind apprehend that which is . . . between, and not of, the parts.* Fuller 1975, sec 508.02.

203, *there is no meaning to the word artificial.* Fuller, EDUCATION AUTOMATION, 1961 (reprinted by Doubleday Anchor, 1971), p 52.

204, *all the chemist can do is to find out what nature permits* Fuller, IDEAS AND INTEGRITIES, 1959 (reprinted by Collier Books 1969), p 75.

207, *when information was stored on carbon molecules in a form of life called "real"* John Barrow, "Big AL", *New Scientist*, 15 July 1989.

208, Yeats quote: after Hardison 1989, pp 347–48.

19. Postbiology

210, *our new symbiosis with computers will develop.* L. Kowarski (Cern, Geneva), THINKERS AND MASTERS, 1966, in *New Scientist*, 27 January 1966.

210, *anything that our industrial machines can do. . . . biological processes in the natural world do . . . more quickly.* Dyson 1988, p 155.

211, *thinking is a blood sport* Stich 1984, *Times Literary Supplement* (London), 24 February 1984.

212, *a pentad, that harvests light energy* from *Science News*, 21 April 1990, p 247.

212, *we are seeing a transfer of power from politics to science.* François Mitterand, as reported in *The New York Times*, 19 January 1988.

213, Footnote: *the Neanderthals made beautiful tools stupidly almost without change for more than 60,000 years* Randall White 1986, DARK CAVES, BRIGHT VISIONS: LIFE IN ICE AGE EUROPE, New York: American Museum of Natural History and W. W. Norton.

213, *plants don't really need brains* Margulis and Sagan 1986, p 174.

20. Birth & death

221, *life begins in the bursting of membranes, and ends with a relaxation of the sphincter muscles* John Updike, THE COUNSELOR.

221, *death . . . is a facet of experience . . . beyond our reach.* Liam Hudson, "Managing Mortality," *Times Literary Supplement* (London) 27 April 1990.

221, *aging and death here engender birth and growth elsewhere.* Fuller 1978, 1052.59.

221, *to offset the shortness of life, living matter grows furiously.* Hoffman 1957, p 314.

222, *bipedalism . . . [and] . . . encephalization . . . combined to make delivery more difficult* Joan B. Silk in *American Scientist*, September 1988, p 524.

222, *life can only be understood backwards but it must be lived forwards.* Kierkegaard quoted by Friedrich Cramer, "Death: From Microscopic to Macroscopic Disorder," in PROCEEDINGS OF INTERNATIONAL SYMPOSIUM ON SYNERGETICS, ed. E. Frehland, Berlin: Springer-Verlag, 1984, p 227.

223, *there is as much uncertainty about the moment of personal death as there is about the moment of personal birth.* W. H. Thorpe 1962, p 117.

224, *it is not life that begins in each human generation, it is self* Clifford Grobstein 1981, pp 79–80.

224–225, *societies and multicellular organisms subordinate the individual to the point of dispensability* from Rodney Cotterill 1985, p 287.

21. Proclivities of death

226, *the most universal and mundane of all human crises* Hockett 1973, p 248.

226, *enzymes cease to function . . . submerged in the sea of background chemistry* Levins and Lewontin 1985, p 49.

227, *to the eye of science, nature is a continuum.* Glanville Williams 1957, pp 3–4.

228, *death and life are symmetrical* Friedrich Cramer, "Death: from microscopic to macroscopic disorder," 1983. From PROCEEDINGS OF INTERNATIONAL SYMPOSIUM ON SYNERGETICS, ed. E. Frehland. Berlin: Springer-Verlag, 1984, pp 220–27.

228, *three commonly held views of what happens at death,* and the descriptions that follow are summarized (with permission) from Dr. Arthur S. Berger, "Three views of death and their implications for life," paper presented at the XVIth International Conference on the Unity of the Sciences, Atlanta GA, 26–29 November 1987.

231, *programmed cell death.... a possible safeguard against unbridled cell proliferation*   Alberts 1983, p 621.

231–232, *absolute certainty of cell death is as important as life itself.*   Hoffman 1957, pp 322–23.

232, *cancer cells and germ cells are the only two mammalian cell types known which avoid the inevitability of death.*   Cotterill 1985, p 297–8.

232, *death is completely explicable ... while the origin of life ... has so far proved completely contrary to the laws of physics and nature.*   Hoffman 1957, pp 270, 286–87.

232, *parts of us begin to die long before we are born ...*   L. Watson 1974, p 21.

233, *death ... has only three possible causes:*   D. E. Price, and C. F. Ross 1963, POST-MORTEM APPEARANCES, Oxford University Press: London (quoted in L. Watson 1974, p 47).

234, *the desire of life to feed on life is the main cause of death*   Hoffman 1957, p 308.

234, *considering modern human beings, accidents and the vulnerability of the body ... are the main causes of death.*   Hoffman 1957, pp 316–17.

235, *the certificates of death... provide for only three forms of unnatural death*   Gonzales-Crussi 1986.

235, *let the jury look at the clock for three minutes.*   The Washington Post, 10 January 1988.

236, *aging is ... deeply programmatic in character*   P. B. and J. S. Medawar 1977, p 153.

236, *senescence is the condition of a system that has come to rely more on habits than on random impulse.*   S. N. Salthe, Smithsonian Seminar, 2–3 June 1989.

236, *senescence is characterized by a decrease in redun-*

dancy.   Eric Chaisson, Smithsonian Seminar, 2–3 June 1989.

237, *man is at his peak of performance in his twenties or early thirties*   Thorpe 1961, pp 117–118.

238, *the elderly require . . . a growing share of society's resources*   Louis Lasagne, Professor at Rochester School of Medicine, in *The Sciences*, July/August 1985.

238, *conventional billion-dollar disease research . . . is becoming progressively more futile*   Denham Harman in *The Scientist*, 19 March 1990.

239, *molecular diseases, . . . the consequence of a molecular tendency toward . . . autonomy.* Lwoff 1968, p 100.

239, *contagious diseases . . . follows from the desire of life to prey on life.*   Hoffman 1957, pp 308–09.

239–240, *the major categories of diseases*   Morowitz & Morowitz 1974, p 292.

240, *the poisonous ingenuity of time in the science of affliction*   Denis Donoghue review of *Waiting for Godot* in *The New York Review of Books*, 8 December 1988.

240, *dying is a misunderstanding . . . it may not be dying we fear so much but the diminished self*   Anatole Broyard, "Good Books about Being Sick," *The New York Times Book Review*, 1 April 1990.

241, *worldwide capacity of zoos would allow for maintenance of no more than 900 species.*   Letter from Arthur L. Spingarn, heritage ecologist at the Indiana Department of Natural Resources, to *BioScience*, October 1987.

242, *extinction is the motor of species evolution*   Peter J. Smith review of Niles Eldredge's Life Pulse in *New Scientist*, 19 November 1987.

242, *by the year 2020 . . . all seafood would be grown in*

mariculture. Dr. Jim Butler, Bermuda Biological Station in the *Royal Gazette*, Hamilton, 29 October 1987.

242, *Consider Sexual Organization and hide thee in the dust* William Blake, *Jerusalem*, Quoted at Mackay 1977 (p 21).

243, *the other necessary condition for the very possibility of evolution is death.* Francois Jacob 1973, pp 309–10.

244, *in a sense, the original amoeba . . . is among us still.* Jonathan Weine in *The Sciences*, July/August 1984.

244, *sex requires two unions . . . neither rendezvous is easy to arrange.* Jonathan Weiner in *The New York Times Book Review*, 27 March 1988, review of THE DANCE OF LIFE by Mark Jerome Walters.

244, *[eukaryotes] once having once tasted the pleasures of individuality, pursue it feverishly unto this day.* William H. Calvin in *Nature*, 5 November 1987.

245, *the debris and excrement and waste of living things provide nourishment* Hoffman 1957, p 313.

245, *no single species could persist alone on the planet. It would eventually exhaust all the nutrients* Robert Augros and George Stanciu, symposium transcript in *Noetic Sciences Review*, Winter 1989.

246, *each organism has first shared the life of another organism* Jacob 1973, p. 91.

246–247, *without the bacteria . . . all life would eventually cease.* Zinsser 1934, pp 39–40.

22. Immortality

248, *in temporal immortality the . . . mind continues after death indefinitely;* Dagobert D. Runes, ed. 1962. DICTION-

ARY OF PHILOSOPHY, Totowa, New Jersey: Littlefield & Adams Co., p 142.

248, *the capacity of the individual consciousness to integrate past, present and future*   paraphrased from Campbell 1986, pp 365–66.

248, *immortality can acquire a meaning . . . through one's feeling that one has duties*   Wittgenstein quoted by N. Malcolm 1958.

249, *if eternity were attained . . . nothing could be left . . . save pure ecstasy of contemplation*   Thorpe 1962, p 117.

250, *that mortals should desire immortality, and yet find difficulty in passing an afternoon*   Schopenhauer quoted at Dixon 1937, p 85.

250, *infinity is the enemy of any system.*   Timothy Dickenson to E.J.A., 4 December 1989.

251, *on the day when man makes himself immortal he makes himself extinct.*   Brad Leithauser, 9 January 1989.

251, *is there not a certain satisfaction in the fact that natural limits are set to the life of the individual, so that at its conclusion it may appear as a work of art?"*   Mallove 1987, ch 17.

251, *life might be unforgivable if it were not for death. . . . Has it ever occurred to you that death is a blessing?*   from UPI obituary of Will Durant, 9 November 1981.

252, *interviews with more than 100 cases . . . identified five phases of NDE:*   From E.J.A. notes of a presentation by Dr. Kenneth E. Ring, a professor of psychology at the University of Connecticut, on 27 October 1985 at a symposium on consciousness and survival sponsored by the Institute of Noetic Sciences at Georgetown University.

253, *being born is like dying from a previous existence*   Carol Zaleski 1987, OTHERWORLD JOURNEYS.

23. The secularity of life & death

254–255, to identify . . . the coming together of sperm and ovum . . . as a point of indecipherable mystery Anthony Dyson in EXPERIMENTS ON EMBRYOS, Dyson & Harris, eds. 1989, London: Routledge (reviewed in *New Scientist*, 6 January 1990).

255, we will have to give up the notion that death is a catastrophe, Lewis Thomas 1974, pp 98–99.

256, the innate resonance of a two-atom molecule of iodine. "Femtosecond observations of molecular vibration and rotation," M. Dantus et al., *Nature* 343, 22 February 1990.

257, death can take more than one form—natural or unnatural Kastenbaum 1986, p 2.

24. The abundance of the elements

262, every atom in our body . . . has already passed through particle, galactic, stellar, planetary, and chemical evolution. Chaissson 1987, p 218.

262, each one of us and all of us are truly and literally a little bit of star dust. Science Impact, March 1988.

264, the next breath you inhale will contain atoms exhaled by Jesus at Gethsemane Preston Cloud and Aharon Gibor, "The oxygen cycle," *Scientific American*, September 1970, p 123.

265, every atom belonging to me as good belongs to you. Whitman 1881, "Song of Myself."

265, once caught up in the network of living matter, atoms are apt to find themselves within living things for a long time Hoffman 1957, p 310.

265, every cubic centimeter of air contains some 10^{19} molecules. Capra 1982, footnote, p 73.

265, *there are 200 times as many molecules in a glass of water as there are glasses of water in the world!*   Kieffer 1971, p 121.

266, *almost all the molecules in our bodies turn over in a matter of days, weeks or at the most a few months.*   Francis Crick, "Memory and molecular turnover," *Nature* 312, 8 November 1984, p 101.

266, *living matter is a specialized form of matter.   There is much less of it.*   Kieffer 1971.

267, *the total weight of humans on earth equals the total weight of ants*   E. O. Wilson at Georgetown University Conference, 4 April 1989.

267, *20 times the present biomass exists in the form of bacteria as exists in the form of animals.*   Marquand 1968, p 52.

267, *each of our intestinal tracts contains more* E. coli *bacteria than the earth houses people.*   Stephen Jay Gould in *The New York Review of Books*, 15 April 1982.

268, *whales weighing up to 150 tons and plankton so numerous that their total mass is thought to exceed that of the whole human race.*   *New Scientist*, 23 September 1989.

268, *20 species provide 90 percent of the world's food, and just three species—wheat, maize and rice—supply more than half.*   E. O. Wilson in *Issues*, Fall 1985.

268, *65–90 percent of all living matter is water.*   *Economist*, 10 October 1987.

268, *It takes about 108,000 cattle a day to supply the nation's grocery stores and restaurants.*   *The Washington Post*, 2 September 1986.

268, *the combined weight of earth's insects is 12 times greater than that of its human population*   Thomas A.

Bass, "Africa's drive to win the battle against insects," *Smithsonian*, August 1988.

268, *there are now more people alive than all those who have lived before added together.* New Scientist, 17 March 1988.

268, *vertebrates are only about five per cent of the animal kingdom* Buchsbaum 1938, Animals without Back-bones, p 13.

268, *As much as one third of tropical biomass circulates through ants and termites* Alun Anderson in *Nature*, 3 September 1987, p 6.

25. The cell as a unit of life

269, *a tendency to identify life with a particular substance* Florkin 1972, p 295.

270, *the cytoplasm is the field of interplay of hereditary and environmental factors.* Whyte 1949, p 120.

270, *everything in the universe consists of something surrounded by a boundary . . .* Cyril Stanley Smith, University Professor Emeritus, MIT, communication to E.J.A., 11 April 1990.

271, *words and meanings evolve together like DNA and proteins* Alan L. Mackay, "Lucretius: atoms and opinions," *Symmetry*, vol I, no 1, 1990, p 3.

271, *the cell is . . . the only unit of biological organization which can multiply itself. . . .* Whyte 1949, p 118.

271–273, *patterning in the single cell is a fundamental biological mechanism that has been taken over by multicellular organisms* Lewis Wolpert, review in *Nature* 346, 23 August 1990.

274, *every living organism is, or at some time has been, a cell.* E. B. Wilson 1925, THE CELL IN DEVELOPMENT AND HEREDITY, 3rd. ed. New York: Macmillan.

276, *Weismann located the germ plasm in the nucleus of the cell.* Goodwin 1988.

277–278, *of the immensely large number of ways of arranging the atoms in a cell . . . only an immensely small fraction can represent viable living systems.* Frederick Seitz 1989, physicist, at ICUS XVII plenary address.

278, *most of us carry about two pounds of bacteria in our intestinal tracts.* The Sciences, May-June 1940.

280, *to say that DNA transmits information is not an analogy* John Maynard Smith "Evolution for those who have ears," *New Scientist,* 20 November 1986.

280, *more like a recipe than a blueprint.* Richard Dawkins, "Creation and natural selection" in *New Scientist,* 25 September 1986.

280, *the organism, and the cells and molecules . . . each evolved in a series of previous environments.* Salk 1972, p 2.

280, *I seem to be a verb* Fuller 1970.

280, *the genetic program . . . evolved in the Earth's evolution over three billion years* Luria, Gould, Singer 1981, pp 14, 17.

281, *DNA has relinquished some of its control to the brain.* Review of Dulbecco 1987, by Ann Roman in *American Scientist,* March-April 1990.

281, *DNA . . . has relinquished some of its powers to the organisms themselves* Dulbecco 1987, p *viii.*

26. The biosphere as a unit of life

282, *a biosphere is a highly ordered system of matter and energy* Gerald Feinberg & Robert Shapiro 1980, p 147.

283, *there are 329 million cubic miles of sea-water*   John Coote, ed. 1990, THE FABER BOOK OF THE SEA, London: Faber.

284, *Lovelock and Margulis published their second paper on the hypothesis*   Icarus 21, 1974, p 471.

284, *human beings are 'genitals'* . . . *incestuously involved with Mother Earth*   Dorion Sagan 1989, BIOSPHERES: METAMORPHOSIS OF PLANET EARTH, New York: McGraw-Hill.

285, *without the moderating effect* . . . *of life* . . . *temperatures might rise*   "Biotic enhancement of weathering," *Nature*, 10 August 1989.

285, *for the past 3.3 billion years the temperature of the earth's atmosphere has remained constant*   *Science News*, 11 May 1974.

285, *the temperature of the earth is a median between the heat of the sun and the cold of outer space*   Harold Morowitz at Georgetown University symposium, 1 May 1990.

285, *there is a direct correlation between the growth in the atmospheric carbon dioxide and the growth of the world's human population*   *Science News*, 12 September 1987.

285–286, *all of the oxygen in the atmosphere, were it not replenished by plants, bacteria and algae, would be totally exhausted*   Dixon 1976, p 46.

286, *oxygen* . . . *was to the early biosphere what* . . . *nuclear power is to the biosphere of today*   Preston Cloud, "The Biosphere," *Scientific American*, September 1983.

286, *the pool of species diversity* . . . *comprises a vast reservoir of potential new crops*   *Issues*, Fall 1985.

287, *we don't know to the nearest order of magnitude how many species there are*   E. O. Wilson quoted in *The New York Times*, 23 October 1988.

288, *the solemnity of the remorseless working of*

things. A. N. Whitehead 1948, SCIENCE AND THE MODERN WORLD, New York: Mentor.

288, *the only way we can preserve and nurture other more precious freedoms is by relinquishing the freedom to breed.* Garrett Hardin, "The Tragedy of the Commons," *Science* 162, 13 December 1968.

288, *the carrying capacity of our living space is not enough to provide a broadened niche for all men who now exist* P. A. Colinvaux 1973, INTRODUCTION TO ECOLOGY, New York: John Wiley & Sons.

288, *politicians are professionally compelled to remain deaf to suggestions that . . . elevation of consumption cannot be perpetual* William R. Catton, Jr., "The World's Most Polymorphic Species," *BioScience*, June 1987.

27. Hierarchy & classification

291, *the most majestic of taxonomic distinctions* Sir Peter Medawar in HARPER DICTIONARY OF MODERN THOUGHT, 1977, New York: Harper & Row, p 64.

292, *functional intricacy on distance scales very small compared to overall size* Mallove 1987, p 120.

293, *we must divide the biped class into featherless and feathered.* Plato, THE STATESMAN, 266 E (quoted in *Bartlett's Quotations*, 15th ed. p 86, footnote 4).

293, *a certain Chinese dictionary divided animals into such categories* from preface to Michel Foucault 1971, THE ORDER OF THINGS, New York.

294, *taxonomy is fundamental . . . to the incorporation of all knowledge into a system* Martin Ingrouille, "The decline and fall of British Taxonomy," *New Scientist*, 7 January 1989.

294, *the basis for the definition of taxa has progressively shifted from the organismal to the cellular to the molecular level* Carl R. Woese, et al. "Towards a natural system of organisms: Proposal for the domains Archaea, Bacteria and Eucarya," *Proceedings of the National Academy of Sciences*, vol 87, p 4576.

296, *modern science, no less than ancient science, proceeds according to the cinematic method. It cannot do otherwise* Henri Bergson 1908, L'Evolution Creatrice, quoted in W. M. Wheeler 1910, p 506.

297, *there are only two types of cells . . . one type has a nucleus, the other type does not* Jeanne McDermott, "A biologist whose heresy redraws Earth's tree of life," *Smithsonian*, August 1989.

298, *for more than half the total span of life on earth the only life for which a fossil record exists was* [prokaryotic] Arthur Fisher, "The wheels within wheels in the Superkingdom Eukaryotae," *Mosaic*, Fall 1989.

298, *each cell in our body has the . . . status of a former colony.* Stephen Jay Gould, "Tires to Sandals," *Natural History*, April 1989.

299, *there is no neutral terminology.* Mary Midgely 1978, Beast and Man.

300, *a book misplaced may be as useless as a book lost.* Dobzhansky 1962, p 266.

28. Disciplines

302, *the natural tendency of educated groups with common interests to band together* Kenneth P. Ruscio, Department of social science and policy studies, Worcester Polytechnic Institute in *BioScience*, January 1988.

303, *a dismissal of irrelevancies* Fuller 1975, sec 509.06.

303, *it is the function of discipline, . . . to submerge the individual fantasy in a greater whole.* Dyson 1988.

303, *John Milton is believed to be the last person to have read every book published in his lifetime.* Hugh Kenner, conversation with E.J.A., 13 September 1989.

304, *The highest wisdom has but one science—the science of the whole* Leo Tolstoy 1869, WAR AND PEACE, as inscribed on wall of McLaughlin Planetarium, Toronto.

304, *the best interdisciplinary work is that carried on within the confines of a single brain.* Nicholas Rescher, *Journal of Economic Literature*, 1982.

304, *polytropic is the idiom applied to Odysseus* Alan L. Mackay, letter to *The Scientist*, 17 October 1988.

305, *I predict the development of some new principles of hierarchy* Cyril Stanley Smith, "Matter versus Materials: A historical View," *Science* 162, 8 November 1968, p 644.

305, *NIBS: for Neural, Informational and Behavioral sciences* news article in *Nature*, 18 February 1988.

306, *it is not given to us mortals to know the unity of knowledge . . .* Edward A. Shils, professor of sociology, University of Chicago, from E.J.A. notes at the conference of ICUS XVIth session, Atlanta, Georgia, 27 November 1987.

307, *by trying to understand everything, one ends up learning little that is solid.* Weinberg 1988.

309, *biology is what chemistry does when . . . the Earth [has] some billions of years to play around with.* Frederick Turner 1986.

309, *the functional part of biology is reducible to physics while the evolutionary aspect is not.* from Mayr 1988.

309, *DNA . . . plays opposite natural selection* Gairdner B. Moment, Professor Emeritus, Goucher College, *Bio-Science*, June 1988.

310, *mathematics is the science of pattern, and there are five sorts of patterns* Rudy Rucker 1987, MIND TOOLS: THE FIVE LEVELS OF MATHEMATICAL REALITY, New York: Houghton Mifflin.

310, *mathematics, a product of human thought independent of experience* Attributed to Albert Einstein by George Farre, a professor of philosophy at Georgetown University, in a paper presented at the Washington Evolutionary Systems Society, 20 June 1990.

311, *as one science uses more fully the conceptual tools provided it by another the dividing line between them blurs.* The quotes and much of the argument here is from William F. Kiefer 1971.

311, *a new theory will be found. . . . In that case, one would say that physics was reduced to biology and not biology to physics.* J. G. Kemeny 1959, A PHILOSOPHER LOOKS AT SCIENCE, New York: Van Nostrand, pp 215–216 (footnoted at Francisco J. Ayala, "Biology as an autonomous science," *American Scientist* 56, 1968, p 221).

313, *the evolutionary later always subsumes the evolutionarily earlier. . . . the arts and humanities are higher physics.* These quotes and most of the argument in this section is taken from Frederick Turner, "Design for a new academy," *Harper's*, September 1986, p 49ff.

313, *long one of the most homespun of disciplines* Clifford Geertz 1984, LOCAL KNOWLEDGE: FURTHER ESSAYS IN INTERPRETATIVE ANTHROPOLOGY. New York: Basic Books.

313, *all ethnography is part philosophy* Geertz, INTERPRETATION OF CULTURES, pp. 345–346.

313, *paradigmlessness a permanent affliction.* Geertz, "Waddling in," *Times Literary Supplement* (London), 7 June 1985, p 623.

314, *biology is not equipped to study those adjuncts of our bodies which make humans human.* Barbara Noske,

Humans and Other Animals, Pluto Press (quoted by Lynda Burke, *New Scientist*, 13 May 1989, p 67).

314, *the layman cannot help thinking that the essence of life is never recovered by biology.*   The Economist, 11 February 1989, p 82.

29. The nature of biological doctrines

316, *the laws of physics are believed to be the same everywhere. . . . This is unlikely to be true of biology.*   Crick 1988.

316, *the majority of physiological laws are of a statistical character*   Max Planck 1959, p 102.

316, *Allen's rule.*   Dobzhansky 1962, p 273.

316, *Bergmann's rule*   Dobzhansky 1962, p 273.

316–317, *Farenholz's rule*   Nature, 17 March 1988.

317, *Bionomogenesis.*   Rensch 1972, p 28.

317, *Dollo's law*   Rosenberg 1985, p 209.

317, *[holism] still survives, albeit in a more quantitative than intuitive mode.*   E. O. Wilson 1975, p 7.

319, *the availability of . . . genetic techniques for the modification of organisms.*   R. Garcia, et al. in *BioScience*, November 1988.

319, *the emerging biotech industry has great potential for cutting pollution.*   James Gustave Speth, president, World Resources Institute, quoted in *The Washington Post*, 20 November 1988.

30. Research frontiers in biology

320, *three basic areas of ignorance pervade the scene* formulation advanced by Lancelot Law Whyte 1965, Internal Factors in Evolution, New York: Braziller, p 29.

320, *the three most likely areas for technological progress*   Dyson 1988, p 273.

321, *since the end of the 19th century biologists have sought a unified theory*   Joseph G. Gall, review of "Molecular Biology of the Gene," in *Nature*, 3 March 1988. (Gall is American Cancer Society Professor of Developmental Genetics, Carnegie Institution, Baltimore, MD.)

322, *Dr. Jonathan Roughgarden has proposed that Congress should create a US Ecological Survey*   *BioScience*, January 1989.

323, *no one knows how embryos progressively take up their forms or how instincts are inherited*   Sheldrake 1988, p 15.

324, *an inventory of the estimated 30,000 to 50,000 different kinds of proteins that make up the human body.*   Albert Rosenfeld, "The Great Protein Hunt," *Science 81*, Jan/Feb 1981, p 61.

324, *the last common ancestor of all living species*   Dyson 1988, p 88.

325, *molecular biology will soon move beyond its present preoccupation*   John Maddox, *Nature* 339, 8 June 1989.

325, *how the unidimensional genetic information encoded in the DNA of a single cell becomes transformed*   Francisco J. Ayala in *Issues*, Spring 1987.

326, *the prediction of the three-dimensional structure of a protein from its amino-acid sequence.*   Janet M. Thornton in *Nature*, 1 September 1988.

326, *every species is the terminus of an ancient lineage*   E. O. Wilson in *Science*, 13 December 1985.

326–327, *an understanding of biological systems requires a knowledge of function and history that chemistry cannot provide.*   Steven Rose quoting Popper in review of Max

F. Perutz in *Times Literary Supplement* (London), 4 August 1989.

327, *molecular biology is still incapable of predicting.* *Science*, 10 February 1989, p 792.

327, *new general principles . . . are becoming ever more elusive.* E. O. Wilson "The coming pluralization of biology," *BioScience*, vol 39, no 4, April 1989.

327, *it seems highly unlikely that we will ever have a grand unified theory of biology.* Harold Morowitz, "Models, theory and the matrix of biological knowledge," *BioScience*, vol 39, no 3, March 1989, p 178.

328, *the key problem of biology . . . is how living matter manages to record and perpetuate experience.* Max Delbruck 1949.

328, *everything interesting happens only once* Stephen Jay Gould, "Mighty Manchester" review of Freeman J. Dyson, INFINITE IN ALL DIRECTIONS; *The New York Review of Books*, 12 October 1988.

328, *investigation of the population structure of homeostatic systems of molecules.* Dyson 1988, p 87.

329, *some new principles of hierarchy . . . will enable the effective resonance between molecule and organism to be explored.* Cyril Stanley Smith, Institute Professor of metallurgy emeritus, MIT, Sarton lecture to AAAS, 28 December 1967.

31. Prospects for a scientific explanation of life

330, *in biology it is still possible to work alone.* Borek 1980, p 189.

330–331, *only by renouncing an explanation about life* Niels Bohr 1958, ATOMIC PHYSICS AND HUMAN KNOWLEDGE, New York: Wiley, pp 67–82.

331, *this life of yours which you are living*   Erwin Schrödinger 1925, MY VIEW OF THE WORLD, quoted at Bernstein
1982, p 150.

331, *natural science does not simply describe*   Werner
Heisenberg 1959, PHYSICS AND PHILOSOPHY.

331, *any one cell . . . represents more a historical than a
physical event*   Max Delbruck, 1949 Lecture: "A physicist looks at biology" (quoted at Stent 1969, p 23).

331, *only if life was very easy to start, . . . are we likely to
be able to reproduce it in the laboratories*   Crick 1981,
p 88.

332, *matter, like logic, is destined to remain forever in part
within, and in part without, the reach of any closed
form.*   Philip Morison interview, *The New York Times,*
12 January 1970.

333, *we are no better intellectually and morally than the
people who lived . . . ten thousand years ago*   Edward
Harrison talk to Cambridge Forum, 1986, as reprinted in
New Scientist, 24 September 1987.

333, *you can never get to the exact, most economical statement of the truth*   Fuller 1978, sec 504.11.

333, *when science has answered all its last questions . . .
life will still be unexplained*   Ludwig Wittgenstein
quoted by a character playing the role of Alan Turing in the
play *Breaking the Code* at the Haymarket Theater, London,
23 May 1987.

334, *there is no phenomenon in a living system that is not
molecular, but there is none that is only molecular, either.*   Paul A Weiss in Koestler & Smythies, eds. 1969,
p 11.

335, *the mind-matter mystery is not likely to be amenable
to scientific analysis*   Gunther S. Stent, "DNA," *Daedalus,* Fall 1970.

336, *a catechism on teleology*   Dr. Harold Morowitz, Conference commemorating Teilhard de Chardin; "Sharing the Great Work"; Georgetown University, 1 May 1990. Dialogue transcribed by E.J.A.

337, *a subtle interplay between indeterminacy in the small and determinacy in the gross.*   George Steiner, "Life-Lines," *The New Yorker*, 6 March 1971.

Appendix: Biological disciplines

340, *comparative anatomy does not evoke a natural fondness*   Henry Gee, *Nature*, 13 October 1988.

345, *an untravelled twilight region*   Grobstein 1981, p 3.

347, *a key problem ... is the dearth of specific predictions*   Eugene P. Odum, *Nature*, 6 July 1989.

347, *the study of the effect on human beings of local characteristics*   Sherlock 1931, p 9.

348, *the interplay of cultural and biological processes*   Stephen Boyden, 1987, WESTERN CIVILIZATION IN BIOLOGICAL PERSPECTIVE: PATTERNS IN BIOHISTORY, Oxford: Clarendon Press: Oxford University Press.

349, *an Aristotelian breakdown*   after Mayr 1982, p 153.

350, *only for bacteria is there unambiguous evidence of ... biomagnetism*   Proceedings of the National Academy of Sciences, vol 85, p 4907.

350, *an examination of the principles of engineering design*   ENCYCLOPAEDIA BRITANNICA 3, vol 7, p 542.

350, *the evolutionary process cannot alter ... the behavior of diffusing molecules.*   Steven Vogel 1989.

351, *the term biomedicine is still problematical.*   Thomas 1974, p 115.

352, *there would be no molecular biology without*

isotopes   John Maynard Smith, "What can't the computer do?" *The New York Review of Books*, 15 March 1990.

352, *the study of the interaction of the psyche*   *Noetic Sciences Review*, Winter 1988.

353, *closed to matter but open to energy.*   Margulis & Sagan 1988.

353, *less concern for good science than for what pleases*   *The Scientist*, 28 November 1988.

358, *changes which . . . transform any biological system . . . into one of increasing complexity*   Delgado 1987.

358, *predictable irreversible changes.*   S. N. Salthe 1985.

360, *the application of physics to ecology*   S. N. Salthe 1985, p 327.

360, *terraforming*   Mallove 1987, p 111.

360, *much of the potential . . . lies in genetically engineering the microorganisms*   C. Vaughan, *BioScience*, June 1988.

362, *reductionism and determinism fail*   S. A. Barnett 1989, BIOLOGY AND FREEDOM: AN ESSAY ON THE IMPLICATIONS OF HUMAN ETHOLOGY.

363, *a marriage of neurobiology and ethology*   Konner 1983, p 146.

363, *the race and class distortions of eugenics*   Dobzhansky 1962, p 13.

363, *modification of human genes through . . . expression.* Stent 1969, p 15.

364, *diagnosis by character-state transitions.*   Levinton in *American Scientist*, January-February 1989, p 72.

364, *biotropic universe*   Mallove 1987, p 119.

365, *a neologism* David Suzuki and Peter Knudtson 1989, GENETHICS, Cambridge: Harvard University Press.

366, *exploring correlations between structure and function in proteins* Hwang & Warshel, *Nature*, 31 July 1988.

366, *one of the most profound mysteries of life: how like begets like.* Stent 1970, p 909.

367, *the difference in lifespan between human and mouse* Joshua Lederburg in *The Scientist*, 11 July 1988.

368, *a complex cascade of proteins.* John M. Weiler, letter in *BioScience*, January 1989.

368, *the scientific basis of psychoneuroimmunology* Dr. Howard R. Weiner, Harvard Medical School, review in *Nature*, 29 September 1988.

370, *molecular biology ... credit for introducing the term* Paul A. Weiss in Koestler & Smythies, eds. 1969, p 10.

370, *molecular biology was to indicate ... the lowest level of investigation* Koestler *op cit.* pp 10–11.

370, *a synthesis of five distinct disciplines* Judson 1979, p 607.

371, *molecular biologists are the astronomers of cells.* Eric Lax in *The New York Times Book Review*: review of Natalie Angier's "Natural Obsessions" 10 July 1988.

372, *fungi probably rival flowering plants in their species diversity* Alan D. M. Rayner in *Nature*, 29 September 1988.

373, *focuses on where organisms are and what they do in their environment* Greene and Losnos in *BioScience*, July 1988.

374, *the chemistry of a single neuron is so*

complex   George Johnson in *The New York Times*, 9 October 1988.

376, *a reduction of body-plan diversity*   from Jeffrey Levinton 1988, GENETICS, PALEONTOLOGY, AND MACROEVOLUTION, Cambridge: Cambridge University Press.

377, *phenology can be used for both botany and zoology.*   Stanwyn G. Shetler in *The New York Times*, 2 April 1989.

379, *the basic task for population biologists*   Ehrlich, keynote address to AIBS annual meeting, 10 August 1987.

380, *an effort to provide psychiatry with an objective basis in the hard sciences*   Sackler in *Smithsonian*, October 1987.

380, *concern with the relationship of physical processes to mental events.*   Restak 1979.

380, *for the first time in history, the interest of science and the interest of the humanities coincide.*   Restak 1979 (p 416).

381, *computational psychology today is rather like the dragon*   Margaret Boden 1988.

381, *how the emotions interact with the immune system*   Dr. George Solomon, *Noetic Sciences Review*, Winter 1988.

382, *it may not be too much to say ... the last branches of biology waiting to be included in the Modern Synthesis*   E. O. Wilson 1975, pp 3–4.

382, *biologic basis for human behavior*   Restak 1979, p 75.

383, *systematics is central to all of biology*   Rosenberg 1985, p 181.

383, *systematics encompasses the characteristics, genetic*

status, and evolutionary history of organisms.   Greene and Losnos in *BioScience*, July 1988.

384, *in physics 50 percent are theoretical physicists ... in chemistry, 90 percent work in the laboratory*   Dr. Michael J. Moravcsik, a professor at the Institute of Theoretical Science, University of Oregon. Statement to International Conference on the Unity of the Sciences, 28 November 1987.

386, *whether a process of co-evolution has resulted in the development of distinct units*   Peter D. Moore in *Nature*, 3 November 1988.

BIBLIOGRAPHY

*Indicates works of particular, possibly unrecognized, merit

ARTIFICIAL LIFE BOOKS

(Including books on self-organizing systems)

Babloyantz, Agnessa. 1986. MOLECULES, DYNAMICS AND LIFE: AN INTRODUCTION TO THE SELF-ORGANIZATION OF MATTER. New York: John Wiley.

Braitenberg, Valentino. 1984. VEHICLES: EXPERIMENTS IN SYNTHETIC PSYCHOLOGY. Cambridge, MA: MIT Press.

Davies, Paul. 1988. THE COSMIC BLUEPRINT: NEW DISCOVERIES IN NATURE'S CREATIVE ABILITY TO ORDER THE UNIVERSE. New York: Simon & Schuster.

Fjermedal, Grant. 1986. THE TOMORROW MAKERS: A BRAVE NEW WORLD OF LIVING-BRAIN MACHINES. New York: Macmillan.

Jantsch, Erich. 1980. THE SELF-ORGANIZING UNIVERSE: SCIENTIFIC AND HUMAN IMPLICATIONS OF THE EMERGING PARADIGM OF EVOLUTION. Oxford: Pergamon Press.

Langton, Christopher G. ed. 1989. ARTIFICIAL LIFE: PROCEEDINGS OF AN INTERDISCIPLINARY WORKSHOP ON THE SYNTHESIS AND SIMULATION OF LIVING SYSTEMS HELD IN 1987,

Los Alamos, New Mexico (Santa Fe Institute Studes, vol. VI). Redwood City, CA: Addison-Wesley.

Lucky, Robert W. 1989. Silicon Dreams: information, man, and machine. New York: St. Martin's Press.

Moravec, Hans. 1988. Mind Children: the future of robot and human intelligence. Cambridge, MA: Harvard University Press.

Pattee, Howard H. 1973. Hierarchy Theory: the challenge of complex systems. New York: Georges Braziller.

Salthe, Stanley N. 1985. Evolving Hierarchical Systems: their structure and representation. New York: Columbia University Press.

Woolridge, Dean E. 1968. Mechanical Man: the physical basis of intelligent life. New York: McGraw-Hill.

BIOLOGY BOOKS

(Books by scientists about life)

Ahmadjian, Vernon, & Surindar Paracer. 1986. Symbiosis: an introduction to biological associations. Hanover and London: University Press of New England.

Antebi, Elizabeth, and David Fishlock. 1986. Biotechnology: strategies for life. Cambridge, MA: MIT Press.

Arthur, Wallace. 1987. Theories of Life: Darwin, Mendel and beyond. New York: Viking Penguin.

Beck, William S. 1957. Modern Science and the Nature of Life. New York: Harcourt Brace.

Bernal, J. D. 1951. The Physical Basis of Life. London: Routledge and Kegan Paul.

Borek, Ernest. 1973. The Sculpture of Life. New York: Columbia University Press.

———. 1980. THE ATOMS WITHIN US. New York: Columbia University Press.

Cairns-Smith, A. G. 1985. SEVEN CLUES TO THE ORIGIN OF LIFE. Cambridge: Cambridge University Press.

Cottrell, Alan. 1975. PORTRAIT OF NATURE: THE WORLD AS SEEN BY MODERN SCIENCE. New York: Scribner's.

Crick, Francis. 1981. LIFE ITSELF: ITS ORIGIN AND NATURE. New York: Simon & Schuster.

———. 1988. WHAT MAD PURSUIT: A PERSONAL VIEW OF SCIENTIFIC DISCOVERY. New York: Basic Books.

*Cudmore, L. L. Larison. 1977. THE CENTER OF LIFE: A NATURAL HISTORY OF THE CELL. New York: Quadrangle/New York Times.

Davis, Philip J., and David Park. 1987. NO WAY: THE NATURE OF THE IMPOSSIBLE. New York: W. H. Freeman.

Dawkins, Richard. 1986. THE BLIND WATCHMAKER. New York: Norton.

Dixon, Bernard. 1976. MAGNIFICENT MICROBES. New York: Atheneum.

Dobzhansky, Theodosius. 1955. EVOLUTION, GENETICS AND MAN. New York: John Wiley.

———. 1962. MANKIND EVOLVING: THE EVOLUTION OF THE HUMAN SPECIES. New Haven, CT: Yale University Press.

———. 1967. THE BIOLOGY OF ULTIMATE CONCERN. New York: New American Library.

Dulbecco, Renato. 1987. THE DESIGN OF LIFE. New Haven, CT: Yale University Press.

Dyson, Freeman J. 1985. ORIGINS OF LIFE. Cambridge: Cambridge University Press.

———. 1984. THE HUMAN MYSTERY: THE GIFFORD LECTURES 1977–1978. London: Routledge & Kegan Paul.

Eldredge, Niles. 1985. UNFINISHED SYNTHESIS: BIOLOGICAL HIERARCHIES AND MODERN EVOLUTIONARY THOUGHT. New York: Oxford University Press.

Elsasser, Walter M. 1958. THE PHYSICAL FOUNDATION OF BIOLOGY: AN ANALYTICAL STUDY. New York: Pergamon Press.

Feinberg, Gerald. 1985. SOLID CLUES: QUANTUM PHYSICS, MOLECULAR BIOLOGY, AND THE FUTURE OF SCIENCE. New York: Simon and Schuster.

Feinberg, Gerald, and Robert Shapiro. 1980. LIFE BEYOND EARTH: THE INTELLIGENT EARTHLING'S GUIDE TO LIFE IN THE UNIVERSE. New York: William Morrow.

Florkin, Marcel. 1972. A HISTORY OF BIOCHEMISTRY (vol. 30 of *Comprehensive Biochemistry*, ed. Florkin and Stotz, eds.). New York: Elsevier.

Gal-Or, Benjamin. 1981. COSMOLOGY, PHYSICS, AND PHILOSOPHY. New York: Springer-Verlag.

Gardner, Martin. 1969. THE AMBIDEXTROUS UNIVERSE: LEFT, RIGHT, AND THE FALL OF PARITY. New York: New American Library.

Gerstein, Dean R. 1988. THE BEHAVIORAL AND SOCIAL SCIENCES: ACHIEVEMENTS AND OPPORTUNITIES. Washington, D.C.: National Academy Press.

Gribbin, John. 1981. GENESIS: THE ORIGINS OF MAN AND THE UNIVERSE. New York: Delta.

Hall, Thomas S. 1969. IDEAS OF LIFE AND MATTER: STUDIES IN THE HISTORY OF PHYSIOLOGY (2 vols.). Chicago: University of Chicago Press.

*Hockett, C. F. 1973. MAN'S PLACE IN NATURE. New York: McGraw-Hill.

*Hoffman, Joseph G. 1957. THE LIFE AND DEATH OF CELLS. New York: Doubleday & Co.

Jacob, François. 1974. THE LOGIC OF LIFE: A HISTORY OF HEREDITY. New York: Pantheon.

———. 1982. THE POSSIBLE AND THE ACTUAL. New York: Pantheon.

———. 1988. THE STATUE WITHIN: AN AUTOBIOGRAPHY. New York: Basic Books.

Jepsen, Glenn L., George Gaylord Simpson, and Ernst Mayr, eds. 1949. GENETICS, PALEONTOLOGY AND EVOLUTION. Princeton, NJ: Princeton University Press (reprint, New York: Atheneum, 1963).

*Koestler, Arthur & J. R. Smythies, eds. 1969. BEYOND REDUCTIONISM: NEW PERSPECTIVES IN THE LIFE SCIENCES. THE ALPBACH SYMPOSIUM, 1968. Boston: Beacon Press.

Konner, Melvin. 1983. THE TANGLED WING: BIOLOGICAL CONSTRAINTS ON THE HUMAN SPIRIT. New York: Harper & Row.

Levins, Richard, and Richard Lewontin. 1985. THE DIALECTICAL BIOLOGIST. Cambridge: Harvard University Press.

Ling, Gilbert N. 1984. IN SEARCH OF THE PHYSICAL BASIS OF LIFE. New York: Plenum.

Lovelock, James E. 1979. GAIA: A NEW LOOK AT LIFE ON EARTH. New York: Oxford University Press.

Lumsden, Charles J., and Edward O. Wilson. 1981. GENES, MIND AND CULTURE: THE COEVOLUTIONARY PROCESS. Cambridge, MA: Harvard University Press.

Luria, S. E. 1975. 36 LECTURES IN BIOLOGY. Cambridge, MA: MIT Press.

*Lwoff, André. 1968. BIOLOGICAL ORDER (The Karl T. Compton Lectures). (Second Paperback edition). Cambridge, MA: MIT Press.

McElroy, William D., and Bentley Glass, eds. 1961. A SYM-

POSIUM ON LIGHT AND LIFE. Baltimore: Johns Hopkins University Press.

Margulis, Lynn, and Dorion Sagan. 1986. MICROCOSMOS: FOUR BILLION YEARS OF EVOLUTION FROM OUR MICROBIAL ANCESTORS. New York: Summit Books.

————. 1986. THE ORIGINS OF SEX: THREE BILLION YEARS OF GENETIC RECOMBINATION. New Haven, CT: Yale University Press.

Margulis, Lynn, and Karlene V. Schwartz. 1982. FIVE KINGDOMS: AN ILLUSTRATED GUIDE TO THE PHYLA OF LIFE ON EARTH. San Francisco: W. H. Freeman.

*Marquand, Josephine. 1968. LIFE: ITS NATURE, ORIGINS AND DISTRIBUTION. New York: Norton.

Mayr, Ernst. 1982. THE GROWTH OF BIOLOGICAL THOUGHT: DIVERSITY, EVOLUTION, AND INHERITANCE. Cambridge, MA: Belknap Press of Harvard Uneversity Press.

————. 1988. TOWARD A NEW PHILOSOPHY OF BIOLOGY: OBSERVATIONS OF AN EVOLUTIONIST. Cambridge, MA: Belknap Press of Harvard University Press.

Mazzeo, Joseph Anthony. 1967. THE DESIGN OF LIFE: MAJOR THEMES IN THE DEVELOPMENT OF BIOLOGICAL THOUGHT. New York: Pantheon Books.

Medawar, P. B. and J. S. 1977. THE LIFE SCIENCE: CURRENT IDEAS OF BIOLOGY. New York: Harper and Row.

————. 1983. ARISTOTLE TO ZOOS: A PHILOSOPHICAL DICTIONARY OF BIOLOGY. Cambridge, MA: Harvard University Press.

Miller, James Grier, 1978. LIVING SYSTEMS. New York: McGraw-Hill.

*Monod, Jacques. 1971. CHANCE AND NECESSITY: AN ESSAY ON THE NATURAL PHILOSOPHY OF MODERN BIOLOGY. New York: Random House, Vintage Books.

Morley, Derek Wragge. 1953. THE ANT WORLD. London: Penguin Books.

Morowitz, Harold J. 1979. THE WINE OF LIFE AND OTHER ESSAYS ON SOCIETIES, ENERGY AND LIVING THINGS. New York: St. Martin's Press.

*Palade, George E., ed. 1964. THE SCIENTIFIC ENDEAVOR: CENTENNIAL CELEBRATION OF THE NATIONAL ACADEMY OF SCIENCES. New York: Rockefeller University Press.

Planck, Max. 1959. THE NEW SCIENCE. Meridian books reprint.

Postgate, John. 1969. MICROBES AND MAN. Hammondsworth, England: Penguin Books.

Rose, Steven. 1966. THE CHEMISTRY OF LIFE. Hammondsworth, England: Penguin Books.

Rosenberg, Alexander. 1985. THE STRUCTURE OF BIOLOGICAL SCIENCE. Cambridge: Cambridge University Press.

*Sagan, Carl. 1978. Article on *Life*. ENCYCLOPAEDIA BRITANNICA, 15th ed., vol. 10.

Salk, Jonas. 1972. MAN UNFOLDING. World Perspectives, vol. 46. New York: Harper and Row.

Schrödinger, Erwin. 1944. WHAT IS LIFE?: THE PHYSICAL ASPECT OF THE LIVING CELL. Cambridge: Cambridge University Press.

Scott, André. 1986. THE CREATION OF LIFE: PAST, FUTURE, ALIEN. Oxford: Basil Blackwell.

Shapiro, Robert. 1986. ORIGINS: A SKEPTIC'S GUIDE TO THE CREATION OF LIFE ON EARTH. New York: Summit Books.

Sheldrake, Rupert E. 1981. A NEW SCIENCE OF LIFE: THE HYPOTHESIS OF FORMATIVE CAUSATION. Los Angeles: J. P. Tarcher.

——— 1988. THE PRESENCE OF THE PAST: MORPHIC RESO-

NANCE AND THE HABITS OF NATURE. New York: Times Books.

*Sherlock, R. L. 1931. MAN'S INFLUENCE ON THE EARTH. London: Thornton Butterworth.

Simon, Michael A. 1971. THE MATTER OF LIFE: PHILOSOPHICAL PROBLEMS OF BIOLOGY. New Haven: Yale University Press.

Simpson, George Gaylord. 1949. THE MEANING OF EVOLUTION: A STUDY OF THE HISTORY OF LIFE AND OF ITS SIGNIFICANCE FOR MAN. New Haven, CT: Yale University Press.

———. 1961. PRINCIPLES OF ANIMAL TAXONOMY. New York: Columbia University Press.

———, and William S. Beck. 1965. LIFE: AN INTRODUCTION TO BIOLOGY. New York: Harcourt, Brace.

Smith, John Maynard. 1986. THE PROBLEMS OF BIOLOGY. Oxford: Oxford University Press.

Sober, Elliott. 1984. CONCEPTUAL ISSUES IN EVOLUTIONARY BIOLOGY An anthology. Cambridge: MIT Press.

Sonea, Sorin, and Maurice Panisett. 1983. A NEW BACTERIOLOGY. Boston Jones & Barlett.

*Stent, Gunther S. 1969. THE COMING OF THE GOLDEN AGE: A VIEW OF THE END OF PROGRESS. Garden City: Natural History Press.

———. 1970. "DNA," *Daedalus*, Fall 1970.

Stryer, Lubert. 1989. MOLECULAR DESIGN OF LIFE. New York: W. H. Freeman.

Thaxton, Charles B., Walter L. Bradley, and Roger L. Olsen. 1984. THE MYSTERY OF LIFE'S ORIGIN: REASSESSING CURRENT THEORIES. New York: Philosophical Library.

Thompson, D'Arcy Wentworth. 1917. ON GROWTH AND

FORM. Cambridge: Cambridge University Press (abridged edition, Bonner, ed., 1961).

Thomson, Sir Arthur J. 1932. RIDDLES OF SCIENCE. New York: Liveright (Revised by Bernard Jaffe. 1958) Hart Publishing: New York.

*Thorpe, W. H. 1962. BIOLOGY AND THE NATURE OF MAN. London: Oxford University Press.

Tributsch, Helmut. 1982. HOW LIFE LEARNED TO LIVE: ADAPTATION IN NATURE. Cambridge, MA: MIT Press.

Vale, Thomas R., ed. 1986. PROGRESS AGAINST GROWTH: DANIEL B. LUTEN ON THE AMERICAN LANDSCAPE. New York: Guilford.

Von Frisch, Karl. 1965. MAN AND THE LIVING WORLD. New York: Time Incorporated.

Waddington C. H. 1961. THE ETHICAL ANIMAL. New York: Atheneum.

Wheeler, William Morton. 1910. ANTS: THEIR STRUCTURE, DEVELOPMENT AND BEHAVIOR. New York: Columbia University Press.

*Whyte, Lancelot Law. 1949. THE UNITARY PRINCIPLE IN PHYSICS AND BIOLOGY. New York: Henry Holt and Co.

———. 1965. INTERNAL FACTORS IN EVOLUTION. New York: Georges Braziller.

Wilson, Edward O. 1975. SOCIOBIOLOGY: THE NEW SYNTHESIS. Cambridge: Belknap/Harvard.

———. 1978. ON HUMAN NATURE. Cambridge, MA: Harvard University Press.

*Young, Louise B. 1986. THE UNFINISHED UNIVERSE. New York: Simon & Schuster.

BIOLOGY TEXTBOOKS

Alberts, Bruce, Dennis Bray, Julian Lewis, Martin Raff, Keith Roberts, James D. Watson. 1983. THE MOLECULAR BIOLOGY OF THE CELL. New York: Garland.

Ford, James M., and James E Monroe. 1971. LIVING SYSTEMS: PRINCIPLES AND RELATIONSHIPS. Third edition. San Francisco: Canfield Press.

Giese, Arthur C. 1973. CELL PHYSIOLOGY. Fifth edition. Philadelphia: Saunders College.

Hawker, Lilian E., and Alan H. Linton, eds. 1971. MICRO-ORGANISMS: FUNCTION, FORM AND ENVIRONMENT. New York: American Elsevier.

Johnson, Willis H., Louis E. Delanney, and Thomas A. Cole. 1969. ESSENTIALS OF BIOLOGY. New York: Holt Rinehart and Winston.

Koob, Derry D. and William E. Boggs, 1972. THE NATURE OF LIFE. Reading, MA: Addison-Wesley.

Luria, Salvador E., Gould, Singer. 1981. A VIEW OF LIFE. Menlo Park, CA: Benjamin/Cummings.

Morowitz, Harold J., and Lucille S. 1974. LIFE ON THE PLANET EARTH. New York: W. W. Norton.

Simpson, George Gaylord, and William S. Beck. 1965. LIFE: AN INTRODUCTION TO BIOLOGY. New York: Harcourt, Brace.

BIRTH & DEATH BOOKS

Birth books

Battaglia, Frederick C., and Giacomo Mescha, 1986. AN INTRODUCTION TO FETAL PHYSIOLOGY. San Diego: Academic Press.

Ford, Norman M. 1988. WHEN DID I BEGIN? CONCEPTION OF THE HUMAN INDIVIDUAL IN HISTORY, PHILOSOPHY AND SCIENCE. Cambridge, MA: Cambridge University Press.

Grobstein, Clifford. 1981. FROM CHANCE TO PURPOSE: AN APPRAISAL OF EXTERNAL HUMAN FERTILIZATION. Reading, MA: Addison-Wesley.

Books on aging

Comfort, Alex. 1965. THE PROCESS OF AGEING. London: Weidenfield and Nicolson.

Vischer, A. L. 1947. OLD AGE, ITS COMPENSATIONS AND REWARDS. London: Allen and Unwin.

Woodward, Kathleen, and Murray M. Schwartz, eds. 1986. MEMORY AND DESIRE: AGING—LITERATURE—PSYCHOANALYSIS. Bloomington, IN: Indiana University Press.

Books on dying

Aries, Phillipe. 1981. THE HOUR OF OUR DEATH. New York: Alfred A. Knopf.

Gonzales-Crussi, F. 1986. THREE FORMS OF SUDDEN DEATH: AND OTHER REFLECTIONS ON THE GRANDEUR AND MISERY OF THE HUMAN BODY. New York: Harper & Row.

Humphrey, Derek. 1983. LET ME DIE BEFORE I WAKE: HEMLOCK'S BOOK OF SELF-DELIVERANCE FOR THE DYING. Second edition. Los Angeles: The Hemlock Society.

Portwood, Doris. 1978. COMMON SENSE SUICIDE: THE FINAL RIGHT. New York: Dodd, Mead & Co.

Sissman, L. E. 1968. DYING: AN INTRODUCTION. New York: Atlantic Monthly Press; Little, Brown & Co.

Death books

Berger, Arthur S. 1987. ARISTOCRACY OF THE DEAD: NEW FINDINGS IN POSTMORTEM SURVIVAL. Jefferson, NC: Mc-Farland & Co., Inc.

Cramer, Friedrich. 1983. DEATH: FROM MICROSCOPIC TO MACROSCOPIC DISORDER. From proceedings of international symposium on Synergetics, E. Frehland, ed. Berlin: Springer-Verlag, 1984.

Kastenbaum, Robert J. 1986. DEATH, SOCIETY, AND HUMAN EXPERIENCE. Columbus, OH: Merrill Publishing.

Sissman, L. E. 1968. SCATTERED RETURNS. New York: Atlantic Monthly Press; Little, Brown & Co.

Watson, Lyall. 1974. THE BIOLOGY OF DEATH. Sceptre edition of 1987. London: Hodder & Stoughton.

Weir, Robert F., ed. 1980. DEATH IN LITERATURE. New York: Columbia University Press.

*Williams, Glanville. 1957. THE SANCTITY OF LIFE AND THE CRIMINAL LAW. New York: Alfred A. Knopf.

Zaleski, Carol. 1987. OTHERWORLD JOURNEYS: ACCOUNTS OF NEAR-DEATH EXPERIENCE IN MEDIEVAL AND MODERN TIMES. New York: Oxford University Press.

BRAIN & MIND BOOKS

Blakemore, Colin. 1977. THE MECHANICS OF THE MIND. Cambridge, MA: Cambridge University Press.

Campbell, Jeremy. 1982. GRAMMATICAL MAN: INFORMATION, ENTROPY, LANGUAGE AND LIFE. New York: Simon & Schuster.

———. 1989. THE IMPROBABLE MACHINE: WHAT THE UPHEAVALS IN ARTIFICIAL INTELLIGENCE RESEARCH REVEAL

ABOUT HOW THE MIND REALLY WORKS. New York: Simon & Schuster.

*Changeux, Jean-Pierre. 1985. NEURONAL MAN: THE BIOLOGY OF MIND. New York: Oxford University Press.

Churchland, Paul M. 1984. MATTER AND CONSCIOUSNESS: A CONTEMPORARY INTRODUCTION TO THE PHILOSOPHY OF MIND. Cambridge, MA: MIT Press.

*Delbruck, Max. 1986. MIND FROM MATTER?: AN ESSAY ON EVOLUTIONARY EPISTEMOLOGY. Gunther S. Stent, ed. Palo Alto, CA: Blackwell Scientific.

Dyson, Freeman J., ed. 1985. MIND AND BRAIN: THE MANY-FACETED PROBLEMS. New York: Paragon.

*Eccles, John C. 1970. FACING REALITY: PHILOSOPHICAL ADVENTURES OF A BRAIN SCIENTIST. Heidelberg: Springer-Verlag.

―――. 1989. EVOLUTION OF THE BRAIN: CREATION OF THE SELF. London: Routledge & Kegan Paul.

Edelman, Gerald M. 1987. NEURAL DARWINISM: THE THEORY OF NEURONAL GROUP SELECTION. New York: Basic Books.

Elvee, Richard Q., ed. 1982. MIND IN NATURE: NOBEL CONFERENCE XVI. San Francisco: Harper & Row.

*Flanagan, Owen J., Jr. 1984. THE SCIENCE OF THE MIND. Cambridge, MA: MIT Press.

Gazzaniga, Michael S. 1988. MIND MATTERS: HOW MIND AND BRAIN INTERACT TO CREATE OUR CONSCIOUS LIVES. Boston: Houghton Mifflin.

Harth, Erich. 1982. WINDOWS ON THE MIND: REFLECTIONS ON THE PHYSICAL BASIS OF CONSCIOUSNESS. New York: William Morrow.

Hooper, Judith, and Dick Teresi, 1986. THE THREE-POUND

Universe: The Brain—from the chemistry of the mind to the new frontiers of the soul. New York: Dell.

Hunter, I. M. L. 1964. Memory. Baltimore: Penguin Books.

Owen, George E. 1971. The Universe of the Mind. Baltimore: Johns Hopkins University Press.

Penfield, Wilder. 1975. The Mystery of the Mind: a critical study of consciousness and the human brain. Princeton, NJ: Princeton University Press.

Penrose, Roger. 1989. The Emperor's New Mind: concerning computers, minds, and the laws of physics. Oxford: Oxford University Press.

Restak, Richard M. 1979. The Brain: the last frontier. New York: Warner Books.

Romanyshyn, Robert D. 1982. Psychological Life: from science to metaphor. Austin, TX: University of Texas Press.

Rose, Steven. 1974. The Conscious Brain. New York: Alfred A. Knopf.

Searle, John. 1984. Minds, Brains and Science. Cambridge, MA: Harvard University Press.

*Whyte, L. L. 1960. The Unconsciousness before Freud. New York: Basic Books.

COLLATERAL SOURCES

(Trade and literary works quoted; not in the scientific literature.)

Asimov, Isaac. 1960. Asimov's New Guide to Science. New York: Basic Books.

Barash, David P. 1986. The Hare and the Tortoise: culture, biology, and human nature. New York: Viking.

Butler, Samuel. 1877. Volume 4: LIFE AND HABIT. CHAPTER 8: "THE ASSIMILATION OF OUTSIDE MATTER." New York: AMS Press, Inc. (edition of 1968).

Campbell, Jeremy. 1987. WINSTON CHURCHILL'S AFTERNOON NAP: A WIDE-AWAKE INQUIRY INTO THE HUMAN NATURE OF TIME. New York: Simon & Schuster.

Capra, Fritjof. 1982. THE TURNING POINT: SCIENCE, SOCIETY, AND THE RISING CULTURE. New York: Simon & Schuster.

Dixon, W. Macneille. 1937. THE HUMAN SITUATION (THE GIFFORD LECTURES). 1958 edition. New York: Oxford University Press/Galaxy.

Flanagan, Dennis. 1988. FLANAGAN'S VERSION: A SPECTATOR'S GUIDE TO SCIENCE ON THE EVE OF THE 21ST CENTURY. New York: Alfred A. Knopf.

Fuller, R. Buckminster. 1975. SYNERGETICS: EXPLORATIONS IN THE GEOMETRY OF THINKING. New York: Macmillan.

———. 1979. SYNERGETICS 2. New York: Macmillian.

———, with Jerome Agel & Quentin Fiore. 1970. I SEEM TO BE A VERB. New York: Bantam Books.

———. 1991. COSMOGRAPHY. New York: Macmillian.

Hardison, O. B. 1989. DISAPPEARING THROUGH THE SKYLIGHT: CULTURE AND TECHNOLOGY IN THE TWENTIETH CENTURY. New York: Viking.

Harrison, Edward. 1985. MASKS OF THE UNIVERSE: A PHYSICIST'S REMARKABLE PORTRAYAL. New York: Macmillan.

Judson, Horace Freeland. 1979. THE EIGHTH DAY OF CREATION: MAKERS OF THE REVOLUTION IN BIOLOGY. New York: Simon & Schuster.

———. 1980. THE SEARCH FOR SOLUTIONS. New York: Holt, Rinehart & Winston.

Levi, Primo. 1984. THE PERIODIC TABLE. New York: Schocken Books.

Murchie, Guy. 1978. THE SEVEN MYSTERIES OF LIFE. Boston: Houghton Mifflin.

Rifkind, Jeremy. 1983. ALGENY. New York: Viking.

Scott, Andrew. 1986. THE CREATION OF LIFE: PAST, FUTURE, ALIEN. Oxford: Basil Blackwell.

Thomas, Lewis. 1974. THE LIVES OF A CELL: NOTES OF A BIOLOGY WATCHER. New York: Viking.

———. 1979. THE MEDUSA AND THE SNAIL: MORE NOTES OF A BIOLOGY WATCHER. New York: Viking.

———. 1983. THE YOUNGEST SCIENCE: NOTES OF A MEDICINE-WATCHER. New York: Viking.

———. 1983. LATE NIGHT THOUGHTS ON LISTENING TO MAHLER'S NINTH SYMPHONY. New York: Viking.

White, Randall. 1986. DARK CAVES, BRIGHT VISIONS: LIFE IN ICE AGE EUROPE. New York: American Museum of Natural History, with W. W. Norton & Co.

Wright, Robert. 1988. THREE SCIENTISTS AND THEIR GODS: LOOKING FOR MEANING IN AN AGE OF INFORMATION. New York: Times Books.

BOOKS ON KNOWLEDGE & CLASSIFICATION

Beniger, James R. 1986. THE CONTROL REVOLUTION: TECHNOLOGICAL AND ECONOMIC ORIGINS OF THE INFORMATION SOCIETY. Cambridge, MA: Harvard University Press.

Chan, Lois Mai. 1981. CATALOGING AND CLASSIFICATION: AN INTRODUCTION. New York: McGraw-Hill.

Emblen, D. L. 1970. PETER MARK ROGET: THE WORD AND THE MAN. New York: Cromwell.

Frangsmyr, Tore, ed. 1983. LINNAEUS: THE MAN AND HIS WORK. Berkeley, CA: University of California Press.

*Innis, Harold A. 1951. THE BIAS OF COMMUNICATION. Toronto: University of Toronto Press.

*————. 1950. EMPIRE & COMMUNICATIONS. Toronto: University of Toronto Press.

Lucky, Robert W. 1989. INFORMATION, MAN AND MACHINE. New York: St. Martin's Press.

Machlup, Fritz. 1982. KNOWLEDGE: ITS CREATION, DISTRIBUTION, AND ECONOMIC SIGNIFICANCE. VOLUME II. THE BRANCHES OF LEARNING. Princeton, NJ: Princeton University Press.

BOOKS ON MAN & THE COSMOS

Anderson, Walter Truett. 1987. TO GOVERN EVOLUTION: FURTHER ADVENTURES OF THE POLITICAL ANIMAL. New York: Harcourt Brace Jovanovich.

Augros, Robert, & George Stanciu. 1988. THE NEW BIOLOGY: DISCOVERING THE WISDOM IN NATURE. Boston: New Science Library: Shambhala.

Barrow, John D., and Frank J. Tipler. 1986. THE ANTHROPIC COSMOLOGICAL PRINCIPLE. Oxford: Oxford University Press; Clarendon Press.

Billingham, John, ed. 1981. LIFE IN THE UNIVERSE: PROCEEDINGS OF THE CONFERENCE ON LIFE IN THE UNIVERSE HELD AT NASA AMES RESEARCH CENTRE, JUNE 19–20, 1979. Cambridge, MA: MIT Press.

Casti, John L. 1989. PARADIGMS LOST: IMAGES OF MAN IN THE MIRROR OF SCIENCE. New York: William Morrow.

Chaisson, Eric. 1981. COSMIC DAWN: THE ORIGINS OF MAT-

TER AND LIFE. Boston: Little, Brown & Co. (Atlantic Monthly Press).

————. 1987. THE LIFE ERA: COSMIC SELECTION AND CONSCIOUS EVOLUTION. New York: Atlantic Monthly Press.

Dyson, Freeman J. 1988. INFINITE IN ALL DIRECTIONS. New York: Harper & Row.

Mallove, Eugene. 1987. THE QUICKENING UNIVERSE. New York: St. Martin's Press.

Mather, Kirtley F. 1986. THE PERMISSIVE UNIVERSE. Albuquerque, NM: University of New Mexico Press.

Mott, Lloyd. 1975. THE UNIVERSE: ITS BEGINNING AND END. New York: Scribner's.

Ornstein, Robert, & Paul Ehrlich. 1989. NEW WORLD, NEW MIND: MOVING TOWARD CONSCIOUS EVOLUTION.

Reeves, Hubert. 1984. ATOMS OF SILENCE: AN EXPLORATION OF COSMIC EVOLUTION. Cambridge, MA: MIT Press.

Smith, E. Lester, ed. 1975. INTELLIGENCE CAME FIRST. Wheaton, IL: Theosophical Publishing House.

*Whyte, Lancelot Law. 1974. THE UNIVERSE OF EXPERIENCE: A WORLD VIEW BEYOND SCIENCE AND RELIGION. New York: Harper Torchbooks.

SCIENCE BOOKS

Barrow, John D., and Joseph Silk. 1983. THE LEFT HAND OF CREATION: THE ORIGIN AND EVOLUTION OF THE EXPANDING UNIVERSE. New York: Basic Books.

Briggs, John P., and F. David Peat. 1984. LOOKING GLASS UNIVERSE: THE EMERGING SCIENCE OF WHOLENESS. New York: Simon & Schuster; A Touchstone Book.

Calder, Nigel. 1977. THE KEY TO THE UNIVERSE: A REPORT ON THE NEW PHYSICS. New York: Viking.

Duncan, Ronald, & Miranda Weston-Smith, eds. 1978. THE ENCYCLOPEDIA OF IGNORANCE. New York: Pocket Books.

Heisenberg, Werner. 1952. PHILOSOPHICAL PROBLEMS OF QUANTUM PHYSICS. Woodbridge, CT: Ox Bow Press, (reprint 1979).

Korzybski, Alfred, 1933. SCIENCE AND SANITY: AN INTRO-DUCTION TO NON-ARISTOTELIAN SYSTEMS AND GENERAL SE-MANTICS. Lancaster and New York: The Science Press.

Kuhn, Thomas S. 1970. THE STRUCTURE OF SCIENTIFIC REV-OLUTIONS. Second edition, enlarged. Chicago: University of Chicago Press.

Speakman, J. C. 1966. MOLECULES. New York: McGraw-Hill.

*Sullivan, J. W. N. 1933. THE LIMITATIONS OF SCIENCE. New York: Viking.

Books on matter

Cotterill, Rodney. 1985. THE CAMBRIDGE GUIDE TO THE MATERIAL WORLD. Cambridge: Cambridge University Press.

Hammond, Albert L. 1969. IDEAS ABOUT SUBSTANCE. Baltimore: Johns University Press, Hopkins.

Haraway, Donna Jeanne. 1976. CRYSTAL, FABRICS, AND FIELDS: METAPHORS OF ORGANICISM IN TWENTIETH-CENTURY DEVELOPMENTAL BIOLOGY. New Haven: Yale University Press.

*Kieffer, William F. 1971. CHEMISTRY: A CULTURAL AP-PROACH. New York: Harper & Row.

*Smith, Cyril Stanley. 1980. FROM ART TO SCIENCE: SEV-

ENTY-TWO OBJECTS ILLUSTRATING THE NATURE OF DISCOVERY. Cambridge, MA: MIT Press.

*————. 1981. A SEARCH FOR STRUCTURE: SELECTED ESSAYS ON SCIENCE, ART, AND HISTORY. Cambridge: MIT Press.

Stevens, Peter S. 1974. PATTERNS IN NATURE. Boston: Atlantic Monthly Press; Little, Brown & Co.

*von Baeyer, Hans Christian. 1984. RAINBOWS, SNOWFLAKES, AND QUARKS: PHYSICS AND THE WORLD AROUND US. New York: McGraw-Hill.

Zoltai, Tibor, and James H. Stout. 1984. MINERALOGY: CONCEPTS AND PRINCIPLES. Minneapolis: Burgess Publishing Co.

ACKNOWLEDGMENTS

Grateful acknowledgment is made for permission to reprint excerpts from the following copyrighted works:

Excerpts from "Three Views of Death and Their Implications for Life" presented at the XVIth International Conference on the Unity of the Sciences, Atlanta, GA, 26–29 November 1987. Copyright © by Arthur S. Berger, J.D. Reprinted by permission of Dr. Berger.

Excerpts from THE SCIENCE OF THE MIND by Owen Flanagan. Copyright © 1984 by MIT. Reprinted by permission of the publisher, The MIT Press.

Excerpts from IDEAS AND INTEGRITIES by R. Buckminster Fuller. Collier Books, 1969. Reprinted by permission of the publisher, Macmillan Publishing Company. Excerpts from SYNERGETICS by R. Buckminster Fuller in collaboration with E. J. Applewhite. Copyright by R. Buckminster Fuller 1975, and SYNERGETICS 2 copyright 1979. Reprinted by permission of the publisher, Macmillan Publishing Company. Excerpts from COSMOGRAPHY by R. Buckminster Fuller, Kyoshi Kuromiya, adjuvant. Copyright by estate of R. Buckminster Fuller 1991. Reprinted by permission of the publisher, Macmillan Publishing Company.

Excerpts from THE LIFE AND DEATH OF CELLS by Joseph G. Hoffman, Dolphin Books, 1957. Reprinted by permission of Doubleday & Co., Inc.

Excerpts from RATS, LICE AND HISTORY by Hans Zinsser. Copyright 1934. Reprinted by permission of the publisher, Little, Brown and Company.

Excerpts from GAIA: A NEW LOOK AT LIFE ON EARTH by

J. E. Lovelock. Copyright 1982. Reprinted by permission of the publisher, Oxford University Press, Walton Street, Oxford OX2 6DP.

Excerpts from BIOLOGICAL ORDER by André Lwoff. Copyright 1968. Reprinted by permission of the publisher, The MIT Press.

Excerpts from a transcript of Professor Morowitz's remarks at Georgetown University conference on Teilhard de Chardin, "Sharing the Great Work," 1 May 1990. By permission of Dr. Harold J. Morowitz.

Excerpts from THE LIVES OF A CELL by Lewis Thomas, Copyright © 1971 by Lewis Thomas. Reprinted by permission of Viking Penguin, a division of Penguin Books USA, Inc. Excerpts from THE MEDUSA AND THE SNAIL by Lewis Thomas. Copyright © 1979 by Lewis Thomas. Reprinted by permission of Viking Penguin, a division of Penguin Books USA, Inc.

Excerpts from A SEARCH FOR STRUCTURE by Cyril Stanley Smith. Copyright 1981 by MIT. Reprinted by permission of the publisher, The MIT Press.

Excerpts from "DNA" in *Daedalus*, Fall 1970, by Dr. Gunther S. Stent. Reprinted by permission of Dr. Gunther S. Stent.

INDEX